Concise
Bible Concordance

COMPILED AND EDITED BY

Jay J. Smith and Mary Smith

HODDER AND STOUGHTON
LONDON SYDNEY AUCKLAND TORONTO

A Word to the Reader

ANY BOOK—and this one is no exception—needs some sort of introduction as to its purposes and how to use it.

First of all, what is a "concordance"? A Bible concordance is an index to the Bible. There are many different sizes and kinds of concordances available. This one was deliberately planned as a concise and handy reference for the average reader or Bible class teacher. The most important biblical words and subjects are arranged alphabetically, and under each is a listing of the most important passages in which this term occurs. Two principles guided the selection of the passages which make up the listings in this index: 1) familiarity, and 2) significance. The most familiar passages were listed, because they are obviously the ones that people will be searching for most frequently. The significant or important passages are needed because of their value in understanding the Bible.

For more than two hundred years the name "Cruden's" has been almost synonymous with concordances. Since Alexander Cruden first compiled his *Complete Concordance* in 1737, it has been recognized as a standard and has appeared in many editions and versions by different publishers. The *Concise Bible Concordance* is based primarily on Cruden's work and later adaptations, but it also owes a debt to *Young's Analytical Concordance* (Funk & Wagnalls) and to *Joy's Topical Concordance* (Harper). A sincere attempt has been made to combine some of the best features of all these fine works into one concise, easily used volume.

HOW TO USE THIS CONCORDANCE

There are three ways this concordance can be used. The most obvious use is to locate some familiar passage by looking up one of its key words in the alphabetical listing. For example, suppose you wanted to find the familiar statement "faith cometh by hearing." If you look under the word *faith*, you will find this phrase, with its reference, in a list of seventy-seven familiar and important passages containing the word (in addition to separate listings for *faithful* and *faithless*). The passages, from Habakkuk 2:4 to Revelation 13:10, are arranged in the order they occur in the Bible. You could also have found "faith cometh by hearing" by looking under the word *hearing*. In addition, after many subjects (e.g., *faithful*) there is a "See also" list of additional verses that relate to the subject but most of which do not actually contain the key word.

A second method of using the concordance is to check listings to find the most important passages on a given subject even when no specific quotation on that topic comes to mind. Although you may not be thinking of any particular verse, you might want to locate the most important passages on *faith, love, God, Christ, baptism,* or dozens of other topics.

A third usage, closely related to the second, arises from using the concordance as a companion to Bible reading. Whenever a word or subject of interest is noted in reading, a quick check in the concordance will reveal other important passages on the same topic—and thereby give a fuller understanding of the subject.

As an additional help to the reader, very simple definitions or identifying phrases are given for many of the key words. These definitions are especially important in the case of older words whose meanings have changed radically since the Bible was translated; in most of these cases the definition is labeled "archaic" to point out that the word is an old form no longer used in this sense. Sometimes a very simple word may have a special definition that best explains its usage in some passages, but in other passages the word has the everyday meaning that we normally think of. In such cases, the word will be repeated as a part of its own definition so the reader will not think the special definition is the only meaning of the word in the Bible. For an example, see *pain.*

A WORD ABOUT ABBREVIATIONS

To conserve space, we have used several abbreviations. In most cases they will cause no difficulties, but, to avoid any misunderstanding, the following list gives all the abbreviations used in this concordance.

An individual italicized letter without a period is used in each listing to signify the word under consideration. Thus, under the entry *eye*, "every *e* shall see Rev 1:7."

Two abbreviations are often used after a scripture reference to avoid additional numbers when attention is to be drawn to a following verse or verses: *f* meaning "verse following," *ff* meaning "two or more verses following."

If a comparison is to be made with some other passage or idea, this is indicated by the Latin abbreviation *cf*, meaning "compare."

And in the definitions and identifying phrases, the abbreviations *lit.*, meaning "literally," and *prob.*, meaning "probably," are sometimes used.

The following abbreviations are used for the names of the books of the Bible:

Gen	Genesis	**Ezra**	Ezra
Ex	Exodus	**Neh**	Nehemiah
Lev	Leviticus	**Esth**	Esther
Num	Numbers	**Job**	Job
Deut	Deuteronomy	**Psa**	Psalms
Josh	Joshua	**Pro**	Proverbs
Judg	Judges	**Ecc**	Ecclesiastes
Ruth	Ruth	**S of S**	Song of Solomon
1 Sam	1 Samuel	**Isa**	Isaiah
2 Sam	2 Samuel	**Jer**	Jeremiah
1 Ki	1 Kings	**Lam**	Lamentations
2 Ki	2 Kings	**Ezek**	Ezekiel
1 Chr	1 Chronicles	**Dan**	Daniel
2 Chr	2 Chronicles	**Hos**	Hosea

Joel	Joel	Gal	Galatians
Amos	Amos	Eph	Ephesians
Ob	Obadiah	Phil	Philippians
Jonah	Jonah	Col	Colossians
Mic	Micah	1 Thes	1 Thessalonians
Nah	Nahum	2 Thes	2 Thessalonians
Hab	Habakkuk	1 Tim	1 Timothy
Zeph	Zephaniah	2 Tim	2 Timothy
Hag	Haggai	Tit	Titus
Zech	Zechariah	Philem	Philemon
Mal	Malachi	Heb	Hebrews
Mat	Matthew	Jas	James
Mk	Mark	1 Pet	1 Peter
Lk	Luke	2 Pet	2 Peter
Jno	John	1 Jno	1 John
Acts	Acts	2 Jno	2 John
Rom	Romans	3 Jno	3 John
1 Cor	1 Corinthians	Jude	Jude
2 Cor	2 Corinthians	Rev	Revelation

THE DEVELOPMENT OF THE ENGLISH BIBLE

This concordance has been developed around the *Authorized* or *King James Version* of the Bible, which was first published in 1611. This version is still the most widely used, in spite of its age and the newer translations that have appeared.

It must be remembered that the Old Testament was written in Hebrew (with a few chapters in Aramaic). The New

Testament was written in Greek. Any translation into another language (called a version) is an attempt to express the original in a language understandable to people of a different culture. Since spoken language constantly changes, there is always the need to produce newer translations to keep up with the language. This does not change the word of God, as some might think, but re-expresses the original Hebrew and Greek in understandable language.

The King James translation was not the first English translation. It *is* the oldest one still in general usage. The following list will be helpful in understanding the development of translations:

The *Wycliffe Bible*—The first complete English translation was made about 1380–1382. It was a manuscript Bible, since printing from movable type had not been invented.

The *Tyndale Bible*—The first printed Bible in English (incomplete) was that of William Tyndale in 1525 (New Testament), and parts of Old Testament in 1530–1531. He was burned at the stake (1536) for his translations.

The *Coverdale Bible*—The first complete printed English Bible was published in 1535. It leaned heavily on Wycliffe and Tyndale, and Myles Coverdale is credited more as an editor than translator.

Matthew's Bible—John Rogers revised the Tyndale Bible slightly, and published it under the pseudonym of Thomas Matthew in 1537. It formed the real basis for later revisions such as the Great Bible, Geneva Bible, Bishop's Bible, and the King James Bible.

The *Great Bible*—Coverdale was authorized by Thomas Cromwell to prepare a Bible to supplant both Matthew's Bible and Coverdale's own first effort. Issued in 1539 on large sheets (13¼ x 17½ inches), it was authorized by King Henry VIII and went through several editions.

Taverner's Bible—Issued by Richard Taverner, also in 1539, this Bible was superseded by the Great Bible and was only reprinted once.

The *Geneva Bible*—A Bible was produced by Puritan exiles in Geneva, Switzerland, about 1557–1560 and smuggled into England. It was bitterly anti-Catholic in its notes and introductions. It was another revision of Tyndale.

The *Bishop's Bible*—This Bible was produced by the clergy of England in 1568 to supplant the Geneva Bible, but it never became popular. It was too stilted and formal.

The *Rheims-Douai*—In 1582 (New Testament) and 1609 (Old Testament) the Catholic Church produced an English translation of the Scriptures from the Latin Vulgate. It was revised in 1750 by Challoner, and has been replaced today by the Confraternity edition (1941).

The *King James* or *Authorized Version*—An Official Bible was commissioned in 1604 (in part to supplant the Geneva Bible, which was still popular). Some forty-seven scholars were selected from several religious persuasions. The Bible was published in 1611 and was declared by James I to be the *Authorized Bible*. Although not popular at first, the Authorized or King James Bible eventually won acceptance. It was the fifth in the line of revisions of the Tyndale Bible.

Since the King James Bible, there have been many translations, but there have only been a few "official" ones, in the sense of being prepared by committees of translators as distinguished from individuals or small private groups.

The *English Revised Version*—A version done by a group of eminent British and American scholars was published in 1881. Owing to differences of British and American usage, an agreement was made to allow an American version to be published twenty years after the ERV.

The *American Standard Version*—In 1901, when the twenty years had expired, the ASV was published. It is the most literal of all translations, and this stiff literalness, as well as the fact that until 1947 it was available from only one publisher by copyright protection, has contributed to a decline in its use in spite of its accuracy.

The *Revised Standard Version*—The RSV made its appearance in 1948 (New Testament) and 1952 (Old Testament), and has been gaining in popularity. It is an excellent translation, even though some passages have been criticized severely.

The *New English Bible*—The NEB New Testament appeared in 1961, and the Old Testament is under preparation. This revision departs from the King James wording even more than the RSV.

There are many modern speech translations of either the whole Bible or the New Testament alone that could be mentioned. Each has its strengths and weaknesses. Among the more important ones still in print are: *Weymouth*

(1903), *Moffatt* (1913–1924), *Goodspeed* (1923), *Phillips* (1947–1958), *Berkeley* (1945–1959), *Williams* (1937), *The Amplified Bible* (1958), *The New American Standard* (1960), *Today's English Version,* or *Good News for Modern Man* (1967), *The Living New Testament* (1967).

WORDS THAT CHANGE MEANING

Since 1609, when the King James Version was first published, the English language has undergone a great deal of change. The average person finds the reading of Shakespeare (from about the same period) somewhat odd, and the same would be true of the Bible were it not so familiar. What we often take to be exalted language is really nothing but old-fashioned language which was perfectly common three hundred years ago. A number of such language changes are listed below for the convenience of the user of this concordance.

Verb Endings. One of the most noticeable features of King James English is the "-eth," "-est" type ending on verbs. Most of these have been dropped in our common language, but, although they sometimes seem strange to pronounce, they usually cause no problem in understanding. For example, "Understandest thou what thou readest?" Acts 8:30, means, "Do you understand what you are reading?"

Pronouns. Another obvious difference in biblical English is the use of the pronouns "thee," "thou," and "thine." In 1609 these forms were already beginning to become old-fashioned, and were used mostly in speaking to children and to intimate friends and members of one's family. But the translators of the King James Bible used them very carefully in their original sense to render accurately the exact meaning of the Hebrew and Greek: "You" and "ye" were used when two or more people were being spoken to, and "thee" and "thou" when only one person was addressed.

Changing Connotations. By far the most troublesome type of words are those whose meaning or significance have changed over the years. The word "charity" as used in 1611 usually meant what we now mean by the word "love." Today "charity" means helping those in poverty (and even has an undesirable connotation). This modern usage of "charity" misses the richness of the meaning of 1 Corinthians 13:1–13. Another example is the word "let" in 2 Thessalonians 2:7. Today the word means to "permit" or "allow," but its usage in this passage is just the opposite, meaning to "prevent" or "hold back"! (We preserve the archaic meaning of "let" in tennis and in law courts today.) Coincidentally, in 1 Thessalonians 4:15 we have the word "prevent," which does not make sense when we think of our meaning of "hindering," but in this verse, it means to "precede" or "go before." There are many other such instances.

Let us re-emphasize that we are not tampering with the Greek or Hebrew originals; we are attempting to select the most meaningful English words to express best those originals' meanings as our language changes and as old words become obsolete.

The person who wishes to search out the precise shades of meanings of the English words used to translate the original Greek and Hebrew scriptures may use one or more of the following: *Young's Analytical Concordance, Strong's Concordance* (both are huge volumes that have excellent and exhaustive treatments of terms), *The Language of the King James Bible* by Melvin Elliott, or *Bible Words That Have Changed Meaning* by Luther Weigle.

A

Aaron, *the brother of Moses and first high priest,* Ex 4:14, 6:23, Lev 8:12, Num 20:28, Heb 5:4

Abaddon, *angel of the bottomless pit,* Rev 9:11

Abana, *a river of Damascus,* 2 Ki 5:12

abase, *to bring low or to humble*
behold proud and *a* him   Job 40:11
lion will not *a* himself   Isa 31:4
and *a* him that is high   Ezek 21:26
exalt himself shall be *a*   Mat 23:12,
                Lk 14:11, 18:14
I know how to be *a*   Phil 4:12
See also: Dan 4:37, Lk 18:13, 1 Cor 1:19, Gal 6:3, Jas 4:10

abated, *decreased, cut off*
the waters were *a*   Gen 8:3,11
nor his natural force *a*   Deut 34:7

Abba, *Aramaic word for father*
A Father, all things   Mk 14:36
we cry, *A* Father   Rom 8:15
into hearts crying *A*   Gal 4:6

Abed-nego, *servant of Nego, one of captives in Babylon,* Dan 1:7, 2:49, 3:23, 3:30

Abel, *the second son of Adam,* Gen 4:4, Mat 23:35, Heb 11:4

Abel, *fresh, grassy, meadow, a place name,* Gen 50:11, Judg 7:22, 1 Sam 6:18, 2 Sam 20:18

abhor, *loathe, detest, reject*
I *a* myself, and repent   Job 42:6
he *a* not evil   Psa 36:4
I hate and *a* lying   119:163

nations shall *a* him   Pro 24:24
thou that *a* idols, dost   Rom 2:22
a that which is evil   12:9
See also: Psa 101:3, Jer 3:19, 25:5, Rom 1:28, 2 Tim 4:4

Abiathar, *priest in the days of David,* 1 Sam 22:20, 23:6,9, 2 Sam 8:17, 20:25

Abib, *the first month of the religious year and seventh of the civil,* Ex 13:4, 23:15, 34:18, Deut 16:1

abide, *to stay, dwell in one place, endure, stand firm*
the earth *a* forever   Ecc 1:4
shepherds *a* in field   Lk 2:8
I must *a* at thy house   19:5
not *a* in darkness   Jno 12:46
send comforter that he *a*   14:16
a in me and I in you   15:4,7
if any man *a* not in me   15:6
now *a* faith, hope   1 Cor 13:13
word of God which *a*   1 Pet 1:23
whoso *a* not in doctrine   2 Jno 9

Abigail, *Nabal's wife,* 1 Sam 25:3, 27:3, 1 Chr 2:16

Abihu, *son of Aaron who offered strange fire,* Lev 10:2

Abijah, or Abijam, *two kings—one of Israel, one of Judah,* 1 Ki 14:1, 31, 15:1,7, 1 Chr 29:1, Neh 10:7, 12:4,17

ability, *power, strength*
they gave after their *a*   Ezra 2:69
according to his *a*   Mat 25:15
according to *a* determined   Acts 11:29
as the *a* God giveth   1 Pet 4:11

Abimelech, *several persons bore the name,* Gen 20:2, 21:22, 26:1,16, Judg 8:31, 9:1, 2 Sam 11:21, 1 Chr 18:16

able, *abundance, power*

give as he is *a*   Deut 16:17
God whom we serve is *a* Dan 3:17
Thy God is *a* to deliver   6:20
God is *a* of stones Mat 3:9, Lk 3:8
believe that I am *a* to   Mat 9:28
that is *a* to destroy soul   10:28
are ye *a* to drink of cup   20:22
no man is *a* to pluck   Jno 10:29
a to separate from   Rom 8:39
above that ye are *a*   1 Cor 10:13
Lord *a* to do abundantly Eph 3:20
a to keep that I   2 Tim 1:12
scriptures *a* to make wise   3:15
word which is *a* to   Jas 1:21

Abner, *general of Saul's army,* 1 Sam 14:51, 17:55, 2 Sam 3:30

abode *(see abide)*

glory of Lord *a* on Sinai Ex 24:16
spirit, and it *a* upon   Jno 1:32
make our *a* with him   14:23
upper room where *a*   Acts 1:32

abolish, *cause to pass away*

righteousness not *a*   Isa 51:6
a in his flesh enmity   Eph 2:15
Christ, who hath *a*   2 Tim 1:10

abomination, *hateful, detestable, often means "an idol"*

every shepherd is *a*   Gen 46:34
the froward is an *a*   Pro 3:32
seven things are an *a*   6:16
lying lips are *a*   12:20
way of the wicked is an *a*   15:9
is proud in heart is an *a*   16:5

sigh and cry for all *a*   Ezek 9:4
a of desolation   Mat 24:15, Mk 13:14
man is *a* with God   Lk 16:15

abound, *many, much, to be above*

faithful men shall *a*   Pro 28:20
iniquity shall *a*   Mat 24:12
grace by Jesus hath *a*   Rom 5:15
continue in sin, grace *a?*   6:1
able to make grace *a*   2 Cor 9:8
your love may *a* more   Phil 1:9
I know how to *a*   4:12
be in you and *a*   2 Pet 1:8

above, *higher up, over, more*

waters *a* the firmament   Gen 1:7
commandments *a* gold Psa 119:127
mountains be exalted *a*   Isa 2:2
be tempted *a* that ye   1 Cor 10:13
one God who is *a* all   Eph 4:6
things which are *a*   Col 3:1
perfect gift is from *a*   Jas 1:17

Abraham, or Abram, *father of Hebrew people,* Gen 11:27, 25:8, Rom 3:9, Gal 3:6, Heb 11:17, Jas 2:23

Absalom, *third son of David,* 2 Sam 3:3, 1 Chr 3:2, 2 Sam 15:4, 18:33

absent, *away from, to be hidden*

to be *a* from the body   2 Cor 5:8
I be *a* in the flesh   Col 2:5

abstain, *to hold off from*

a pollutions of idols   Acts 15:20
a from all appearance of evil   1 Thes 5:22
commanding to *a* from 1 Tim 4:3
a from fleshly lusts   1 Pet 2:11

abundance *(see abound)*

waters bring forth *a*   Gen 1:20 f
Israel increased *a*   Ex 1:7

our God will *a* pardon   Isa 55:7

out of *a* of the heart   Mat 12:34

consisteth not in *a*   Lk 12:15

have life more *a*   Jno 10:10

receive *a* of grace   Rom 5:17

able to do exceeding *a*   Eph 3:20

according to *a* mercy   1 Pet 1:3

accept, *receive, be well pleased*

meditation be *a*   Psa 19:14

thee, O Lord, in an *a* time   69:13

Justice and judgment is *a*   Pro 21:3

in *a* time have I heard   Isa 49:8

to proclaim the *a* year   61:2, Lk
                              4:19

no prophet is *a* in his   4:24

worketh righteousness is *a*   Acts
                              10:35

living sacrifice, holy, *a*   Rom 12:1

Now is the *a* time   2 Cor 6:2

good and *a* before God   1 Tim 5:4

access, *leading unto*

also we have *a* by faith   Rom 5:2

through him we have *a*   Eph 2:18

boldness and *a* by faith   3:12

accomplish, *to end, complete*

shall *a* that I please   Isa 55:11

accord, *like-minded,* Acts 1:14, 2:1,
2:46, 4:24, 5:12, 8:6, 12:20, 15:25,
Phil 2:2

according, *like as*

judge me, O God, *a* to   Psa 35:24

a to your faith be it   Mat 9:29

he will reward every man *a*   16:27,
                              Rom 2:6, 2 Tim 4:14

judge not *a* to the   Jno 7:24

Christ died *a* to   1 Cor 15:3

a as he purposeth   2 Cor 9:7

a to good pleasure   Eph 1:5

a to riches of his grace   1:7

a as his divine power   2 Pet 1:3

account, *answer, reckon, respond*

we may give an *a* of   Acts 19:40

we are as sheep *a* for   Rom 8:36

everyone shall give *a*   14:12

shall give *a* to him   1 Pet 4:5

accursed, *thing lightly esteemed*

hanged, is *a* of God   Deut 21:23

gospel, let him be *a*   Gal 1:8 f

accuse, *to insult, speak down*

over his head this *a*   Mat 27:37

they began to *a* him   Lk 23:2

receive not an *a*   1 Tim 5:19

falsely *a* your good   1 Pet 3:16

Aceldama, *field of blood,* Acts 1:19

Achaia, *classic name for southern
Greece. See:* Acts 18:12, 19:21, Rom
15:26, 1 Cor 16:15, 2 Cor 1:1, 1 Thes
1:7

Achan, or Achar, *violated command at
Jericho. See:* Josh 7:18, 22:20, 1 Chr
2:7

acknowledge, *to know, make known*

I *a* my sin   Psa 32:5

I *a* my trangression   51:3

a the Son hath Father   1 Jno 2:23

Adam, *of the ground, man. See:* Gen
5:2, Rom 5:14, 1 Cor 15:22,45
See also: Josh 3:16 (town)

add, *to increase, to give*

and he *a* no more   Deut 5:22

a thou not to his words   Pro 30:6

Lord *a* to the church   Acts 2:47

disannulleth or *a*   Gal 3:15

a because of transgressions   3:19

adder, *serpent*

a poison is under lips   Psa 140:3

stingeth like an *a*   Pro 23:32

adjure, *to cause to take an oath* 1 Ki 22:16, Mat 26:63, Mk 5:7, Acts 19:13

admonish, *put in mind, say again*
by these, my son, be *a*   Ecc 12:12
also to *a* one another   Rom 15:14
a one another in psalms   Col 3:16

admonition *(see admonish)*
written for our *a*   1 Cor 10:11
bring them up in the *a*   Eph 6:4
See also: Pro 10:17, Ezek 3:14, Amos 4:12

Adonijah, *fourth son of David,* 2 Sam 3:4, 1 Ki 1:5, 2:17 ff

adoption, *make as a son*
received spirit of *a*   Rom 8:15
might receive *a* of sons   Gal 4:5
us to the *a* of children   Eph 1:5

adorn, *to decorate, polish*
woman *a* in modest   1 Tim 2:9
a the doctrine of God   Tit 2:10
a let it be outward   1 Pet 3:3

adulterer, *one who violates the marriage vows; symbolically idol worship*
thou shalt not commit *a*   Ex 20:14
divorced committeth *a*   Mat 5:32
out of heart proceed *a*   15:19
neither *a* inherit   1 Cor 6:9
works of the flesh, *a*   Gal 5:19

adversary, *opponent, accuser*
long shall *a* reproach?   Psa 74:10
agree with *a* quickly   Mat 5:25
avenge me of mine *a*   Lk 18:3
no occasion to the *a*   1 Tim 5:14
a devil as roaring   1 Pet 5:8

adversity, *distress, straitness*
I shall never be in *a*   Psa 10:6

but in the day of *a*   Ecc 7:14
give you bread of *a*   Isa 30:20

advocate, *one alongside to help*
we have an *a* with   1 Jno 2:1

Aenon, *one of the sites where John baptized. See:* Jno 3:23

afar, *far away, distant*
my thoughts *a* off   Psa 139:2
and not a God *a* off?   Jer 23:23
peace to you *a* off   Eph 2:17
seen the promise *a* off   Heb 11:13
and cannot see *a* off   2 Pet 1:9

affairs, *thing, business, matter*
he will guide his *a*   Psa 112:5
ye also may know my *a*   Eph 6:21
with the *a* of life   2 Tim 2:4

affection, *feeling, passion*
gave them up to vile *a*   Rom 1:26
kindly *a* one to another   12:10
the flesh with the *a*   Gal 5:24
set your *a* on things   Col 3:2

afflict, *press, grieve, do evil*
a them 400 years   Gen 15:13
taskmasters to *a* them   Ex 1:11
ye shall not *a* any widow   22:22
the Egyptians *a* us   Deut 26:6
smitten of God and *a*   Isa 53:4,7
be *a* and mourn   Jas 4:9
is any among you *a*?   5:13

affliction *(see afflict)*
Lord hath heard thy *a*   Gen 16:11
fruitful in the land of *a*   41:52
many are the *a*   Psa 34:19
consider mine *a* and   119:153
in the furnace of *a*   Isa 48:10
in those days shall *a*   Mk 13:19
our light *a* which   2 Cor 4:17
endure *a*   2 Tim 4:5

suffer *a* with people   Heb 11:25

fatherless in their *a*   Jas 1:27

aforetime, *before this, previously*

things were written *a*   Rom 15:4

afraid, *terrified, tremble*

it is I, be not *a*   Mat 14:27, Mk 6:50, Jno 6:20

I was *a* and hid talent   Mat 25:25

afresh, *again, anew*

crucify Son of God *a*   Heb 6:6

Agabus, *prophet in early church,* Acts 11:28, 21:10

against, *opposite*

hand will be *a* every   Gen 16:12

not with me, is *a* me   Mat 12:30

every where spoken *a*   Acts 28:22

ages, *era, dispensation*

in *a* to come he might   Eph 2:7

in the church through all *a*   3:21

hath been hid from *a*   Col 1:26

agree, *be like or similar*

together except they *a*   Amos 3:3

a with thine adversary   Mat 5:25

if two of you shall *a*   18:19

blood, these *a* in one   1 Jno 5:8

Agrippa (II), *king of northern Palestine under Romans,* Acts 25:22 ff

Ahab, *king of Israel,* 1 Ki 16:29 ff, 18:17, 22:6 ff

Ahaz, *king of Judah,* 2 Ki 16:1 ff, 2 Chr 28:1 ff, Isa 7:1 ff

Ai, *place name meaning the heap, ruin,* Gen 13:3, Josh 7:4

air, *heavens, wind, atmosphere*

the birds of the *a* have   Mat 8:20

birds of the *a* come and lodge   13:32, Mk 4:32, Lk 9:58

one that beateth *a*   1 Cor 9:26

meet the Lord in *a*   1 Thes 4:17

alienate, *to be disjointed*

a from the life of God   Eph 4:18

sometimes *a*, enemies of   Col 1:21

alike, *just as, same*

contentious woman are *a* Pro 27:15

all things come *a* to   Ecc 9:2

esteemeth every day *a*   Rom 14:5

alive, *living*

heard that he was *a*   Mk 16:11

was dead and is *a*   Lk 15:24,32

shewed himself *a* after   Acts 1:3

a to God through Christ Rom 6:11

in Christ made *a*   1 Cor 15:22

are *a* and remain   1 Thes 4:15,17

which was dead, and is *a*   Rev 2:8

allow, *know, recognize*

that I do, I *a* not   Rom 7:15

that thing which he *a*   14:22

almighty, *powerful, sufficient*

I am the *a* God, walk   Gen 17:1

doth *a* pervert justice?   Job 8:3

great day of God *a*   Rev 16:14

God *a* and the Lamb are   21:22

almost, *to be about to, nearly*

a thou persuadest me   Acts 26:28

alms, *kindness, kind act*

that ye do not your *a*   Mat 6:1

sell, and give *a*   Lk 12:33

seeing Peter, asked *a*   Acts 3:3

Cornelius gave much *a* to   10:2

alone, *one, to be separate, apart*

that man should be *a*   Gen 2:18

his name *a* is excellent Psa 148:13

Lord *a* be exalted   Isa 2:11,17

have trodden wine press *a*   63:3

live by bread *a*   Mat 4:4, Lk 4:4

let *a* they be blind   Mat 15:14

forgive sins but God *a*?   Lk 5:21
I am not *a* but   Jno 8:16, 16:32
works is dead, being *a*   Jas 2:17

alpha, *first letter of Greek alphabet,*
   Rev 1:8, 21:6, 22:13

Alphaeus, *the father of James,* Mat
   10:3, Mk 3:18, Lk 6:15, Acts 1:13;
   the father of Levi, Mk 2:14

altar, *place of sacrifice*
   Noah builded an *a*   Gen 8:20
   Abraham built an *a*   12:7, 22:9
   a of burnt offering   Ex 40:10
   the dedication of the *a*   Num 7:84
   bring thy gift to the *a*   Mat 5:23
   I found an *a* with   Acts 17:23

alway, *always, continually, ever*
   keep my commands *a*   Deut 5:29
   learn to fear the Lord *a*   14:23
   I am with you *a*   Mat 28:20
   as ye have *a* obeyed   Phil 2:12

am, *existing, being*
   a I brother's keeper?   Gen 4:9
   I *a* that I *a* hath sent   Ex 3:14
   I *a* and   Isa 47:8, Zeph 2:15
   say that I the Son of man *a*?   Mat
      16:13, Mk 8:27, Lk 9:18
   there *a* I in midst   Mat 18:20
   I *a* the bread of life   Jno 6:35
   I *a* the light of the world   8:12
   before Abraham was, I *a*   8:58
   where I *a* there shall   12:26
   altogether as I *a*   Acts 26:29
   I *a* what I *a*   1 Cor 15:10

amiss, *out of place, wickedly*
   we have done *a.*   2 Chr 6:37
   man hath done nothing *a* Lk 23:41
   because ye ask *a*   Jas 4:3

Amos, *prophet to Israel about 750 B.C.,*
   Amos 1:1, 7:14

Ananias, *husband of Sapphira,* Acts
   5:1 ff; *disciple of Damascus,* Acts
   9:10; *high priest,* Acts 23:2, 24:1

anathema, *accursed*
   let him be *a*   1 Cor 16:22
   See also: Gal 1:8,9

anchor, *anchor, weight*
   would have cast *a*   Acts 27:30
   hope we have as an *a*   Heb 6:19

ancient, *aged, old*
   remove not the *a* land   Pro 22:28
   the *a* of days did sit   Dan 7:9

Andrew, *an apostle,* Mat 4:18, Mk
   13:3, Jno 1:40, 6:8, 12:22, Acts 1:13

angel, *messenger*
   there came two *a* to   Gen 19:1
   a of the Lord said   22:11
   Balaam saw *a* standing Num 22:31
   Son of Man, and all the holy *a*
      Mat 25:31, Mk 8:38, Lk 9:26
   a answered the woman   Mat 28:5
   the *a* said, fear not   Lk 1:13
   sixth month the *a* Gabriel   1:26
   a said to the shepherds   2:10
   an *a* strengthening him   22:44
   a spake to Cornelius   Acts 10:7
   the *a* said to Peter, bind   12:8
   tongues of men and *a*   1 Cor 13:1
   into an *a* of light   2 Cor 11:14
   an *a* from heaven preach   Gal 1:8

anger, *fury, indignation*
   ready to pardon, slow to *a*   Neh
      9:17
   cease from *a* and forsake   Psa 37:8
   grievous words stir up *a*   Pro 15:1
   that is slow to *a*   15:18, 16:32

gift in secret pacifieth *a*   21:14
wrath is cruel, and *a* is   27:4
the Lord is slow to *a*   Nah 1:3

angry *(see anger)*

and Moses was *a* with   Lev 10:16
God is *a* with the wicked   Psa 7:11
friendship with *a* man   Pro 22:24
so doth an *a* countenance   25:23
a man stirreth up strife   29:22
Didst thou well to be *a?*   Jonah 4:4,9
whosoever is *a* with his   Mat 5:22
he was *a* and would not   Lk 15:28
be *a* and sin not   Eph 4:26

anise, *dill*

pay tithe of mint, *a*   Mat 23:23

Annas, *high priest,* Lk 3:2, Jno 18:13, Acts 4:6

anoint, *smear (with oil)*

a and consecrate   Ex 28:41, 30:30, 40:15
David the *a* of God   2 Sam 23:1
saith the Lord to his *a*   Isa 45:1
Lord hath *a*   61:1, Lk 4:18
a themselves with   Amos 6:6
salvation with thine *a*   Hab 3:13
spices that they might *a*   Mk 16:1
kissed his feet and *a*   Lk 7:38
he *a* the eyes of blind   Jno 9:6
a Jesus of Nazareth   Acts 10:38
hath *a* us in God   2 Cor 1:21

answer, *reply, return a word*

a soft *a* turneth away   Pro 15:1
a not a fool according   26:4
he *a* nothing   Mat 27:12,14, Mk 14:61, 15:5, Lk 23:9
were astonished at his *a*   2:47
they marvelled at his *a*   20:26

be ready to give an *a*   1 Pet 3:15
a of a good conscience   3:21

Antioch, *city of Syria,* Acts 11:26, 13:1; *city of Pisidia,* Acts 13:14

Apollos, *eloquent Christian preacher,* Acts 18:24 ff, 1 Cor 1:12, 3:4

apostle, *one sent forth*

names of the twelve *a*   Mat 10:2
whom he named *a*   Lk 6:13
with the eleven *a*   Acts 1:26
scattered abroad, except *a*   8:1
called an *a*   Rom 1:1, 1 Cor 1:1
God hath set first *a*   12:28
some *a,* some prophets   Eph 4:11

apparel, *clothing, robe, garment*

stood by in white *a*   Acts 1:10
themselves in modest *a*   1 Tim 2:9
if a man in goodly *a*   Jas 2:2
gold, or putting on *a*   1 Pet 3:3

appear, *reveal, to be seen*

God said, let dry land *a*   Gen 1:9
what time the star *a*   Mat 2:7
that they may *a* to men   6:16
ye outwardly *a* righteous   23:28
he *a* to the eleven   Mk 16:14
there *a* to them cloven   Acts 2:3
quick and dead at his *a*   2 Tim 4:1
them also that love his *a*   4:8
grace of God hath *a*   Tit 2:11
looking for glorious *a* of   2:13

appearance, *sight, manifestation*

as the *a* of fire   Num 9:15,16
not according to the *a*   Jno 7:24
abstain from all *a*   1 Thes 5:22

apple, *quince*

like *a* of gold   Pro 25:11

applied *(see apply)*

I *a* my heart to know   Ecc 7:25, 8:9, 8:16

apply, *apply, give, cause to go in*
   we may *a* our hearts   Psa 90:12
   and *a* thine heart to   Pro 2:2
   hear words, *a* thine heart   22:17
   a heart to instruction   23:12

appoint, *choose, decree*
   he hath *a* a day   Acts 17:31
   elders every city as *a*   Tit 1:5
   a to men once to die   Heb 9:27

apprehend, *to receive thoroughly*
   I may *a* that for which   Phil 3:12
   I am *a* of Christ Jesus   3:12
   not myself to have *a* but   3:13

approve, *be pleased with*
   Jesus, a man *a* of God   Acts 2:22
   a the things that are   Rom 2:18
   study to shew thyself *a*   2 Tim 2:15
   that ye may *a* things   Phil 1:10

Aquila, *husband of Priscilla,* Acts 18:2,
   18:26, 16:3, 1 Cor 16:19

Ararat, *mountain where ark rested,*
   Gen 8:4

archangel, *chief messenger*
   with voice of the *a*   1 Thes 4:16
   Michael the *a* when   Jude 9

aright, *right, properly*
   set not their heart *a*   Psa 78:8
   the wise useth knowledge *a*   15:2

arise, *to go up, wake up*
   therefore *a* go over   Josh 1:2
   a O Lord, save me   Psa 3:7
   a for our help, and redeem   44:26
   shall the dead *a?*   88:10
   a shine, for thy light   Isa 60:1
   when persecution *a*   Mat 13:21
   shall *a* false Christs   24:24
   a and go to my father   Lk 15:18
   for out of Galilee *a*   Jno 7:52

   said, Tabitha, *a*   Acts 9:40
   why tarriest thou? *a* and   22:16
   till the day star *a*   2 Pet 1:19

ark, *chest, boat*
   an *a* of gopher wood   Gen 6:14
   and the *a* went on the face   7:18
   she took for him an *a*   Ex 2:3
   a of the Lord   Josh 4:11, 6:12,
       1 Sam 4:6, 6:1, 2 Sam 6:9
   waited while *a* was   1 Pet 3:20

Armageddon, *Greek for "hill of
   Megiddo,"* Rev 16:6. Cf. Josh 17:11,
   Judg 1:27, 2 Ki 23:29, Zech 12:11

armour
   David put Goliath's *a* 1 Sam 17:54
   let us put on the *a*   Rom 13:12
   put on the *a* of God to   Eph 6:11
   take to you whole *a* of God   6:13

arose *(see rise)*
   a a new king   Ex 1:8, Acts 7:18
   a generation that knew   Judg 2:10
   a and took young   Mat 2:14,21
   he *a* and rebuked the winds   8:26,
       Mk 4:39, Lk 8:24
   a and followed   Mat 9:1,19, Mk
       2:14
   flood *a*, the storm beat   Lk 6:48

array, *to clothe, prepare*
   not *a* like   Mat 6:29, Lk 12:27
   woman was *a* in purple   Rev 17:4

arrow
   Jonathan shot an *a*   1 Sam 20:36
   a of the Almighty are   Job 6:4
   false witness is sharp *a*   Pro 25:18
   mad man who casteth *a*   26:18

Asa, *king of Judah,* 1 Ki 15:8, 2 Chr 16

ascend, *go up*
   if I *a* up into   Psa 24:3, 139:8

who hath *a* into heaven   Pro 30:4
no man hath *a* to heaven   Jno 3:13
a to my Father, and your   20:17
when he *a* up on high   Eph 4:8

ashamed, *to blush, put to shame*
and his wife were not *a*   Gen 2:25
forsake thee shall be *a*   Jer 17:13
be *a* of me   Mk 8:38, Lk 9:26
cannot dig, to beg I am *a*   16:3
I am not *a* of gospel   Rom 1:16
hope maketh not *a* because   5:5
I am not *a*   2 Tim 1:12
Onesiphorus was not *a*   2 Tim 1:16
God is not *a* to be   Heb 11:16

Ashdod, *city of Philistines,* 1 Sam 5,
2 Chr 26:6, Amos 1:8, Zech 9:6

Ashtaroth, *goddess of Canaanites,* Judg
2:13, 1 Sam 12:10, 1 Ki 11:5 ff

aside, *apart, away*
he riseth and laid *a*   Jno 13:4
lay *a* every weight   Heb 12:1

ask, *inquire, seek, search out*
a for the old paths   Jer 6:16
give to him that *a*   Mat 5:42, Lk
     6:30
need of before ye *a* him   Mat 6:8
a, and it shall be   7:7, Lk 11:9
he *a* his disciples   Mat 16:13, Mk
     8:27, Lk 9:18
whatsoever ye *a*   Jno 14:13, 15:16
if ye abide in me, *a* what   15:7
above all we can *a*   Eph 3:20
lack wisdom, let him *a*   Jas 1:5,6
have not, because ye *a*   4:2
to every one that *a*   1 Pet 3:15
if we *a* according   1 Jno 5:14

asleep, *sleeping*
are *a* in Christ   1 Cor 15:18

them that are *a*   1 Thes 4:13
since fathers fell *a*   2 Pet 3:4

ass, *beast of burden*
the jawbone of an *a*   Judg 15:16
ox his owner, and *a* his   Isa 1:3
riding on a   Zech 9:9, Mat 21:5
the dumb *a* speaking   2 Pet 2:16

assemble, *to be gathered*
a whole year they *a*   Acts 11:26
forsake not the *a*   Heb 10:25

assure, *to persuade, make certain*
house of Israel know *a*   Acts 2:36
shall *a* our hearts   1 Jno 3:19

Assyria, *empire northeast of Palestine,*
Nineveh capital city, 2 Ki 15:29,
19:4, Isa 37:36, Jonah 1:1, Nah 1:1

Athaliah, *daughter of Ahab and Jeze-*
bel, 2 Ki 8:26, 11:1 ff, 2 Chr 22:10 ff

Athens, *capital of Greece,* Acts 17:15,
1 Thes 3:1

athirst, *to be thirsty*
when saw we these *a*?   Mat 25:24
give to him that is *a*   Rev 21:6
let him that is *a*   22:17

atonement, *to cover, reconcile*
eat things wherewith *a*   Ex 29:33
to make an *a*   30:15, Lev 17:11
we have now received *a*   Rom 5:11

attain, *reach, lay hold of*
it is high, I cannot *a*   Psa 139:6
Gentiles have a *to*   Rom 9:30
a to the resurrection   Phil 3:11
whereto we have already *a*   3:16
doctrine thou hast *a*   1 Tim 4:6

attend, *understand, give attention*
a to my cry   Psa 17:1, 61:1, 142:6
a to me, hear me, I mourn   55:2
son, *a* to my words   Pro 4:20, 7:24

C.B.C.—2

my son, *a* to my wisdom 5:1
may *a* on the Lord 1 Cor 7:35
attendance *(see attend)*
till I come, give *a* 1 Tim 4:13
author, *beginner, creator*
God is not the *a* of 1 Cor 14:33
became the *a* of eternal Heb 5:9
the *a* and finisher of 12:2
authority, *strength, power*
taught them as one having *a* Mat
7:29, Mk 1:22
exercise *a* Mat 20:25, Mk 10:42
by what *a* doest thou these things?
Mat 21:23, Mk 11:28
exercise *a* are called Lk 22:25
hath given his *a* to Jno 5:27
a woman to usurp *a* 1 Tim 2:12
and rebuke with all *a* Tit 2:1
availeth, *accomplish, be strong*
circumcision *a* not Gal 5:6, 6:15
righteous man *a* much Jas 5:16
avenge, *revenge, give full justice*
shall God *a* his elect Lk 18:7
a not yourselves Rom 12:19
avoid, *keep free of*
cause divisions, and *a* Rom 16:17
a profane and vain 1 Tim 6:20
unlearned questions *a* 2 Tim 2:23
a foolish questions Tit 3:9
awake, *waken, stir up*
a, why sleepest thou? Psa 44:23
a, put on strength Isa 51:9, 52:1
high time to *a* Rom 13:11
a to righteousness 1 Cor 15:34
a thou that sleepest Eph 5:14
awoke *(see awake)*
Noah *a* from his wine Gen 9:24
Pharaoh *a* 41:4,7,21

(handwritten in margin: Full a. Mat 28:18 P.1.)

Samson *a* out of sleep Judg 16:20
axe, *cutting tool*
to sharpen his *a* 1 Sam 13:20
the *a* head fell into 2 Ki 6:5
a is laid to root of trees Mat 3:10,
Lk 3:9
Azariah, or Uzziah, *king of Judah,* 2 Ki
14:21, 2 Chr 26

B

Baal, *god of the Canaanites,* Judg 2:13,
3:7, 10:6,10, 1 Ki 16:31, 18:21,
19:18, Rom 11:4
Baasha, *king of Israel,* 1 Ki
15:16,27,32, 16:6
babbler, *vain speaker*
a *b* is no better Ecc 10:11
what will this *b* say? Acts 17:18
babbling, *empty sound*
who hath *b*? Pro 23:29
profane and vain *b* 1 Tim 6:20
shun profane *b* 2 Tim 2:16
babe, *baby*
mouths of *b* Psa 8:2, Mat 21:16
b wrapped in swaddling clothes Lk
2:12,16
as newborn *b* desire 1 Pet 2:2
See also: Mat 11:25, Rom 2:20,
Heb 5:13
Babel, *Babylon,* Gen 10:10, 11:9, 2 Ki
17:30, 20:17, Psa 137:1, Jer 25:11,
1 Pet 5:13, Rev 17:5
back, *behind*
plough, and looking *b* Lk 9:62

See also: Mat 24:18, Lk 17:31

back *(of person)*

gave my *b* to smiters   Isa 50:6

have turned their *b*   Jer 2:27

backbiters, *slanderers*

b, haters of God   Rom 1:30

wraths, strifes, *b*   2 Cor 12:20

backsliding, *turning back*

b Israel committed   Jer 3:8

people are bent to *b*   Hos 11:7

I will heal their *b*   14:4

bad, *base, evil*

cast the *b* away   Mat 13:48

whether good or *b*   2 Cor 5:10

bade, *invited, asked*

made a supper and *b*   Lk 14:16

the Spirit *b* me go   Acts 11:12

bag, *purse, sack*

b of deceitful weights   Mic 6:11

thief, and had the *b*   Jno 12:6

Judas had the .*b*   13:29

See also: Deut 25:13, Pro 7:20, 16:11

Balaam, *Midianite prophet,* Num 22:5, 24:2, Deut 23:4, 2 Pet 2:15

Balak, *king of Moab,* Num 22:4, Josh 24:9

balance, *scale for weighing*

just *b*   Lev 19:36, Ezek 45:10

a false *b* is   Pro 11:1, 20:23

weighed in the *b*   Dan 5:27

See also: Job 31:6, Pro 16:11

balm, *medicinal gum, salve*

Is there no *b* in Gilead?   Jer 8:22

to Gilead, and take *b*   46:11

band, *bond, cord*

drew with *b* of love   Hos 11:4

all the body by *b*   Col 2:19

baptism *(see baptize)*

Pharisees come to his *b*   Mat 3:7

b of John, whence was it   21:25, Mk 11:30, Lk 20:4

and preach the *b*   Mk 1:4, Lk 3:3

preached *b* of repentance   Acts 13:24

Apollos knowing only the *b* 18:25

John baptized with the *b*   19:4

buried with him by *b*   Rom 6:4

One Lord, one *b*   Eph 4:5

buried with him in *b*   Col 2:12

doctrine of *b*   Heb 6:2

figure whereunto, *b*   1 Pet 3:21

Baptist John, Mat 3:1, 11:11, 14:8, Lk 7:28,33

baptize, *to wash, immerse, dip*

I *b* you with water   Mat 3:11, Mk 1:8, Lk 3:16, Jno 1:26

b of him in   Mat 3:6, Mk 1:5

Jesus to John to be *b*   Mat 3:13

teach all nations, *b* them   28:19

John did *b* in the   Mk 1:4

Jesus was *b* of John   1:9

he that believeth and is *b*   16:16

Jesus being *b* and praying Lk 3:21

lawyers, not *b* of him   7:30

that sent me to *b* said   Jno 1:33

Jesus himself *b* not   4:2

b with water   Acts 1:5, 11:16

repent, and be *b* every one   2:38

received his word were *b*   2:41

what hinder me to be *b*?   8:36

Philip and eunuch, he *b*   8:38

sight, and arose and was *b*   9:18

Peter commanded to be *b*   10:48

Lydia when she was *b*   16:15

and was *b,* he and all his   16:33

believed and were *b* 18:8

arise, and be *b* and wash 22:16

b into Jesus, were *b* Rom 6:3

were ye *b* in name? 1 Cor 1:13

by one Spirit are we *b* 12:13

been *b* into Christ Gal 3:27

Barak, *judge, helper of Deborah,* Judg 4:6, 5:1

barbarian, *non-Greek*

both to Greeks and *b* Rom 1:14

neither Greek, Jew, *b* Col 3:11

bare, *carried, lifted up (see bear)*

how I *b* you on eagles' Ex 19:4

he *b* the sins of many Isa 53:12

b false witness Mk 14:56,57

b witness of him Jno 1:15,32,34

John *b* witness to truth 5:33

he *b* our sins 1 Pet 2:24

barley, *small grain,* Jno 6:9, Rev 6:6

barn, *storage house*

nor gather into *b* Mat 6:26

the wheat into my *b* 13:30

I will pull down my *b* Lk 12:18

Barnabas, *companion of Paul,* Acts 4:36, 11:22, 12:25, 13:1, 15:2, Gal 2:9

barren, *sterile*

but Sarai was *b* Gen 11:30

Rebekah was *b* 25:21

Rachel was *b* 29:31

base, *humble, ignoble*

b things of world 1 Cor 1:28

basket, *woven container*

a *b* of summer fruit Amos 8:1,2

took up twelve *b* Mat 14:20, Mk 6:43, Lk 9:17, Jno 6:13

wall in a *b* Acts 9:25, 2 Cor 11:33

See also: Mat 15:37, 15:9, Mk 8:8

bath, *Hebrew measure of about nine gallons. See:* Isa 5:10, Ezek 45:10 ff

Bath-sheba, *mother of Solomon,* 2 Sam 11:3, 12:24, 1 Ki 1:15, 2:13

battle, *conflict, struggle*

before us and fight *b* 1 Sam 8:20

front of hottest *b* 2 Sam 11:15

b of great day Rev 16:14, 20:8

beam, *thick board, rafter*

not the *b* Mat 7:3, Lk 6:41,42

bear, *carry, lift up*

greater than I can *b* Gen 4:13

land not able to *b* 13:6, 36:7

how long shall I *b* Num 14:27

shoes not worthy to *b* Mat 3:11

found Simon, compelled him to *b* Mat 27:32, Mk 15:21, Lk 23:26

doth not *b* his cross 14:27

chosen to *b* my name Acts 9:15

b infirmities of weak Rom 15:1

were not able to *b* it 1 Cor 3:2

b one another's burdens Gal 6:2

every man shall *b* his own 6:5

b in my body marks of Lord 6:17

fig tree *b* olive Jas 3:12

bear, *to give birth*

a virgin shall *b* a son Isa 7:14

Elisabeth shall *b* a son Lk 1:13

bear witness, *testify*

shalt not *b* false *w* Ex 20:16, Deut 5:20, Mat 19:18, Rom 13:9

the Spirit that *b w* 1 Jno 5:6

three that *b w* in earth 5:8

See also: Mk 10:19, Jno 1:7, 5:36, 10:25

beast, *living creature*

let earth bring forth *b* Gen 1:24

God formed every *b* 2:19

of every clean *b* take   7:2,8
b ascendeth out of pit   Rev 11:7
where *b* and false prophet   20:10

beat, *pound, smite*
  b him with rod   Pro 23:13,14
  b plowshares into swords Joel 3:10
  b on that house   Mat 7:25,27, Lk
                   6:48,49
  one that *b* the air   1 Cor 9:26
  thrice, was I *b* with   2 Cor 11:25

beautiful, *fair, of good form*
  Rachel was *b*   Gen 29:17
  Abigail *b* countenance 1 Sam 25:3
  Bath-sheba was *b*   2 Sam 11:2
  Esther was fair and *b*   Esth 2:7
  b feet of them that   Isa 52:1,7
  sepulchres, appear *b*   Mat 23:27
  the gate called *b*   Acts 3:2,10

became
  man *b* a living soul   Gen 2:7
  Lot's wife *b* pillar of salt   19:26
  to the Jews I *b* a Jew 1 Cor 9:20

because, *for this reason*
  b I live ye shall live also Jno 14:19
  b we love brethren   1 Jno 3:14
  love him *b* he first loved   4:19

become
  excellent speech *b* not   Pro 17:7
  is *b* head of corner Mat 21:42, Mk
    12:10, Lk 20:17, Acts 4:11
  all things are *b* new   2 Cor 5:17
  behaviour as *b* holiness   Tit 2:3

bed, *couch, mattress*
  if I make my *b* in hell Psa 139:8
  lie on *b* of ivory   Amos 6:4
  take up thy *b* and walk Mat 9:6,
          Mk 2:9, Jno 5:11,12
  honourable and *b*   Heb 13:4

Beelzebub, *heathen deity,* Mat 10:25,
  12:24,27, Mk 3:22, Lk 11:15 ff

before, *in front, until*
  come to torment us *b*? Mat 8:29
  law judge man *b* it hear? Jno 7:51
  men's sins open *b*   1 Tim 5:24
  works are manifest *b*   5:25

beg, *seek, ask*
  have not seen his seed *b* Psa 37:25
  to *b* I am ashamed   Lk 16:3

began, *started, commenced*
  since the world *b* Jno 9:32, Acts
             3:21, Rom 16:25
  in Christ before the world *b* 2 Tim
                1:9, Tit 1:2
  salvation at first *b*   Heb 2:3

begat *(see begotten)*
  of his own will *b* he   Jas 1:18

begin, *start, commence*
  in the *b* God created   Gen 1:1
  fear of the Lord is *b*   Pro 1:7
  from the *b* it was not so Mat 19:8
  among all nations, *b* at Lk 24:47
  in *b* was the word   Jno 1:1
  who is the *b*, the firstborn Col 1:18
  judgment *b* at house   1 Pet 4:17
  continue as from the *b* 2 Pet 3:4
  I am the *b*   Rev 1:8, 21:6, 22:13

begotten, *caused to bring forth, to be
  born*
  this day have I *b* thee   Psa 2:7
  glory as of the only *b* Jno 1:14
  only *b* Son, he hath   1:18
  he gave his only *b* Son   3:16
  offered up only *b*   Heb 11:17
  who hath *b* us again   1 Pet 1:3
  sent his only *b* Son   1 Jno 4:9
  he that is *b* of God keepeth 5:18

Jesus who is first *b*   Rev 1:5

beguile, *deceive, entrap*
  said, serpent *b* me   Gen 3:13
  lest the serpent *b*   2 Cor 11:3
  any *b* you with words   Col 2:4
  See also: Col 2:18, 2 Pet 2:14

behave, *act*
  charity doth not *b*   1 Cor 13:5
  b not disorderly   2 Thes 3:7
  how thou oughtest to *b* 1 Tim 3:15
beheaded
  b John Mat 14:10, Mk 6:16,27, Lk
                9:9

beheld, *see, view*
  he *b* serpent of brass   Num 21:9
  b Satan as lightning   Lk 10:18
  and we *b* his glory   Jno 1:14
  while they *b* Jesus was   Acts 1:9

behind, *back of*
  cast all my sins *b*   Isa 38:17
  she came in press *b*   Mk 5:27
  forgetting things *b*   Phil 3:13

behold, *see, look*
  b eye of the Lord is on Psa 33:18
  b the Lamb of God   Jno 1:29,36
  b what manner of love   1 Jno 3:1
  b I stand at the door   Rev 3:20
  b I come as a thief, blessed   16:15
  b I come quickly   22:7,12

behoved, *to be necessary*
  it *b* Christ to suffer   Lk 24:46
  b him to be made like   Heb 2:17

being, *to be*
  her husband *b* a just   Mat 1:19
  lifted up his eyes *b*   Lk 16:23
  b in agony, he prayed   22:44
  who *b* in form of God   Phil 2:6

believe, *trust, rely on, be persuaded*
  they may *b* Lord hath   Ex 4:5
  that they may hear and *b*   19:9
  b in the Lord God   2 Chr 20:20
  ye may know and *b* me   Isa 43:10
  who hath *b* our report?   53:1, Jno
             12:32, Rom 10:16
  ask in prayer *b*   Mat 21:22
  repent and *b* the gospel   Mk 1:15
  be not afraid *b*   5:36, Lk 8:50
  that *b* and is baptized   Mk 16:16
  thou canst *b* all things   9:23
  Lord, I *b* help mine 9:24, Jno 9:38
  b ye receive, and ye   Mk 11:24
  b in him not perish   Jno 3:15,16
  b on him is not condemned   3:18
  b hath everlasting   3:36, 6:47
  work of God, that ye *b* on   6:29
  that seeth the son and *b*   6:40
  written that ye might *b*   20:31
  whoso *b* on me should not   12:46
  b Jesus Christ is Son   Acts 8:37
  b on the Lord Jesus   16:31
  to every one that *b*   Rom 10:4
  for with the heart man *b*   10:10
  how shall they *b* in him?   10:14
  all joy and peace in *b*   15:13
  Love *b* all things   1 Cor 13:7
  promise to them that *b*   Gal 3:22
  I know whom I have *b* 2 Tim 1:12
  cometh to God must *b*   Heb 11:6
  b Jesus is Christ   1 Jno 5:1

belly, *inward parts*
  b shall thou go, and   Gen 3:14
  Jonah was in *b* . Jonah 1:17, Mat
                12:40
  fain have filled his *b*   Lk 15:16.
  meats for the *b*   1 Cor 6:13.

whoso God is their *b*   Phil 3:19

belong, *related to, things of*
   secret things *b* to God   Deut 29:29
   to me *b* vengeance 32:35, Psa 94:1,
           Heb 10:30
   salvation *b* unto the Lord   Psa 3:8
   to our God *b* the issues   68:20
   meddleth with strife *b*   Pro 26:17
   the things which *b* to   Lk 19:42

beloved, *to be loved*
   two wives, the one *b*   Deut 21:15
   b of the Lord shall dwell   33:12
   I will call *b* which not   Rom 9:25
   Luke the *b* physician   Col 4:14
   b Son   Mat 3:17, 17:5, Mk 1:11,
     9:7, Lk 3:22, 9:35, 2 Pet 1:17

Belshazzar, *prince of Babylon,* Dan 5:1, 7:1

Belteshazzar, *Daniel's Babylonian name,* Dan 1:7, 2:26

Benhadad, *king of Damascus,* 1 Ki 15:18, 1 Chr 16:2; *another king,* 1 Ki 20:1, 2 Ki 6:24

Benjamin, *youngest son of Jacob,* Gen 35:18, Ex 1:3

Berea, *city of Macedonia,* Acts 17:10

Bernice, *sister of Agrippa II,* Acts 25:13

beseech, *ask, pray*
   we *b* thee, O Lord   Jonah 1:14
   I *b* you by the mercies   Rom 12:1

beset, *attack, harrass*
   thou hast *b* me behind   Psa 139:5
   sin doth so easily *b*   Heb 12:1

beside, *addled, insane*
   friends said, he is *b*   Mk 3:21
   thou art *b* thyself   Acts 26:24

beside, *near, alongside*
   he leadeth me *b* still   Psa 23:2

besought, *asked, pleaded (see beseech)*
   b the Lord   Ex 32:11, Deut 3:23
   b him to depart   Mat 8:34, Lk 8:37

best, *good, foremost*
   bring forth the *b* robe   Lk 15:22
   covet earnestly *b*   1 Cor 12:31

bestow, *give, bring together*
   that he may *b* a blessing   Ex 32:29
   no room where to *b* my   Lk 12:17,18
   though I *b* my goods   1 Cor 13:3
   love Father *b* on us   1 Jno 3:1

Bethabara, *traditional site of Jesus' baptism,* Jno 1:28

Bethany, *town east of Jerusalem on Mt. of Olives,* Mat 21:17, 26:6, Mk 11:1,12, 14:3, Lk 19:29, 24:50, Jno 11:1, 12:1

Beth-el, *town 12 miles north of Jerusalem,* Gen 28:19, 35:6 ff, 1 Sam 7:16, Amos 3:14

Bethlehem, *town 4 miles south of Jerusalem, birthplace of Jesus,* Gen 35:19, Ruth 1:19, 1 Sam 16:4, Mat 2:1,6,16, Lk 2:4,15, Jno 7:42

Bethpage, *town near Bethany,* Mat 21:1, Mk 11:1, Lk 19:29

Bethsaida, *town on northwest shore of sea of Galilee,* Mat 11:21, Mk 6:45, 10:13, Jno 1:44, 12:21

betray, *to give over to an enemy*
   Judas who *b*   Mat 10:4, Mk 3:19
   Son of man *b* into   Mat 17:22, 20:18, 26:2,45, Mk 14:41
   sought opportunity to *b* Mat 26:16, Mk 14:11, Lk 22:6

one of you shall *b* me   Mat 26:21,
Mk 14:18, Jno 13:21
woe to man by whom Son of man is
b Mat 26:24, Mk 14:21, Lk 22:22
he that *b*   Mat 26:48, Mk 14:44
Jesus knew who *b* Jno 6:64, 13:11
heart of Judas to *b*   13:2
night he was *b* he   1 Cor 11:23

better, *good, to be above*
b to have served   Ex 14:12
former days were *b*   Ecc 7:10
and a babbler is no *b*   10:11
are you not much *b?* Mat 6:26, Lk
12:24
b that a millstone   Mat 18:6, Mk
9:42, Lk 17:2
are we *b* than they?   Rom 3:9
b for me to die   1 Cor 9:15
let each esteem other *b*   Phil 2:3
bringing in a *b* hope   Heb 7:19
mediator of a *b* covenant   8:6
in heaven a *b* and enduring   10:34
they desire a *b* country   11:16
b for them not to   2 Pet 2:21

(better is)
b is little with fear   Pro 15:16
b is a dinner of herbs   15:17
b is little with   16:8
b is it to get wisdom   16:16
b is a dry morsel   17:1
b is the poor   19:1, 28:6
b is a neighbour near   27:10
b is an handful   Ecc 4:6
b is a poor wise child   4:13
b is the sight of eyes   6:9
b is the end of a thing   7:8
b is love than   S of S 4:10

(is better)
obey is *b* than sacrifice   1 Sam
15:22
wisdom is *b* than rubies   8:11
slow to anger is *b* than   16:32
a poor man is *b*   19:22
good name is *b* than   Ecc 7:1
patient in spirit is *b*   7:8
living dog is *b* than dead   9:4
wisdom is *b* than strength   9:16
with Christ, is far *b*   Phil 1:23

(it is better) *See:* Psa 118:8,9, Pro
16:19, 21:9,19, 25:24, Ecc 7:2,5,
Mat 18:8,9, Mk 9:43,45,47, 1 Pet
3:17

between, *betwixt, in middle*
I will put enmity *b*   Gen 3:15
the covenant *b* God   9:16
how long halt ye *b*   1 Ki 18:21
no difference *b* Jew   Rom 10:12
I am in a strait *b*   Phil 1:23
one mediator *b* God   1 Tim 2:5

beware, *be warned against*
b of false prophets   Mat 7:15
b of the leaven   16:6,11, Mk 8:15,
Lk 12:1
b of dogs, *b* of   Phil 3:2
b lest ye also   2 Pet 3:17

beyond, *over, further*
and *b* their power   2 Cor 8:3
that no man go *b*   1 Thes 4:6

bind, *tie, fasten*
broken in heart, *b* up   Psa 147:3
b them about thy neck   Pro 7:3
hath sent me to *b* up   Isa 61:7
b tares in bundles   Mat 13:30
whatsoever thou *b*   16:19, 18:18
b heavy burdens   23:4

bird, *fowl*

flee as a *b* to your   Psa 11:1
and as a *b* from the hand   6:5
rise up at voice of *b*   Ecc 12:4
heritage is speckled *b*   Jer 12:9
b of the air   Mat 8:20, Lk 9:58
b lodge in the branches Mat 13:32

birth, *be born, break forth*

better than day of *b*   Ecc 7:1
the *b* of Jesus Christ   Mat 1:18
shall rejoice at his *b*   Lk 1:14

birthright, *status of first-born*

sell me this day thy *b*   Gen 25:31
for one morsel sold *b*   Heb 12:16

bishop, *overseer*

b must be   1 Tim 3:2, Tit 1:7
to *b* of your souls   1 Pet 2:25

bit, *bridle*

put *b* in horses' mouths   Jas 3:3

bite, *devour*

at the last it *b* like   Pro 23:32
if ye *b* and devour one   Gal 5:15

bitter, *nasty, rancid*

hungry soul *b* is sweet   Pro 27:7
strong drink shall be *b*   Isa 24:9
Peter wept *b* Mat 26:75, Lk 22:62
if ye have *b* envying   Jas 3:14
See also: Ezek 27:31, Col 3:19

bitterness *(see bitter)*

a foolish son is *b*   Pro 17:25
let all *b* be put away   Eph 4:31
root of *b* springing   Heb 12:15

black, *darkness*

I clothe heavens with *b*   Isa 50:3
one hair white or *b*   Mat 5:36
I beheld, lo a *b* horse   Rev 6:5
See also: Jer 4:28, Jude 13

blameless, *guiltless, not accused*

ordinances of the Lord *b*   Lk 1:6
ye may be *b* in the day 1 Cor 1:8
soul and body, *b*   1 Thes 5:23
bishop be *b*   1 Tim 3:2, Tit 1:7
without spot and *b*   2 Pet 3:14
See also: Eph 1:4, Phil 3:6

blaspheme, *revile, speak against*

enemies of Lord *b*   2 Sam 12:14
foolish have *b* thy name Psa 74:18
my name continually is *b* Isa 52:5
heart proceed *b*   Mat 7:22, 15:19
b against Holy Ghost   Mat 12:31,
          Mk 3:29
the name of God is *b*   Rom 2:24
last days men be *b*   2 Tim 3:2
word of God be not *b*   Tit 2:5
do not *b* that worthy?   Jas 2:7

blemish, *spot, defect*

lamb without *b*   Ex 12:5, Lev 9:3,
          14:10, 23:12, Num 6:14
holy and without *b*   Eph 5:27
as a lamb without *b*   1 Pet 1:19
See also: Ex 29:1, Lev 5:15,18, 6:6,
9:2, 22:20, Ezek 46:4, Deut 15:21

bless, *to declare happy*

I will *b* thee   Gen 12:2, 26:3,24
our God, shall *b* us   Psa 67:1,6,7
b them that fear Lord   115:13
I will *b* thy name   145:1
b them that curse you   Mat 5:44,
          Lk 6:28
b them which persecute Rom 12:14

blessed *(see bless)*

in thee all families be *b* Gen 12:3,
18:18, 22:18, 26:4, 28:14, Acts
          3:25
b are the poor in spirit   Mat 5:3

he *b* and brake   14:19, 26:26, Mk 6:41, 14:22, Lk 9:16, 24:30
Jesus said, *b* art thou   Mat 16:17
more *b* to give than to   Acts 20:35

blessed are they. *See:* Psa 2:12, 119:2, Jno 20:29, Rom 4:7, Rev 19:9

blessed are ye. *See:* Mat 5:11, 21:9, 23:39, Mk 11:9, Lk 6:22, 13:35

blessed is the man. *See:* Psa 1:1, 32:2, 34:8, 84:12, 112:1, Pro 8:34, Isa 56:2, Jer 17:7, Rom 4:8, Jas 1:12

blessing *(see bless)*
thou shall be a *b*   Gen 12:2
showers of *b*   Ezek 34:26
and pour you out a *b*   Mat 3:10
blessed with spiritual *b*   Eph 1:3
same mouth proceed *b*   Jas 3:10

blind, *sightless, closed*
two *b* men followed   Mat 9:27, 20:30
b leaders of *b*   15:14, Lk 6:39
woe to you, *b* guides   23:16,26
b Bartimaeus sat by   Mk 10:46
recovery of sight to *b*   Lk 4:18
he hath *b* their eyes   Jno 12:40
a guide to the *b*   Rom 2:19
god of world hath *b*   2 Cor 4:4
lacketh these is *b*   2 Pet 1:9
the darkness *b* eyes   1 Jno 2:11

blood
thy brother's *b* crieth   Gen 4:10
the life which is the *b*   9:4
sheddeth man's *b*, his *b*   9:6
when I see *b*   Ex 12:13
b, fire, smoke   Joel 2:30, Acts 2:19
moon turned to *b*   Joel 2:31, Acts 2:20
b of the new testament   Mat 26:28, Mk 14:24

new testament in my *b*   Lk 22:20, 1 Cor 11:25
sweat as drops of *b*   Lk 22:44
hath made of one *b*   Acts 17:26
being justified by his *b*   Rom 5:9
through his *b*   Eph 1:7, Col 1:14
made nigh by *b* of Christ   Eph 2:13
peace through *b* of   Col 1:20
the *b* of the testament   Heb 9:20
without shedding of *b*   Heb 9:22
b of Christ as a lamb   1 Pet 1:19
redeemed us by thy *b*   Rev 5:9

blot, *to wipe out or away*
not, *b* me out of book   Ex 32:32
have mercy, O God, *b* our   Psa 51:1
b out the handwriting   Col 2:14
I will not *b* his name   Rev 3:5

blow
b the trumpet in Zion   Joel 2:13
wind *b* where it listeth   Jno 3:8

boast, *praise oneself*
workers of iniquity *b*   Psa 94:4
b not against branches   Rom 11:18
not of works lest any *b*   Eph 2:9
See also: Rom 1:30, 2 Tim 3:2, Jas 3:5

Boaz, *husband of Ruth,* Ruth 2:1

bodies *(see body)*
that ye present your *b*   Rom 12:1
b are members of   1 Cor 6:15

bodily *(see body)*
fulness of the Godhead *b*   Col 2:9
b exercise profiteth   1 Tim 4:8

body, *body, flesh*
consume both soul and *b*   Isa 10:18
light of *b*   Mat 6:22, Lk 11:34
b more than   Mat 6:25, Lk 12:23

which kill *b*   Mat 10:28, Lk 12:24
disciples took *b*   Mat 14:12
this is my *b* Mat 26:26, Mk 14:22,
                     Lk 22:19, 1 Cor 11:24
Joseph begged the *b* of Jesus   Mat
        27:58, Mk 15:43, Lk 23:52
dead to the law by *b* of   Rom 7:4
deliver me from *b* of this   7:24
b not for fornication   1 Cor 6:13
b temple of Holy Ghost   6:19
I keep under my *b*   9:27
ye are the *b* of Christ   12:27
though I gave my *b* to be   13:3
natural *b* raised *b*   15:44
edifying of *b* of Christ   Eph 4:12
whole *b* fitly joined   4:16
he is the saviour of the *b*   5:23
he is the head of the *b*   Col 1:18
b without Spirit is dead   Jas 2:26
bare our sins in his *b*   1 Pet 2:24

(one body) *See:* Rom 12:4,5, 1 Cor
10:17, 12:13,20, Eph 2:16, 4:4, Col
3:15

bold, *confident, daring*
righteous *b* as a lion   Pro 28:1
we were *b* in our God   1 Thes 2:2
See also: Acts 9:27,29, 18:26, Heb
4:16

boldness *(see bold)*
in whom we have *b*   Eph 3:12
having *b* to enter   Heb 10:19
that we may have *b*   1 Jno 4:17

bond, *fetter, joining*
in the *b* of iniquity   Acts 8:23
unity of Spirit, in *b*   Eph 4:3
put on charity, the *b*   Col 3:14

bondage, *service, slavery*
lives bitter with hard *b*   Ex 1:14

by reason of *b*   2:23
Lord brought us out of *b*   13:14,
        20:2, Deut 5:6, 6:2, 8:14,
              13:5,10, Josh 24:17
laid upon us hard *b*   Deut 26:6
we were never in *b* to   Jno 8:33
spirit of *b*   Rom 8:15,21
with yoke of *b*   Gal 5:1
b under the elements   4:3,9

bone
this is *b* of my bones   Gen 2:23
carry up my *b*   50:25, Ex 13:19
the *b* of Joseph   Josh 24:32
pleasant words health to *b*   Pro
                                16:24
broken spirit drieth *b*   17:22
soft tongue breaketh *b*   25:15
valley full of *b*   Ezek 37:1,3
full of dead men's *b*   Mat 23:27
a *b* shall not be broken   Jno 19:26

book, *writings, scrolls*
blot me out of thy *b*   Ex 32:32
his law in a *b*   Deut 17:18
Hilkiah gave the *b*   2 Ki 22:8
Shaphan carried *b* to   2 Chr 34:16
Ezra opened the *b*   Neh 8:5
not written in *b*   Jno 20:30
write in *b*   Rev 1:11
take away from words of *b*   22:19

books *(see book)*
of making many *b*   Ecc 12:12
b were opened   Dan 7:10, Rev
                                20:12
dead judge out of *b*   20:12

border, *enclosure, edge*
he will establish the *b*   Pro 15:25
behind, and touch *b*   Lk 8:44
enlarge *b* of garments   Mat 23:5

born *(see birth)*

man is *b* to trouble   Job 5:7
man that is *b* of a woman   14:1
go astray as soon as *b*   Psa 58:3
a time to be *b*   Ecc 3:2
for unto us a child is *b*   Isa 9:6
where is he *b* king?   Mat 2:2
is *b* this day in city   Lk 2:11
can a man be *b* when?   Jno 3:4
to this end was I *b*   18:37
as new *b* babes desire   1 Pet 2:2

born again, *see:* Jno 3:3,7, 1 Pet 1:23
born of God, *see:* Jno 1:13, 1 Jno 3:9,
4:7, 5:1, 5:4, 5:18

borne, *carried*

he hath *b* griefs   Isa 53:4
fathers sinned, we have *b* Lam 5:7
grievous to be *b*   Mat 23:4, Lk
                11:46
we have *b* image of 1 Cor 15:49

borrow

wicked *b* and payeth not Psa 37:21
him that would *b*   Mat 5:42

bosom, *hidden place, hollow, lap*

put thy hand into thy *b* Ex 4:6
prayer returned to my *b* Psa 35:13
Abraham's *b*   Lk 16:22,23
in the *b* of the Father Jno 1:18
leaning on Jesus' *b*   13:23

both, *two*

were *b* naked   Gen 2:25, 3:7
do evil with *b* hands Mic 7:3
b shall fall Mat 15:14, Lk 6:39
reconcile *b* unto God Eph 2:16

bottles, *animal skin containers*

into old *b* Mat 9:17, Mk 2:22, Lk
             5:37,38

boughs, *tree branches*

mule went under the *b* 2 Sam 18:9
nests in *b*   Ezek 31:6, Dan 4:12

bought, *purchased*

Jacob *b* a field   Gen 33:19, Josh
             24:32
Joseph *b* all land of   47:20
David *b* threshingfloor 2 Sam
             24:24
Omri *b* the hill Samaria 1 Ki 16:24
all that he had, and *b* Mat 13:46
cast out them that sold and *b* Mat
    21:12, Mk 11:15, Lk 19:45
I have *b* a piece of Lk 14:18,19
b with a price 1 Cor 6:20, 7:23
denying Lord that *b* 2 Pet 2:1

bound, *tied, fastened*

b Isaac his son, and Gen 22:9
they *b* Samson   Judg 15:13
b Jesus   Mat 27:2, Mk 15:1
b Satan thousand years Rev 20:2
be *b* in heaven Mat 16:19, 18:18
b by law of Rom 7:2, 1 Cor 7:39
word of God is not *b* 2 Tim 2:9

bountifully, *richly, lavishly*

soweth *b* shall reap *b* 2 Cor 9:6

bow, *kneel, bend down*

thou shalt not *b* down to Ex 23:24
eyes darkened, *b* down Rom 11:10
every knee shall *b* Isa 45:23, Rom
          14:11, Phil 2:10
I *b* my knees to Father Eph 3:14

bowels, *intestines, also thought to be seat of emotions*

Judas burst, all his *b* Acts 1:18
put on *b* of mercies   Col 3:12
See also: Phil 1:8, 2:1, 1 Jno 3:17

bowl, *dish, container*

the golden *b* be broken Ecc 12:6

box
  alabaster *b* Mat 26:7, Mk 14:3, Lk
                                        7:37

brake *(see break)*
  Baal's images *b*   2 Ki 11:18
  Josiah *b* the images   23:14
  blessed and *b*   Mat 14:19, 15:36,
     26:26, Mk 6:41, 8:6, 14:22, Lk
     9:16, 22:19, 24:30, 1 Cor 11:24
  b the box and poured   Mk 14:3
  soldiers *b* legs   Jno 19:32,33

bramble, *thorn*
  said the trees to *b*   Judg 9:14 ff
  not of a *b* gather   Lk 6:44

branch, *shoot, bough*
  righteous flourish as *b*   Pro 11:28
  a *b* shall grow out   Isa 11:1
  to David a righteous *b*   Jer 23:5
  b of righteousness grow   33:15
  forth my servant the *b*   Zech 3:8
  the man whose name is the *b* 6:12
  b that beareth not   Jno 15:2
  he is cast forth as a *b*   15:6

branches *(see branch)*
  birds lodge in the *b* Mat 13:32, Mk
                                       13:19
  I am the vine, ye are *b* Jno 15:5
  root be holy, so the *b* Rom 11:16

brass, *copper*
  made a serpent of *b*   Num 21:9
  hills thou mayest dig *b*   Deut 8:9
  belly and thighs were *b*   Dan 2:32
  sounding *b* of cymbal   1 Cor 13:1

brawler, *fighter, contentious person*
  with *b* woman in   Pro 25:24
  a bishop must be no *b*   1 Tim 3:3
  to be no *b*   Tit 3:2

breach, *cleft, breakthrough*
  b for *b*, eye for eye   Lev 24:20
  repaired *b* of city   1 Ki 11:27

bread, *food, sustenance*
  sweat of thy face eat *b*   Gen 3:19
  seven days eat unleavened *b*   Ex
     12:15, 13:6,7, 23:15, 34:18, Lev
     23:6, Num 28:17, Deut 16:3
  I will rain *b* from heaven Ex 16:4
  man doth not live by *b* only Deut
     8:3, Mat 4:4, Lk 4:4
  honoureth himself and lacketh *b*
                                 Pro 12:9
  if enemy hunger, give *b*   25:21
  b of deceit is sweet   20:17
  eateth not *b* of idleness   31:27
  cast *b* upon the water   Ecc 11:1
  the *b* of adversity   Isa 30:20
  seed to sower, *b* to eater   55:10
  not a famine of *b* but   Amos 8:11
  stones made *b*   Mat 4:3, Lk 4:3
  our daily *b*   Mat 6:11, Lk 11:11
  if son ask *b* will he   Mat 7:9
  Jesus took *b*   26:26, Mk 14:22
  took *b* gave thanks   Lk 22:19,
                          24:30, Acts 27:35
  I am the *b* of life   Jno 6:35,48
  breaking of *b*   Acts 2:42,46
  disciples came to break *b* 20:7,11
  as often as ye eat this *b*   1 Cor
                                   11:26,27

break, *crush, bruise*
  if they *b* my statutes   Psa 89:31
  reed will he not *b*   Isa 42:3, Mat
                                   12:20
  b down thy high places Ezek 16:39
  b one of these least   Mat 5:19
  thieves *b* through   6:19

else the bottles *b* 9:17
came together to *b* Acts 20:7
See also: Num 30:2

breaking *(see break)*
known of them in *b* of Lk 24:35
continued in *b* of bread Acts 2:42
in the temple, *b* bread from 2:46
through *b* the law Rom 2:23

breast, *chest*
head of gold, his *b* Dan 2:32
publican smote upon *b* Lk 18:13
on Jesus' *b* Jno 13:25, 21:20

breastplate
put righteousness as *b* Isa 59:17
having on the *b* Eph 6:14
putting on the *b* of 1 Thes 5:8

breath
his nostrils *b* of life Gen 2:7
giveth life and *b* Acts 17:25

breathed
b into man's nostrils Gen 2:7
Saul yet *b* out Acts 9:1

brethren, *kinsmen, brothers*
be no strife, we be *b* Gen 13:8
if *b* dwell together Deut 25:5
answered, we are *b* 2 Ki 10:13
pleasant for *b* to dwell Psa 133:1
soweth discord among *b* Pro 6:19
neither did his *b* believe Jno 7:5
seen of above 500 *b* 1 Cor 15:6
perils among false *b* 2 Cor 11:26
because of false *b* Gal 2:4
unfeigned love of *b* 1 Pet 1:22
because we love *b* 1 Jno 3:14
lay down lives for the *b* 3:16

brick
us make *b* Gen 11:3
lives bitter in *b* Ex 1:14, 5:7,16

bride, *"the perfect one"*
as a *b* adorneth herself Isa 61:10
a *b* forget her attire? Jer 2:32
he that hath the *b* is Jno 3:29

bridegroom
as *b* rejoiceth over Isa 62:5
children mourn while *b* Mat 9:15,
Mk 2:19, Lk 5:34
went forth to meet *b* Mat 25:1,5
governor called *b* Jno 2:9

bridle, *muzzle, rein, control*
seem religious and *b* Jas 1:26
able to *b* whole body Jas 3:2

bright, *light, shining*
behold a *b* cloud Mat 17:5
man stood in *b* Acts 10:30
b and morning star Rev 22:16
See also: Amos 5:20, 2 Thes 2:8,
Heb 1:3

brimstone, *bitumen, sulfur*
rained *b* Gen 19:24, Lk 17:29
lake burneth with fire and *b* Rev
21:8

bring, *cause to come*
waters *b* forth Gen 1:20
b a flood of waters 6:17
two of every sort *b* 6:19
when I *b* a cloud over earth 9:14
shall *b* forth a son Mat 1:21,23
b forth fruit meet 3:8, Lk 3:8
cannot *b* forth evil fruit Mat 7:18
for I *b* you good tidings Lk 2:10
keep my body, *b* it 1 Cor 9:27
b them up in nurture of Eph 6:4
See also: Mat 3:10, 7:19, 12:35,
13:53, Lk 3:9, 6:45, Tit 2:11, Jas 1:15

bringing, *See:* Rom 7:23, 2 Cor 10:5,
Heb 7:19

broad, *wide*
b is the way   Mat 7:13
make b their phylacteries   23:5

broidered, *twined*
adorn, not with b   1 Tim 2:9

broken, *destroyed*
b my covenant   Gen 17:14, Psa
    55:20, Isa 24:5, 33:8, Jer 11:10
nigh them of b   Psa 34:18
sacrifices are a b spirit   51:17
of heart spirit is b   Pro 15:13
golden bowl be b   Ecc 12:6
on this stone, shall be b Mat 21:44,
                                       Lk 20:18
law of Moses not be b   Jno 7:23
and scripture cannot be b   10:35
my body b for you   1 Cor 11:24
Christ b down middle   Eph 2:14
branches be b off   Rom 11:17 ff

brokenhearted, *grieved*
to bind up the b   Isa 61:1
to heal b to preach   Lk 4:18

brood, *offspring*
as a hen gathers her b   Lk 13:34

brother, *relative, friend*
am I my b keeper?   Gen 4:9
a b offended is harder   Pro 18:19
sticketh closer than b   18:24
mote in thy b eye   Mat 7:3,5, Lk
                                       6:41,42
b shall deliver   Mat 10:21, Mk
                                       13:12
judge thy b?   Rom 14:10
any man called a b   1 Cor 5:11
withdraw from every b   2 Thes 3:6
admonish him as b   3:15

and hateth his b   1 Jno 2:9, 10,11
he that loveth not his b   3:10,14
loveth God, love his b   4:21

brotherhood, *united as brothers*
love the b fear God   1 Pet 2:17

brotherly, *brotherlike*
with b love   Rom 12:10
as touching b love   1 Thes 4:9
let b love continue   Heb 13:1
to godliness b kindness   2 Pet 1:7

brought *(see bring)*
earth b forth grass and   Gen 1:12
strength of hand Lord b Ex 13:3 ff,
                                     Deut 6:21
b them out of Egypt Ex 29:46, Lev
                               25:38, 26:13,45
Lord b us forth   Deut 26:8
lifted up, be b low   Isa 2:12
b forth fruit   Mat 13:8, Mk 4:8
b forth firstborn son   Lk 2:7

bruise, *to crush*
b thy head   Gen 3:15
pleased Lord to b him   Isa 53:10
b for our iniquities   Isa 53:5
liberty them that are b   Lk 4:18

buffeted, *to strike*
and b him   Mat 26:67, Mk 14:65
to present we are b   1 Cor 4:11
if when ye be b for   1 Pet 2:20

build, *construct*
let us b us a city   Gen 11:4
except Lord b house   Psa 127:1
on this rock will I b   Mat 16:18
b it in 3 days   26:61, Mk 14:58
down my barns and b   Lk 12:18

builders *(see build)*
stone which b refused   Psa 118:22,
           Mat 21:42, Mk 12:10, Lk 20:17,
                         Acts 4:11, 1 Pet 2:7

whose *b* and maker   Heb 11:10

building, *creation, thing built*
husbandry, God's *b*   1 Cor 3:9
we have a *b* of God   2 Cor 5:1
in whom all the *b*   Eph 2:21

built *(see build)*
rooted and *b* up in him   Col 2:7
so *b* we the wall   Neh 4:6
b his house on   Mat 7:24, Lk 6:48

bullock, *bull*
not in the blood of *b*   Isa 1:11
not possible blood of *b*   Heb 10:4

bulrushes, *papyrus rush*
an ark of *b*   Ex 2:3

burden, *weight, load*
cast thy *b* on the Lord   Psa 55:22
grasshopper shall be a *b*   Ecc 12:5
and my *b* is light   Mat 11:30
bind heavy *b*   23:4, Lk 11:46
bear ye one another's *b*   Gal 6:2
every man bear his own *b*   6:5
we groan being *b*   2 Cor 5:4

buried, *entombed*
there was Abraham *b*   Gen 25:10
the bones of Joseph *b*   Josh 24:32
rich man died and was *b*   Lk 16:22
David is dead and *b*   Acts 2:29
b with him by baptism   Rom 6:4
b with him in baptism   Col 2:12

burn
bush *b* with fire   Ex 3:2
the mountain *b* with fire   Deut 4:11
was in my heart as *b* fire   Jer 20:9
into midst of *b* furnace   Dan 3:6,11
tares in bundles to *b*   Mat 13:30
but chaff he will *b* with   Lk 3:17
I give my body to be *b*   1 Cor 13:3
in lake which *b* with   Rev 21:8

a great mountain *b*   8:8

bury, *entomb*
let dead *b* dead   Mat 8:22, Lk 9:60
potters field to *b*   Mat 27:7

bush, *plant*
in fire in the *b*   Ex 3:2, Acts 7:30
how in *b* God spake   Mk 12:26

bushel, *measuring container*
put it under a *b*   Mat 5:15, Mk 4:21, Lk 11:33

business, *work, matter*
about my Father's *b*?   Lk 2:49
not slothful in *b*   Rom 12:11

busy, *active*
servant was *b* here   1 Ki 20:40

busybody, *meddler*
some are *b*   2 Thes 3:11, 1 Tim 5:13
none suffer as a *b*   1 Pet 4:15

but, *yet, only, except*
b a step between me   1 Sam 20:3
said, if I may touch *b*   Mk 5:28
affliction, which is *b*   2 Cor 4:17

butler, *cup bearer*
b of king of Egypt   Gen 40:1

butter
words smoother than *b*   Psa 55:21
b and honey shall   Isa 7:15,22

buy, *acquire, purchase*
land of Canaan to *b*   Gen 42:7, 43:20
b truth and sell not   Pro 23:23
we will *b* and sell   Jas 4:13

buyeth *(see buy)*
considereth a field, *b* it   Pro 31:16
selleth all, and *b*   Mat 13:44

byword, *sharp saying*
thou shalt become *b*   Deut 28:37

Israel shall be a *b*   1 Ki 9:7
thou makest us a *b*   Psa 44:14

C

Caesar, *emperor of Rome*
to *C* the things that are *C*'s   Mat
22:21, Mk 12:17, Lk 2:1, Acts
25:11

Caiaphas, *high priest,* Mat 26:3, Jno
11:49, 18:4

Cain, *first son of Adam,* Gen 4:2, Heb
11:4, 1 Jno 3:12, Jude 11

calamity, *misfortune, evil*
my refuge until these *c*   Psa 57:1
that is glad at *c* shall   Pro 17:5
a foolish son is the *c*   19:13

Caleb, *one of two faithful spies,* Num
13:6,30, 14:38, Josh 14:13

calf
Abraham fetched a *c*   Gen 18:7
he made it a molten *c*   Ex 32:4
c and the young lion   Isa 11:6
hither the fatter *c*   Lk 15:23

call, *say, name, invite*
c upon name of the Lord Gen 4:26
them that *c* evil good   Isa 5:20
c his name Immanuel   7:14, Mat
1:23
c on name of Lord Joel 2:32, Acts
2:21, Rom 10:13
shalt *c* his name Jesus   Mat 1:21
not come to *c* righteous   9:13, Mk
2:17, Lk 5:32
c no man your father   Mat 23:9

Why *c* ye me Lord?   Lk 6:46
ye *c* me Master and   Jno 13:13
many as Lord shall *c*   Acts 2:39
how then shall they *c* Rom 10:14

called *(see call)*
c light day, darkness he *c* Gen 1:5
shall be *c* woman   2:23
shall be *c* wonderful   Isa 9:6
c house of prayer 56:7, Mat 21:13
peacemakers shall be *c*   5:9
many be *c* few chosen 20:16, 22:14
his name was *c* Jesus   Lk 2:21
no more worthy to be *c*   15:19 ff
disciples *c* Christians   Acts 11:26
not many mighty are *c*   1 Cor 1:26
calling wherein he was *c*   7:20
are *c* in one hope   Eph 4:4
God hath not *c* us to   1 Thes 4:7
faithful is he that *c*   5:24
that we should be *c*   1 Jno 3:1

calling, *profession*
one hope of your *c*   Eph 4:4
prize of the high *c*   Phil 3:14
c and election sure   2 Pet 1:10

Calvary, *place of skull,* Lk 23:33

came, *arrived (see come)*
smote rock, water *c*   Num 20:11
I *c* not to send peace   Mat 10:34
Son of Man *c* not to be   20:28
when he *c* to himself   Lk 15:17
c to his own, and his   Jno 1:11
c death, by man *c*   1 Cor 15:21
that Christ *c* to save   1 Tim 1:15
prophecy *c* not in   2 Pet 1:21

camel, *camel, dromedary*
raiment of *c* hair   Mat 3:4, Mk 1:6
easier for a *c* to go Mat 19:24, Mk
10:25, Lk 18:25

at gnat and swallow *c*   Mat 23:24

can, *be able*
  c two walk together   Amos 3:3
  who *c* be saved?   Mat 19:25, Mk
                        10:26, Lk 18:26
  c ye drink of the cup?   Mk 10:38
  c the blind lead blind?   Lk 6:39
  how *c* a man be born?   Jno 3:4
  c any forbid water?   Acts 10:47
  works, *c* faith save?   Jas 2:14

Cana, *town of Galilee,* Jno 2:1, 4:46

Canaan, *son of Ham,* Gen 9:18;
  country of Palestine, Gen 12:5, 17:8,
  37:1, Lev 25:38, Ex 15:15, Num
  13:17, 34:2

Canaanite, *pre-Israelite inhabitants of
  Palestine,* Gen 12:6, 13:7, 15:21, Ex
  23:28, 33:2, 34:11, Josh 17:18

Candace, *queen of Ethiopia about A.D.
  40,* Acts 8:27

candle, *candle, lamp*
  spirit of man is *c*   Pro 20:27
  c of wicked be put out   24:20
  light a *c* and put it under Mat 5:15,
            Mk 4:21, Lk 8:16, 11:33
  doth not she light a *c*   15:8

Capernaum, *town on north shore of Sea
  of Galilee,* Mat 4:13, 11:23, Lk 4:23,
  Jno 4:46

captivity, *bondage*
  carried *c* to Babylon   2 Ki 24:15
  went out of *c*   Ezra 2:1, Neh 7:6
  and bringing me into *c*   Rom 7:23
  bringing into *c* every   2 Cor 10:5

care, *concern, anxiety*
  c of world chokes   Mat 13:22, Mk
                          4:19
  casting your *c* on him   1 Pet 5:7

careful, *filled with cares, worry*
  Martha, thou art *c*   Lk 10:41
  c for nothing, but by   Phil 4:6

cares *(see care)*
  they are choked with *c*   Lk 8:14
  be overcharged with the *c*   21:34
  c thou not we perish?   Mk 4:38

carnal, *fleshly, of the world*
  spiritual, but I am *c*   Rom 7:14
  for to be *c* minded is   8:6
  of our warfare not *c*   2 Cor 10:4

carpenter, *woodworker*
  this the *c* son?   Mat 13:55, Mk 6:3

carried, *lift up, carry, bear*
  borne our griefs, *c* our   Isa 53:4
  c into Babylon   Jer 27:22, 28:3,
                        52:11,17
  c about with every wind   Eph 4:14
  clouds *c* with   2 Pet 2:17, Jude 12

cast, *throw, hurl*
  they *c* lots upon my vesture   Psa
          22:18, Mat 27:35, Jno 19:24
  c thy burden on the Lord   Psa
                        55:22
  c out the beam   Mat 7:5, Lk 6:42
  nor *c* your pearls before   Mat 7:6
  in thy name *c* out devils?   7:22
  if Satan *c* out Satan   12:26
  c out all that sold   21:12, Mk
               11:15, Lk 19:45
  poor widow *c* two mites   21:2
  let him first *c* a stone   Jno 8:7
  c your care upon him   1 Pet 5:7
  perfect love *c* fear   1 Jno 4:18

castaway, *one put forth, refused*
  I myself should be a *c*   1 Cor 9:27

cause, *matter, reason*
  away wife for every *c*   Mat 19:3

for this *c* shall a man   19:5, Mk
                          10:7, Eph 5:31
found no *c* of death   Lk 23:22
for this *c* came   Jno 12:27, 18:37
Mark them who *c*   Rom 16:17
this *c* I bow my knees   Eph-3:14

cease, *stop*
and night shall not *c*   Gen 8:22
no talebearer, strife *c*   Pro 26:20
grinders *c* because   Ecc 12:3
c to do evil   Isa 1:16
tongues, they shall *c*   1 Cor 13:8
I *c* not to give thanks   Eph 1:16
pray without *c*   1 Thes 5:17

Cenchrea, *seaport at Corinth,* Acts
18:14, Rom 16:11

centurion, *captain in Roman army*
c said, Lord, I am not   Mat 8:8
Cornelius was a *c* of   Acts 10:1
See also: Mat 27:54, Lk 7:2, 21:32,
27:1

Cephas, *Aramaic form of Peter,* Jno
1:42, 1 Cor 3:22, Gal 2:9

chain, *bond, fetter*
gold *c* about his neck   Gen 41:42,
                          Dan 5:7,16,29
I am bound with this *c* Acts 28:20
not ashamed of my *c*   2 Tim 1:16

change, *alter*
can Ethiopian *c* his skin? Jer 13:23
I am the Lord, I *c* not   Mal 3:6
c the glory of   Rom 1:23
c the truth of God into   1:25
we shall all be *c*   1 Cor 15:51,52

charge, *credit to, command*
give his angels *c*   Psa 91:11, Mat
                          4:6, Lk 4:10
lay not sin to their *c*   Acts 7:60

lay any thing to *c*   Rom 8:33
c that they teach no   1 Tim 1:3
I *c* thee   5:21, 2 Tim 4:1

chariot, *two-wheeled vehicle*
appeared a *c* of fire   2 Ki 2:11
c and horses are cast   Psa 76:6
go join thyself to *c*   Acts 8:29

charity, *love* (archaic)
but *c* edifieth   1 Cor 8:1
and have not *c*   13:1,2,3
the greatest of these is *c*   13:13
follow after *c* and desire   14:1
above all put on *c*   Col 3:14
end of commandments is *c*   1 Tim
                                1:5
be example in *c* in spirit   4:12
to brotherly kindness *c*   2 Pet 1:7
See also: 1 Cor 16:14, 1 Tim 2:15,
2 Tim 2:22, 3:10, 1 Pet 4:8, Rev
2:19

chaste, *pure*
you as a *c* virgin   2 Cor 11:2
young women be *c*   Tit 2:5
your *c* conversation   1 Pet 3:2

chasten, *to correct*
c thy son while there   Pro 19:18
love, I rebuke and *c*   Rev 3:19
c his son, so Lord *c*   Deut 8:5
despise not the *c* of Almighty   Job
            5:17, Pro 3:11, Heb 12:5
whom Lord loveth he *c*   12:6
See also: Psa 6:1, 38:1, 1 Cor 11:32,
2 Cor 6:9

cheek, *face, jaw*
smiteth one *c*, offer   Lk 6:29

cheer, *glad, well-minded*
merry heart maketh a *c* Pro 15:13
I exhort be of good *c*   Acts 27:22

for God loveth a *c* 2 Cor 9:7

cherisheth, *loves*
c his own flesh Eph 5:29

chickens, *fowl*
a hen gathereth her *c* Mat 23:37

chief, *foremost*
whosoever will be *c* Mat 20:27
c seats in 23:6, Mk 12:39
c corner stone Eph 2:20, 1 Pet 2:6
sinners, I am *c* 1 Tim 1:15
when *c* Shepherd shall 1 Pet 5:4

child
divide the living *c* 1 Ki 3:25
train up a *c* in the way Pro 22:6
c left to himself bringeth 29:15
better is a wise *c* Ecc 4:13
before the *c* shall know Isa 7:16
for unto us a *c* is born 9:6
little *c* shall lead 11:6
Jesus called little *c* Mat 18:2
took a *c* and set Mk 9:36, Lk 9:47
I spake as a *c* 1 Cor 13:11
See also: Mk 10:15, Lk 9:48, 18:17

children *(see child)*
iniquity of fathers upon *c* Ex 20:5,
34:7, Num 14:18, Deut 5:9
ye are the *c* of Lord 14:1
when your *c* ask Josh 4:6, 21
c are an heritage Psa 127:3,4
glory of *c* are Pro 17:6
c teeth set on edge Jer 31:29, Ezek
18:2
Herod slew all the *c* Mat 2:16
become as little *c* 18:3
suffer little *c* to come 19:14, Mk
10:14, Lk 18:16
blood be on us and our *c* Mat
27:25

c of this world wiser Lk 16:8
promise to you and your *c* Acts
2:39
if *c* then heirs Rom 8:17
no more *c,* tossed to Eph 4:14
c obey parents 6:1, Col 3:20
provoke not your *c* Eph 6:4

Chloe, *acquaintance of Paul,* 1 Cor
1:11

choke, *strangle, overcome*
riches *c* the word Mat 13:22, Mk
4:19
thorns *c* them Mat 13:7, Mk 4:7,
Lk 8:7

choose, *select*
c this day whom you Josh 24:15
refuse evil, and *c* Isa 7:15,16
c rather to suffer Heb 11:25

chose *(see choose)*
Lot *c* the plain Gen 13:11
good name rather to be *c* Pro 22:1
called, few *c* Mat 20:16, 22:14
and Mary hath *c* Lk 10:42
for he is a *c* vessel Acts 9:15
God hath *c* foolish 1 Cor 1:27
ye are a *c* generation 1 Pet 2:9
hath not God *c* poor? Jas 2:5

Christ, *anointed*
thou art *C* the Son Mat 16:16
art thou the *C?* Mk 14:61
art thou the *C?* tell us Lk 22:67
if thou be *C* save 23:39
if thou be *C* tell Jno 10:24
Made Jesus Lord and *C* Acts 2:36
we preach *C* crucified 1 Cor 1:23
C the power of God 1:24
ye are *C* and *C* is God's 3:23
God was in *C* reconciling 2 Cor
5:19

C in you the hope   Col 1:27
Jesus *C* same yesterday   Heb 13:8
Christian, *a follower of Christ*
  disciples first called *C*   Acts 11:26
  almost persuadest me to be *C*
                                      26:28
  any man suffer as *C*   1 Pet 4:16
church, *assembly, those called*
  rock I will build my *c*   Mat 16:18
  Lord added to *c* daily   Acts 2:47
  feed the *c* of God   20:28
  the *c* of Christ   Rom 16:16
  neither *c* of Christ   1 Cor 11:16
  head over all to the *c*   Eph 1:22
  Christ is head of the *c*   5:23
  as the *c* is subject   5:24
  Christ loved *c* and   5:25
  present a glorious *c*   5:27
  head of the body the *c*   Col 1:18
  body's sake, which is the *c*   1:24
  to *c* of first-born   Heb 12:23
Cilicia, *province of Asia Minor, Paul's
  home,* Acts 6:9, 21:39, 22:3, 23:4
circumcise, *to cut off ritually*
  ye shall *c* the flesh   Gen 17:11
  every male was *c* 34:24, Ex 12:48
  except ye be *c* ye   Acts 15:1,24
  Paul *c* Timothy because   16:3
  neither Titus be *c*   Gal 2:3
  c profit nothing   5:2,6, 6:15
circumspectly, *carefully, watchfully*
  see that ye walk *c*   Eph 5:15
cistern, *well*
  wheel broken at the *c*   Ecc 12:6
city, *town*
  Cain builded a *c* and   Gen 4:7
  let us build us a *c*   11:4
  except Lord keep *c*   Psa 127:1

he looked for *c*   Heb 11:10,16
c was pure gold   Rev 21:18,23
I John saw holy *c* coming   21:2
clamour, *noise, outcry*
  a foolish woman is *c*   Pro 9:13
  all anger and *c* be put   Eph 4:31
clean, *pure*
  of every *c* beast   Gen 7:2
  c hands and a pure heart Psa 24:4
  create in me a *c* heart   51:10
  make *c* the outside   Mat 23:25, Lk
                                     11:39
  all things are *c* unto   11:41
cleanse, *to clean*
  wash me throughly, and *c* Psa 51:2
  c them from iniquity   Jer 33:8,
                               Ezek 37:23
  heal sick, *c* lepers   Mat 10:8
  what God hath *c* Acts 10:15, 11:9
  blood of Jesus Christ *c*   1 Jno 1:7
cleave, *cling to*
  man shall *c* to wife Gen 2:24, Mat
                             19:5, Mk 10:7
  abhor evil, *c* to   Rom 12:9
climb, *go up*
  Zaccheus *c* up into   Lk 19:4
  c up some other way   Jno 10:1
cloke, *coat, other garment*
  let him have thy *c* also   Mat 5:40
  him that taketh thy *c*   Lk 6:29
  using liberty for *c*   1 Pet 2:16
closer, *near*
  friend that sticketh *c*   Pro 18:24
closet, *inner chamber*
  enter into thy *c*   Mat 6:6
cloth
  piece of new *c* Mat 9:16, Mk 2:21
  wrapped it in a linen *c*   Mat 27:59

clothe, *to put on clothing*
 coats of skins and *c* Gen 3:21
 God so *c* grass Mat 6:30, Lk 12:28
 c in soft raiment Mat 11:8, Lk 7:25
 naked and ye *c* me Mat 25:36,43
 John was *c* with camel's Mk 1:6
 c with humility 1 Pet 5:5

clothes, *garments*
 in sheep's *c* Mat 7:15
 in swaddling *c* Lk 2:7,12

cloud, *mist, vapor*
 set my bow in the *c* Gen 9:13
 a pillar of *c* Ex 13:21,22
 it was *c* and darkness 14:20
 bright *c* overshadowed them Mat
   17:5, Mk 9:7, Lk 9:34,35
 coming in *c* Mat 24:30, 26:64, Mk
   13:26, 14:62
 up with them in *c* 1 Thes 4:17
 c received him out of Acts 1:9
 they are *c* carried 2 Pet 2:17
 c without water Jude 12

cloven, *divided*
 not *c* footed Lev 11:26, Deut 14:7
 c tongues as fire Acts 2:3

coasts, *borders*
 depart their *c* Mat 8:34, Mk 5:17

coat, *clothing*
 God made *c* of skins Gen 3:21
 Jacob make Joseph *c* 37:3
 and take away thy *c* Mat 5:40
 forbid not to take thy *c* Lk 6:29

cock, *rooster*
 night before *c* crow Mat 26:34,75,
  Mk 14:30,72, Lk 22:34,61, Jno
   13:38, 18:27

coffin, *ark, chest*
 Joseph was put in *c* in Gen 50:26

cold
 c cometh out of north Job 37:9
 as *c* waters to thirsty Pro 25:25
 a cup of *c* water Mat 10:42
 neither *c* nor hot Rev 3:15,16

collection, *gathering*
 concerning the *c* 1 Cor 16:1

colour, *hue, tint*
 when wine giveth his *c* Pro 23:31
 coat of many *c* for Gen 37:3

colt
 riding upon *c* Zech 9:9, Mat 21:5,
   Jno 12:15
 find ass tied *c* with her Mat 21:2,
  Mk 11:2, Lk 19:30

come, *arrive*
 end of all flesh is *c* Gen 6:13
 Judah till Shiloh *c* 49:10
 out of Jacob shall *c* Num 24:19
 all nations shall *c* Psa 86:9
 c ye to the waters Isa 55:1
 thy kingdom *c* Mat 6:10, Lk 11:2
 c all ye that labour Mat 11:28
 if any man will *c* after 16:24
 all things are ready, *c* 22:4
 whosoever will *c* after me Mk 8:34,
  Lk 9:23, 14:47
 suffer little children to *c* Mk 10:14,
  Lk 18:16
 c take up the cross Mk 10:21
 hour not yet *c* Jno 2:4, 7:6, 8:20
 Lazarus, *c* forth 11:43
 do evil, that good *c*? Rom 3:8
 whence *c* wars Jas 4:1
 day of Lord will *c* as a thief 2 Pet
  3:10, Rev 3:3, 16:15
 I *c* quickly 3:11, 22:7,20

comeliness, *beauty, elegance*
he hath no form nor *c* — Isa 53:2

cometh *(see come)*
from whence *c* my help — Psa 12:1,2
when pride *c* then *c* shame — Pro 11:2
day of the Lord *c* — Joel 2:1, Isa 13:9, Zech 14:1, 1 Thes 5:2
he that *c* after me — Mat 3:11, Mk 1:7, Lk 3:16
he that *c* in name of Lord — Mat 21:9, Mk 11:9, Lk 13:35, 19:38
the night *c* when no man can — Jno 9:4
c unto the Father but by me — 14:6
faith *c* by hearing — Rom 10:17
he that *c* to God must — Heb 11:6

comfort (verb), *to strengthen, console*
rod and thy staff, they *c* — Psa 23:4
c ye, *c* ye my people — Isa 40:1
c one another — 1 Thes 4:18

comfort *(see comfort, verb)*
not leave you *c* less — Jno 14:18
through patience and *c* — Rom 15:4
even the God of all *c* — 2 Cor 1:3,4
any *c* of love — Phil 2:1,19

comforter *(see comfort)*
c which is Holy Ghost — Jno 14:26
when the *c* is come — 15:26, 16:7

coming *(see come)*
see Son of man *c* Mat 16:28, 24:30, 26:64
so shall *c* of Son — 16:27,37,39
the hour is *c* — Jno 5:25,28
brightness of his *c* — 2 Thes 2:8
promise of his *c* — 2 Pet 3:4

command, *speak, give order*
tree I *c* not to eat — Gen 3:11,17

and God *c* thee so — Ex 18:23
hear what Lord will *c* — Num 9:8
not add to the word I *c* — Deut 4:2
I *c* thee this day 7:11, 8:11, 10:13, 11:8,27, 13:18, 30:8
c these stones — Mat 4:3, Lk 4:3
all things I have *c* — Mat 28:20
if ye do what I *c* — Jno 15:14,17
c all men to repent — Acts 17:30
these *c* and teach — 1 Tim 4:11

commandments, *precepts, statutes*
wrote on tables ten *c* — Ex 34:28, Deut 4:13, 10:4
he gave them in *c* all — Ex 34:32
go beyond *c* of Lord — Num 24:13
the *c* of Lord is pure — Psa 19:8
for doctrines that *c* of men — Mat 15:9, Mk 7:7
first *c* — Mat 22:38, Mk 12:30
on these two *c* hang all — Mat 22:40
a new *c* I give unto — Jno 13:34
if there be any other *c* — Rom 13:9
first *c* with promise — Eph 6:2
end of *c* is charity — 1 Tim 1:5
I write no new *c* — 1 Jno 2:7,8
he that keepeth his *c* — 3:24

commend, *put in charge, praise*
into thy hands I *c* my — Lk 23:46
but God *c* his love — Rom 5:8
not he that *c* himself — 2 Cor 10:18

commit, *to do, deliver to*
not *c* adultery Ex 20:14, Deut 5:18, Mat 5:27, 19:18, Rom 13:9
if a soul *c* a trespass — Lev 5:15
into thine hand I *c* my — Psa 31:5
which *c* such things — Rom 1:32
keep that which I *c* — 2 Tim 1:12
the same *c* thou to — 2:2

c sin transgresseth   1 Jno 3:4,8
born of God doth not *c*   3:9

common, *profane, belonging to all*
had all things *c*   Acts 2:44, 4:32
never eaten anything *c*   10:14, 11:8
no temptation but *c*   1 Cor 10:13

commonwealth, *community*
being aliens from *c* of   Eph 2:12

communication, *word, sometimes companions (as 1 Cor 15:33)*
evil *c* corrupt good   1 Cor 15:33
no corrupt *c*   Eph 4:29, Col 3:8

communion, *act of sharing*
c of body of Christ   1 Cor 10:16
what *c* hath light   2 Cor 6:14
c of the Holy Ghost be   13:14

compacted, *joined*
body fitly joined and *c*   Eph 4:16

companion, *friend*
but a *c* of fools shall   Pro 13:20
but a *c* of riotous men   28:7

company, *association*
Jew to keep *c*   Acts 10:28
not to keep *c* with   1 Cor 5:11
and have no *c* with   2 Thes 3:14

compare, *set alongside*
who in heaven can be *c?*   Psa 89:6
what likeness will ye *c?*   Isa 40:18
are not worthy to *c*   Rom 8:18
c spiritual things   1 Cor 2:13
c themselves amongst   2 Cor 10:12

compass, *encircle*
ye shall *c* the city   Josh 6:3,4
woe to you, ye *c* sea   Mat 23:15
evils have *c* me about   Psa 40:12
c about with a cloud   Heb 12:1

compassion, *mercy*
thou art a God of *c*   Psa 86:15,
111:4, 112:4, 145:8

Jesus moved with *c*   Mat 9:36,
14:14, 15:32, 20:34, Mk 1:41,
6:34, 8:2
of one mind, having *c*   1 Pet 3:8

compel, *force*
c thee to go a mile   Mat 5:41
they *c* one Simon to   Mk 15:21
go into highways, *c*   Lk 14:23

comprehend, *contain, receive*
the darkness *c* it not   Jno 1:5
is briefly *c* in this   Rom 13:9

conceal, *hide, cover*
of a faithful spirit *c*   Pro 11:13
prudent man *c* knowledge   12:23
it is the glory of God to *c*   25:2

conceits, *opinion*
wise in his own *c* Pro 26:5 ff, 28:11
ye be wise in own *c*   Rom 11:25
be not wise in your own *c*   12:16

conceive, *become pregnant*
in sin did my mother *c*   Psa 51:5
virgin shall *c* and   Isa 7:14

conceived *(see conceive)*
Eve *c* and bare Cain   Gen 4:1
Sarah *c* and bare Isaac   21:2
Jochebed *c* and bare   Ex 2:2
c in her is of Holy Ghost Mat 1:20
Elisabeth hath *c* a son   Lk 1:36
when lust hath *c*   Jas 1:15

conclusion, *end*
let us hear the *c*   Ecc 12:13

concord, *agreement*
what *c* hath Christ?   2 Cor 6:15

concubines, *half wife*
David took more *c*   2 Sam 5:13
Solomon had 300 *c*   1 Ki 11:3

concupiscence, *inordinate desire*
wrought all manner of *c*   Rom 7:8

mortify members, evil *c*   Col 3:5
not in lust of *c*   1 Thes 4:5

condemn, *declare wrong*
judged, let him be *c*   Psa 109:7
by words thou be *c*   Mat 12:37
c not, and ye shall not   Lk 6:37
God sent not Son to *c*   Jno 3:17
he that believeth not is *c*   3:18
neither do I *c* thee   8:11
judgest another thou *c*   Rom 2:1
who is he that *c?*   8:34
that *c* not himself in that   14:22
if our heart *c* us   1 Jno 3:20 f

condemnation *(see condemn)*
thou art in the same *c*   Lk 23:40
this is *c* that light   Jno 3:19
there is no *c* to them   Rom 8:1
lest he fall into the *c*   1 Tim 3:6

condescend, *regard, consider*
high things, but *c*   Rom 12:16

confess, *assent, admit*
c their iniquity   Lev 26:40
they shall *c* their sins   Num 5:7
him will I *c*   Mat 10:32, Lk 12:8
shalt *c* with thy mouth   Rom 10:9
every tongue shall *c* to God   14:11
every tongue shall *c*   Phil 2:11
c your faults one to   Jas 5:16
if we *c* our sins   1 Jno 1:9
whoso shall *c* that Jesus   4:15

confession *(see confess)*
with the mouth *c* is   Rom 10:10

confidence, *assurance, persuasion*
trust Lord than put *c*   Psa 118:8,9
in fear of Lord is *c*   Pro 14:26
we have *c* in Lord   2 Thes 3:4
this is *c* that we   1 Jno 5:14

confident *(see confidence)*
fool rageth and is *c*   Pro 14:16
art *c* thou thyself art   Rom 2:19

confirmed, *established, steadfast*
preached, *c* word with   Mk 16:20
testimony of Christ *c*   1 Cor 1:6
covenant that was *c*   Gal 3:17

conformed, *fashioned same way*
predestinate to be *c*   Rom 8:28
be not *c* to this world   12:2

confound, *mix, confuse*
let us go down and *c*   Gen 11:7,9

confusion
God not author of *c*   1 Cor 14:44
strife is, there is *c*   Jas 3:16

congregation, *assembly*
make atonement for *c*   Lev 16:33

conscience
convicted by their own *c*   Jno 8:9
their *c* also bearing   Rom 2:15
pure heart, and good *c*   1 Tim 1:5
holding faith and good *c*   1:19
mystery of faith in pure *c*   3:9
having their *c* seared   4:2
answer of a good *c*   1 Pet 3:21

consecrate, *devoted*
c Aaron   Ex 28:3
Son, *c* for evermore   Heb 7:28

consent, *agree*
sinners entice, *c* not   Pro 1:10
I *c* unto the law   Rom 7:16

consider, *think about, regard*
when I *c* the heavens   Psa 8:3
c the lilies   Mat 6:28, Lk 12:27
c one another to   Heb 10:24
c not the beam that is   Mat 7:3

consist, *to be*
a man's life *c* not in   Lk 12:15

consolation, *comfort, encouragement*
interpreted, son of *c*   Acts 4:36
if there be any *c*   Phil 2:1

constrained, *to press*
Jesus *c* his disciples Mat 14:22, Mk
     6:45, Lk 24:29
love of Christ *c* us   2 Cor 5:14

consume, *devour, melt*
ye ask that ye may *c*   Jas 4:3
fire of Lord *c* 1 Ki 18:38, 2 Chr 7:1
take heed ye be not *c*   Gal 5:15
God is *c* fire Deut 4:24, Heb 12:29

contain, *hold, bear*
heavens cannot *c* 1 Ki 8:27, 2 Chr
     2:6, 6:18
do by nature things *c*   Rom 2:14
having abolished law *c*   Eph 2:15

contend, *strive*
earnestly *c* for faith   Jude 3

content, *be pleased*
in every state to be *c*   Phil 4:11
raiment, let us be *c*   1 Tim 6:8
be *c* with such things   Heb 13:5

contention, *strife*
only by pride cometh *c*   Pro 13:10
a fool's lips enter into *c*   18:6
c of a wife are   19:13, 27:15
cast out scorner, and *c*   22:10
who hath woe? who *c*?   23:29
as wood to fire, so *c*   26:21
there are *c* among   1 Cor 1:11
if any seem *c*   11:16
avoid *c* and strivings   Tit 3:9

contentment *(see content)*
godliness with *c* is   1 Tim 6:6

continual, *remaining, enduring*
this shall be a *c* burnt   Ex 29:42
merry heart *c* feast   Pro 15:15

continually *(see continual)*
imagination evil *c*   Gen 6:5
goodness God endureth *c*   Psa 52:1
he deviseth mischief *c*   Pro 6:14
abideth a priest *c*   Heb 7:3

continue *(see continual)*
shall we *c* in sin that?   Rom 6:1
if ye *c* in the faith   Col 1:23
c in prayer, and watch   4:2
c in the things which   2 Tim 3:14
let brotherly love *c*   Heb 13:1
all things *c*   2 Pet 3:4

contrary, *against*
if walk *c*   Lev 26:21,23,27,40
do many things *c* to   Acts 26:9
writing which was *c*   Col 2:14

contribution, *given for common use*
to make *c* for poor   Rom 15:26

contrite, *humble, bruised*
saveth such as be of *c*   Psa 34:18
a *c* heart, O God, thou   51:17
c and humble spirit   Isa 57:15
that is of a *c* spirit   66:2

convenient
I have a *c* season   Acts 24:25

conversation, *manner of life*
put off former *c*   Eph 4:22.
only let your *c* be as   Phil 1:27
example in *c*   1 Tim 4:12
shew out of a good *c*   Jas 3:13
having your *c* honest   1 Pet 2:12
in all holy *c*   2 Pet 3:11

conversion, *turning about*
c of the Gentiles   Acts 15:3

convert *(see conversion)*
law of Lord perfect, *c*   Psa 19:7
and sinners shall be *c*   51:13
repent and be *c*   Acts 3:19

err from truth, one *c* .   Jas 5:19

convicted, *to make obvious*
    c by own conscience   Jno 8:9

convince, *to convict, persuade*
    which of you *c* me of?   Jno 8:46
    he may be able to *c* .   Tit 1:9

cool
    walking in garden in *c*   Gen 3:8
    dip tip of finger and *c*   Lk 16:24

cord, *small rope*
    silver *c* be loosed   Ecc 12:6
    a scourge of small *c*   Jno 2:15

Corinth, *city of Greece,* Acts 18:1, 19:1,
    1 Cor 1:2, 2 Cor 1:1

corn, *small cereal grains*
    came to buy *c*   Gen 41:57
    was *c* in Egypt   42:2, Acts 7:12
    not muzzle ox treadeth out *c* Deut
       25:4, 1 Cor 9:9, 1 Tim 5:18
    c fields on sabbath   Mk 2:23, Mat
       12:1, Lk 6:1
    except a *c* of wheat   Jno 12:24

Cornelius, *first Gentile convert,* Acts
    10:1

corner
    better to dwell in *c* Pro 21:9, 25:24
    stone rejected become head of *c*
       Mat 21:42, Psa 118:22, Mk
       12:10, Lk 20:17, Acts 4:11, 1
       Pet 2:7
    was not done in a *c*   Acts 26:26
    Christ chief *c* stone   Eph 2:20 .

correct
    whom Lord loveth, he *c*   Pro 3:12
    c thy son, and he shall   29:17
    c me, but with   Jer 10:24

correction, *instruction, reproof*
    neither be weary of his *c*   Pro 3:11

c is grievous to him that   15:10
withhold not *c* from child   23:13
scripture is profitable for *c*   2 Tim
       3:16

corrupt (adj.), *evil, putrid*
    earth also was *c*   Gen 6:11,12
    a *c* tree   Mat 7:17, Lk 6:43
    let no *c* communication   Eph 4:29

corrupt (verb)
    moth and rust doth *c*   Mat 6:19
    evil communications *c* 1 Cor 15:33
    which *c* word of God   2 Cor 2:17

corruptible, *decayable*
    for this *c* must put   1 Cor 15:53
    not redeemed with *c*   1 Pet 1:18
    born again, not of *c*   1:23
    See also: 2 Pet 1:4

cost, *expense*
    and counteth *c*   Lk 14:28

couch, *bed, mattress*
    stretch themselves on *c*   Amos 6:4
    arise, take up thy *c*   Lk 5:24

council, *assembly*
    c sought false   Mat 26:59, Mk
       14:55
    elders led Jesus into *c*   Lk 22:66
    priests gathered *c* Jno 11:47, Acts
       5:21

counsel, *advice*
    c of wicked   Job 21:16, 22:18
    walketh not in the *c*   Psa 1:1
    c of Lord standeth   33:11
    walked in their own *c*   81:12
    c of wicked are deceit   Pro 12:5
    c against Jesus   Mk 3:6, Jno 11:53
    Jews took *c* to kill   Acts 9:23

counsellor, *adviser*
    called Wonderful, *c*   Isa 9:6

count, *to number*

he *c* it   Gen 15:6, Psa 106:31, Rom 4:3, Gal 3:6

fool is *c* wise   Pro 17:28

down first, *c* cost   Lk 14:28

his faith is *c*   Rom 4:5

c all things loss   Phil 3:8,13

c it joy when ye fall   Jas 1:2

some men *c* slackness   2 Pet 3:9

countenance, *face, appearance*

wroth, and his *c* fell   Gen 4:5

Jacob beheld *c* of Laban   31:2

maketh cheerful *c*   Pro 15:13

country, *land, nation*

out of thy *c*   Gen 12:1, Acts 7:3

men to search out *c*   Josh 2:2,3

save in his own *c*   Mat 13:57, Mk 6:4, Lk 4:24

went into a far *c*   Mat 21:33, Mk 12:1, Lk 15:13

desire a better *c*   Heb 11:16

countryman, *fellow citizen*

perils by own *c*   2 Cor 11:26

courage, *confidence*

be of good *c* let us   2 Sam 10:12, 1 Chr 19:13, Ezra 10:4, Isa 41:6

good *c* and he shall strengthen   Psa 27:14, 31:24

course, *division, race*

Zacharias was of the *c*   Lk 1:5

might finish my *c*   Acts 20:24

I have finished my *c*   2 Tim 4:7

court, *enclosed area, border*

c of tabernacle   Ex 27:9, 35:17, 38:9, 39:40

enter into *c* with   Psa 100:4

courteous, *friendly minded*

be pitiful, be *c*   1 Pet 3:8

cousin, *relative*

thy *c* Elisabeth hath   Lk 1:36

covenant, *agreement*

I establish my *c*   Gen 6:18, 9:9

he wrote words of the *c*   Ex 34:28

declared unto you his *c*   Deut 4:13

Lord gave tables of *c*   9:11,15

that the *c* was confirmed   Gal 3:17

mediator of a better *c*   Heb 8:6,7

a new *c* he hath made   8:13

Jesus the mediator of new *c*   12:24

these are the two *c*   Gal 4:24

strangers from *c* of   Eph 2:12

cover, *conceal, overlay*

love *c* all sins   Pro 10:12

a prudent man *c* shame   12:16

for charity shall *c*   1 Pet 4:8

nothing *c* not be revealed   Mat 10:26, Lk 12:2

whose sin is *c*   Psa 32:1, Rom 4:7

covet, *desire*

thou shalt not *c* thy   Ex 20:17, Deut 5:21, Rom 7:7, 13:9

but *c* earnestly   1 Cor 12:31

c no man's silver or   Acts 20:33

of heart proceedeth *c*   Mk 7:22

but *c* let not be named   Eph 5:3

craftiness, *shrewdness*

no more carried by *c*   Eph 4:14

create, *fashion, make*

in the beginning God *c*   Gen 1:1

c man in his own image   1:27, 5:2

he had rested from all he *c*   2:3

c in me a clean heart   Psa 51:10

we are his workmanship, *c*   Eph 2:10

by him were all things *c*   Col 1:16

image of him that *c*   3:10

thou hast *c* all things   Rev 4:11

creation, *thing made*
> we know that the whole *c*   Rom 8:22
> continue as from *c*   2 Pet 3:4

creator, *maker*
> remember thy *c* in the   Ecc 12:1
> creature more than *c*   Rom 1:25

creature, *created being*
> bring forth moving *c*   Gen 1:20,21
> gospel to every *c*   Mk 16:15, Col 1:23
> in Christ, a new *c*   2 Cor 5:17
> but a new *c*   Gal 6:15
> first-born of every *c*   Col 1:15

creep, *crawl*
> every thing that *c*   Gen 1:25,26
> Peter saw *c* things Acts 10:12, 11:6

Crete, *island in Mediterranean Sea*,
Acts 27:7, Tit 1:5

crew, *crowed*
> immediately the cock *c* Mat 26:74, Mk 14:68,72, Lk 22:60, Jno 18:27

cried, *shouted, groaned*
> Israel *c* to the Lord Ex 14:10, Judg 3:9,15, 4:3, 6:7, 10:10
> the people *c* to Moses   Num 11:2
> in my distress I *c* unto   Psa 18:6
> Jesus *c* with loud voice Mat 27:46, 50, Mk 15:34,37, Lk 23:46, Jno 11:43

crieth *(see cry, cried)*
> thy brother's blood *c*   Gen 4:10
> voice of him that *c*   Isa 40:3

crimson, *scarlet*
> sins be red like *c*   Isa 1:18

crooked, *perverse, twisted*
> and *c* generation   Deut 32:5
> *c* be straight   Isa 40:4, 42:16, Lk 3:5
> midst of *c* nation   Phil 2:15

cross
> taketh not his *c*   Mat 10:38, Lk 14:27
> take up his *c* Mat 16:24, Mk 8:34, 10:21, Lk 9:23
> compelled to bear his *c* Mat 27:32, Mk 15:21, Lk 23:26
> come down from *c*   Mat 27:40,42, Mk 15:30,32
> preaching of *c* is   1 Cor 1:18
> reconcile both by *c*   Eph 2:16
> obedient unto death of *c*   Phil 2:8
> enemies of *c* of Christ   3:18
> peace through blood of *c* Col 1:20
> nailing it to his *c*   2:14

crown, *diadem*
> a virtuous woman is a *c*   Pro 12:4
> *c* of the wise is their   14:24
> *c* of thorns Mat 27:29, Mk 15:17, Jno 19:2
> is laid up for me a *c*   2 Tim 4:8
> shall receive *c* of life   Jas 1:12
> I will give a *c* of life   Rev 2:10
> cast their *c* before   4:10

crowned
> thou hast *c* him with glory Psa 8:5
> he is not *c* except he   2 Tim 2:5
> we see Jesus *c* with   Heb 2:9

crucified *(see crucify)*
> let him be *c*   Mat 27:22,23
> delivered him to be *c* 27:26, Jno 19:16
> *c* him   Mat 27:35, Jno 19:23

two thieves *c*　　Mat 27:38,44, Mk
　15:32, Lk 23:33, Jno 19:18
wicked hands have *c*　Acts 2:23
Jesus, whom ye *c*　　2:36, 4:10
our old man is *c* with　Rom 6:6
was Paul *c* for you?　1 Cor 1:23
Jesus Christ and him *c*　2:2,8
I am *c* with Christ　Gal 2:20
are Christ's have *c*　　5:24

crucify, *put to death on a cross*
　him to Gentiles to *c*　Mat 20:19
　led him away to *c* 27:31, Mk.15:20
　cried out again, *c*　　15:13,14
　c him, *c* him Lk 23:21, Jno 19:6,15
　they *c* to themselves　Heb 6:6

cruel, *fierce, violent*
　he that is *c* troubleth　Pro 11:17
　mercies of wicked are *c*　12:10

crumbs, *little bits*
　c which fall from　Mat 15:27, Mk
　　　　　　　　　　　7:28
　fed with *c* which　　Lk 16:21

cry (noun), *shout, plea*
　c of Sodom　Gen 18:20, 19:13
　their *c* came up　Ex 2:23, 3:9
　a great *c* through Egypt　11:6
　ears are open to *c*　Psa 34:15
　at midnight a *c* made　Mat 25:6

cry (verb)
　c but none answer　Job 35:12
　hear, when I *c*　Psa 27:7, 28:2
　what shall I *c*?　Isa 40:6
　shall not strive, nor *c*　Mat 12:19
　Spirit, whereby we *c*　Rom 8:15
　stones would *c* out　Lk 19:40

crying *(see cry)*
　voice of one *c* in wilderness　Mat
　　3:3, Mk 1:3, Lk 3:4, Jno 1:23

Spirit into hearts, *c*　Gal 4:6
no more death nor *c*　Rev 21:4

crystal, *clear*
　sea of glass like unto *c*　Rev 4:6
　light of city clear as *c*　21:11
　water of life, clear as *c*　22:1

cubit, *length of the forearm, 18 inches*
　add one *c* to　Mat 6:27, Lk 12:25

cucumber, *prob. watermelon*
　we remember the *c* and　Num 11:5

cumbered, *distracted, useless*
　Martha was *c* about　Lk 10:40
　cut it down, why *c* it?　13:7

cummin, *a spice*
　ye pay tithes of *c*　Mat 23:23

cunningly, *skillfully*
　not followed *c* devised　2 Pet 1:16

cup, *goblet, bowl*
　my *c* runneth over　Psa 23:5
　c of cold water　Mat 10:42, Mk
　　　　　　　　　　9:41
　are ye able to drink of the *c*?　Mat
　　　　　　　20:22, Mk 10:38
　make clean outside of *c*　Mat
　　　　　　　　　23:25,26
　took *c* and gave thanks　Mat 26:27,
　　Mk 14:23, Lk 22:17,20, 1 Cor
　　　　　　　　　　11:25
　let this *c* pass from　Mat 26:39, Mk
　　　　　　　14:36, Lk 22:42
　c is new testament Lk 22:20, 1 Cor
　　　　　　　　　　11:25
　as often as ye drink of this *c*
　　　　　　　　　11:26,27

curse, *take oath, vilify, condemn*
　Lord said, I will not *c*　Gen 8:21
　hired Balaam to *c* thee　Deut 23:4,
　　　　　　　　　　Neh 13:2

said his wife, c God   Job 2:9
bless them that c you Mat 5:44, Lk
6:28
he began to c   Mat 26:74, Mk
14:71
bless and c not   Rom 12:14
therewith c we man   Jas 3:9

cursed *(see curse)*
c is the ground   Gen 3:17
now art thou [Cain] c   4:11
Noah said, c be Canaan   9:25
c be the man obeyeth not   Jer 11:3
c that work deceitfully   48:10
depart from me, ye c   Mat 25:41
the fig tree thou c is   Mk 11:21

curseth *(see curse)*
c his father or   Ex 21:17, Lev 20:9,
Pro 20:20
whosoever c his God   Lev 24:15
generation that c father   Pro 30:11
that c father   Mat 15:4, Mk 7:10

cursing
blessing and c   Deut 30:19, Josh
8:34
mouth full of c   Psa 10:7, Rom 3:14
same mouth blessing c   Jas 3:10

Cush, *son of Ham,* Gen 10:6, 1 Chr 1:8

custom, *common usage, habit*
Jesus' c was, he went   Lk 4:16
we have no such c   1 Cor 11:16
teach c which are not lawful   Acts
16:21

cut, *hew, cleave*
like flower, c down   Job 14:2
evil doers be c off   Psa 37:9
right hand offend, c it off Mat 5:30,
18:8, Mk 9:43,45
and c off his ear   Mk 14:47, Lk
22:50, Jno 18:10,26

c to the heart   Acts 5:33, 7:54
I would they were c off   Gal 5:12

cymbal, *musical instrument*
brass, or a tinkling c   1 Cor 13:1

Cyprus, *island of Mediterranean,* Acts
4:36, 11:19,20, 13:4

Cyrene, *country of north Africa,* Mat
27:32, Mk 15:21, Acts 6:9, 11:20

Cyrus, *emperor of Persia about 550–
529 B.C.,* 2 Chr 36:22, Ezra 1:1,
1:7,8, 5:14, Isa 45:1, Dan 1:21

D

Dagon, *idol of Philistines,* Judg 16:23,
1 Sam 5:2

daily, *each day*
give us this day our d bread   Mat
6:11, Lk 11:3
continuing d with one   Acts 2:46
Lord added to church d   2:47
searched scriptures d   17:11

Damascus, *capital of Syria,* Gen 15:2,
2 Sam 8:6, 1 Ki 11:24, 2 Ki 16:10,
Amos 1:3, Acts 9:2, 22:6, 26:12, Gal
1:17

damnable, *condemnable*
bring in d heresies   2 Pet 2:1

damnation, *condemnation*
receive the greater d   Mat 23:14,
Mk 12:40, Lk 20:47
and drinketh d   1 Cor 11:29

damned, *condemned*
believeth not be d   Mk 16:16
he that doubteth is d   Rom 14:23

DAMSEL

40

damsel, *maid, young girl*
brought in a charger, and given to *d*
Mat 14:11, Mk 6:28
a *d* came to Peter   Mat 26:69, Jno
18:17
the *d* is not dead   Mk 5:39

Dan, *son of Jacob,* Gen 30:6, 35:25,
49:16; *city of northern Palestine,*
Gen 14:14, Josh 19:47, Judg 18:29,
20:1, 1 Sam 3:20, 2 Sam 3:10, 17:11,
24:2,5, 1 Ki 4:25, 1 Chr 21:2, 30:5

dance
and David *d* before   2 Sam 6:14
daughter of Herodias *d*   Mat 14:6,
Mk 6:22

danger, *peril*
shall be in *d* of   Mat 5:21,22
is in *d* of eternal   Mk 3:29

Daniel, *prophet in Babylon,* Ezek
14:14,20, 28:3, Dan 1:7, Mat 24:15,
Mk 13:14

dare
good man some would *d* Rom 5:7
d not make ourselves   2 Cor 10:12

Darius, *king of Persia,* Ezra 4:5,24,
6:1,12, Hag 1:1,15, Zech 7:1

dark
d water   2 Sam 22:12, Psa 18:11
utter *d* saying of old   78:2
and moon shall be *d*   Joel 2:10
I will *d* the earth   Amos 8:9
light shineth in *d*   2 Pet 1:19

darkened, *become dark*
look out of the windows be *d* Ecc
12:3
then shall the sun be *d* Mat 24:29,
Mk 13:24
and the sun was *d*   Lk 23:45

foolish heart was *d*   Rom 1:21
the understanding *d*   Eph 4:18

darkly
through glass *d*   1 Cor 13:12

darkness
d was upon face of deep   Gen 1:2
light day, and the *d* night   1:5
there be *d* over Egypt   Ex 10:21
Lord spake out of *d*   Deut 5:22
sun turned to *d*   Joel 2:31, Acts
2:20
day of the Lord be *d*   Amos 5:20
them that sit in *d*   Isa 42:7
cast out into outer *d*   Mat 8:12,
22:13, 25:30
from sixth hour was *d*   27:45, Mk
15:33
us from power of *d*   Col 1:13
and walk in *d* we lie   1 Jno 1:6
hateth his brother, is in *d*   2:9
light shine out of *d*   2 Cor 4:6
communion hath light with *d?* 6:14
d into marvellous light   1 Pet 2:9
God is light, and no *d*   1 Jno 1:5
d is past, and true light   2:8

daughter, *daughter, child*
Jephthah's *d* come out Judg 11:34
Solomon took Pharaoh's *d* 1 Ki 3:1
d have done virtuously   Pro 31:29
Naomi said to her two *d*-in-law
Ruth 1:8
that loveth son or *d*   Mat 10:37
the *d* of Herodias danced   14:6

David, *second king of Israel,* Ruth
4:22, 1 Sam 16:13, 16:23, 17:23,
2 Sam 2:4, 2:10, 5:1, Mat 22:42, Mk
12:35, Rom 1:3, 2 Tim 2:8

dawn, *early morning*

as it began to *d*   Mat 28:1
day *d* and day star   2 Pet 1:19

day, *day, era*

God called the light *d*   Gen 1:5
and morning were first *d*   1:5
God blessed seventh *d*   2:3, Ex
                                20:11
few and evil are *d* of   Gen 47:9
remember sabbath *d* to   Ex 20:8
honour father and mother that thy
  d   20:12
in mount forty *d* and forty   24:18,
            34:28, Deut 9:9, 10:10
cloud by *d* fire by   Ex 40:38, Num
                                 9:16
meditate therein *d* and   Josh 1:8,
                               Psa 1:2
born of woman of few *d*   Job 14:1
thou art my Son, this *d* have I Psa
          2:7, Acts 13:33, Heb 1:5
d unto *d* uttereth speech   Psa 19:2
d in thy courts is better   84:10
d which the Lord hath made
                               118:24
sun shall not smite by *d*   121:6
remember Creator in *d*   Ecc 12:1
while evil *d* come not   12:1
d of the Lord is at hand   Isa 13:6,
            Joel 1:15, Zeph 1:7
d of the Lord cometh Isa 13:9, Joel
               2:1, Zech 14:1
petition three times a *d*   Dan 6:10
a *d* of darkness   Joel 2:2
Jonah in fish three *d*   Jonah 1:17,
                            Mat 12:40
who may abide *d* of his coming
                              Mal 3:2
fasted forty *d* and   Mat 4:2

Son of man is Lord of sabbath *d*
                                12:8
lawful to heal on sabbath *d*
                              12:10,12
raised again the third *d*   16:21,
                 17:23, Lk 9:22
third *d* rise again   Mat 20:19, Mk
    9:31, 10:34, Lk 18:33, 24:7,46
build it in three *d*   Mat 23:61,
      27:40, Mk 14:58, 15:29, Jno
                                2:19
that *d* knoweth no man Mat 24:36,
                         Mk 13:32
come in a *d* when he looketh not
             Mat 24:50, Lk 12:46
neither know the *d* nor   Mat 25:13
after three *d* I will rise again 27:63,
                         Mk 8:31
Jesus was forty *d* in the wilderness
                        1:13, Lk 4:2
rising before *d*, prayed   Mk 1:35
do good on sabbath *d*   3:4, Lk 6:9
to you is born this *d*   2:11
d come when ye shall   17:22
raise it again at last *d*   Jno 6:39
Abraham rejoiced to see *d*   8:56
he hath appointed a *d*   17:31
walk honestly as in *d*   Rom 13:13
now is the *d* of salvation 2 Cor 6:2
because the *d* are evil   Eph 5:6
d of the Lord cometh as a thief
            1 Thes 5:2, 2 Pet 3:10
ye are children of *d*   1 Thes 5:5
to him against that *d*   2 Tim 1:12
more as ye see the *d*   Heb 10:25
till *d* dawn and   2 Pet 1:19
in Spirit on Lord's *d*   Rev 1:10

day star, *morning star, light bearer*

and the *d* arise in   2 Pet 1:19

deacon, *servant, slave*
with bishops and *d*   Phil 1:1
the *d* must be grave   1 Tim 3:8

dead
let the *d* bury their *d*   Mat 8:22
touching resurrection of the *d*
    22:31, Mk 12:26
full of *d* men's bones   Mat 23:27
seek living among *d*?   Lk 24:5
rise from *d* third   24:46, Jno 20:9
after he rose from *d*   Acts 10:41
judge of quick and *d*   10:42,
    2 Tim 4:1
God who quickeneth *d*   Rom 4:17
we that are *d* to sin   6:2
if we be *d* with Christ   6:8,11, Col
    2:20, 2 Tim 2:11
ye are *d* and your life   Col 3:3
hath not works is *d*   Jas 2:17,20
body without Spirit is *d*   2:26
we being *d* to sin   1 Pet 2:24
to judge the quick and *d*   4:5
name that thou livest, and art *d*
    Rev 3:1
blessed are the *d* who die   14:13
saw *d* stand before God   20:12
sea gave up *d* in it   20:13

deadly, *death-bearing*
drink *d* thing, it shall   Mk 16:18
unruly evil, full of *d*   Jas 3:8

deaf, *dull, deaf, silent*
is *d* as my messenger?   Isa 42:19
the *d* hear   Mat 11:5, Lk 7:22
he maketh *d* to hear   Mk 7:37

dealt, *to deal, treat*
God had *d* graciously   Gen 33:11
had *d* deceitfully   Job 6:15

Lord hath *d* bountifully   Psa 13:6,
    116:7
according God hath *d*   Rom 12:3

dear, *precious*
count I my life *d*   Acts 20:24
kingdom of his *d* Son   Col 1:13

dearth, *lack, famine*
d began to come   Gen 41:54
there was a *d* in land   2 Ki 4:38
should be great *d*   Acts 11:28

death
die *d* of righteous   Num 23:10
step between me and *d*   1 Sam 20:3
valley of shadow of *d*   Psa 23:4
precious is *d* of   116:15
d and life are in   Pro 18:21
no pleasure in *d* of wicked   Ezek
    18:32, 33:11
let him die the *d*   Mat 15:4, Mk
    7:10
shall not taste of *d* till   Mat 16:28,
    Mk 9:1, Lk 9:27
soul is sorrowful to *d*   Mat 26:38,
    Mk 14:34
he is guilty of *d*   Mat 26:66, Mk
    14:64
should not see *d* before   Lk 2:26
is passed from *d* to life   Jno 5:24,
    1 Jno 3:14
shall never see *d*   Jno 8:51,52
having loosed pains *d*   Acts 2:24
Saul consenting to *d*   8:1, 22:20
reconciled to God by the *d* of his Son
    Rom 5:10, Col 1:22
and *d* by sin, and so *d*   Rom 5:12
d reigned from Adam   5:14,17,21
baptized into his *d*   6:3,4
for wages of sin is *d*   6:23

me from body of this *d?*   7:24

free from law of sin and *d*   8:2

ye do shew the Lord's *d*   11:26

last enemy destroyed is *d*   15:26

d swallowed up in victory   15:54

sting of *d* is sin   15:56

sorrow of world worketh *d*   2 Cor
                                   7:10

through fear of *d*   Heb 2:15

bringeth forth *d*   Jas 1:15

faithful unto *d*   Rev 2:10

d and hell cast into lake   20:14

there shall be no more *d*   21:4

Deborah, *Rebekah's nurse,* Gen 35:8;
    a prophetess, Judg 4:4

debt, *loan, owed*

reckoned of grace but *d*   Rom 4:4

I am *d* to the Greeks   1:14

as we forgive our *d*   Mat 6:12

deceit, *deception, falseness*

counsels of wicked are *d*   Pro 12:5

folly of fools is *d*   14:8

bread of *d* is sweet to a   20:17

of murder, debate, *d*   Rom 1:29

deceitful *(see deceit)*

abhor bloody and *d* man   Psa 5:6

deliver me from the *d*   43:1

the mouth of the *d* are   109:2

deliver my soul from a *d*   120:2

favour is *d* and beauty   Pro 31:30

deceitfulness *(see deceit)*

d of riches choke the word   ·Mat
                              13:22, Mk 4:19

hardened through *d*   Heb 3:13

deceive, *lead astray*

no man *d* you   Mat 24:4, Mk 13:5

let no man *d* you   Eph 5:6, 2 Thes
                         2:3, 1 Jno 3:7

we have no sin, we *d*   1:8

be not *d* 1 Cor 6:9, 15:33, Gal 6:7

d his own heart   Jas 1:26

decently, *becomingly*

all things done *d*   1 Cor 14:40

decision, *determination*

in valley of *d*   Joel 3:14

declare, *make known*

the heavens *d* the glory   Psa 19:1

set watchman, let him *d*   Isa 21:6

who shall *d* his generation?   53:8,
                              Acts 8:33

I *d* unto you gospel   1 Cor 15:1

which we have seen *d*   1 Jno 1:3

d to be the Son of God   Rom 1:4

decrease, *lessen*

waters *d* continually   Gen 8:5

increase, I must *d*   Jno 3:30

decree, *command*

king Cyrus made *d*   Ezra 5:13,17

Darius made a *d*   6:1,12

there went out a *d*   Lk 2:1

they delivered them *d*   Acts 16:4

deed, *act*

because their *d* were   Jno 3:19

Dorcas full of alms *d*   Acts 9:36

man according to his *d*   Rom 2:6

d of the law shall no   3:20

obedient by word and *d*   15:18

put off old man with *d*   Col 3:9

ye do in word or *d*   3:17

shall be blessed in *d*   Jas 1:25

love in *d* and truth   1 Jno 3:18

deep

God caused a *d* sleep   Gen 2:21

d sleep fell on Abram   15:12

Spirit searcheth *d*   1 Cor 2:10

deep, *sea*
darkness on face of *d*   Gen 1:1
fountains of *d* were   7:11
launch out into the *d*   Lk 5:4

deepness
they had no *d* of earth   Mat 13:5

defence, *protection*
my *d* is of God who   Psa 7:10
for God is my *d*   59:9,17, 94:22

deferred, *delayed*
hope *d* maketh heart sick   Pro
                       13:12
discretion of a man *d*   19:11

defile, *pollute*
d not yourselves with idols   Ezek
                      20:7,18
and they *d* the man Mat 15:18, Mk
                      7:15,23
if any man *d* temple   1 Cor 3:17
conscience being weak is *d*   8:7
is tongue, that is *d*   Jas 3:6

defraud, *oppress, deprive*
false witness, *d* not   Mk 10:19
no man *d* his brother   1 Thes 4:6
suffer to be *d*   1 Cor 6:7

degree, *station*
exalted them of low *d*   Lk 1:52
let brother of low *d*   Jas 1:9

delight, *joy*
if have no *d* in her   Deut 21:14
but his *d* is in the law   Psa 1:2
fool no *d* in understanding   Pro
                       18:2
I *d* in law of God   Rom 7:22
See also: Psa 119:77,174, Pro 11:1,
20, 12:22, 15:8

Delilah, *Samson's Philistine consort,*
Judg 16:4,12

deliver, *to rescue, to give*
Lord *d* unto me two tables   Deut
                       9:10
and Moses *d* the law unto   31:9
he hath *d* my soul   Psa 55:18
d me from oppression   119:134
d us from evil   Mat 6:13, Lk 11:4
d him to Gentiles to crucify   Mat
   20:19, Mk 10:33, Lk 20:20, Acts
                       21:11
for envy they had *d* him   Mat
              27:18, Mk 15:10
d him to be crucified   Mat 27:26,
                  Jno 19:16
his Son whom ye *d* up   Acts 3:13
doctrine which was *d* you   Rom
                       6:17
now we are *d* from law   7:6
who shall *d* me from?   7:24
but *d* him up for us   8:32
I received that which I *d* unto you
           1 Cor 11:23, 15:3
that he might *d* us from   Gal 1:4
hath *d* us from power of   Col 1:13
the Lord shall *d* me   2 Tim 4:18
Lord knoweth how to *d*   2 Pet 2:9
faith which was once *d*   Jude 3
death and hell *d* up   Rev 20:13

deliverance, *salvation*
upon mount Zion shall be *d* Ob 17
sent me to preach *d* to   Lk 4:18

deliverer, *protector*
Lord is my rock and *d* 2 Sam 22:2,
                  Psa 18:2
my help and my *d*   40:17, 70:5

delusion, *delusion, error*
  send them strong *d*   2 Thes 2:11

Demas, *companion of Paul,* Col 4:14,
  Phil 24, 2 Tim 4:10

Demetrius, *at least two bore this name
  in N.T.,* Acts 19:24,38, 3 Jno 12

demonstration, *showing*
  in *d* of the Spirit   1 Cor 2:4

den, *cave, habitation*
  of Israel made them *d*   Judg 6:2
  cast into *d* of lions   Dan 6:7,12
  made it a *d* of thieves   Mat 21:13,
      Mk 11:17

deny, *deny, disown, keep back*
  d me, him will I *d*   Mat 10:33
  let him *d* himself   16:24, Mk 8:34,
      Lk 9:23
    thou shalt *d* me thrice   Mat
      26:34,75 Mk 14:30,72
    Peter *d*   Mat 26:70,72, Mk 14:70,
      Lk 22:57, Jno 18:25,27
  who *d* shall be *d*   Lk 12:9
  d there is resurrection   20:27
  till thou hast *d* me   Jno 13:38
  he hath *d* the faith   1 Tim 5:8
  d him, he will *d* us   2 Tim 2:12
  form of godliness but *d*   3:5
  a liar, that *d* Jesus   1 Jno 2:22

depart, *leave*
  sceptre shall not *d*   Gen 49:10
  d from me, workers   Psa 6:8, Mat
      7:23, Lk 13:27
  d from me, evil doers   Psa 119:115
  when old he will not *d*   Pro 22:6
  d out of their coasts   Mat 8:34, Mk
      5:17
  d from me, ye cursed   Mat 25:41
  if I *d* I will send   Jno 16:7

not *d* from Jerusalem   Acts 1:4
shall *d* from faith   1 Tim 4:1
d from iniquity   2 Tim 2:19

departure
  time of my *d* is at   2 Tim 4:6

depth, *deepness*
  drowned in the *d* of the   Mat 18:6
  because it had not *d* of   Mk 4:5
  O the *d* of riches   Rom 11:33
  what is breadth and *d*   Eph 3:18

depths, *sea*
  the *d* were congealed in   Ex 15:8
  out of *d* have I cried   Psa 130:1

descend, *go down*
  because the Lord *d*   Ex 19:18
  spirit of God *d*   Mat 3:16, Mk 1:10
  the Holy Ghost *d* in   Lk 3:22
  vessel *d* as great sheet   Acts 11:15
  Lord shall *d* from   1 Thes 4:16
  wisdom *d* not from   Jas 3:15

desert, *deserted place*
  streams in the *d*   Isa 35:6
  make straight in *d* a   40:3
  make rivers in the *d*   43:19,20
  departed into a *d* place   Mat 14:13,
      Mk 6:32, Lk 4:42
  did eat manna in the *d*   Jno 6:31
  to Gaza, which is *d*   Acts 8:26

desire, *want, seek*
  d of wicked perish   Psa 112:10
  d of righteous shall   Pro 10:24
  no beauty that we should *d*   Isa
      53:2
  for I *d* mercy and not   Hos 6:6
  woe to you that *d* day   Amos 5:18
  if any man *d* to be first   Mk 9:35
  follow after charity, *d*   1 Cor 14:1
  in strait, have a *d*   Phil 1:23

ye kill, ye *d* to have   Jas 4:2
as newborn babes, *d* sincere   1 Pet
2:2

desolate, *forsaken*
none that trust in him shall be *d*
Psa 34:22
let his habitation be *d*   Acts 1:20

desolation (*see desolate*)
kingdom divided against itself is
brought to *d* Mat 12:25, Lk 11:17
abomination of *d*   Mat 24:15, Mk
13:14

despair, *have no outlet, no hope*
cause my heart to *d*   Ecc 2:20
perplexed, but not *d*   2 Cor 4:8
insomuch that we *d*   1:8

despise, *loathe, hate*
fools *d* wisdom   Pro 1:7
d not chastening of Lord 3:11, Heb
12:5
void of wisdom *d*   Pro 11:12
fool *d* father's instructions   15:5
d and rejected of men   Isa 53:3
I hate, I *d* your feast   Amos 5:21
or *d* thou riches of?   Rom 2:4
let none *d* thy youth   1 Tim 4:12
but ye have *d* the poor   Jas 2:6
d dominion, and speak evil Jude 8

despiteful, *use spitefully*
pray for them that *d*   Mat 5:44, Lk
6:28
haters of God, *d* proud   Rom 1:30

destroy
I will *d* man whom I   Gen 6:7
flood of waters to *d* all   6:17
prosperity of fools *d*   Pro 1:32
Lord will *d* house of proud   15:25
think not that I am come to *d* Mat
5:17

fear him able to *d*   10:28
d this temple   Mk 14:58, Jno 2:19
body of sin might be *d*   Rom 6:6
for meat *d* not work   14:20
I will *d* wisdom of   1 Cor 1:19
last enemy *d* is death   15:26
cast down, but not *d*   2 Cor 4:9
d with brightness   2 Thes 2:8
d him that had power of Heb 2:14
that he might *d* works   Jno 3:8

destruction (*see destroy*)
thou turnest man to *d*   Psa 90:3
pride goeth before *d*   Pro 16:18
a fool's mouth is his *d*   18:7
Hell and *d* are never full   27:20
way that leadeth to *d*   Mat 7:13
d and misery are in   Rom 3:16
walk whose end is *d*   Phil 3:19
with everlasting *d*   2 Thes 1:9
wrest to own *d*   2 Pet 3:16

determine, *decide, mark out*
seeing his days are *d*   Job 14:5
hath *d* times before   Acts 17:26
I *d* not to know anything   1 Cor
2:2

devil, *demon, destroyer*
forty days tempted of *d*   Mat 4:1,
Lk 4:2
those possessed with *d*   Mat 4:24,
8:6,28,33, Mk 1:32, Lk 8:36
say he hath a *d*   Mat 11:18, Lk
7:33
saw one casting out *d* in thy name
Mk 9:38, Lk 9:49
of whom went seven *d*   8:2
thou hast a *d*   Jno 7:20, 8:48
against wiles of *d*   Eph 6:11
resist *d* and he will   Jas 4:7

your adversary the *d* 1 Pet 5:8
sin is of the *d* 1 Jno 3:8
old serpent called *d* Rev 12:9

devise, *design, plan*
he *d* mischief on his bed Psa 36:4
d mischief continually Pro 6:14
woe to them that *d* Mic 2:1
not followed cunningly *d* 2 Pet 1:16

devour, *eat, consume*
fowls came and *d* them Mat 13:4,
Mk 4:4, Lk 8:5
but if ye bite and *d* one Gal 5:15
seeking whom he may *d* 1 Pet 5:8

devout, *reverent, worshipful*
at Jerusalem Jews, *d* Acts 2:5
d men carried Stephen to 8:2
Cornelius was a *d* man 10:2

dew
God give thee of *d* Gen 27:28,39
hast *d* of thy youth Psa 110:3
goodness is as *d* Hos 6:4, 13:3

Diana, *goddess of Ephesus,* Acts 19:24
did, *(see do)*
d evil in sight of Lord Judg 2:11,
1 Ki 14:22, 2 Ki 8:27, 2 Chr 22:4,
etc.
d it not to these Mat 25:45
who *d* not sin, nor 1 Pet 2:22

die *(see death),* to expire
touch it, lest ye *d* Gen 3:3
every thing shall *d* 6:17
d death of righteous Num 23:10
curse God and *d* Job 2:9
d shall he live again? 14:14
fools *d* for want of Pro 10:21
to be born, a time to *d* Ecc 3:2
both great and small *d* Jer 16:6

soul that sinneth, it shall *d* Ezek 18:4,20
eat thereof, and not *d* Jno 6:50
ye shall *d* in sins 8:21,24
righteous man will one *d* Rom 5:7
it is Christ that *d* 8:34
no man *d* to himself 14:7
Christ both *d* and rose 14:9
for as in Adam all *d* 1 Cor 15:22
live in Christ, to *d* Phil 1:21
believe that Jesus *d* 1 Thes 4:14
to men once to *d* Heb 9:27
blessed are dead that *d* Rev 14:13

difference, *distinction*
and put no *d* between Acts 15:9
for there is no *d* Rom 3:22
is no *d* between Jew and 10:12

dig
of those hills mayst *d* Deut 8:9
cannot *d*, to beg I am Lk 16:3

dignities, *reputation, esteem*
speak evil of *d* 2 Pet 2:10, Jude 8

diligence, *determination*
keep heart with all *d* Pro 4:23
giving all *d*, add 2 Pet 1:5,10

diligent, *determined, careful*
hand of *d* bear rule Pro 12:24
but the soul of *d* shall 13:4
rewarder of them that *d* Heb 11:6
prophets search *d* 1 Pet 1:10

diminish, *become less*
you shall not *d* Ex 5:8
nor shall you *d* Deut 4:2, 12:32

Dinah, *daughter of Jacob,* Gen 30:21, 34:5

dinner, *meal*
better is a *d* of herbs Pro 15:7

Diotrephes, *opponent of John,* 3 Jno 9
dip
he that *d* his hand with me   Mat
26:23, Mk 14:20, Jno 13:26
Lazarus that he may *d*   Lk 16:24
direct, *guide*
he shall *d* thy paths   Pro 3:6
man that walketh to *d*   Jer 10:23
Lord *d* your hearts   2 Thes 3:5
disallow, *reject*
stone which builders *d*   1 Pet 2:7
disannul, *make void*
covenant law cannot *d*   Gal 3:17
discern, *understand*
can I *d* between good 2 Sam 19:35
senses exercised to *d*   Heb 5:14
they are spiritually *d*   1 Cor 2:14
word is *d* of thoughts   Heb 4:12
disciple, *follower, learner*
d not above master Mat 10:24, Lk
6:40
cannot be my *d*   14:26,27,33
thou art his *d* we are   Jno 9:28
d Jesus loved   20:2, 21:7,20
disciples *(see disciple)*
unto him his twelve *d*   Mat 10:1
Jesus took the twelve *d*   20:17
then all *d* forsook him   26:56
he began to wash *d* feet Jno 13:5
so shall ye be my *d*   15:8
d were called Christians   Acts
11:26
first day of week *d* came   20:7
discord, *strife, contention*
mischief, he soweth *d*   Pro 6:14
and him that soweth *d*   6:19
disease, *sickness*
vanity is an evil *d*   Ecc 6:2

healing all manner of *d* Mat 4:23,
9:35, 10:1
dish, *bowl, dish*
as a man wipeth a *d*   2 Ki 21:13
dippeth with me in *d*   Mat 26:23,
Mk 14:20
dishonour, *shame*
clothed with shame and *d*   Psa
35:26, 71:13
d thou God   Rom 2:23
to honour, another *d*   9:21
sown in *d*, raised   1 Cor 15:43
disobedience *(cf. obey)*
by one man's *d* many   Rom 5:19
to revenge all *d*   2 Cor 10:6
children of *d*   Eph 5:6, Col 3:6
d received a just   Heb 2:2
disobedient
not *d* to heavenly   Acts 26:19
boasters, *d* to parents   Rom 1:30,
2 Tim 3:2
disorderly, *not in order*
them that are *d*   1 Thes 5:14
brother who walks *d*   2 Thes 3:6
some who walk among you *d*   3:11
dispensation, *law, arrangement*
a *d* of the gospel is   1 Cor 9:17
d of fulness of times   Eph 1:10
ye have heard of *d* of grace   3:2
according to *d*   Col 1:25
dispute, *reason, argue*
d against Grecians   Acts 9:29
Paul *d* in synagogue with   17:17
where is *d* of world?   1 Cor 1:20
without murmurings and *d*   Phil
2:14
dissension, *contention*
Barnabas had *d*   Acts 15:2

49   DOCTRINE

arose a *d* between Pharisees 23:7
when there arose *d* 23:10

dissimulation, *hypocrisy*
let love be without *d* Rom 12:9
carried away with *d* Gal 2:13

dissolve, *melt away*
tabernacle were *d* 2 Cor 5:1
heavens shall be *d* 2 Pet 3:12

distress, *distress, suffering*
day of trouble and *d* Zeph 1:15
there shall be great *d* Lk 21:23
d separate us from love Rom 8:35
over you in your *d* 1 Thes 3:7

distribute, *apportion, give*
sell all, and *d* Lk 18:22
rich be ready to *d* 1 Tim 6:18
but as God hath *d* 1 Cor 7:17

ditch, *ditch, pit*
both shall fall into *d* Mat 15:14,
Lk 6:39

divers, *different, various*
deceived, serving *d* lusts Tit 3:6
who in *d* manners spake Heb 1:1
fall into *d* temptations Jas 1:2

divide, *separate, cleave*
and let the firmament *d* Gen 1:6
lights, to *d* day from 1:14,18
d land by lot Num 33:54,
34:17,18,29
in his days was earth *d* Gen 10:25,
1 Chr 1:19
and waters were *d* Ex 14:21
which *d* the Red Sea Psa 136:13
kingdom or house *d* Mat 12:25,
Mk 3:24,25, Lk 11:17
he *d* unto them his living 15:12
is Christ *d*? 1 Cor 1:13
a workman rightly *d* 2 Tim 2:15

piercing to *d* asunder Heb 4:12

divine, *godlike*
as his *d* power hath 2 Pet 1:3
be partakers of the *d* nature 1:4

division *(see divide)*
them which cause *d* Rom 16:17
that there be no *d* 1 Cor 1:10
is among you strife and *d* 3:3
I hear there be *d* among 11:18

divorce, *cast out*
not take *d* woman Lev 21:14
bill of *d* Deut 24:1,3
and given a bill of *d* Jer 3:8
marry her that is *d* Mat 5:32
suffered bill of *d* Mk 10:4

do, *act*
Judge of earth *d* right? Gen 18:25
but to *d* justly, and Mic 6:8
d will of my Father Mat 12:50, Mk
3:35
as ye would that men *d* Lk 6:31
hear word of God and *d* it 8:21
this *d* in remembrance 22:19,
1 Cor 11:24,25
my meat is to *d* will Jno 4:34
d by nature things Rom 2:14
let us *d* evil that good 3:8
whatsoever ye *d* in word Col 3:17
ye *d, d* it heartily 3:23
I can *d* all things Phil 4:13

doctor, *teacher*
Jesus in midst of the *d* Lk 2:46
there were Pharisees and *d* 5:17
Gamaliel, a *d* Acts 5:34

doctrine, *teaching*
people astonished at his *d* Mat 7:28,
22:33, Mk 1:22, 11:18, Lk 4:32
for *d* commandments of men Mat
15:9, Mk 7:7

continued in apostles' *d* Acts 2:42
obeyed that form of *d* Rom 6:17
with every wind of *d* Eph 4:14
contrary to sound *d* 1 Tim 1:10
heed to thyself, and to thy *d* 4:16
is profitable for *d* 2 Tim 3:16
not endure sound *d* 4:3
which become sound *d* Tit 2:1
may adorn the *d* 2:10
leaving principles of *d* Heb 6:1
abideth not in *d* 2 Jno 9

doer, *one who acts*
but the *d* of law Rom 2:13
be ye *d* of the word Jas 1:22
hearer, not *d* of word 1:23
not a *d* of law 4:11

doest, doeth *(see do)*
there is none that *d* good Psa
14:1,3, 53:1, Rom 3:12
blessed is he that *d* Psa 106:3
a merry heart *d* good Pro 17:22
d thou well to be angry? Jonah
4:4,9
heareth sayings and *d* Mat 7:24
if any man *d* his will Jno 9:31
thou *d*, do quickly 13:27
believest God, thou *d* Jas 2:19

dog, *canine, but sometimes euphemism for prostitute (as in Deut 23:18)*
not bring price of *d* Deut 23:18
living *d* is better than Ecc 9:4
give not holy unto *d* Mat 7:6
d eat of crumbs 15:27, Mk 7:28
d came and licked Lk 16:21

doing *(see do)*
who went about *d* good Acts 10:38
not be weary in well *d* Gal 6:9,
2 Thes 3:13.

suffer for well *d* 1 Pet 3:17
dominion, *rule over*
have *d* over fish Gen 1:26,28
not iniquity have *d* Psa 119:133
Gentiles exercise *d* Mat 20:25
sin not have *d* over you Rom 6:14
law hath *d* over a man as long 7:1
to only wise God be *d* Jude 25
done, *accomplished, finished*
thy will be *d* Mat 6:10, 26:42, Lk
11:2, 22:42
these ought ye to have *d* Mat
23:23, Lk 11:42
well *d* good Mat 25:21,23
d it to one of these 25:40
having *d* all to stand Eph 6:13
nothing be *d* through Phil 2:3
door, *entrance, gate*
sin lieth at the *d* Gen 4:7
d was shut Mat 25:10
entereth not by the *d* Jno 10:1
I am the *d* 10:7,9
great *d* and effectual 1 Cor 16:9
d was opened to me 2 Cor 2:12
at *d* and knock, if any Rev 3:20
Dorcas, *woman raised by Peter,* Acts
9:36,39
Dothan, *town of northern Palestine,*
Gen 37:17, 2 Ki 6:13
double, *twice, two*
with a *d* heart do speak Psa 12:2
deacons grave, not *d* 1 Tim 3:8
counted worthy of *d* honour 5:17
d-minded man is unstable Jas 1:8
your hearts, ye *d*-minded 4:8
doubt, *waver*
have faith, and *d* not Mat 21:21
not *d* in his heart Mk 11:23

d is damned if he eat   Rom 14:1
without wrath and *d*   1 Tim 2:8

dove, *bird of pigeon family*
   Noah sent *d*   Gen 8:8,10,12
   had wings like *d*   Psa 55:6
   flee as *d* to their   Isa 60:8
   Ephraim is like silly *d*   Hos 7:11
   descending like a *d*   Mat 3:16, Mk
     1:10, Lk 3:22, Jno 1:32
   that sold *d*   Mat 21:12, Mk 11:15,
     Jno 2:14,16

dragon, *sea serpent*
   wine is the poison of *d*   Deut 32:33
   praise Lord ye *d*   ·   Psa 148:7
   behold, a great red *d*   Rev 12:3

draught, *catch of*
   let down nets for *d*   Lk 5:4

drave, *archaic form of drove*
   they *d* them out   Josh 24:12, Judg
     6:9
   Lord *d* out before us all Josh 24:18
   he *d* them from   Acts 18:16

draw, *attract*
   nor years *d* nigh   Ecc 12:1
   d near with their lips   : Isa 29:13
   this people *d* nigh with· Mat 15:8
   Father which sent me *d*   Jno 6:44
   I be lifted up, *d* all   12:32
   to *d* away disciples   Acts 20:30
   d near with a true   Heb 10:22
   d nigh to God, will *d* nigh Jas 4:8

dread, *fear*
   d of you shall be on   Gen 9:2
   fear and *d* shall fall   Ex 15:16
   this day will I begin to put *d* Deut
     2:25, 11:25

dream, *sometimes: vision*
   Joseph dreamed a *d* Gen 37:5,9,10

butler and baker dreamed a *d* 40:5
Pharaoh *d*   41:1,15
Nebuchadnezzar *d* dreams Dan 2:1
your old men *d* dreams Joel 2:28,
     Acts 2:17
appeared to Joseph in a *d*   Mat
     1:20, 2:13,19

dreamer *(see dream)*
   not hearken to *d*   Deut 13:3

dregs, *lees, sediment*
   hast drunken the *d*   Isa 51:17 ff

dress, *care for*
   man into garden to *d*   Gen 2:15

dried
   until waters were *d* up Gen 8:7,13
   our bones *d* and hope Ezek 37:11

drink (noun), *liquid to drink*
   do not drink strong *d*   Lev 10:9
   wine is mocker, strong *d* Pro 20:1
   erred through strong *d*   Isa 28:7
   thirsty, and ye gave me *d*   Mat
     25:35
   drink wine nor strong *d* Lk 1:15
   my blood is *d* indeed   Jno 6:55
   enemy thirst, give him *d*   Rom
     12:20
   not meat and *d*   14:17
   judge in meat or *d*   Col 2:16

drink (verb)
   Moses made Israel *d*   Ex 32:20
   Nazarite *d* no vinegar   Num 6:3
   gave me vinegar to *d*   Psa 69:21
   for they *d* the wine of   Pro 4:17
   enemy be thirsty, give *d*   25:21
   gave Nazarite wine to *d*   Amos
     2:12
   whoso shall give to *d* Mat 10:42
   able to *d* cup   20:22, Mk 10:38

gave cup, saying *d*   Mat 26:27
not *d* henceforth   26:29, Mk 14:25
vinegar to *d*   Mat 27:34, Mk 15:36
John shall *d* neither   Lk 1:15
oft as ye *d*   1 Cor 11:25
d no longer water, but   1 Tim 5:23

drinketh
who *d* iniquity like water Job 15:16
d of this water shall   Jno 4:13,14
he that *d* unworthily *d* 1 Cor 11:29

drive, *cause to go or flee*
I will *d* out the Canaanite   Ex 33:2
to *d* out nations   Deut 4:39, 9:4,5,
    Josh 3:10
spirit *d* him   Mk 1:12
d of devil   Lk 8:29
like wave of sea *d*   Jas 1:6
ships though great are *d*   3:4

drop, *to flow, pour out*
heavens shall *d* down dew   Deut
    33:28, Pro 3:20
contentions of a wife are continual
    d   19:13, 27:15

drops
sweat was as great *d*   Lk 22:44

drown, *overflow*
better he were *d* in   Mat 18:6
foolish lusts, that *d*   1 Tim 6:9

drunk, *inebriated*
be not *d* with wine   Eph 5:18
made *d* with the wine   Rev 17:2

drunkard *(see drunk)*
son is a glutton and *d*   Deut 21:20
for *d* and glutton shall   Psa 23:21
to and fro like a *d*   Isa 24:20
nor *d* shall inherit   1 Cor 6:10

drunken *(see drunk)*
Noah was *d* and he   Gen 9:21

stagger like a *d*   Job 12:25, Psa
    107:27
for these are not *d*   Acts 2:15

drunkenness *(see drunk)*
not in rioting and *d*   Rom 13:13
flesh are murders, *d*   Gal 5:21

dry, *dry, waterless*
better is a *d* morsel   Pro 17:1
rivers of water in a *d*   Isa 32:2
root out of a *d* ground   53:2
O ye *d* bones   Ezek 37:4

due, *owed, appropriate*
word spoken in *d* season Psa 15:23
in *d* time Christ died   Rom 5:6
to whom tribute is *d.*   13:7
one born out of *d* time   1 Cor 15:8
in *d* season we shall   Gal 6:9

dull, *insensitive*
ears are *d*   Mat 13:15, Acts 28:27
seeing ye are *d*   Heb 5:11

dumb, *silent*
I was as a *d* man   Psa 38:13
sheep before shearers *d*   Isa 53:7
like a lamb *d* before   Acts 8:32
d ass speaking with   2 Pet 2:16

dungeon, *prison, pit*
Joseph hastily out of *d*   Gen 41:14
drew Jeremiah out of *d*   Jer 38:13

dust, *clay, earth*
Lord formed man of the *d* Gen 2:7
d thou art, and unto *d* shalt   3:19
make thy seed as *d*   13:16, 28:14,
    2 Chr 1:9
pant after the *d*   Amos 2:7
shake off the *d* of your   Mat 10:14,
    Mk 6:11, Lk 9:5

duty, *obligation*
this is whole *d* of man   Ecc 12:13

dwell, *to inhabit, sit*

Japhet shall *d* in tents   Gen 9:27
if brethren *d* together   Deut 25:5
I *d* among own people   2 Ki 4:13
brethren to *d* together   Psa 133:1
if I *d* in uttermost parts of   139:9
better *d* in the corner   Pro 21:9,
     25:24
I *d* in midst of a people   Isa 6:5
Spirit of God *d* in you   Rom 8:9,11
Christ may *d* in your   Eph 3:17
word of Christ *d* in you richly   Col
     3:16

dwelleth *(see dwell)*

Father that *d* in me   Jno 14:10
Spirit, for he *d* in you   14:17
d not in temples made with hands
     Acts 7:48, 17:24
sin that *d* in me   Rom 7:17,20
Holy Ghost which *d*   2 Tim 1:14
new earth wherein *d*   2 Pet 3:13
how *d* love of God?   1 Jno 3:17
keepeth his commandments, *d* 3:24
love one another, God *d*   4:12

dwelt *(see dwell)*

word made flesh and *d*   Jno 1:14

dying, *to die*

bearing in body the *d* of   2 Cor
     4:10
as *d* and behold we live   6:9

E

each, *one*

e esteem other better   Phil 2:3
charity toward *e* other   2 Thes 1:3

eagle

I bare you on *e* wings   Ex 19:4
riches fly away as an *e*   Pro 23:5
thou exalt thyself as *e*   Ob 4
e be gathered   Mat 24:28, Lk 17:37

ear

by hearing of the *e*   Job 42:5
my son, incline thine *e*   Pro 4:20
e of the wise seeketh   18:15
that taketh a dog by the *e*   26:17
they have *e* to hear   Ezek 12:2
he that hath *e*, let him hear   Mat
   11:15, 13:9,43, Mk 4:9,23, 7:16,
   Lk 8:8, 14:35, Rev 2:7,11,17,29,
     3:16,13,22, 13:9
smote off *e*   Mat 26:51, Mk 14:47
having *e* hear ye not?   Mk 8:18
not seen, nor *e* heard   1 Cor 2:9
if *e* shall say, Because   12:16
having itching *e*   2 Tim 4:3
his *e* are open to   1 Pet 3:12

ear, *head of grain*

seven thin *e* devoured seven full *e*
     Gen 41:7,24
disciples began to pluck the *e*   Mat
     12:1

early, *early, dawn*

my God, *e* will I seek   Psa 63:1
seek me *e*   Pro 1:28, 8:17
cometh Mary Magdalene *e*   Jno
     20:1

earnest, *sincere, intense*
　e expectation of the　　　Rom 8:19
　covet *e* best gifts　　　1 Cor 12:31
　e expectation and hope　　Phil 1:20
　ought to give the more *e*　Heb 2:1
　that ye should *e* contend　　Jude 3

earnest, *surety, pledge*
　e of the Spirit　　　2 Cor 1:22, 5:5
　e of our inheritance　　　Eph 1:14

earth, *world, soil, ground*
　e was without form　　　Gen 1:2
　God called the dry land *e*　　1:10
　dominion over all the *e*　　1:26
　be fruitful, replenish *e*　　1:28, 9:1
　while *e* remaineth, seedtime　8:22
　nations of *e* shall be blessed in
　　　　18:18, 22:18, 26:4, 28:14
　know that *e* is the Lord's　Ex 9:29,
　　　Deut 10:14, Psa 24:1, 1 Cor
　　　　　　　　　　　　10:26
　going way of all the *e*　Josh 23:14,
　　　　　　　　　　1 Ki 2:2
　to and fro in the *e*　　Job 1:7, 2:2
　uttermost parts of *e*　Psa 2:8, 65:8
　not fear though *e* be　　　46:2
　the *e* abideth for ever　　Ecc 1:4
　the *e* is my　　　　　Isa 66:1
　let all *e* keep silence　　Hab 2:20
　they shall inherit *e*　　Mat 5:5
　not up treasures upon *e*　　6:19
　bind on *e*　　　16:19, 18:18
　to send fire on the *e*　　Lk 12:49
　he that is of *e* is　　　Jno 3:31
　I be lifted up from *e*　　12:32
　e and works therein　2 Pet 3:10
　three that bear witness in the *e*
　　　　　　　　　　1 Jno 5:8

earthen, *clay, made of earth*

　treasure in *e* vessels　　2 Cor 4:7
earthly, *of the earth*
　if I have told you *e*　　Jno 3:12
　who mind *e* things　　Phil 3:19
　wisdom is *e*, sensual　　Jas 3:15
earthquake, *shaking*
　two years before *e*　　Amos 1:1
　e in divers places　　Mat 24:7, Mk
　　　　　　13:8, Lk 21:11
　there was a great *e* Mat 28:2, Acts
　　　　16:26, Rev 6:12, 11:13
　thunderings and an *e*　8:5, 11:19
ease, *quiet, rest*
　his soul shall dwell at *e*　Psa 25:13
　woe to them that are at *e*　.Amos
　　　　　　　　　　6:1
　take thine *e*, eat, drink　Lk 12:19
east, *"sun rising"*
　as far as *e* from west　Psa 103:12
　come wise men from *e*　Mat 2:1
　we have seen star in the *e*　2:2,9
Easter, *mistranslation of Passover,*
　Acts 12:4
easy, *light, not difficult*
　my yoke is *e* my burden Mat 11:30
　e for a camel to go　　19:24, Mk
　　　　　　10:25, Lk 18:25
　charity is not *e* provoked　1 Cor
　　　　　　　　　　13:5
　sin which doth so *e* beset Heb 12:1
　wisdom from above is *e*　Jas 3:17
eat, *devour*
　of every tree freely *e*　　Gen 2:16
　tree of knowledge of good and evil,
　　not *e*　　　　2:17, 3:1 ff
　Eve took and did *e*　　　3:6
　blood thereof shall ye not *e*　9:4,
　　Lev 19:26, Deut 12:16,23,24,25,
　　　　　　　　　　15:23

children of Israel did *e* manna   Ex
       16:35, Jno 6:31,49,58
let us *e* and drink   Isa 22:13, 1 Cor
       15:32
what shall *e* Mat 6:25,31, Lk 12:29
and said, take *e*   Mat 26:26, Mk
       14:22, 1 Cor 11:24
John did *e* locusts and   Mk 1:6
take ease, *e*, drink   Lk 12:19
a man may *e* thereof   Jno 6:50
except ye *e* flesh of Son   6:53
they did *e* their meat   Acts 2:46
is damned if he *e*   Rom 14:23
e and drink unworthily 1 Cor 11:28
neither should he *e*   2 Thes 3:10
give to *e* of tree   Rev 2:7
give to *e* hidden manna   2:17

eaten *(see eat)*
hast thou *e* of tree?   Gen 3:11
zeal *e* me up   Psa 69:9, Jno 2:17
bread *e* in secret   Pro 9:17
e sour grapes Jer 31:29, Ezek 18:2
Lord, I have never *e*   Acts 10:14
he was *e* of worms, and   12:23

Eber, *ancestor of Abraham,* Gen
10:21,25, 1 Chr 1:19, Num 24:24

Eden, *garden where God placed Adam,*
Gen 2:15, 3:23, Isa 51:3, Ezek 36:35,
Joel 2:3, Amos 1:5

edged, *having edges*
and a two-*e* sword in   Psa 149:6
sharp as a two-*e* sword   Pro 5:4
sharper than two-*e*   Heb 4:12
out of mouth two-*e*   Rev 1:16

edify, *build up, strengthen*
charity   1 Cor 8:1
lawful, but *e* not   10:23
all things be done to *e*   14:26

for the *e* of the body   Eph 4:12
increase of body to *e*   4:16
e one another, even   1 Thes 5:11

Edom, *another name for Esau and the
country he settled,* Gen 25:30, 36:1,
Num 20:14,21, 24:18, Judg 11:17,
2 Sam 8:14, 1 Chr 18:13

effect, *result, consequence, effectiveness*
commandment of none *e* Mat 15:6
word of God of none *e*   Mk 7:13
of none *e*   Rom 4:14, Gal 3:17
Christ be of none *e*   1 Cor 1:17
Christ became of no *e*   Gal 5:4

effectual, *effective*
a great door and *e*   1 Cor 16:9
e working of his power   Eph 3:7
e prayer of righteous   Jas 5:16

egg
if he ask an *e*, will he   Lk 11:12

Egypt, *land of the Nile in North Africa,*
Gen 12:10, Ex 1:1, etc.

Egyptian, *of Egypt*
handmaid an *E*   Gen 16:1,3, 21:9
Moses spied *E* smiting   Ex 2:11
art not thou that *E*   Acts 21:38

Ehud, *judge of Israel,* Judg 3:15

eight
e days old   Gen 17:12, 21:4, Lk
       2:21
wherein *e* souls were   1 Pet 3:20

either, *or, each*
e he will   Mat 6:24, Lk 16:13
e make the tree good   Mat 12:33
crucified, on *e* side   Jno 19:18
e can a vine bear figs?   Jas 3:12

Elah, *valley west of Jerusalem*
by valley of *E*   1 Sam 17:2
Goliath in valley of *E*   21:9

elder, *older, presbyters*
e serve   Gen 25:23, Rom 9:12
tradition of the *e?*   Mat 15:2
many things of *e*   16:21, 27:12
the tradition of the *e*   Mk 7:3
rejected of *e*   8:31, Lk 9:22
rebuke not an *e* but   1 Tim 5:1
against an *e* receive not   5:19
who am also an *e*   1 Pet 5:1
younger, submit to *e*   5:5

Eleazer, *son of Aaron,* Ex 6:25, 28:1,
  Num 3:2,32

elect, *chosen*
behold mine *e* in whom   Isa 42:1
Israel mine *e* I have called   45:4
to charge of God's *e?*   Rom 8:33
put on as the *e* of God   Col 3:12
all things for *e*'s sakes   2 Tim 2:10
to faith of God's *e*   Tit 1:1
e according to   1 Pet 1:2.

election, *choice*
a remnant according to *e*   Rom
   11:5
calling and *e* sure   2 Pet 1:10

elements, *rudiments*
weak and beggarly *e*   Gal 4:9
the *e* shall melt   2 Pet 3:10,12

eleven
then the *e* disciples   Mat 28:16
he appeared to the *e*   Mk 16:14
all these things to *e*   Lk 24:9
was numbered with *e*   Acts 1:26
Peter standing up with *e*   2:14

Eli, *priest of Israel about 1050 B.C.,*
  1 Sam 1:25, 2:12, 3:5, 6:8

Eli *(Heb.); Eloi (Aramaic) "My God"*
  Mat 27:46, Mk 15:34

Eliezer, *servant of Abraham,* Gen 15:2;
  son of Moses, Ex 18:4, 1 Chr 23:15

Elijah, or Elias, *prophet about 850
  B.C.,* 1 Ki 17:1, 18:2, 19:1, 2 Ki 1:8,
  2:11, Mat 11:14, 16:14, 17:4, Mk
  6:15, 9:5, Lk 9:8,19,33

Elisabeth, *mother of John the Baptist,*
  Lk 1:5, 1:24,36

Elisha, or Eliseus, *prophet and
  successor of Elijah,* 1 Ki 19:16,19,
  2 Ki 2:15, 4:8, 6:20, 13:14

eloquent, *expressive with words*
O my Lord, I am not *e*   Ex 4:10
named Apollos, and *e*   Acts 18:24

Elymas, *Jewish magician,* Acts 13:8

Emmanuel, or Immanuel, *God with us*
call name *E*   Isa 7:14, Mat 1:23

Emmaus, *town west of Jerusalem,* Lk
  24:13

empty, *vain, hollow*
Israel is an *e* vine   Hos 10:1
Nineveh is *e* and void   Nah 2:10
he findeth it *e*   Mat 12:44
sent away *e*   Mk 12:3, Lk 20:10
rich he sent *e* away   1:53

end, *completion, finish*
the *e* of all flesh is   Gen 6:13
e of wicked shall be   Psa 37:38
e thereof are   Pro 14:12, 16:25
better *e* of a thing   Ecc 7:8
making books is no *e*   12:12
the sign of the *e?*   Mat 24:3
kingdom shall be no *e*   Lk 1:33
Christ is *e* of the law   Rom 10:4
neither beginning nor *e*   Heb 7:3
what shall be the *e*   1 Pet 4:17
Alpha and Omega, beginning and *e*
   Rev 21:6, 22:13

endeavouring, *attempt*
e to keep the unity of   Eph 4:3

ended *(see end)*
seventh day God e work   Gen 2:2
when Jesus had e these   Mat 7:28
when forty days were e   Lk 4:2
when the devil had e all   4:13

En-dor, *town in Galilee,* 1 Sam 28:7

ends *(see end)*
e of earth shall fear   Psa 67:7
eyes of a fool are in e   Pro 17:24
salvation to e of   Acts 13:47
words to e of world   Rom 10:18
on whom e of world   1 Cor 10:11

endued, *clothed with*
God hath e me with   Gen 30:20
till ye be e with   Lk 24:49
and e with knowledge?   Jas 3:13

endure, *to continue, to bear*
his mercy e   1 Chr 16:34, 2 Chr
   5:13, Ezra 3:11, Psa 106:1, Jer
   33:11
Lord shall e for ever   Psa 9:7
his name shall e for ever   72:17
his truth e for ever   117:2
hopeth all things, e   1 Cor 13:7
therefore e hardness   2 Tim 2:3
therefore I e all things   2:10
will not e sound doctrine   4:3
blessed is man that e   Jas 1:12
count them happy who e   5:11
he e the cross   Heb 12:2
word of Lord e for   1 Pet 1:25

enemies *(see enemy)*
table in presence of e   Psa 23:5
a man's e are the men of   Mic 7:6
love your e   Mat 5:44, Lk 6:27,35
if when we were e   Rom 5:10

are e of the cross   Phil 3:18
e be made footstool   Heb 10:13

enemy, *foe, adversary*
became David's e   1 Sam 18:29
rejoice not when e   Pro 24:17
if e hunger   25:21, Rom 12:20
kisses of an e are   Pro 27:6
last e destroyed   1 Cor 15:26
am I become your e?   Gal 4:16
a friend of world is e   Jas 4:4

engrafted, *implanted*
with meekness e word   Jas 1:21

enjoy, *pleased with*
giveth things to e   1 Tim 6:17
than e pleasure of sin   Heb 11:25

enlarge, *make broad, large*
God shall e Japheth   Gen 9:27
thou shalt e my heart   Psa 119:32
and e the borders of   Mat 23:5

enlighten, *to give light*
Lord is pure, e the eyes   Psa 19:8
understanding being e   Eph 1:18
for those who were e   Heb 6:4

enmity, *hostility, opposition*
put e between thee   Gen 3:15
carnal mind is e   Rom 8:7
abolished in flesh e   Eph 2:15
cross, having slain the e   2:16
friendship of world e   Jas 4:4

Enoch, *father of Methuselah,* Gen
5:22,24, Heb 11:5

enough, *sufficient*
say not, it is e   Pro 30:15
servants have bread e   Lk 15:17

enriched, *made rich*
every thing ye are e   1 Cor 1:5
e in every thing   2 Cor 9:11

enrolled, *recorded in a list*

all world should be *e*	Lk 2:1

See also: Heb 12:23

ensample, *example*

happened for *e*	1 Cor 10:11
have us for an *e*	Phil 3:17
make ourselves an *e*	2 Thes 3:9
being *e* to the flock	1 Pet 5:3
an *e* to those that	2 Pet 2:6

ensue, *pursue*

seek peace, and *e* it	1 Pet 3:11

entangle, *trap, snare*

how they might *e* him	Mat 22:15
not *e* again with yoke	Gal 5:1
e himself with affairs	2 Tim 2:4

enter, *go in*

a fool's lips *e* into	Pro 18:6
no case *e* into kingdom	Mat 5:20
e in at strait	7:13, Lk 13:24
not every one shall *e* in	Mat 7:21
better to *e* life halt	18:8, Mk 9:43,45,47
e into life, keep	Mat 19:17
rich man to *e* kingdom	19:24, Mk 10:25, Lk 18:25
e into joy of Lord	Mat 25:21
lest ye *e* into	Mk 14:38, Lk 22:46
woe lawyers, ye *e* not	11:52
cannot *e* into kingdom	Jno 3:5
if any man *e* in he	10:9
sin *e* into the world	Rom 5:12
neither have *e* heart	1 Cor 2:9
see they could not *e*	Heb 3:19
e not in because of	4:6
may *e* in gates	Rev 22:14

entice, *persuade, deceive*

said to Delilah, *e* him	Judg 16:5
if sinners *e* thee	Pro 1:10

a violent man *e* his	16:29
when drawn away and *e*	Jas 1:14

entire, *whole, complete*

ye be perfect and *e*	Jas 1:4

entrance, *way in, opening*

so an *e* shall be	2 Pet 1:11

entreat, *to treat*

Egyptians evil *e* us	Deut 26:6
e them spitefully	Mat 22:6, Lk 18:32
we were shamefully *e*	1 Thes 2:2

See also: intreat

envy (verb), *to be jealous*

Rachel *e* her sister	Gen 30:1
Joseph's brethren *e* him	37:11
e thou not oppressor	Pro 3:31
let not heart *e* sinners	23:17
charity *e* not	1 Cor 13:4

envy (noun), *jealousy*

wrath killeth, and *e*	Job 5:2
e rottenness of bones	Pro 14:30
able to stand before *e?*	27:4
love, hatred, and *e* is	Ecc 9:6
for *e* delivered him	Mat 27:18, Mk 15:10
full of *e*, murder	Rom 1:29
not in strife and *e*	13:13
there is among you *e*	1 Cor 3:3
works of flesh are *e*	Gal 5:21
whereof cometh *e*	1 Tim 6:4
if ye have *e*	Jas 3:14,16
lusteth to *e*	4:5
all malice, guile, *e*	1 Pet 2:1

ephah, *unit of measure in O.T.*, Ex 16:36, Amos 8:5

Ephesians, *inhabitants of Ephesus*

Diana of *E*	Acts 19:28,34

Ephesus, *city of Asia Minor,* Acts
18:19, 20:16, 1 Cor 15:32, 16:8, Eph
1:1, 1 Tim 1:3, Rev 2:1

ephod, *priestly garment*
shall make an *e*   Ex 28:4,6
he made the *e* of gold   39:2
and Gideon made an *e*   Judg 8:27
girded with linen *e*   2 Sam 6:14,
    1 Chr 15:27

Ephraim, *one of sons of Joseph,* Gen
41:52, 48:14; *a tribe of Israel,* Josh
16:9, 17:9, 20:7, 21:21, Judg 2:9,
1 Sam 9:4, 2 Sam 2:9, Isa 7:9, Jer
31:9, Hos 7:8

Ephrath, *old name of Bethlehem, also
Ephratah,* Gen 35:19, 48:7, Mic 5:2

Epicureans, *Greek philosophers,* Acts
17:18

epistle, *letter*
I wrote you in an *e*   1 Cor 5:9
e written in hearts   2 Cor 3:2
e be read to all   1 Thes 5:27
as also in all his *e*   2 Pet 3:16

equal, *same as, just*
legs of lame not *e*   Pro 26:7
way of Lord not *e*   Ezek 18:25,29,
    33:17,20
himself *e* with God   Jno 5:18
not robbery to be *e*   Phil 2:6

equity, *uprightness, impartiality*
judge the people with *e*   Psa 98:9
of wisdom and *e*   Pro 1:3
ye that pervert *e*   Mic 3:9

err, *go astray*
cause thee to *e*   Isa 3:12, 9:16
wayfaring man not *e*   35:8
e not knowing scriptures   Mat
    22:29, Mk 12:24,27

if *e* from truth   Jas 5:19
concerning truth *e*   2 Tim 2:18

error, *mistake, fault*
work of *e*   Jer 10:15, 51:18
last *e* shall be worse   Mat 27:64
sinner from *e*   Jas 5:20

Esau, *brother of Jacob,* Gen 25:25,
27:41, 33:4, 36:43, Deut 2:5,12, Josh
24:4, Rom 9:13

escape, *flee, slip from*
think not thou *e*   Esth 4:13
wicked shall not *e*   Job 11:20
make a way to *e*   1 Cor 10:13
e if we neglect?   Heb 2:3

eschew, *turn aside, incline*
e evil and do good   1 Pet 3:11

especially, *most of all*
e them of household   Gal 6:10
Saviour, *e* of those   1 Tim 4:10

espoused, *betrothed, engaged*
his mother Mary was *e*   Mat 1:18
to a virgin *e* to a man   Lk 1:27
I have *e* you to one   2 Cor 11:2

establish, *to found, prepare*
I *e* my covenant   Gen 6:18, 9:9,
    17:7, Lev 26:9, Ezek 16:62
covenant I have *e*   Gen 9:17
have also *e* my covenant   Ex 6:4
witnesses, matter shall be *e*   Deut
    19:15, 2 Cor 13:1
Lord shall *e* thee   Deut 28:9
of house shall be *e*   Isa 2:2
house of Lord shall be *e*   Mic 4:1
e an everlasting   Ezek 16:60
every word be *e*   Mat 18:16
to *e* their own   Rom 10:3
may *e* your hearts   1 Thes 3:13
e you in every good   2 Thes 2:17

estate, *condition, state*
last *e* of Mat 12:45, Lk 11:26
to men of low *e* Rom 12:16
in whatsoever *e* I am Phil 4:11

esteem, *to think, judge*
we *e* him smitten of Isa 53:4
one man *e* one day above Rom 14:5
each *e* other better Phil 2:3
e reproach of Christ Heb 11:26

Esther, *Jewish wife of Xerxes,* Esth 2:7

eternal, *everlasting*
even his *e* power Rom 1:20
worketh an *e* weight 2 Cor 4:17
things not seen are *e* 4:18
an house *e* in the heavens 5:1
according to *e* purpose Eph 3:11
author of *e* salvation Heb 5:9
obtained *e* redemption 9:12
promise of *e* inheritance 9:15
us unto his *e* glory 1 Pet 5:10

eternal life *(see eternal)*
I may have *e* life? Mat 19:16
righteous go to life *e* 25:46
that I may inherit *e* life? Mk 10:17, Lk 10:25, 18:18
world to come *e* life Mk 10:30
hast words of *e* life Jno 6:68
give unto my sheep *e* life 10:28
gift of God is *e* life Rom 6:23
lay hold on *e* life 1 Tim 6:12,19
e life which was with 1 Jno 1:2
he promised, *e* life 2:25
hath given to us *e* life 5:11
know that ye have *e* life 5:13

Ethiopian, *of Ethiopia*
because of *E* woman Num 12:1
Lord smote the *E* 2 Chr 14:12

can *E* change his skin? Jer 13:23
Ebed-melech *E* 38:7,10,12, 39:16
a man of *E,* eunuch of Acts 8:27

eunuch, *castrated male*
e who were so born Mat 19:12
e said, what doth Acts 8:36

Euphrates, *river of Mesopotamia,* Gen 2:14, 15:18, Deut 1:7, Josh 1:4, Rev 16:12

evangelist, *announcer of good news*
house of Philip the *e* Acts 21:8
do the work of an *e* 2 Tim 4:5
some apostles, some *e* Eph 4:11

Eve, *first woman, Adam's wife,* Gen 3:20, 2 Cor 11:3, 1 Tim 2:13

even, *evening, dusk*
fourteenth day, at *e* Lev 23:5, Num 9:3, Deut 16:6
praise Lord every *e* 1 Chr 23:30

evening, *dusk*
e and morning were Gen 1:5 ff
in the *e* it is cut down Psa 90:6

ever, *always, eternally, constantly*
and live for *e* Gen 3:22
Lord shall endure for *e* Psa 9:7
house of Lord for *e* 23:6
counsel standeth for *e* 33:11
my sin is *e* before me 51:3
word of God stand for *e* Isa 40:8
son, thou art *e* with Lk 15:31
eat shall live for *e* Jno 6:51,58
but the Son abideth *e* 8:35
glory for *e* Rom 11:36, 16:27
so shall we *e* be 1 Thes 4:17
e learning and never 2 Tim 3:7
e liveth to make Heb 7:25
endureth for *e* 1 Pet 1:25
be glory, now and *e* Jude 25

reign for *e* and *e*   Rev 11:15
tormented for *e* and *e*   20:10

everlasting, *perpetual, lasting*
the *e* God   Gen 21:33, Isa 40:28,
                              Rom 16:26
e arms   Deut 33:27
be called, the *e* Father   Isa 9:6
with an *e* salvation   45:17
into *e* fire   Mat 18:8,25,41
shall inherit *e* life   19:29
into *e* punishment   25:46
believeth have *e* life   Jno 3:16,36
heareth words hath *e* life   5:24
with *e* destruction   2 Thes 1:9
having the *e* gospel   Rev 14:6

every, *each*
e imagination of heart   Gen 6:5
I hate *e* false way Psa 119:104,128
e word of God is pure   Pro 30:5
e knee bow   Isa 45:23, Rom 14:11
e one give account   14:12
by *e* word that   Mat 4:4
be baptized, *e* one of   Acts 2:38
not far from *e* one of us   17:27
e joint supplieth   Eph 4:16
unto *e* good   2 Tim 2:21
lay aside *e* weight   Heb 12:1
e good and perfect gift   Jas 1:17
believe not *e* spirit   1 Jno 4:1
e one that loveth is   4:7

evidence, *testimony, proof*
faith is the *e* of things   Heb 11:1

evil, *evil, badness*
tree of good and *e*   Gen 2:9,17
I will fear no *e*   Psa 23:4
that love Lord, hate *e*   97:10
feet run to *e*   Pro 1:16, Isa 59:7
he that pursueth *e*   Pro 11:19

e pursueth sinners   13:21
while *e* days come   Ecc 12:1
imagination of *e* heart   Jer 3:17
for it is an *e* time   Amos 5:13
deliver from *e*   Mat 6:13, Lk 11:14
sufficient for day is *e*   Mat 6:34
e man out of *e* treasure bringeth
forth *e*   12:35, Lk 6:45
abhor that which is *e*   Rom 12:9
recompense to no man *e*   12:17
not overcome of *e*   12:21
thinketh no *e*   1 Cor 13:5
because days are *e*   Eph 5:16
none render *e* for *e*   1 Thes 5:15
from all appearance of *e*   5:22
is root of all *e*   1 Tim 6:10
to discern good and *e*   Heb 5:14
not rendering *e* for *e*   1 Pet 3:9

exalt, *make high*
rebellious *e* themselves   Psa 66:7
righteousness *e* nation   Pro 14:34
e him that is low   Ezek 21:26
whoso shall *e* himself   Mat 23:12
if a man *e* himself   2 Cor 11:20
Lord's house be *e*   Isa 2:2, Mic 4:1
my servant shall be *e*   Isa 52:13
humble himself be *e* Mat 23:12, Lk
                        14:11, 18:14
e them of low degree   1:52
God hath highly *e* him   Phil 2:9
rejoice that he is *e*   Jas 1:9

examine, *test, investigate*
e me, O Lord, prove me   Psa 26:2
let a man *e* himself   1 Cor 11:28

example, *sample, exhibition*
not make her public *e*   Mat 1:19
have given you an *e*   Jno 13:15
be thou an *e* of   1 Tim 4:12

leaving us an *e*   1 Pet 2:21

exceed, *to be above*
except righteousness *e*   Mat 5:20

exceeding, *abundant, much*
iniquity *e* great   Ezek 9:9
up into *e* high   Mat 4:8
rejoice and be *e* glad   5:12
worketh for us an *e*   2 Cor 4:17
might shew *e* riches   Eph 2:7
able to do *e* abundantly   3:20
given to us *e* great   2 Pet 1:4

excellency, *honor, greatness*
e of knowledge is   Ecc 7:12
not with *e* of speech   1 Cor 2:1
all things loss for *e*   Phil 3:8

excellent, *great, high*
how *e* is thy name   Psa 8:1,9
his name alone is *e*   148:13
e speech becometh not   Pro 17:7
things more *e*   Rom 2:18, Phil 1:10
obtained a more *e* name   Heb 1:4
Abel offered more *e*   11:4

excellest, *is greater than*
but thou *e* all   Pro 21:29
wisdom *e* folly as   Ecc 2:13

except, *if not, but*
e your righteousness   Mat 5:20
e ye be converted   18:3
put away his wife, *e* for   19:9
e ye repent, ye shall   Lk 13:3,5
e a man be born again   Jno 3:3
e a man be born of water   3:5
e they be sent?   Rom 10:15
e there come a   2 Thes 2:3

excess, *incontinence, overflowing*
extortion and *e*   Mat 23:25
wine, wherein is *e*   Eph 5:18
run not to same *e*   1 Pet 4:4

excuse, *apology, reason*
began to make *e*   Lk 14:18
they are without *e*   Rom 1:20
accusing or else *e*   2:15

exercise, *to do, train*
Gentiles *e* dominion over   Mat
    20:25, Mk 10:42, Lk 22:25
e profiteth little   1 Tim 4:8
senses *e* to discern   Heb 5:14

exhort, *encourage*
these teach and *e*   1 Tim 6:2
e with long suffering   2 Tim 4:2
e, rebuke with authority   Tit 2:15
e one another   Heb 3:13
but *e* one another, and   10:25

expectation, *hope, anticipation*
the *e* of the poor shall   Psa 9:18
e of wicked   Pro 10:28, 11:7
for the *e* of creature   Rom 8:19
to my earnest *e* and   Phil 1:20

expedient, *best, proper*
e that one man die   Jno 18:14
things not *e*   1 Cor 6:12, 10:23

experience, *proof, testing*
worketh *e,* and *e* hope   Rom 5:4

expounded, *explained*
he *e* all things   Mk 4:34
he *e* to them in all   Lk 24:27
and Priscilla *e*   Acts 18:26

express, *exact*
being the *e* image of   Heb 1:3
the Spirit speaketh *e*   1 Tim 4:1

extol, *exalt, praise*
I will *e* thee, O Lord   Psa 30:1

extortion, *oppression*
they are full of *e*   Mat 23:25

extortioner, *one who snatches away*
not as other men, *e*   Lk 18:11

any be drunkard, *e*   1 Cor 5:11
nor *e* inherit kingdom   6:10

eye
   e for *e* · Ex 21:24, Lev 24:20, Deut
           19:21, Mat 5:38
   e of the Lord is on   Psa 33:18
   the seeing *e*, hearing   Pro 20:12
   e is not satisfied   Ecc 1:8
   they shall see *e* to *e*   Isa 52:8
   neither hath *e* seen Isa 64:4, 1 Cor
           2:9
   if right *e* offend thee   Mat 5:29
   light of body is *e*   Mat 6:22, Lk
           11:34
   e be single   Mat 6:22, Lk 11:34
   mote in thy brother's *e*   Mat 7:3,
           Lk 6:41,42
   if *e* offend   Mat 18:9, Mk 9:47
   camel go through *e* Mat 19:24, Mk
           10:25, Lk 18:25
   twinkling of an *e*   1 Cor 15:52
   every *e* shall see   Rev 1:7

eyes
   like fire in *e*   Ex 24:17
   e of the Lord   Deut 11:12, Psa
           34:15, 1 Pet 3:12
   right in own *e*   Deut 12:8, Judg
           17:6, 21:25
   a gift doth blind the *e*   Deut 16:19
   pure, enlightening *e*   Psa 19:8
   not wise in thine own *e*   Pro 3:7
   as smoke to the *e* so is   10:26
   of fool right in own *e*   12:15
   way of man right in own *e*   21:2
   who hath redness of *e*?   23:29
   e are never satisfied   27:20
   e and see not   Jer 5:21, Ezek 12:2
   having *e* see ye not?   Mk 8:18

not lift up so much as his *e*   Lk
           18:13
darkness blinded his *e*   1 Jno 2:11
all tears from *e*   Rev 7:17, 21:4

eyeservice, *work done only when*
    watched
   not with *e* as   Eph 6:6, Col 3:22

eyewitnesses, *one who has seen with his*
    own eyes
   from beginning were *e*   Lk 1:2
   e of his majesty   2 Pet 1:16

Ezra, *priest and scribe,* Ezra 7:25, Neh
  8:2

F

fables, *tales, legends*
   nor give heed to *f*   1 Tim 1:4
   shall be turned to *f*   2 Tim 4:4
   not giving heed to *f*   Tit 1:14
   cunningly devised *f*   2 Pet 1:16

face
   in sweat of *f* eat bread   Gen 3:19
   I have seen God *f* to *f*   32:30
   Moses hid his *f*   Ex 3:6
   spake unto Moses *f* to *f*   33:11
   skin of his *f* shone   34:29
   veil on his *f*   34:33, 2 Cor 3:13
   Lord make his *f* shine   Num 6:25
   turn not away thy *f*   2 Chr 6:42,
           Psa 132:10
   make thy *f* to shine   31:16
   wisdom maketh *f* to shine Ecc 8:1
   hid our *f* from him   Isa 53:3
   anoint head, wash *f*   Mat 6:17

his ƒ did shine as sun   17:2
then see ƒ to ƒ   1 Cor 13:12
natural ƒ in a glass   Jas 1:23

fade, *perish, fail*
grass wither, flower ƒ   Isa 40:7
rich man shall ƒ away   Jas 1:11
inheritance ƒ not   1 Pet 1:4, 5:4

fail, *perish, be lacking*
as water ƒ from sea   Job 14:11
faithful ƒ among men   Psa 12:1
the grass ƒ   Isa 15:6
he shall not ƒ, nor   42:4
treasure in heaven ƒ not   Lk 12:33
hearts of them ƒ for fear   21:26
that thy faith ƒ not   22:32
charity never ƒ   1 Cor 13:8
lest any man ƒ of grace   Heb 12:15
See also: Ecc 10:15, Lk 5:5, 1 Cor 15:14

fain, *desire to*
ƒ fill belly with husks   Lk 15:16

faint, *weary, feeble*
creator of earth ƒ not   Isa 40:28 f
always to pray, not ƒ   Lk 18:1
which cause we ƒ not   2 Cor 4:16
shall reap, if ƒ not   Gal 6:19

fair, *beautiful, good*
daughters of man were ƒ   Gen 6:2
ƒ among women S of S 1:8, 5:9, 6:1
they speak ƒ words   Jer 12:6
by ƒ speeches deceive   Rom 16:18

faith, *belief (the faith = the gospel)*
just shall live by ƒ   Hab 2:4, Rom 1:17, Gal 3:11, Heb 10:38
ye of little ƒ Mat 6:30, 8:26, 14:31, 16:8, Lk 12:28
so great ƒ   Mat 8:10, Lk 7:9
thy ƒ hath made thee whole   Mat

9:22, Mk 5:34, 10:52, Lk 8:48, 17:19
great is thy ƒ   Mat 15:28
if ye have ƒ, and   21:21
judgment, mercy, and ƒ   23:23
have ƒ in God   Mk 11:22
thy ƒ hath saved thee   Lk 7:50
where is your ƒ?   8:25
Lord, increase our ƒ   17:5
shall Son find ƒ on earth   18:8
continue in the ƒ   Acts 14:22
purifying hearts by ƒ   15:9
revealed from ƒ to ƒ   Rom 1:17
make ƒ of God without effect   3:3
justified by ƒ   3:28, 5:1, Gal 2:16, 3:24
ƒ counted righteousness   Rom 4:5
we have access by ƒ   5:2
ƒ cometh by hearing   10:17
what is not of ƒ is sin   14:23
though I have all ƒ   1 Cor 13:2
now abideth ƒ   13:13
stand fast in the ƒ   16:13
walk by ƒ not sight   2 Cor 5:7
I live by the ƒ of   Gal 2:20
ƒ which worketh by love   5:6
fruit of the spirit is ƒ   5:22
access by ƒ   Eph 3:12
one Lord, one ƒ   4:5
in the unity of the ƒ   4:13
taking shield of ƒ   6:16
your work of ƒ   1 Thes 1:3, 2 Thes 1:11
breastplate of ƒ   1 Thes 5:8
fulfil work of ƒ   2 Thes 1:11
all men have not ƒ   3:2
ƒ unfeigned   1 Tim 1:5, 2 Tim 1:5
some depart from ƒ   1 Tim 4:1
erred from the ƒ   6:10,21

fight good fight of *f*   6:12
I have kept the *f*   2 Tim 4:7
the foundation of *f*   Heb 6:1
in full assurance of *f*   10:22
f is substance of things   11:1
without *f* it is impossible   11:6
and finisher of our *f*   12:2
trying of *f*   Jas 1:3, 1 Pet 1:7
let him ask in *f*   Jas 1:6
can *f* save him?   2:14
poor of world, rich in *f*   2:5
f without works is dead   2:17
by works was *f* made   2:22
resist stedfast in *f*   1 Pet 5:9
add to *f* virtue   2 Pet 1:5
overcometh world, even *f*   1 Jno
    5:4
earnestly contend for *f*   Jude 3
hast not denied my *f*   Rev 2:13
patience and *f* of saints   13:10

faithful, *stable, steadfast*
commandments are *f*   Psa 119:86
thy testimonies are *f*   119:138
well done, good and *f*   Mat 25:21
f in few things   25:23, Lk 19:17
f in least is *f* also   16:10
God is *f*   1 Cor 1:9
man be found *f*   4:2
f is he that calleth   1 Thes 5:24
f saying   1 Tim 1:15, 4:9, 2 Tim
    2:11, Tit 3:8
holding fast *f* word   1:9
be thou *f* unto death   Rev 2:10
words true and *f*   21:5
See also: Ruth 1:16, 2 Ki 2:2, Jno
13:1, 1 Cor 16:13

faithless, *unbelieving (see unbelief)*
O *f* generation   Mat 17:17, Mk
    9:19, Lk 9:41

not *f* but believing   Jno 20:27
See also: Deut 32:20, Rom 3:3,
2 Cor 4:4, Heb 3:12

fall

haughty spirit before *f*   Pro 16:18
just man *f* seven times   24:16
great was the *f* of it   Mat 7:27
for *f* and rising of many   Lk 2:34
not hair of head *f* to ground 1 Sam
    14:45, 2 Sam 14:11, 1 Ki 1:52,
    Acts 27:34
how are mighty *f*   2 Sam 1:19,25
let us *f* unto hand of God   2 Sam
    24:14, 1 Chr 21:13
though he *f* not   Psa 37:24
no counsel, people *f*   Pro 11:14
rejoice not when enemy *f*   24:17
dig a pit shall *f* therein   26:27, Ecc
    10:8
say to hills *f* on us   Hos 10:8, Lk
    23:30, Rev 6:16
f in pit on Sabbath   Mat 12:11
crumbs *f* from table   15:27
stars *f* from heaven   24:29, Mk
    13:25
Satan *f* from heaven   Lk 10:18
occasion to *f* in brother's way
    Rom 14:13
take heed lest he *f*   1 Cor 10:12
ye are *f* from grace   Gal 5:4
to *f* into hands   Heb 10:31
when *f* into temptations   Jas 1:2

falling
deliver from *f*   Psa 56:13, 116:8
drops of blood *f*   Lk 22:44
Judas *f* headlong   Acts 1:18
there come *f* away   2 Thes 2:3

false, *empty, untrue, deceit*
> thou shall not bear *f* witness   Ex 20:16, Deut 5:20, Mat 19:18
> I hate every *f*   Psa 119:104,128
> *f* Christs, *f* prophets   Mat 24:24, Mk 13:22
> *f* witnesses of God   1 Cor 15:15
> among *f* brethren   2 Cor 11:26
> shall be *f* teachers   2 Pet 2:1
> *See also:* Pro 13:5, Eph 4:25, Col 3:9

falsely *(see false)*
> prophesy *f*   Jer 5:31, 29:9
> say evil against you *f*   Mat 5:11
> *f* accuse good   1 Pet 3:16

fame, *name, reputation*
> *f* of Solomon   1 Ki 10:1, 2 Chr 9:1
> heard *f* with ears   Job 28:22
> *f* of Jesus   Mat 4:24, Mk 1:28, Lk 4:14,37, 5:15
> *f* thereof went abroad   Mat 9:26
> Herod heard *f* of Jesus   14:1
> *See also:* Pro 22:1, 25:27, Rom 1:8, 14:16

family
> in thee all *f* be blessed   Gen 12:3, 28:14
> you only of all *f*   Amos 3:2
> whole *f* in heaven   Eph 3:15
> *See also:* Psa 133:1, Mat 10:36, 12:49, 13:57

famine, *hunger*
> *f* was grievous in   Gen 12:10
> seven years of *f*   41:27
> destruction, *f,* and   Isa 51:19
> sword without, *f* within   Ezek 5:16
> a *f,* not of bread   Amos 8:11
> *f* in divers places   Mat 24:7, Mk 13:8, Lk 21:11

> mighty *f* in that land   15:14
> *See also:* Rev 7:16

famish *(see famine)*
> not suffer righteous to *f*   Pro 10:3

fan, *winnowing fork*
> I will *f* them with *f*   Jer 15:7
> *f* is in hand   Mat 3:12, Lk 3:17

far, *distant*
> be it *f* from me 1 Sam 2:30, 22:15, 2 Sam 20:20, 23:17
> iniquity *f* away   Job 11:14, 22:23
> *f* as east from west   Psa 103:12
> *f* above rubies   Pro 31:10
> *f* as light excelleth   Ecc 2:13
> peace to him *f* off   Isa 57:19
> not *f* from kingdom   Mk 12:34
> not *f* from every one   Acts 17:27
> *f* more exceeding weight   2 Cor 4:17
> were *f* off, made nigh   Eph 2:13

farthing, *small coin, one-tenth denarius*
> paid the uttermost *f*   Mat 5:26
> sparrows sold for a *f*   10:29
> which make a *f*   Mk 12:42

fashion, *likeness, type*
> he *f* hearts alike   Psa 33:15
> clay say to him that *f*   Isa 45:9
> *f* of his countenance changed   Lk 9:29
> *f* of this world passeth   1 Cor 7:31
> found in *f* as a man   Phil 2:8
> *f* like to his glorious   3:21
> *See also:* Phil 3:20 f

fast, *firm*
> commanded, and stood *f*   Psa 33:9

fast (verb), *abstain from food*
> humbled my soul with *f*   Psa 35:13

he had *f* forty days   Mat 4:2
when ye *f* be not as   6:16
I *f* twice in the week   Lk 18:12
See also: Ex 34:28

fasten, *lay hold, join*
eyes of all were *f* on   Lk 4:20

fasting *(see fast, verb)*
humbled my soul with *f* Psa 35:13
kind goeth out by *f*   Mat 17:21,
                                 Mk 9:29

fat, *fat, richness, the best part*
shall eat the *f* of the land   Gen
                                  45:18
liberal soul be made *f*   Pro 11:25
good report maketh bones *f* 15:30
trust in Lord be *f*   28:25

father
f of nations   Gen 17:4, Rom 4:17
iniquity of *f* upon   Ex 20:5, Num
                                 14:18
I will be his *f*   1 Chr 28:6
f of fatherless is God   Psa 68:5
as *f* pitieth children   103:13
wise son maketh a glad *f* Pro 10:1,
                                 15:20
fool despiseth *f* instructions 15:5
glory of children are *f*   17:6
name shall be everlasting *F* Isa 9:6
f eaten sour grapes Jer 31:29, Ezek
                                  18:2
our *F* which art   Mat 6:9, Lk 11:2
loveth *f* or mother more Mat 10:37
call no man *f*   23:9
Abba, *F* Mk 14:36, Rom 8:15, Gal
                                   4:6
F if thou be willing   Lk 22:42
F, forgive them   23:34
only begotten of *F*   Jno 1:14

worship the *F* in spirit   4:23
hath seen the *F*   6:46
no man cometh to *F* but by   14:6
I ascend to my *F* and   20:17
one God, the *F*   1 Cor 8:6
F of mercies, God of   2 Cor 1:3
one God and *F* of all   Eph 4:6
f, provoke not children   6:4
to glory of the *F*   Phil 2:11
without *f*, without mother Heb 7:3
the *F* of light   Jas 1:17
an advocate with *F*   1 Jno 2:1
love the *F* hath bestowed   3:1
three bear record, the *F*   5:7

fatherless, *orphans*
not afflict *f*   Ex 22:22
religion to visit *f*   Jas 1:27

fault, *error, failure*
cleanse secret *f*   Psa 19:12
I find no *f* Lk 23:4, Jno 18:38, 19:4
overtaken in a *f*   Gal 6:1
confess your *f* one to   Jas 5:16
buffeted for your *f*   1 Pet 2:20
See also: Rom 9:19; Jas 3:2

faultless *(see fault)*
first covenant been *f*   Heb 8:7
able to present you *f*   Jude 24

favour, *grace, kindness*
Joseph found *f* in   Gen 39:21
good man sheweth *f*   Psa 112:5
Jesus increased in *f*   Lk 2:52
having *f* with people   Acts 2:47

fear, *terror; usually "reverence," "awe"*
with reference to God
f of you on every   Gen 9:2
f of God not in   20:11
for I *f* God   42:18
f not, stand still   Ex 14:13

serve the Lord with *f* Psa 2:11
f of the Lord is clean 19:9
I will *f* no evil 23:4
no *f* of God 36:1, Rom 9:18
f of Lord beginning of wisdom Psa
111:10, Pro 9:10
f of Lord beginning of knowledge
1:7
in *f* of Lord is confidence 14:26
f of Lord tendeth to life 19:23
f of man bringeth a snare 29:25
f God, keep commandments Ecc
12:13
Lord give rest from *f* Isa 14:3
of fearful hearts, *f* not 35:4
f not, I am 41:10, 43:5
f. him who Mat 10:28, Lk 12:5
f not, little flock 12:32
f and trembling Eph 6:5, Phil 2:12
not given spirit of *f* 2 Tim 1:7
no *f* in love 1 Jno 4:18

fearful *(see fear)*
f and wonderfully made Psa 139:14
f looking for judgment Heb 10:27
f thing to fall into hands 10:31

feast, *festival*
keep *f* to Lord Num 29:12
merry heart continual *f* Pro 15:15
uppermost rooms at *f* Mat 23:6,
Mk 12:39, Lk 20:46
release one at the *f* Lk 23:17
keep *f* not with old 1 Cor 5:8

fed *(see feed)*
he *f* thee with manna Deut 8:3
have *f* you with milk 1 Cor 3:2

feeble *(see weak)*
what do these *f* Jews Neh 4:2
comfort *f* minded 1 Thes 5:14

feed, *cause to eat*
f with bread of affliction 1 Ki
22:27, 2 Chr 18:26
f his flock like Isa 40:11
f my lambs Jno 21:15
if enemy hunger, *f* Rom 12:20
f the flock of God 1 Pet 5:2

feeling, *emotion, sensitivity*
who being past *f* Eph 4:19
touched with *f* of Heb 4:15

feet
all things under his *f* Psa 8:6,
1 Cor 15:27, Eph 1:22
pierced hands and *f* Psa 22:16
set my *f* on a rock 40:2
deliver my *f* 56:13, 116:8
word is lamp to my *f* 119:105
f run to evil Pro 1:16, 6:18, Isa
59:7
ponder path of thy *f* Pro 4:26
beautiful are thy *f* S of S 7:1
f of him that bringeth good tidings
Isa 52:7, Nah 11:15, Rom 10:15
guide *f* in way of peace Lk 1:79
wiped *f* with hair Jno 11:2, 12:3
wash disciples' *f* 13:5
at *f* of Gamaliel Acts 22:3
f of them that preach Rom 10:15
f shod with preparation Eph 6:15

feign, *pretend*
David *f* himself mad 1 Sam 21:13
with *f* words make 2 Pet 2:3

Felix, *governor of Judea,* Acts 23:23,
24:10 ff

fell
his countenance *f* Gen 4:5
wall *f* down Josh 6:20, Heb 11:30
wise men *f* down Mat 2:11

fellow, *person, friend*
this *f* perverting nation	Lk 23:2
this man pestilent *f*	Acts 24:5
f labourers	Phil 4:3
f helpers to the truth	3 Jno 8

fellowship, *.communion, joined*
in doctrine and *f*	Acts 2:42
f hath righteousness	2 Cor 6:14
f of ministering	8:4
gave right hand of *f*	Gal 2:9
have no *f* with works of	Eph 5:11
f in the gospel	Phil 1:5
we have *f* one with	1 Jno 1:7

See *also:* Pro 13:20, Mat 18:20,
Acts 4:13

female, *woman*
male and *f*	Mat 19:4, Mk 10:6
neither male nor *f*	Gal 13:28

See *also:* Gen 2:22

fervent, *intense*
f in spirit	Acts 18:25, Rom 12:11
with a pure heart *f*	1 Pet 1:22
have *f* charity among	4:8
melt with *f* heat	2 Pet 3:10

Festus, *governor of Judea,* Acts 24:27,
25:1 ff, 26:31

few, *small number*
seemed but a *f* days	Gen 29:20
man is of *f* days	Job 14:1
let thy words be *f*	Ecc 5:2
grinders cease because *f*	12:3
f there be that find	Mat 7:14
labourers are *f*	9:37, Lk 10:2
many called, *f* chosen	Mat 20:16
f that be saved	Lk 13:23

field, *open place*
f and cave made sure	Gen 23:20
the *f* of the slothful	Pro 24:30

consider lilies of *f*   Mat 6:28
f is the world	13:38
treasure hid in a *f*	13:44
f of blood	27:8
lift eyes, look on *f*	Jno 4:35

fierce, *dangerous, hot*
men shall be *f*	2 Tim 3:3
ships driven of *f* winds	Jas 3:4

fiery, *burning*
Lord send *f* serpents	Num 21:6
able to quench *f* darts	Eph 6:16
and *f* indignation	Heb 10:27

fig, *a common fruit in Palestine*
sewed *f* leaves for	Gen 3:7
trees said to *f* tree	Judg 9:10
whoso keepeth *f* tree	Pro 27:18
do men gather *f* of	Mat 7:16, Lk 6:44
saw *f* tree	Mat 21:19, Mk 11:13
can *f* tree bear olive	Jas 3:12

fight, *strive, contend*
Lord *f* for you	Ex 14:14, Deut 1:30, 3:22, 20:4
quit like men, and *f*	1 Sam 4:9
f against God	Acts 5:39, 23:9
so *f* I, not as one	1 Cor 9:26
f good *f* of faith	1 Tim 6:12
I have fought good *f*	2 Tim 4:7
wars and *f* among you	Jas 4:1

See *also:* Pro 6:19

figure, *form, antetype*
like *f* even baptism	1 Pet 3:21

fill
f waters in the seas	Gen 1:22
earth *f* with glory of Lord	Num 14:21, Psa 72:19, Hab 2:14
hunger, shall be *f*	Mat 5:6
f with Holy Ghost	Lk 1:15, Acts 4:8, 9:17, 13:9

f with all knowledge   Rom 15:14
that *f* all in all   Eph 1:23
be *f* with the Spirit   5:18
f with fruit of righteousness   Phil 1:11

filth, *dirt, uncleanness*
as the *f* of the world   1 Cor 4:13
put off *f* communication   Col 3:8
f lucre   1 Tim 3:3, Tit 1:7, 1 Pet 5:2

filthiness *(see filth)*
lay apart all *f*   Jas 1:21

find, *discover*
sin will *f* you out   Num 32:23
words life unto those that *f*   Pro 4:22
seek early shall *f*   8:17, Jer 29:13
whoso *f* me *f* life   Pro 8:35
f a wife *f* good thing   18:22
what thy hand *f* to do   Ecc 9:10
f rest   Jer 6:16, Mat 11:29
seek, ye shall *f*   7:7, Lk 11:9
loseth life, shall *f*   Mat 10:9

fine, *refined, pure*
desired than *f* gold   Psa 19:10
wisdom better than *f* gold   Pro 8:19
precious than *f* gold   Isa 13:12

finger
this is the *f* of God   Ex 8:19
written with *f* of God   31:18, Deut 9:10
heavens, work of thy *f*   Psa 8:3
bind them on *f*   Pro 7:2,3
Jesus with *f* wrote   Jno 8:6
f in print of nails   20:25

finish, *complete, end*
heavens and earth were *f*   Gen 2:1
began to build not able to *f*   Lk 14:30

I have *f* the work   Jno 17:4
he said, it is *f*   19:30
author and *f* of faith   Heb 12:2
sin, when it is *f*   Jas 1:15

fire, *burning*
the bush burned with *f*   Ex 3:2
f from Lord, devoured   Lev 10:2
Lord not in *f*   1 Ki 19:12
no wood is, *f* goeth out   Pro 26:20
neither *f* quenched   Isa 66:24, Mk 9:44
words as *f* in my bones   Jer 20:9
brand plucked out of *f*   Zech 3:2
not good fruit cast in *f*   Mat 3:10, 7:19, Lk 3:9, Jno 15:6
baptize with *f*   Mat 3:11, Lk 3:16
everlasting *f*   Mat 18:8, 25:41, Mk 9:43
come to send *f* on earth   Lk 12:49
cloven tongues like *f*   Acts 2:3
f taking vengeance   2 Thes 1:8
little *f* kindleth   Jas 3:5
heavens being on *f*   2 Pet 3:12
pulling them out of *f*   Jude 23
hell cast into *f*   Rev 20:14

first, *beginning, foremost*
f be reconciled to   Mat 5:24
seek ye *f* the kingdom   6:33
f cast beam out   7:5, Lk 6:42
man worse than *f*   Mat 12:45
f commandment   22:38, Mk 12:28
f shall be last   Mat 19:30, Mk 9:35
called Christians *f* at   Acts 11:26
f born among many   Rom 8:29
Christ the *f* fruit   1 Cor 15:20,23
f a willing mind   2 Cor 8:12
f born of every creature   Col 1:15
dead in Christ rise *f*   1 Thes 4:16

falling away *f*   2 Thes 2:3
Adam *f* formed   1 Tim 2:13
which be *f* principles   Heb 5:12
wisdom from above *f* pure Jas 3:17
judgment *f* began at   1 Pet 4:17
because he *f* love us   1 Jno 4:19
f heaven and *f* earth   Rev 21:1
See also: Gen 1:1, Jno 1:1

fish
dominion over *f* Gen 1:26, Psa 8:8
if he ask a *f*   Mat 7:10

fisher
f of men   Mat 4:19, Mk 1:17

fit, *ready, appropriate*
is *f* for kingdom of God   Lk 9:62
vessels of wrath *f* to   Rom 9:22

fitly, *appropriately*
a word *f* spoken   Pro 25:11
all building *f* framed   Eph 2:21
whole body *f* joined   4:16
See also: Pro 26:1, Phil 1:27

flame, *fire*
in *f* of fire   Ex 3:2, Acts 7:30
tormented in this *f*   Lk 16:24

flatter, *deceptive praise*
speaketh *f* to friends   Job 17:5
f lips and double heart   Psa 12:2
he *f* himself   36:2
they did *f* him   78:36
meddle not with *f*   Pro 20:19
a *f* mouth worketh ruin   26:28
f neighbour, spreadeth net   29:5
neither used we *f* words 1 Thes 2:5
See also: Acts 12:22, 1 Thes 2:4

flee, *run away*
f when none pursueth   Lev 26:17,36
whither shall I *f* from   Psa 139:7

wicked *f* when no man   Pro 28:1
f from wrath to   Mat 3:7, Lk 3:7
f youthful lusts   2 Tim 2:22
resist devil, he will *f*   Jas 4:7

flesh, *meat, body*
one *f*   Gen 2:24, Mat 19:5, Mk 10:8, 1 Cor 6:16, Eph 5:31
end of all *f* is come   Gen 6:13
life of *f* is blood   Lev 17:14
in *f* shall I see God   Job 19:26
f shall rest in hope   Psa 16:9, Acts 2:26
study weariness of *f*   Ecc 12:12
all *f* is grass   Isa 40:6, 1 Pet 1:24
f and blood hath not   Mat 16:17
spirit willing, *f* weak   26:41, Mk 14:38
Word was made *f*   Jno 1:14
f profiteth nothing   6:63
shall not *f* be justified   Rom 3:20
f law of sin   7:25
not in *f,* but in spirit   8:9
f and blood cannot   1 Cor 15:50
a thorn in *f*   2 Cor 12:7
by law no *f* be justified   Gal 2:16
f lusteth against Spirit   5:17
lusts of *f,* desires of *f*   Eph 2:3
Christ is come in *f*   1 Jno 4:3, 2 Jno 7

fleshly *(see flesh)*
not with *f* wisdom   2 Cor 1:12
puffed up by *f* mind   Col 2:18
abstain from *f* lusts   1 Pet 2:11

flock, *herd*
feed *f* like a shepherd   Isa 40:11
gather remnant of *f*   Jer 23:3
shepherd seeketh out *f* Ezek 34:12
f of my pasture, are men   34:31

fear not little *f*   Lk 12:32
take heed to all *f*   Acts 20:28
feed the *f* of God   1 Pet 5:2
being ensamples of *f*   5:3

flood, *deluge, river*
I bring a *f* of waters   Gen 6:17
neither be any more *f*   9:11
Lord sitteth upon *f*   Psa 29:10
neither can *f* drown love   S of S 8:7
I will pour *f* on dry ground   Isa
                                    44:3
f came, and winds blew   Mat 7:25
f on world of ungodly   2 Pet 2:5

flourish, *blossom, thrive*
his days shall righteous *f*   Psa 72:7
righteous shall *f* like   92:12
righteous shall *f* as   Pro 11:28

flow
all nations shall *f* unto it   Isa 2:2
shall see, and *f* together   60:5
f to mountain of Lord   Mic 4:1
shall *f* living water   Jno 7:38

flower, *blossom*
cometh forth as a *f*   Job 14:2
f appear on earth   S of S 2:12
f fadeth   Isa 40:7, Nah 1:4, Jas
                          1:10, 1 Pet 1:24
See also: S of S 2:1, 35:1, Hos 14:5

fly
as sparks *f* upward   Job 5:7
riches *f* away   Pro 23:5
f as a cloud   Isa 60:8

fold, *fenced place*
one *f*, and one shepherd   Jno 10:16

follow, *go after*
hot *f* multitude do evil   Ex 23:2
If Lord be God, *f* him   1 Ki 18:21
and mercy shall *f* me   Psa 23:6

ye that *f* righteousness   51:1
I will *f* thee   Mat 8:19
He that *f* me   Jno 8:12
Peter *f* afar off   Lk 22:54
hear my voice, and *f* me   10:27
thou canst not *f*   13:36
f things that make peace   Rom
                                    14:19
f after charity   1 Cor 14:1
I *f* after, if I   Phil 3:12
f that which is good   1 Thes 5:15
f after righteousness   1 Tim 6:11
f peace with all men   Heb 12:14
ye should *f* his steps   1 Pet 2:21
f not which is evil   3 Jno 11

follower *(see follow)*
be ye *f* of God, as dear   Eph 5:1
f of that which is good   1 Pet 3:13

folly, *senselessness*
fool layeth open *f*   Pro 13:16
f of fools is deceit   14:8
instruction of fools is *f*   16:22
rather than a *f*   17:12
fool according to his *f*   26:4
See also: Pro 27:22, 1 Cor 1:25

food, *nourishment*
tree good for *f*   Gen 3:6
having *f* and raiment   1 Tim 6:8
destitute of daily *f*   Jas 2:15
See also: Mat 4:4, Isa 55:2, Lk 11:3

fool *(see foolish)*
I have played the *f*   1 Sam 26:21
f said in heart   Psa 14:1, 53:1
f despise wisdom   Pro 1:7
f die for want of wisdom   10:21
way of *f* in own eyes   12:15
instruction of *f* is folly   16:22
f is counted wise   17:28

f no delight in understanding 18:2
f voice known by   Ecc 5:3
wayfaring men, though *f*   Isa 35:8
whoso shall say, thou *f*   Mat 5:22
suffer *f* gladly   2 Cor 11:19
walk not as *f*, but as   Eph 5:15
See also: Mat 7:26

foolish, *lacking wisdom, morally blind*
nor charged God *f*   Job 1:22
forsake the *f*, and live   Pro 9:6
a *f* son is grief   17:25
five wise, and five *f*   Mat 25:2
f heart was darkened   Rom 1:21
an instructor of the *f*   2:20
f questions avoid   2 Tim 2:23

foolishness *(see foolish)*
beginning of words is *f*   Ecc 10:13
to them that perish *f*   1 Cor 1:18
the *f* of preaching   1:21
f of God wiser than men   1:25
wisdom of world *f* with God   3:19

foot
dash *f* against a stone   Psa 9:112,
                              Mat 4:6, Lk 4:11
not suffer *f* to be moved Psa 121:3
salt trodden under *f*   Mat 5:13,
if *f* offend   18:8, Mk 9:45
trodden under *f* the Son Heb 10:29
See also feet

forbear, *to hold back*
through *f* of God   Rom 3:25
f one another   Eph 4:2, Col 3:13
See also: Eph 4:32, 1 Thes 5:14,
1 Pet 3:10

forbid, *restrain*
children, *f* them not Mk 10:14, Lk
                                    18:16
can any *f* water   Acts 10:47

force, *strength, power*
violent take it by *f*   Mat 11:12
testament of *f* after   Heb 9:17
See also: Job 6:25

foreigner, *stranger*
ye are no more *f*   Eph 2:19

foreknow, *know beforehand*
whom he did *f*, he also Rom 8:29 f
according to *f* of God   1 Pet 1:2
See also: Eph 1:4, 1 Pet 1:2,20

foreordained, *appointed beforehand*
who verily was *f*   1 Pet 1:20

forest, *wooded area*
beast of *f* is mine   Psa 50:10
lion roar in the *f*   Amos 3:4

forewarn, *say before*
also have *f* you   1 Thes 4:6

forgave *(see forgive)*
Christ *f* you, so do   Col 3:13

forget, *not remember*
beware lest *f* Lord Deut 6:12, 8:11
can a woman *f* child   Isa 49:15
f what manner of man   Jas 1:24

forgive, *cover, pardon*
f iniquity and transgression Ex 34:7
transgression is *f*   Psa 32:1, Rom
                                    4:7
f us as we *f*   Mat 6:12, Lk 11:4
f him seven times   Mat 18:21
while praying *f*   Mk 11:25
f and ye shall be *f*   Lk 6:37
whom little is *f*   7:47
we also *f* every   11:4
if he repent, *f* him   17:3
f them, they know not   23:34
as God hath *f* you   Eph 4:32
faithful and just to *f*   1 Jno 1:9
See also: Mat 5:24, 12:31

forgiveness *(see forgive)*
  is preached *f* of sin   Acts 13:38
  in whom we have *f*   Eph 1:7, Col
                       1:14

forgotten *(see forget)*
  why hast thou *f* me   Psa 42:9
  Israel hath *f* maker   Hos 8:14
  not one *f* before God   Lk 12:6
  f that he was purged   2 Pet 1:9

form, *appearance, shape*
  earth was without *f*   Gen 1:2
  hath no *f* nor comeliness Isa 53:2
  hast *f* of knowledge   Rom 2:20
  obeyed that *f* of doctrine   6:17
  being in *f* of God   Phil 2:6
  f of sound words   2 Tim 1:13
  having a *f* of godliness   3:5

formed, *made, shaped*
  God *f* man of the dust   Gen 2:7
  forgotten God that *f*   Deut 32:18
  God *f* all things   Pro 26:10
  shall thing *f* say to   Rom 9:29
  till Christ be *f* in you   Gal 4:19

former, *previous*
  remember not *f* iniquities Psa 79:8
  where are thy *f* loving   89:49
  remember not *f* things   Isa 43:18
  declared *f* things from   48:3
  f conversation   Eph 4:22

forsake, *leave, abandon*
  he will not *f* thee   Deut 4:31, 31:6,
                    1 Chr 28:20
  not fail nor *f*   Josh 1:5, Heb 13:5
  why hast thou *f* me Psa 22:1, Mat
               27:46, Mk 15:34
  let wicked *f* his way   Isa 55:7
  we have *f* all   Mat 19:27, Lk 5:11
  disciples *f* him   Mat 26:56, Mk
                       14:50

  persecuted, but not *f*   2 Cor 4:9
  not *f* assembling of   Heb 10:25

forswear, *swear against*
  not *f* thyself   Mat 5:33

found *(see find)*
  Noah *f* grace in eyes   Gen 6:8
  f me, mine enemy   1 Ki 21:20
  f of them that Isa 65:1, Rom 10:20
  weighed, and *f* wanting Dan 5:27
  not *f* so great   Mat 8:10, Lk 7:9
  f pearl of great price   Mat 13:46
  have *f* the Messiah   Jno 1:41,45

foundation, *base*
  I lay in Zion a *f*   Isa 28:16
  secret from *f* of world Mat 13:35
  laid *f* on rock   Lk 6:48
  on another man's *f*   Rom 15:20
  other *f* against time   1 Tim 6:19
  f of God standeth   2 Tim 2:19
  not laying *f* of repentance Heb 6:1
  See also: Mat 16:18, 1 Pet 2:6

fountain, *spring, cistern*
  f of deeps   Gen 7:11, 8:2
  with thee is *f* of life   Psa 36:9
  law of wise *f* of life   Pro 13:14
  fear of Lord *f* of life   14:27
  pitcher broken at *f*   Ecc 12:6
  doth a *f* send forth   Jas 3:11
  of *f* of life freely   Rev 21:6

fragment, *piece*
  took up *f* Mat 14:20, Mk 6:43, Lk
                   9:17, Jno 6:13

frame, *to join together, make*
  shall thing *f* say of   Eph 2:21
  worlds *f* by word of God Heb 11:3

free
  uphold me with *f* Spirit Psa 51:12
  f ye have received   Mat 10:8

truth shall make you *f*   Jno 8:32
Son make you *f*, ye shall   8:36
I was *f* born   Acts 22:28
justified *f* by his grace   Rom 3:24
not as offence, so is *f* gift   5:15
being made *f* from sin   6:18
f from law of sin and   8:2
with him *f* give all things   8:32
bond or *f*   1 Cor 12:13, Eph 6:8
neither bond nor *f*   Gal 3:28, Col 3:11
liberty Christ made *f*   Gal 5:1
f and not using liberty   1 Pet 2:16
of fountain of life *f*   Rev 21:6
See also: Isa 55:1, Jas 1:25, Eph 6:6, 1 Pet 2:16

fret, *to be angry, troubled*
f not thyself   Psa 37:1,7,8, Pro 24:19

friend, *companion*
as a man to his *f*   Ex 33:11
love enemies and hate *f*   2 Sam 19:6
the rich hath many *f*   Pro 14:20
a *f* loveth at all times   17:17
f that sticketh closer   18:24
seed of Abraham my *f*   Isa 41:8
trust not in a *f*   Mic 7:5
f of publicans   Mat 11:19, Lk 7:34
f of the mammon   16:9
f of bridegroom rejoice   Jno 3:29
lay down his life for *f*   15:13
thou are not Caesar's *f*   19:12
Abraham called *f* of God   Jas 2:23
f of world is enemy of God   4:4

froward, *perverse*
a very *f* generation   Deut 32:20
a *f* heart shall depart   Psa 101:4

a *f* man soweth strife   Pro 16:28
the way of a man is *f*   21:8

fruit, *produce, result*
f of righteous a tree of   Pro 11:30
a basket of summer *f*   Amos 8:1
f meet for repentance   Mat 3:8, Lk 3:8
good tree bringeth good *f*   Mat 7:17
by *f* shall know them   7:20
make tree, and *f* good   12:33
f of the vine   26:29, Mk 14:25
f of life eternal   Jno 4:36
branch cannot bear *f* of   15:4
bring forth *f* unto God   Rom 7:4
f of Spirit   Gal 5:22, Eph 5:9
yield peaceable *f*   Heb 12:11
full of mercy and good *f*   Jas 3:17

frustrate, *oppose*
I do not *f* the grace of   Gal 2:21

fulfil, *accomplish, complete*
to *f* all righteousness   Mat 3:15
not to destroy, but to *f*   5:17
till all be *f*   5:18, 24:34
my joy is *f*   Jno 3:29, 17:13
righteousness law be *f*   Rom 8:4
love is the *f* of the law   13:10
law is *f* in one word   Gal 5:14
so *f* the law of Christ   6:2
f ye my joy   Phil 2:2
to *f* the word of God   Col 1:25
if ye *f* the royal law   Jas 2:8

full, *filled, complete*
Joshua was *f* of wisdom   Deut 34:9
few days, *f* of trouble   Job 14:1
mouth *f* of cursing   Psa 10:7, Rom 3:14
earth is *f* of mercy   Psa 119:64

hell and destruction never *f*   Pro 27:20

lest I be *f* and deny thee   30:9

f of knowledge of Lord   Isa 11:9

body *f* of light   Mat 6:22, Lk 11:36

f of grace and truth   Jno 1:14

f of Holy Ghost   Acts 6:3, 7:55

meat to them of *f* age   Heb 5:14

your joy may be *f*   1 Jno 1:4

See also: Jno 10:10, Jas 1:4

fully *(see full)*

heart *f* set to do evil   Ecc 8:11

every man be *f* persuaded   Rom 14:5

fulness *(see full)*

earth is Lord's and *f*   Psa 24:1, 1 Cor 10:26,28

when *f* of time was come   Gal 4:4

f of him that filleth   Eph 1:23

stature of the *f* of Christ   4:13

f of the Godhead bodily   Col 2:9

furious, *angry*

f man aboundeth in transgression   Pro 29:22

furnace, *oven*

as smoke of a *f*   Gen 19:28

in *f* of affliction   Isa 48:10

into midst of fiery *f*   Dan 3:6,11

into a *f* of fire   Mat 13:42

furnish, *provide, supply*

can God *f* table in wilderness   Psa 78:19

f unto all good works   2 Tim 3:17

fury, *anger*

with *f* poured out   Ezek 20:33

See also: Pro 22:24, Mic 5:15

future, *See:* Zeph 1:14, Heb 6:1, 13:14

G

Gad, *son of Jacob, tribe of Israel,* Gen 30:11, 35:26, Josh 4:12, Num 1:25, Rev 7:5; *prophet,* 2 Sam 24:11

gain, *profit, increase*

greedy of *g*   Pro 1:19

g is better than fine gold   3:14

is greedy of *g* troubleth   15:27

g whole world and lose   Mat 16:26, Mk 8:36, Lk 9:25

did I make *g* of you?   2 Cor 12:17

to live is Christ, die *g*   Phil 1:21

what things were *g* to me   3:7

with contentment is *g*   1 Tim 6:6

buy, sell and get *g*   Jas 4:13

See also: Job 1:6, Mic 3:11, Mat 6:19

Gadarenes, or Gergesenes, *east of Sea of Galilee,* Mat 8:28, Mk 5:1, Lk 8:26

gainsay, *to speak against*

not able to *g*   Lk 21:15

might be able to convince *g* Tit 1:9

Gaius, *possibly several people of the same name,* Acts 19:29, 20:4, Rom 16:23, 1 Cor 1:14, 3 Jno 1

Galilee, *northern part of Palestine,* Josh 20:7, 1 Ki 9:11, Mat 2:22, 3:13, 4:15, Mk 1:9,39, Lk 23:5, Jno 7:41, Acts 10:37, etc.

gall, *bitter, bile*

are grapes of *g*   Deut 32:32

mingled with *g*   Mat 27:34

in *g* of bitterness   Acts 8:23

Gallio, *Roman deputy of Corinth, brother of Seneca,* Acts 18:12,17

gallows, *See:* Esth 6:4, 7:10

Gamaliel, *rabbinic teacher of Paul,* Acts 5:34, 23:3

garden
God planted a *g*   Gen 2:1
and put him in the *g*   2:15
Lord sent him forth from *g*   3:23
in *g* a sepulchre   Jno 19:41

gardener
supposing him to be *g*   Jno 20:15

garlands, *wreaths of flowers used in sacrifices,* Acts 14:13

garment, *clothing*
caught Joseph by *g*   Gen 39:12
goodly Babylonish *g*   Josh 7:21
wax old like *g*   Psa 102:26, Isa 50:9, Heb 1:11
with *g* of salvation   Isa 61:10
rend heart, not *g*   Joel 2:13
new cloth in old *g*   Mat 9:16, Mk 2:21, Lk 5:36
touch hem of *g*   Mat 9:20, Mk 5:27, Lk 8:44
multitude spread *g*   Mat 21:8
had not wedding *g*   22:11
enlarge borders of *g*   23:5
parted his *g*   Mk 15:24
See also: Mat 6:29, Lk 7:25, Jno 19:25

garnish, *set in order, beautify*
swept and *g*   Mat 12:44, Lk 11:25

gate, *opening, door*
Lot sat in *g* of Sodom   Gen 19:1
the *g* of heaven   28:17
the *g* of Lord   Psa 118:20
wisdom crieth at *g*   Pro 8:1

establish judgment in *g*   Amos 5:15
enter at strait *g*   Mat 7:13, Lk 13:24
g of hell not   Mat 16:18
Lazarus laid at *g*   Lk 16:20
daily at *g* of temple   Acts 3:2

Gath, *Philistine city,* 1 Sam 5:8, 2 Sam 1:20, Mic 1:10

gather, *collect, heap up*
time to *g* stones   Ecc 3:5
g grapes of   Mat 7:16, Lk 6:44
g not scattereth   Mat 12:30
g first the tares   13:30
two or three *g*   18:20
hen *g* brood   23:37, Lk 13:34
g together in   Jno 11:52, Eph 1:10

gathering *(see gather),* Mat 25:24, 1 Cor 16:2

gave *(see give)*
Adam *g* names   Gen 2:20
g he power to become sons   Jno 1:12
God so loved he *g*   3:16
God *g* increase   1 Cor 3:6
first *g* selves   2 Cor 8:5
loved church *g* himself   Eph 5:25
g himself ransom   1 Tim 2:6
g up ghost   Mk 15:37, Lk 23:46, Jno 19:30

Gaza, *Philistine city,* Judg 16:1, Acts 8:26

Gedaliah, *governor of Judah under Nebuchadnezzar,* 2 Ki 25:24, Jer 40:9

genealogy, *family record*
not heed to endless *g*   1 Tim 1:4
avoid foolish *g*   Tit 3:9

generation, *those living at a given time, offspring*

these are *g* of heavens — Gen 2:4
a stubborn *g* — Psa 78:8
g pure in own eyes — Pro 30:12
salvation from *g* to *g* — Isa 51:8
g of vipers — Mat 3:7, 12:34, 23:33, Lk 3:7
adulterous *g* seeketh — Mat 12:39, 16:4, Mk 8:12, Lk 11:29
this *g* not pass — Mat 24:34, Mk 13:30, Lk 21:32
all *g* call me blessed — 1:48
ye are a chosen *g* — 1 Pet 2:9

Gennesaret, *another name for the Sea of Galilee,* Mat 14:34, Mk 6:53, Lk 5:1

gentile, *the nations, i.e., non-Jews*

light to *g* — Isa 42:6, 49:6, Lk 2:32, Acts 13:47
these things *g* seek — Mat 6:32
g received word of God — Acts 11:1
God to *g* hath granted — 11:18
we turn to *g* — 13:46
opened door of faith to *g* — 14:27
I will go to *g* — 18:6
to Jew first, also *g* — Rom 2:9
salvation come to *g* — 11:11
See also: Mat 4:15, Acts 10:45, 28:28, Rom 3:5

gentle, *mild, yielding, quiet*

servant of Lord be *g* — 2 Tim 2:24
wisdom from above, *g* — Jas 3:17
See also: Eph 4:32, 1 Pet 3:8

gentleness *(see gentle)*

fruit of spirit *g* — Gal 5:22
See also: 2 Cor 10:1-7

Gergesenes *(see Gadarenes)*

Gerizim, *mount of blessing at Shechem,* Deut 11:29, 27:12, Josh 8:33, Judg 9:7

Gershom, *son of Levi,* Gen 46:11, Ex 2:22, 6:16

get, *obtain, acquire*

there is a time to *g* — Ecc 3:6
buy, sell *g* gain — Jas 4:13
g thee behind me Satan — Mat 16:23, Mk 8:33, Lk 4:8
See also: Pro 9:7, 18:15

Gethsemane, *lit. "oil press" on Mt. of Olives east of Jerusalem,* Mat 26:36, Mk 14:32, Lk 22:39, Jno 18:1

ghost, *spirit* (archaic)

Jacob yielded up *g* — Gen 49:33
Jesus yielded up *g* — Mat 27:50
Sapphira yielded *g* — Acts 5:10

Ghost, Holy, *See:* Mat 21:31, Lk 3:16, 3:22, Acts 2:4,38, Rom 5:5, 8:9,26, 1 Cor 2:10,13, 6:19, Heb 10:15

giant, *man of abnormal size, fierce*

there were *g* in earth — Gen 6:4
we saw *g* sons of — Num 13:33
king of Bashan, *g* — Deut 3:11
See also: 1 Sam 17:4, Isa 10:33

Gibeah, *city of King Saul,* Judg 19:14, 1 Sam 10:26, Isa 10:29

Gibeon, *city that made treaty with Israel,* Josh 10:12, 2 Sam 3:30

Gideon, *judge of Israel,* Judg 6:11

gift, *offering, present*

bring *g* to altar — Mat 5:23
it is a *g* — 15:5, Mk 7:11
presented to him *g* — Mat 2:11
so is free *g* — Rom 5:15
g of God is eternal? — 6:23

concerning spiritual *g*   1 Cor 12:1
it is *g* of God   Eph 2:8
neglect not *g*   1 Tim 4:14
every good *g* is   Jas 1:17
every man received *g*   1 Pet 4:10
See also: Mat 7:1–12

Gilboa, *mount in northern Palestine where Saul was killed,* 1 Sam 31:1, 2 Sam 21:12, 1 Chr 10:1

Gilead, *land across the Jordan east of Sea of Galilee,* Num 32:1, Jer 8:22, Hos 12:11

Gilgal, *encampment near Jericho in Jordan Valley,* Josh 4:19, 1 Sam 7:16, Amos 4:4

gird, *clothe, restrain*
she *g* her loins   Pro 31:17
old, another *g* thee   Jno 21:18
took towel and *g*   13:4
loins *g* with truth   Eph 6:14

give *(see gift)*
I will *g* thee land   Gen 11:8
g grace to lowly Pro 3:34, Jas 4:6,
   1 Pet 5:5
if enemy hunger *g* him Pro 25:21,
   Rom 12:20
g to him that asketh   Mat 5:42
g us our daily   6:11
g not that which is holy unto dogs
   7:6
ask bread, *g* stone?   7:9
g gifts to child   7:11, Lk 11:13
I will *g* thee keys   Mat 16:19
g in exchange for soul 16:26, Mk
   8:37
God *g* not the Spirit by measure
   Jno 3:34
who *g* life unto world   6:33

I *g* to them eternal   10:28
my peace I *g* not as world *g* 14:27
more blessed to *g* than   20:35
letter killeth, spirit *g* life 2 Cor 3:6
ask God who *g* to all   Jas 1:5
in everything *g*   1 Thes 5:18
I will *g* the crown   Rev 2:10

given *(see give)*
it shall be *g*   Mat 7:7
all power *g* to me   28:19
give, and it shall be *g*   Lk 6:38
I have *g* example   Jno 13:15
ask God, it shall be *g*   Jas 1:5

giver
God loveth cheerful *g*   2 Cor 9:7

giving *(see give)*
g no offence   2 Cor 6:3
g all diligence   2 Pet 1:5

glad, *joyful*
be *g* in the Lord   Psa 104:34
a *g* father   Pro 10:1
rejoice and be *g*   Mat 5:12
to show *g* tidings   Lk 1:19
g tidings of kingdom   8:1
Gentiles heard were *g*   Acts 13:48
let us be *g* and rejoice   Rev 19:7
See also: Neh 8:10, Lk 2:10

gladly *(see glad)*
people heard *g*   Mk 12:37
g received words, were baptized
   Acts 2:41

gladness *(see glad)*
in day of *g*   Num 10:10
make me hear joy and *g* Psa 51:8
serve the Lord with *g*   100:2
the voice of *g*   Jer 33:10,11
who receive it with *g*   Mk 4:16
eat meat with *g*   Acts 2:46

glass, *mirror, transparent*

see through *g* darkly 1 Cor 13:12
beholding in a *g* 2 Cor 3:18
beholding face in *g* Jas 1:23
city of gold, like *g* Rev 21:18

glean, *gather*

not gather *g* Lev 19:9, 23:22
let me *g* in field Ruth 2:2

gloominess, *thick darkness*

darkness and *g* Joel 2:2, Zeph 1:15

glorified *(see glory)*

they *g* him not as God Rom 1:21
word be *g* 2 Thes 3:1
Christ *g* not himself Heb 5:5
God in all things *g* 1 Pet 4:11
See also: Mat 9:8, Mk 2:12, Lk 5:26

glorify, *weighty, honored*

thou shalt *g* me Psa 50:15
g Father in heaven Mat 5:6
Father *g* thy name Jno 12:28
g thy Son 17:1
g God in thy body 1 Cor 6:20
See also: Phil 1:20

glory, *honor, splendor, beauty*

ye shall see *g* of Lord Ex 16:7
heavens declare *g* of God Psa 19:1
g of Lord shall endure 104:31
earth full of his *g* Isa 6:3
people have changed *g* Jer 2:11
their *g* shall fly away Hos 9:11
Solomon in all his *g* Mat 6:29
son of man in *g* 19:28, Lk 9:26
coming with *g* Mat 24:30, Mk 13:26, Lk 21:27
beheld his *g* Jno 1:14
he gave not God *g* Acts 12:23
riches of his *g* Rom 9:23
received us to *g* of God 15:7

short of *g* of God 3:23
image and *g* of God 1 Cor 11:7
g of man as flower 1 Pet 1:24
spirit of *g* of God 4:14

glorious *(see glory)*

into *g* liberty Rom 8:21
present it a *g* church Eph 5:27
like his *g* body Phil 3:21
according to *g* gospel 1 Tim 1:11

glory (verb), *boast*

let no wise man *g* in Jer 9:23
you *g* is not good 1 Cor 5:6
g of my infirmities 2 Cor 11:30
I should *g* in cross Gal 6:14
if have envy, *g* not Jas 3:14

glutton, *intemperate*

our son a *g* Deut 21:20
g shall come to poverty Pro 23:21
See also: Pro 23:2, Mat 11:19, Lk 7:34, 1 Cor 10:31, Phil 3:19

gnash, *bite, grind teeth*

g of teeth Mat 8:12, 13:42, 23:13, 24:51, 25:30, Lk 13:28
g on him with teeth Acts 7:54

gnat, *insect, either gnat or mosquito*

strain at *g* Mat 23:24

go

on thy belly shalt *g* Gen 3:14
whither wilt thou *g?* 16:8
g forward Ex 14:5, Job 23:8
presence *g* not with me Ex 33:15
whither thou *g* I will Ruth 1:16
whither shall I *g* Psa 139:7
three things which *g* Pro 30:29
to *g* a mile *g* twain Mat 5:41
I *g* sir, and went not 21:30
g and do likewise Lk 10:37
I *g* to the Father Jno 14:12

goat

delight not in blood of *g*   Isa 1:11
sheep on right, *g* on left   Mat 25:33
blood of bulls and *g*   Heb 10:4

God

in the beginning *G*   Gen 1:1
G is not a man   Num 23:19
is a *G* in Israel   1 Sam 17:46
if the Lord be *G*   1 Ki 18:21
fool said, no *G*   Psa 14:1, 53:1
my *G*, why hast?   22:1, Mat 27:46
thou art *G*   Psa 86:10, Isa 37:16
G is in heaven   Ecc 5:2
I am *G*   Isa 45:22, 46:9
walk humbly with *G*   Mic 6:8
G with us   Mat 1:23
G is a spirit   Jno 4:24
let *G* be true   Rom 3:4
if *G* be for us   8:31
G is faithful   1 Cor 1:9
G is one   Gal 3:20
G is not mocked   6:7
G manifest in flesh   1 Tim 3:16
G is light   1 Jno 1:5
G is love   4:8
no man hath seen *G*   4:12

God, access to, *see:* Rom 5:2, Eph 2:18,
3:12, Jas 4:8

God, belief in, *see:* Gen 15:6, Job 13:15,
Psa 7:1, 46:10, 53:1, Isa 26:4, Rom
15:13, 1 Tim 4:10, Heb 11:6, Jas 2:19

God, benevolence of, *see:* Psa 84:11,
Jno 3:16, 2 Cor 9:15, Jas 1:17

God, children of, *see:* Deut 14:1, Psa
103:13, Mat 5:9, Jno 1:12, Rom
8:16, 1 Jno 3:2

God, dominion of, *see:* Ex 15:18, Deut
10:14, Psa 145:13, Rev 19:6

God, grace of, *see:* Num 6:25, Rom
3:24, 1 Cor 15:10, Tit 2:11, Heb 4:16

God, image of, *see:* Gen 1:27, 2 Cor 4:4,
Col 1:15

Godhead, *divinity:* Acts 17:29, Rom
1:20, Col 2:9

godliness, *God-like-ness*

the mystery of *g*   1 Tim 3:16
exercise thyself to *g*   4:7
g is profitable   4:8
a form of *g*   2 Tim 3:5
pertain to life and *g*   1:3
holy conversation and *g*   3:11
See also: 1 Tim 2:2,10, 6:6,11

godly, *like God*

the *g* man ceaseth   Psa 12:1
g sorrow worketh   2 Cor 7:9
that live *g* in Christ   2 Tim 3:12
live *g* in this world   Tit 2:12
how to deliver the *g*   2 Pet 2:9
See also: Psa 4:3, 32:6, 2 Cor 11:2

going *(see go)*

g way of all earth   Josh 23:14
pondereth all his *g*   Pro 5:21
man's *g* are of the Lord   20:24
g about to establish   Rom 10:3
g before to judgment   1 Tim 5:24

gold, *"shining," money*

nor [wisdom] valued in *g*   Job
28:19
more desired than *g*   Psa 19:10
like apples of *g*   Pro 25:11
try as *g* is tried   Zech 13:9
silver and *g* have I none   Acts 3:6
not think of Godhead like *g*   17:29
not many vessels of *g*   2 Tim 2:20

man with ring of *g*   Jas 2:2
your *g* is cankered   5:3
not redeemed with *g*   1 Pet 1:18
city was pure *g*   Rev 21:18

Golgotha, *place of skull,* Mat 27:33, Mk 15:22, Lk 23:33, Jno 19:17

Goliath, *giant killed by David,* 1 Sam 17, 21:9, 22:10

Gomorrah, *one of cities destroyed by God,* Gen 19:24,28, Isa 1:9, Mat 10:15

gone *(see go)*

busy he was *g*   1 Ki 20:40
wind passeth, and is *g*   Psa 103:16
g astray like sheep   119:176, Isa 53:6
spirit *g* out   Mat 12:34, Lk 11:24
lamps are *g* out   Mat 25:8
virtue *g* out of him   Mk 5:30, Lk 8:46
they are all *g* out of way Rom 3:12
g in the way of Cain   Jude 11

good (noun), *benefit*

God meant it for *g*   Gen 50:20
thereby *g* shall come   Job 22:21
none doeth *g* Psa 14:1, 53:1, Rom 3:12
withold not *g*   Pro 3:27
no *g* in them   Ecc 3:12
went about doing *g*   Acts 10:38
all things work together for *g* Rom 8:28
abhor evil, cleave to *g*   12:9
overcome evil with *g*   12:21
minister of God for *g*   13:4
do *g* to all men   Gal 6:16
hold fast to *g*   1 Thes 5:21
rich, and increased with *g*   Rev 3:17

See also: Amos 5:24, Mat 7:12

good (adj.)

God saw it was *g*   Gen 1:4, 12:31
not *g* that man be alone   2:18
I will teach you *g* way   1 Sam 12:23
g is word of Lord   2 Ki 20:19, Isa 39:8
g and upright is Lord   Psa 25:8
taste and see Lord is *g*   34:8
steps of *g* man ordered by   37:23
g word maketh heart glad   Pro 12:25
g name rather to be chosen   22:1
g way and walk therein   Jer 6:16
how to give *g* gifts   Mat 7:11, Lk 11:13
none *g*, save one   Mat 19:17, Lk 18:19
well done, *g* and faithful Mat 25:21
why call me *g?*   Mk 10:18, Lk 18:19
peace on earth, *g* will   2:14
many hath chosen *g* part   10:42
g thing come out of Nazareth? Jno 1:46
I am *g* shepherd   10:11
g and perfect will of God   Rom 12:2
corrupt *g* morals   1 Cor 15:33
fruitful to every *g* work   Col 1:10
hold fast that which is *g*   1 Thes 5:21
zealous of *g* works   Tit 2:14
every *g* gift   Jas 1:17

goodness, *quality of being good, uprightness, lovingkindness*

surely *g* and mercy shall Psa 23:6

earth is full of *g* of Lord   33:5
the riches of his *g*   Rom 2:4
g and severity of God   11:22

Goshen, *frontier or eastern delta region of Egypt where Israelites lived,* Gen 45:10, 46:34, 47:4, Ex 8:22, 9:26

gospel, *good news*
repent and believe *g*   Mk 1:15
lose life for my sake and *g*   8:35
g of grace of God   Acts 20:24
I am not ashamed of *g*   Rom 1:16
g wherein ye stand   1 Cor 15:1
pervert *g* of Christ   Gal 1:7
truth of *g*   2:14
preparation of *g* of peace   Eph 6:15
hope of the *g*   Col 1:23
g of blessed God   1 Tim 1:4
See also: Pro 25:25, Isa 40:9, 52:7

government, *rule*
increase of *g*   Isa 9:7
See also: Rom 13:1,7, 1 Pet 2:13 f

grace, *favor, kindness*
giving *g* to the lowly   Pro 3:34, Jas 4:6
full of *g* and truth   Jno 1:14
g and truth came by   1:17
justified freely by his *g*   Rom 3:24
access into his *g*   5:2
g did much more abound   5:20
that *g* may abound?   6:1
by *g* I am what I am   1 Cor 15:10
my *g* is sufficient   2 Cor 12:9
ye are fallen from *g*   Gal 5:4
by *g* ye are saved   Eph 2:5,8
partakers of my *g*   Phil 1:7
giveth *g* to the humble   1 Pet 5:5
grow in *g*   2 Pet 3:18

gracious *(see grace)*
a God *g,* merciful   Neh 9:17
tasted that the Lord is *g*   1 Pet 2:3

grain, *kernel*
g of mustard seed   Mat 13:31
faith as *g* of   17:20

grant, *permit, give*
g that my two sons may sit   Mat 20:21, Mk 10:37
g to sit on throne   Rev 3:21

grape, *fruit of vine*
vines have tender *g*   S of S 2:13
fathers have eaten sour *g*   Jer 31:29, Ezek 18:32
gather *g* of thorns   Mat 7:16
of brambles gather *g*   Lk 6:44

grass, *herbs, hay, plants*
earth bring forth *g*   Gen 1:11
man, days are as *g*   Psa 103:15
all flesh is *g*   Isa 40:6, 1 Pet 1:24
if God so clothe *g*   Mat 6:30, Lk 12:28
as *g* he shall pass away   Jas 1:10

grave, *burial, unseen world*
in *g* who shall give   Psa 6:5
jealousy is cruel as *g*   S of S 8:6
his *g* with wicked   Isa 53:9
all in *g* shall hear voice   Jno 5:28
g where is thy victory   1 Cor 15:55

great, *high, mighty*
make a *g* nation   Gen 12:2, 18:18, 46:3
g men not always wise   Job 32:9
him a portion with *g*   Isa 53:12
g is your reward   Mat 5:12, Lk 6:23
whosoever will be *g*   Mat 20:26
first and *g* commandment   22:38
g is Diana of Ephesians   Acts 19:28,34

g is mystery of godliness 1 Tim
3:16
so g salvation Heb 2:3
so g a cloud of witnesses 12:1
how g a matter little fire Jas 3:5

greater *(see great)*
art thou g than Jno 4:12, 8:53
Father is g than 10:29, 14:28
g love hath no man 15:13
God is g than heart 1 Jno 3:20
g is he that is in you 4:4

greatest *(see great)*
who is g in kingdom Mat 18:1
who should be g Mk 9:34, Lk 9:46
g of these is charity 1 Cor 13:13

Greece, *usually called Achaia in N.T.,*
Dan 8:21, 10:20, 11:2, Zech 9:13,
Acts 16:20

greedy, *grasping, avaricious*
g of gain Pro 1:19, 15:27
not g of filthy lucre 1 Tim 3:3
See also: Ecc 5:10, Mic 2:2, Mat
26:5, Lk 12:15, 1 Tim 6:10

grief, *sorrow, burdened*
my life is spent with g Psa 31:10
much wisdom is much g Ecc 1:18
a man acquainted with g Isa 53:3
if a man endure g 1 Pet 2:19

grieve *(see grief)*
if brother be g with meat Rom
14:15
g not Holy Spirit Eph 4:30

grievous, *burdensome*
g words stir up anger Pro 15:1
work wrought under sun g Ecc
2:17
burdens g to be borne Mat 23:4,
Lk 11:46

commandments are not g 1 Jno 5:3

grind
it will g him to powder Mat 21:44,
Lk 20:18

groan, *moan*
God heard their g Ex 2:24
whole creation g and Rom 8:22
we ourselves g within 8:23
with g which cannot be uttered
8:26
we g desiring to be clothed 2 Cor
5:2

ground, *earth, foundation*
not a man to till g Gen 2:5
root out of dry g Isa 53:2
fell into good g Mat 13:8, Lk 8:8
I have bought a piece of g 14:18
corn of wheat fall into g Jno 12:24
pillar and g of truth 1 Tim 3:15

grounded, *established*
rooted and g in love Eph 3:17
in faith, g and settled Col 1:23

grow, *increase, sprout up*
shall g up before him Isa 53:2
he shall g as the lily Hos 14:5
consider the lilies how they g Mat
6:28, Lk 12:27
no fruit g on thee for ever Mat
21:19
may g up in him Eph 4:15
faith g exceedingly 2 Thes 1:3
milk of word, that ye may g 1 Pet
2:2
g in grace 2 Pet 3:18
See also: Mk 4:28, 30:32

grudge, *feel resentment*
g not one against Jas 5:9
hospitality without g 1 Pet 4:9

guide, *lead, direct*
lord shall g thee — Isa 58:11
ye blind g — Mat 23:16,24
g feet in way of peace — Lk 1:79
g you into all truth — Jno 16:13
a g of the blind — Rom 2:19

guile, *deceit*
in whose spirit is no g — Psa 32:2
keep lips from speaking g — 34:13, 1 Pet 3:10
laying aside malice, g — 2:1
nor g found in his mouth — 2:22
See also: Pro 20:17, 2 Pet 1:16

guilty
all world g before God — Rom 3:19
g of the body and — 1 Cor 11:27
one point, he is g of all — Jas 2:10
See also: Gen 3:8, Deut 24:16, Psa 51:3, Isa 1:18, 59:2, Acts 2:37

H

Habakkuk, *prophet about 626 B.C.,* see: Hab 1:1

habitation, *dwelling place*
I have loved h of thy — Psa 26:8
determined bounds of h — Acts 17:26
an h of God — Eph 2:22
See also: Psa 84:3, Pro 11:29

Hagar, *Egyptian servant of Sarah and mother of Ishmael by Abraham,* Gen 16:1 ff, 21:9 ff

Haggai, *prophet about 520 B.C., see:* Ezra 5:1, 6:14, Hag 1:1

hail, *falling lumps of ice*
a very grievous h — Ex 9:18
fire and h, snow — Psa 148:8
h and fire mingled — Rev 8:7

hair
let h of his head grow — Num 6:5
more than the h of — Psa 40:12, 69:4
of camel's h — Mat 3:4, Mk 1:6
not make one h white — Mat 5:36
h numbered — 10:30, Lk 12:7
wiped feet with h — Jno 11:2, 12:3
if man have long h — 1 Cor 11:14

half, *half, middle*
divide child, h to one — 1 Ki 3:25
not live h days — Psa 55:23
leaving him h dead — Lk 10:30
h of my goods — 19:8
See also: 1 Ki 18:21, Hos 10:2, Mat 6:24, Jas 4:8, Rev 3:15 f

hallelujah, *praise to God,* Rev 19:1-6
See also: Psa 105:45, 106:48, 149:1

hallow, *to set apart*
blessed Sabbath, and h — Ex 20:11
I have h this house — 1 Ki 9:3
h be thy name — Mat 6:9, Lk 11:2

halt, *to limp; lame, crippled*
how long h ye between — 1 Ki 18:21
better to enter life h — Lk 14:21

Ham, *son of Noah,* Gen 5:32, 6:10, 7:13, 9:18, 10:1 ff, 1 Chr 1:4

Haman, *minister of Ahasuerus about 510 B.C. in Persia,* Esth 3:1 ff

hand, *hand, palm*
h against every man — Gen 16:12
with a high h — Ex 14:8, Num 33:3
what evil is in h — 1 Sam 26:18
put my life in my h — 28:21
let us fall in h of Lord — 2 Sam 24:14, 1 Chr 21:13

cloud like a man's *h*   1 Ki 18:44
clean *h* and pure heart   Psa 24:4
into thy *h* I commit   31:5
whatsoever thy *h* findeth   Ecc 9:10
kingdom of heaven at *h*   Mat 3:2,
     4:17, 10:7
if *h* offend   18:8, Mk 9:43
sat on right *h* of God   16:19
out of my Father's *h*   Jno 10:29
eye say to *h*   1 Cor 12:21
work with own *h*   1 Thes 4:11
cleanse your *h*, ye   Jas 4:8
end of things at *h*   1 Pet 4:7
our *h* have handled   1 Jno 1:1

handle, *handle, touch, feel*
father of such as *h* harp   Gen 4:21
h me, and see   Lk 24:39
not *h* word deceitfully   2 Cor 4:2

handmaid, *female servant*
she had an *h*   Gen 16:1
Sarah's *h*   25:12
Zilpah his *h*   29:24
Bilhah his *h*   29:29
let thine *h*   1 Sam 1:18
behold the *h*   Lk 1:38

hang, *to hang up*
he that is *h*   Deut 21:23, Gal 3:13
h earth on nothing   Job 26:7
h harps upon willows   Psa 137:2
millstone *h* about neck   Mat 18:6,
     Mk 9:42, Lk 17:2
h the law and prophets   Mat 22:40
Judas *h* himself   27:5

haply, *if then*
lest *h* after laid foundation   Lk
     14:29
h ye fight God   Acts 5:39

happen, *to come about*
h for ensample   1 Cor 10:11
as though strange things *h*   1 Pet
     4:12

happy, *happy, fortunate*
h is that people   Psa 144:15
h that findeth wisdom   Pro 3:13
h is he that hath mercy   14:21
trusteth in Lord, *h* is   16:20
h if ye do them   Jno 13:17
h is he that   Rom 14:22
count *h* that endure   Jas 5:11
h are ye   1 Pet 3:14, 4:14
See also: Psa 1:1, 100:2, Mat 5:10,
Rom 14:17, 1 Jno 1:4

hard, *firm, difficult*
any thing too *h* for Lord   Gen
     18:14
laid *h* bondage   Deut 26:6
way of transgressors is *h*   Pro 13:15
thou art an *h* man   Mat 25:24
h for them that trust   Mk 10:24
this is a *h* saying   Jno 6:60
many things *h* to be   Heb 5:11
h to be understood   2 Pet 3:16

harden *(see hard)*
I will *h* Pharaoh's heart   Ex 4:21,
     7:3, 14:4
h hearts of Egyptians   14:17
h not your hearts   Psa 95:8, Heb
     3:8, 15:4,7
he hath *h* their hearts   Jno 12:40
lest any of you be *h*   Heb 3:13

hardness *(see hard)*
because of *h* of hearts   Mat 19:8
h and impenitent heart   Rom 2:5
endure *h*, as good soldier   2 Tim
     2:3

See also: Pro 21:13, Jer 5:3, Lk 16:31

harlot, *prostitute*
Rahab the *h*   Josh 2:1, 6:17
keepeth company with *h*   Pro 29:3
publicans and *h*   Mat 21:31
joined to *h*   1 Cor 6:16
See also: Pro 7:22, 23:27, Heb 13:4

harm, *injure, do evil*
no more do thee *h*   1 Sam 26:21
do prophets no *h* 1 Chr 16:22, Psa 105:15
do thyself no *h*   Acts 16:28
who will *h* you, if   1 Pet 3:13

harmless *(see harm)*
wise as serpents, *h* as   Mat 10:16
may be *h*, the sons of   Phil 2:15
holy, *h*, and undefiled   Heb 7:26

harp, *stringed musical instrument*
hanged *h* on willows   Psa 137:2
harping with their *h*   Rev 14:2

harvest, *reaping*
h shall not cease   Gen 8:22
he that sleepeth in *h*   Pro 10:5
h past, summer ended   Jer 8:20
the *h* is plenteous   Mat 9:37
Lord of *h*   9:38, Lk 10:2
grow together until *h*   Mat 13:30
h is end of world   13:39
fields are white to *h*   Jno 4:35
See also: Zech 8:21, Mat 5:25, Acts 19:36

hasty, *rash, impatient*
he that is *h* of spirit   Pro 14:29
let not thy heart be *h*   Ecc 5:2

hate, *hate, oppose*
shall not *h* brother   Lev 19:17
that *h* righteous be desolate   Psa 34:21

I *h* every false way   119:104
that love Lord, *h* evil   139:21
fear of Lord is *h* evil   Pro 8:13
h stirreth up strife   10:12
he that spareth rod, *h* son   13:24
a time to *h*   Ecc 3:8
h evil and love good   Amos 5:15
do good to them that *h* you   Mat 5:44, Lk 6:27
either he will *h* one   Mat 6:24
ye shall be *h*   10:23, Mk 13:13, Lk 21:17
blessed when men *h* you   6:22
he that *h* his life   Jno 12:25
if world *h* you   15:18, 1 Jno 3:13
h his brother   2:9, 3:15
See also: Rom 12:9, 1 Jno 4:20

haughty, *high, arrogant*
h spirit before a fall   Pro 16:18
heart of man is *h*   18:12
h shall be humbled   Isa 10:33
See also: Job 24:24, Ezek 31:10, Lk 18:11, 1 Tim 6:4, 1 Jno 2:16

head, *head, first*
it shall bruise thy *h*   Gen 3:15
coals of fire on his *h*   Pro 25:22, Rom 12:20
helmet of salvation on *h*   Isa 59:17
h thou didst not anoint   Lk 7:46
not hair on *h* perish   21:18
h of man is Christ   1 Cor 11:3
h of the Church   Eph 1:22, 4:15, Col 1:18
husband is *h* of wife   Eph 5:23

heal, *heal, make whole*
h my soul, for I sinned   Psa 41:4
h the broken in heart   147:3
with his stripes we are *h*   Isa 53:5

lawful to *h* on Sabbath   Mat 12:10,
    Lk 14:3
be converted, and I *h* them   Mat
   13:15, Jno 12:40, Acts 28:27
to *h* the brokenhearted   Lk 4:18
had faith to be *h*   Acts 14:9
by stripes ye were *h*   1 Pet 2:24
for *h* of nations   Rev 22:2

healing *(see heal)*
with *h* in his wings   Mal 4:2

heap, *mound*
be an *h* for ever   Deut 13:16
h coals of fire   Pro 25:22
h to themselves teachers 2 Tim 4:3
ye have *h* treasures   Jas 5:3

hear, *hear, give ear*
make them *h* my words Deut 4:10
h and fear the Lord   31:12
come *h*, all ye that   Psa 66:16
ears but *h* not   115:6
h instruction and be   Pro 8:33
be more ready to *h*   Ecc 5:1
h but understand Isa 6:9, Mk 4:12
h, and your soul Isa 55:3, Jno 5:25
deaf *h* Mat 11:5, Mk 7:37, Lk 7:22
things which ye *h*   Mat 13:17
my beloved Son, *h*   17:5, Mk 9:7
heed what ye *h*   4:24, Lk 8:18
dead shall *h* voice of   Jno 5:25
God *h* not sinners   9:31
if any man *h* my words   12:47
h without a preacher   Rom 10:14
and them that *h* thee   1 Tim 4:16
swift to *h*   Jas 1:19
if any man *h* my voice   Rev 3:20

heard *(see hear)*
they *h* voice of the Lord   Gen 3:8
God *h* their groaning   Ex 2:24

nor any tool of iron *h*   1 Ki 6:7
where voice is not *h*   Psa 19:3
I sought the Lord, and he *h* 34:4
voice of turtle is *h*   S of S 2:12
when they *h* this   Acts 2:37
many which *h* believed   4:4
thou hast seen and *h*   22:15
not seen, or ear *h*   1 Cor 2:9
which we have *h* and   1 Jno 1:1

hearer, *one who hears*
not *h* of law are just   Rom 2:13
be doers of word, not *h*   Jas 1:22

hearing *(see hear)*
by the *h* of the ear   Job 42:5
h, they hear not   Mat 13:13
h a voice, but seeing   Acts 9:7
faith cometh by *h*   Rom 10:17
or by the *h* of faith   Gal 3:2
seeing ye are dull of *h*   Heb 5:11

hearken, *to attend to*
if *h* to commandments Deut 28:13,
    1 Ki 11:38
to *h* better than   1 Sam 15:22

heart, *heart, man's innermost being*
love Lord with all *h*   Deut 6:5 f
serve with all your *h*   11:13, Josh
    22:5, 1 Sam 12:20
love Lord with all your *h*   Deut
  13:3, 30:6, Mat 22:37, Mk 12:30
Lord looketh on the *h* 1 Sam 16:7
let *h* seek the Lord   1 Chr 16:10,
    Psa 105:3
them of broken *h*   34:18
trust Lord with all *h*   Pro 3:5
keep *h* with all diligence   4:23
hope deferred maketh *h* sick 13:12
h knoweth own bitterness   14:10
merry *h* maketh   15:13,15

merry *h* doeth good like   17:22
as he thinketh in his *h*   23:7
wise man's *h* discerneth   Ecc 8:5
them of fearful *h*   Isa 35:4
h is deceitful above   Jer 17:9
make a new *h* and new Ezek 18:31
blessed are pure in *h*   Mat 5:8
there will *h* be   6:21, Lk 12:34
meek and lowly in *h*   Mat 11:29
out of abundance of *h*   12:34, Lk
                            6:45
out of *h* proceed evil   Mat 15:19,
                         Mk 7:21
let not *h* be troubled   Jno 14:1,27
with *h* man believeth   Rom 10:10
neither entered into *h*   1 Cor 2:9
Christ dwell in *h* by   Eph 3:17
in singleness of *h*   Col 3:22
intents of the *h*   Heb 4:12
draw near with true *h*   10:22
purify your *h*   Jas 4:8
hidden man of the *h*   1 Pet 3:4

heat, *warmth*
cold and *h*, summer and   Gen 8:22
elements melt with *h*   2 Pet 3:10

heathen, *"the nations," i.e., non-Jews*
why do *h* rage   Psa 2:1, Acts 4:25
vain repetitions, as *h*   Mat 6:7
that God would justify *h*   Gal 3:8

heaven, *sky, abode of God*
God created *h* and earth   Gen 1:1
h of *h* is Lord's   Deut 10:14, 1 Ki
                  8:27, Psa 115:16
when I consider thy *h*   8:3
h declare glory of God   19:1
God is in *h*, and you   Ecc 5:2
new *h* and new   Isa 65:17, Rev
                         21:1

h is my throne   Isa 66:1, Acts 7:49
till *h* and earth pass   Mat 5:18
coming in clouds of *h* 24:30, 26:64,
                         Mk 14:62
names written in *h*   Lk 10:20
bread from *h*   Jno 6:31
no other name under *h*   Acts 4:12
wrath revealed from *h*   Rom 1:18
family in *h* is named   Eph 3:15
things created, in *h*   Col 1:16
silence in *h*   Rev 8:1
temple of God in *h*   11:19
new *h*, and new earth   21:1

heavenly *(see heaven)*
h father feedeth them   Mat 6:26
partakers of *h* calling   Heb 3:1

heaviness, *sorrow, grief*
h in heart maketh it   Pro 12:25
great *h* and sorrow   Rom 9:2
joy be turned to *h*   Jas 4:9

heavy, *weighty, sorrowful*
Moses' hands were *h*   Ex 17:12
iniquities too *h* for me   Psa 38:4
songs to a *h* heart   Pro 25:20
fool's wrath *h* than   27:3
all that are *h* laden   Mat 11:28
they bind *h* burdens   23:4
he began to be very *h*   26:37

Heber, *various people,* Gen 46:17, Judg
   4:11 ff, 1 Chr 4:18, 5:13, 8:17,22

Hebrew, *alternate name for Israelites,*
   Gen 14:13, 39:14, Ex 1:15, etc.

Hebron, *city 22 miles south of Jerusa-*
   lem, Gen 13:18, Num 13:22, Josh
   10:36, 14:13, 2 Sam 5:3

hedge, *fence*
as an *h* of thorns   Pro 15:19

heed, *to give attention*

take *h* what ye hear   Mk 4:24
neither give *h* to fables   1 Tim 1:4,
                       Tit 1:14
to give more earnest *h*   Heb 2:1
See also: Pro 23:12, Mk 13:33

heel

shalt bruise his *h*   Gen 3:15
hold on brother's *h*   25:26, Hos
                              12:3

height *(see high)*

h nor depth be able   Rom 8:39
h of love of Christ   Eph 3:18,19

heir, *one who receives portion*

this is the *h*   Mat 21:38, Mk 12:7,
                          Lk 20:14
h of God, joint *h* with   Rom 8:17
h according to promise   Gal 3:29
an *h* of God through Christ   4:7
Gentiles be fellow *h*   Eph 3:6
h according to hope of   Tit 3:7
h of all things   Heb 1:1
h of the kingdom   Jas 2:5
h together of grace   1 Pet 3:7
See also: 1 Pet 1:4, Rev 1:5

hell, *place or condition of punishment after death for unregenerate souls*

h is naked before him   Job 26:6
not leave soul in *h* Psa 16:10, Acts
                              2:27
if I make my bed in *h*   Psa 139:8
deliver soul from *h*   Pro 23:14
h never full   27:20
h hath enlarged herself   Isa 5:14
in danger of *h* fire   Mat 5:22
destroy soul in *h*   10:28, Lk 12:5
brought down to *h*   Mat 11:23, Lk
                              10:15

gates of *h* not prevail   Mat 16:18
twofold more child of *h*   23:15
in *h* he lift up eyes   Lk 16:23
tongue set on fire of *h*   Jas 3:6
keys of *h* and death   Rev 1:18
death and *h* cast   20:14
See also: Mat 25:46, 2 Thes 1:9,
Jude 7, Rev 14:10, 21:8

help, *assistance*

he is our *h* and shield   Psa 23:20
God a *h* in trouble   46:1
Lord had been my *h*   94:17
from whence cometh my *h*   121:1
trust not man, who is no *h*   146:3,5
h thou mine unbelief   Mk 9:24
to Macedonia and *h*   Acts 16:9

helper *(see help)*

Lord is my *h*, I will   Heb 13:6

hem, *border*

touched *h* of his   Mat 9:20
might touch the *h*   14:31

hen, *fowl*

h gathereth chickens   Mat 23:37,
                             Lk 13:34

heresy, *opinion, false teaching*

way which they call *h*   Acts 24:14
be also *h* among you   1 Cor 11:19
strife, seditions, *h*   Gal 5:20
bring in damnable *h*   2 Pet 2:1
See also: Mat 15:9, 22:29, Rom
16:17, Eph 4:14, 1 Tim 1:10, 2 Pet
3:16, 2 Jno 2:9

heretick, *opinionated person*

a man that is *h*   Tit 3:10

heritage, *possession, inheritance*

children are *h* of Lord   Psa 127:3
lords over God's *h*   1 Pet 5:3
See also: Psa 37:9, Rom 8:16, 1 Cor
15:50, 1 Pet 1:4

Hermon, *mountain northeast of Sea of Galilee,* Deut 3:8, Josh 11:3, 1 Chr 5:23, Psa 89:12, 133:3

Herod, *"the Great," king of Palestine under Romans,* Mat 2:1 ff, Lk 1:5; *Antipas, son of Herod the Great,* Mat 14:1 ff, Mk 6:14 ff, Lk 3:1 ff, 23:7 ff; *Agrippa I, grandson of Herod the Great,* Acts 12:1 ff (to be distinguished from Agrippa II—See Acts 25:13 ff)

Herodians, *political party,* Mat 22:16, Mk 3:6, 12:13

Herodias, *wife of Herod Antipas,* Mat 14:3 ff, Mk 6:17 ff, Lk 3:19

Hezekiah, *king of Judah about 700 B.C.,* 2 Ki 16:20, 18:1 ff, 2 Chr 28:27 ff, Isa 1:1, 36:1 ff

hid *(see hide)*
Adam and his wife *h*   Gen 3:8
h Moses three months   Ex 2:2
Moses *h* his face   3:6
thy word I *h* in heart   Psa 119:11
we *h* our faces from him   Isa 53:3
nothing *h*   Mat 10:26, Mk 4:22
went and *h* money   Mat 25:18
mystery *h* from ages   Col 1:26
your life is *h* with Christ   3:3
h man of the heart   1 Pet 3:4

hide, *to conceal*
h me under thy wings   Psa 17:8
how long wilt thou *h*   89:46
h a multitude of sins   Jas 5:20

high, *high, lofty*
as heaven is *h* above   Psa 103:11
it is *h*, I cannot   139:6
Lord *h* and lifted up   Isa 6:1
mind not *h* things   Rom 12:16

prize of *h* calling of   Phil 3:14

higher *(see high)*
to rock that is *h* than I   Psa 61:2
heavens *h* than earth   Isa 55:9
be subject to *h* powers   Rom 13:1

highway, *raised roadway*
an *h* shall be there   Isa 35:8
make straight a *h* for God   40:3
went out into *h*   Mat 22:10
go out into *h*   Lk 14:23
See also: Jer 31:21, Mat 3:3

hill, *hill, mountain*
ascend the *h* of Lord   Psa 24:3
little *h* rejoice on every side   65:12
lift up mine eyes to *h*   121:1
be exalted above *h*   Isa 2:2
every *h* made low   40:4
city set on an *h*   Mat 5:14
every *h* be brought low   Lk 3:5
Paul stood on Mars' *h*   Acts 17:22
See also: Psa 97:5, 98:8, Joel 3:18

hinder, *delay, prevent*
h me to be baptized   Acts 8:36
h the gospel   1 Cor 9:12
Satan *h* us   1 Thes 2:18
prayers be not *h*   1 Pet 3:7
See also: Heb 12:1

hire, *wage, reward*
priests teach for *h*   Mic 3:11
labourer worthy of *h*   Lk 10:7

hireling, *one hired*
h looketh for reward   Job 7:2
as years of *h*   Isa 16:14, 21:16
he is an *h*   Jno 10:12 f

hitherto, *until now*
my Father worketh *h*   Jno 5:17

Hittites, *descendants of Heth,* Gen 15:20, 23:10, Ex 3:8, 13:5, etc.

hold, *keep*

understanding *h* peace Pro 11:12
fool, when he *h* peace 17:28
never *h* their peace Isa 62:6
h truth in unrighteousness Rom 1:18
h fast which is good 1 Thes 5:21
h fast sound words 2 Tim 1:13
h fast profession Heb 4:14, 10:23

hole

put it in bag with *h* Hag 1:6
foxes have *h* Mat 8:20, Lk 9:58

holiness *(see holy)*

beauty of *h* 1 Chr 16:29, 2 Chr 20:21, Psa 29:2, 96:9
God throne of his *h* 47:8
the way of *h* Isa 35:8
according to spirit of *h* Rom 1:4
h in fear of God 2 Cor 7:1
stablish hearts in *h* 1 Thes 3:13
h without which man Heb 12:14

holy, *separate, set apart*

an *h* nation Ex 19:6, 1 Pet 2:9
Sabbath keep it *h* Ex 20:8, 31:14
between *h* and unholy Lev 10:10
none *h* as Lord 1 Sam 2:2
preserve soul, I am *h* Isa 86:2
between *h* and profane Ezek 22:26
commandment is *h*, just Rom 7:12
firstfruit be *h*, if 11:16
living sacrifice, *h* acceptable to God 12:1
temple of God is *h* 1 Cor 3:17
h in all conversation 1 Pet 1:15, 2 Pet 3:11
be *h*, for I am *h* 1 Pet 1:16

on *h* priesthood 2:5
See also: Psa 34:12–14, 1 Cor 3:17

Holy Ghost, *Holy Spirit, the third member of the Godhead*

baptize with *H G* Mat 3:11, Mk 1:8, Lk 3:16, Jno 1:33, Acts 1:5
Jesus being full of *H G* Lk 4:1
H G shall teach you 12:12
comforter, who is *H G* Jno 14:26
filled with *H G* Acts 2:4, 4:31
men full of the *H G* 6:3
that they might receive *H G* 8:15
H G made you overseers 20:28
words which *H G* teacheth 1 Cor 2:13
communion of *H G* 2 Cor 13:14
H G sent from heaven 1 Pet 1:12

home, *house, dwelling place*

man goeth to his long *h* Ecc 12:5
ask husbands at *h* 1 Cor 14:35
shew piety at *h* 1 Tim 5:4
keepers at *h* Tit 2:5
See also: Num 10:30, Pro 5:15, 17:1

honest, *excellent, upright*

an *h* and good heart Lk 8:15
things *h* Rom 12:17, 2 Cor 8:21
whatsoever things are *h* Phil 4:8
conversation *h* among Gentiles 1 Pet 2:12
See also: Deut 25:13, 1 Ki 22:16, Psa 101:7, Pro 12:22, Eph 4:25

honour, *honor, respect, reverence, majesty, beauty*

h thy father and mother Ex 20:12, Deut 5:16, Mat 15:4, 19:19, Mk 7:10, 10:19, Lk 18:20, Eph 6:2
wives give husbands *h* Esth 1:20
crowned him with *h* Psa 8:5, Heb 2:7

h them that fear Lord — Psa 15:4
before *h* is humility — Pro 15:33, 18:12
h to cease from strife — 20:3
with lips do *h* me — Isa 29:13
prophet not without *h* — Mat 13:57, Mk 6:4, Jno 4:44
h me with lips — Mat 15:8, Mk 7:6
in *h* preferring one — Rom 12:10
h to whom *h* is due — 13:7
some to *h* some to — 2 Tim 2:20
h all men, *h* the king — 1 Pet 2:17
giving *h* to the wife — 3:7

hope, *expectation, confidence*
my days spent without *h* — Job 7:6
might set their *h* in God — Psa 78:7
happy whose *h* is in Lord — 146:5
h deferred maketh sick — Pro 13:12
blessed whose *h* Lord is — Jer 17:7
who against *h* believed — Rom 4:18
h maketh not ashamed — 5:5
we are saved by *h* — 8:24
rejoicing in *h* — 12:12
may abound in *h* — 15:13
should plow in *h* — 1 Cor 9:10
faith, *h*, charity — 13:13
life only we have *h* — 15:19
the *h* of his calling — Eph 1:18
having no *h*, and without — 2:12
Christ in you, the *h* of — Col 1:27
helmet, *h* of salvation — 1 Thes 5:8
looking for blessed *h* — Tit 2:13
the *h* of eternal life — 3:7
rejoicing *h*, firm to end — Heb 3:6
substance of things *h* for — 11:1
begotten to lively *h* — 1 Pet 1:3
h to the end — 1:13
reason of *h* that is in you — 3:15

that hath this *h* — 1 Jno 3:3

horror, *terror, abhorrence*
a *h* of great darkness — Gen 15:12
h hath overwhelmed me — Psa 55:5
h hath taken hold upon me — 119:53
See also: Deut 32:25, Psa 91:5, Hos 6:10

horse
h and rider into sea — Ex 15:21
be not as *h* or mule — Psa 32:9
h is a vain thing for — 33:17
whip for *h* — Pro 26:3
we put bits in *h* mouths — Jas 3:3

hospitality, *generosity*
given to *h* — Rom 12:13
a lover of *h* — Tit 1:8
use *h* one to another — 1 Pet 4:9
See also: Ex 2:22, Pro 25:17, Mat 25:35, Lk 14:13, 1 Tim 5:10, Heb 13:2

hot, *heat, burning*
can one go *h* coals — Pro 6:28
seared with *h* iron — 1 Tim 4:2
neither cold nor *h* — Rev 3:15

hour, *time, period of time*
that *h* knoweth no man — Mat 24:36, Mk 12:32
ye know neither day nor *h* — Mat 25:13
mine *h* is not yet come — Jno 2:4
h is coming — 4:23, 5:25, 16:32
save me from this *h* — 12:27

house, *house, household*
not covet neighbour's *h* — Ex 20:17, Deut 5:21
zeal of thine *h* — Psa 69:9, Jno 2:17
doorkeeper in *h* of Lord — Psa 84:10
h of righteous shall — Pro 12:7

h of wicked shall   14:11
keeper of *h* shall tremble   Ecc 12:3
let us go to *h* of God   Mic 4:2
h divided cannot stand   Mat 12:25,
                     Mk 3:25
Father's *h* are many   Jno 14:2
h not made with hands   2 Cor 5:1
judgment begin at *h*   1 Pet 4:17

household, *family (see house)*
foes of his own *h*   Mat 10:36
the *h* of faith   Gal 6:10
of the *h* of God   Eph 2:19

humble, *lowly, gentle*
to *h* thee and prove   Deut 8:2
forgetteth not cry of *h*   Psa 9:12
better of *h* spirit   Pro 16:19
contrite and *h* spirit   Isa 57:15
h himself   Mat 18:4, 23:12, Lk
                   14:11, 18:14
h himself and become   Phil 2:8
grace to *h*   Jas 4:6, 1 Pet 5:5
See also: Lk 18:13, Rom 12:16, Col
3:17, 1 Tim 6:17

humility *(see humble)*
before honour *h*   Pro 15:33, 18:12
h are riches and honour   22:4

hunger, *need for food, desire*
idle soul suffer *h*   Pro 19:15
not *h* not thirst   Isa 49:10
blessed that *h*   Mat 5:6, Lk 6:21
I perish with *h*   15:17
cometh to me never *h*   Jno 6:35
if enemy *h*, feed   Rom 12:20
we both *h* and thirst   1 Cor 4:11
they shall *h* no more   Rev 7:16
See also: Amos 8:11, Rev 2:17

hungry *(see hunger)*
filleth *h* soul with   Psa 107:9

to *h* bitter is sweet   Pro 27:7
to be full and to be *h*   Phil 4:12

hurt, *injure, break*
ruleth another to own *h*   Ecc 8:9
nothing shall *h* you   Lk 10:19
h not earth, neither sea   Rev 7:3
See also: Rom 13:10, 1 Pet 3:3

husband, *man, spouse, master*
a bloody *h* art thou   Ex 4:25
wife crown to her *h*   Pro 12:4
heart of *h* doth trust   31:11
thou save thy *h*   1 Cor 7:16
wives, submit to *h*   Eph 5:22
h, love wives   5:25, Col 3:19
the *h* of one wife   1 Tim 3:12
young women to love *h*   Tit 2:4
subjection to own *h*   1 Pet 3:1
bride adorned for *h*   Rev 21:2

husbandman, *farmer*
I am vine, Father is *h*   Jno 15:1
the *h* that laboureth   2 Tim 2:6

hymn, *song of praise*
sung an *h*   Mat 26:30, Mk 14:26
psalms and *h*   Eph 5:19, Col 3:16
See also: 1 Cor 14:15, Rev 15:3

hypocrisy, *deception, acting*
iniquity, to practise *h*   Isa 32:6
ye are full of *h*   Mat 23:28
leaven of Pharisees, is *h*   Lk 12:1
speaking lies in *h*   1 Tim 4:2
pure, and without *h*   Jas 3:17
See also: Psa 62:4, Pro 27:6

hypocrite, *actor, deceiver*
h hope shall perish   Job 8:13
joy of *h* but for moment   20:5
h with mouth destroyeth   Pro 11:9
thou *h*, first cast   Mat 7:5, Lk 6:42
woe unto *h*   Mat 23:13 ff, Lk 11:44

hyssop, *reed used as sponge*
bunch of *h* and dip it   Ex 12:22
purge me with *h*, I shall   Psa 51:7

I

Iconium, *city of central Asia Minor (Turkey),* Acts 13:51, 14:1, 16:2, 2 Tim 3:11

idle, *inactive, lazy, useless*
an *i* soul shall hunger   Pro 19:15
eateth not bread of *i*   31:27
every *i* word men speak Mat 12:36
standing *i* in market place   20:3
they learn to be *i*   1 Tim 5:13
See also: Pro 6:9, 10:26, Rom 12:-11, 1 Thes 4:11

idol, *image of gods*
gods of nations are *i*   Psa 96:5
from pollutions of *i*   Acts 15:20
an *i* is nothing   1 Cor 8:4
hath temple with *i*   2 Cor 6:16
turned to God from *i*   1 Thes 1:9
keep from *i*   1 Jno 5:21
See also: Deut 32:17, Judg 2:19, Isa 48:5, Eph 5:5

idolatry, *worship of idols*
flee from *i*   1 Cor 10:4
covetousness, which is *i*   Col 3:5

ignorance, *without knowledge*
forgiven for it is *i*   Num 15:25
times of *i* God winked at   Acts 17:30
from God through *i*   Eph 4:18
put to silence *i* of   1 Pet 2:15

See also: Judg 2:10, Job 38:2, Pro 1:22, Hos 4:6, Lk 23:34

ignorant *(see ignorance)*
perceived they were *i*   Acts 4:13
i of God's righteousness   Rom 10:3
if any man be *i*   1 Cor 14:38
be not *i* of this   2 Pet 3:8

Illyricum, *section of northwestern Greece,* Rom 15:19

image, *likeness, often: an idol*
make man in our *i*   Gen 1:26
whose *i*? Mat 22:20, Mk 12:16, Lk 20:24
glory of God to *i*   Rom 1:23
conformed to *i* of son   8:29
also bear *i* of heavenly 1 Cor 15:49
Christ is *i* of God   2 Cor 4:4
express *i* of his person   Heb 1:3

imagination, *thought, idea*
i of heart evil   Gen 6:5, 8:22
walk in *i* of heart   Deut 29:19
i heart deviseth wicked   Pro 6:18
Lord understandeth *i*   1 Chr 28:9
became vain in *i*   Rom 1:21

imagine, *to think, devise*
why do people *i* Psa 2:1, Acts 4:25
let none *i* evil   Zech 7:10, 8:17

Immanuel, or Emmanuel, *God with us,* Isa 7:14, Mat 1:23

immortality, *deathlessness, eternal life*
to them who seek *i*   Rom 2:7
mortal must put on *i*   1 Cor 15:53
See also: Job 14:14, Psa 49:5, Ecc 12:7, Jno 8:51, 11:25, 14:19, 1 Jno 2:25

impenitent, *without change of mind*
after thy *i* heart   Rom 2:5
See also: Psa 95:8, Jer 5:3, Mat 11:20, Heb 3:13

impossible

nothing be *i* unto you   Mat 17:20

with men it *i* 19:26, Mk 10:27, Lk
18:27

i for those enlightened   Heb 6:4

without faith *i* to please   11:6

See also: Jer 10:23, Mat 6:24, 1 Jno
4:20

impute, *reckon, account*

Lord *i* not   Psa 32:2, Rom 4:8

sin is not *i* where no   5:13

incline, *turn toward, tend*

i heart unto Lord   Josh 24:23

he may *i* our hearts   1 Ki 8:58

i not to evil   Psa 141:4

incorruptible, *imperishable, not subject to change*

changed glory of *i* God   Rom 1:23

to obtain an *i* crown   1 Cor 9:25

an inheritance *i*   1 Pet 1:4

See also: 1 Cor 15:42 ff, 1 Pet 1:23

increase, *increase, abound*

riches *i*, set not heart   Psa 62:10

wise man *i* learning   Pro 1:5, 9:9

he that *i* knowledge   Ecc 1:18

Jesus *i* in wisdom   Lk 2:52

Lord, *i* our faith   17:5

he must *i*, I decrease   Jno 3:30

word of God *i*   Acts 6:7

churches *i* daily   16:5

God gave the *i*   1 Cor 3:6

I am rich, *i* with goods   Rev 3:17

indeed, *truly, certainly*

will God *i* dwell on earth   1 Ki
8:27, 2 Chr 6:18

the Lord is risen *i*   Lk 24:34

Israelite *i*, in whom   Jno 1:47

my flesh is meat *i*   6:55

ye shall be free *i*   8:36

indignation, *anger*

moved with *i*   Mat 20:24

looking for fiery *i*   Heb 10:27

the cup of his *i*   Rev 14:10

inexcusable, *without excuse*

thou art *i*, O man   Rom 2:1

infidel, *not believing*

is worse than *i*   1 Tim 5:8

infirmity, *sickness, weakness*

himself took our *i*   Mat 8:17

the *i* of the flesh   Rom 6:19

the spirit helped our *i*   8:26

strong bear *i* of weak   15:1

touched with our *i*   Heb 4:15

See also: Pro 18:14, 2 Cor 11:30

ingrafted, *engrafted*

receive the *i* word   Jas 1:21

inherit, *gain, receive*

seed shall *i* earth   Psa 25:13

meek shall *i* earth   37:11, Mat 5:5

wise shall *i* glory   Pro 3:35

i everlasting life   Mat 19:29

i the kingdom prepared   25:34

i eternal life   Mk 10:17, Lk 10:25,
18:18

not *i* the kingdom   1 Cor 6:9,
15:50, Gal 5:21

that overcometh shall *i*   Rev 21:7

inheritance *(see inherit)*

the earnest of our *i*   Eph 1:14

i of saints   Col 1:12

promise of eternal *i*   Heb 9:15

an *i* incorruptible   1 Pet 1:4

iniquity, *sin, perverseness*

visiting *i* of fathers   Deut 5:9

they that plow *i* reap   Job 4:8

pardon mine *i*, for it   Psa 25:11

wash me from my *i* — 51:2
I was shapen in *i* — 51:5
he that soweth *i* shall — Pro 22:8
bruised for our *i* — Isa 53:5
your *i* have separated — 59:2
add *i* to *i* — 69:27
in bond of *i* — Acts 8:23
servants of *i* — Rom 6:19
rejoice not in *i* — 1 Cor 13:4,6
mystery of *i* doth — 2 Thes 2:7
depart from *i* — 2 Tim 2:19
redeem us from *i* — Tit 2:14
tongue is a world of *i* — Jas 3:6
See also: Amos 5:15, Rom 12:9

inn, *lodging place*
no room for them in *i* — Lk 2:7
brought him to an *i* — 10:34

innocent, *clean, guiltless*
whoever perished, being *i*? — Job 4:7
I am *i* of the blood — Mat 27:24
See also: Pro 20:9, Mat 5:8, 1 Tim 1:5, Jas 1:27, Rev 14:5

inscription, *something marked or engraved*
an altar with this *i* — Acts 17:23

inspiration, *lit. God-breathed*
scripture given by *i* — 2 Tim 3:16
See also: Lk 1:70, 2 Pet 1:21, Heb 1:1

instant, *persevering, continuing*
continuing *i* in prayer — Rom 12:12
i in season, out of — 2 Tim 4:2

instruct, *teach, make known*
who *i* him, and taught — Isa 40:14
being *i* out of law — Rom 2:18

instruction *(see instruct)*
seeing thou hatest *i* — Psa 50:17
fools despise *i* — Pro 1:7

whoso loveth *i* — 12:1
fool despiseth father's *i* — 15:5
the *i* of fools is folly — 16:22
apply thy heart to *i* — 23:12
scripture is profitable for *i* — 2 Tim 3:16

instrument, *musical instrument, tool*
praise him with stringed *i* — Psa 150:4
members *i* of unrighteousness — Rom 6:13

intangle, *entangle* (archaic)
how they might *i* him — Mat 22:5
be not *i* with yoke of — Gal 5:1
i with affairs of — 2 Tim 2:4

integrity, *sincerity, perfection*
let *i* preserve me — Psa 25:21
the *i* of the upright — Pro 11:3
better is poor in *i* — 19:1
just man walketh in his *i* — 20:7

intent, *purpose*
i to build a tower — Lk 14:28
discerner of *i* of heart — Heb 4:12

intercession, *pleading for*
spirit maketh *i* for us — Rom 8:26
ever liveth to make *i* — Heb 7:25
See also: Jno 14:6, 1 Jno 2:1

intreat, *ask, plead*
i him as a father — 1 Tim 5:1
wisdom is easy to be *i* — Jas 3:17
See also: entreat

invisible, *unseen*
i things are clearly — Rom 1:20
the image of *i* God — Col 1:15
king immortal, *i* — 1 Tim 1:17
seeing him who is *i* — Heb 11:27
See also: Ex 33:23, Jno 1:18

inward, *within*

    law in their *i* parts   Jer 31:33

    law of God after *i* man   Rom 7:22

    the *i* man is renewed   2 Cor 4:16

iron

    thy neck is *i* sinew   Isa 48:4

    conscience seared with hot *i* 1 Tim
                              4:2

Isaac, *son of Abraham,* Gen 15:4,
17:16, 21:2, 22:7, 35:29

Isaiah, *son of Amoz, prophet about
750–690 B.C.,* 2 Ki 19:2 ff, 2 Chr
26:22 ff, Isa 1:1, 7:1, 37:6

Iscariot *(see Judas)*

Ishbosheth, *son of Saul,* 2 Sam 2:8 ff

Ishmael, *son of Abraham by Hagar,*
Gen 16:15, 17:20, 25:12

Israel, *name given to Jacob and of people he fathered. Also northern kingdom after 931 B.C. as distinguished
from Judah.* Gen 32:28, 35:10, Hos
12:3

issue, *that which comes forth*

    to God belong the *i*   Psa 68:20

    of heart are *i* of life   Pro 4:23

J

Jabbok, *river which empties into the
Jordan,* Gen 32:22

Jabel, *son of Lamech,* Gen 4:20 f

Jabesh-Gilead, *city east of the Jordan,*
Judg 21, 1 Sam 11

Jabin, *two different kings of Hazor
(city north of Sea of Galilee),* Josh
11:1, Judg 4

Jacob, *son of Isaac, father of 12 tribes
of Israel,* Gen 25:26—49:33

Jael, *Kenite woman who killed Sisera,*
Judg 4:17, 5:24

Jairus, *father of girl raised by Jesus,*
Mat 9:18, Mk 5:22, Lk 8:41

James, *the son of Zebedee,* Mat 4:21,
Mk 1:19, Lk 5:10 *(see also:* Mat 10:2,
17:1, 26:36, Acts 12:2); *the son of
Alphaeus,* Mat 10:3, Mk 3:18, Lk
6:15, Acts 1:13; *the Lord's brother,*
Mat 13:55, Mk 6:3, Acts 15:13 ff,
21:18, Gal 1:19, Jas 1:1; *the Less,*
Mat 27:56, Mk 15:40, Lk 24:10

Jannes and Jambres, *Egyptian magi-
cians who opposed Moses,* 2 Tim 3:8,
(cf. Ex 7:11)

Japheth, *son of Noah,* Gen 5:32, 9:27,
10:1 ff

Jason, Acts 17:5, Rom 16:21

jealous, *jealous, often: zealous*

    a *j* God Ex 20:5, 34:14, Deut 4:24,
                   5:9, 6:15, Josh 24:19

    j for my holy name   Ezek 39:25

    See also: Gen 37:4, 2 Cor 11:2

jealousy *(see jealous)*

    j is the rage of a man   Pro 6:34

    j is as cruel as grave   S of S 8:6

    provoke Lord to *j?*   1 Cor 10:22

Jebusites, *pre-Israelite inhabitants of
Jerusalem,* Gen 15:21, Num 13:29,
Josh 15:63

Jedidiah, *Solomon's other name,*
2 Sam 12:25

Jehoahaz, *king of Israel,* 2 Ki 10:35, 13:4

Jehoiachin, *king of Judah,* 2 Ki 24:6, 2 Chr 36:8

Jehoiada, *priest who saved Jehoash,* 2 Ki 11:4, 12:7; *father of Beniah,* 2 Sam 8:18, 1 Ki 1:8; *(other minor characters also bore the name)*

Jehoiakim, *king of Judah,* 2 Ki 23:34, 24:1, 2 Chr 36:4

Jehoram, *king of Judah,* 1 Ki 22:50, 2 Ki 8:16; *Joram, king of Israel,* 2 Ki 1:17, 3:1, 9:24

Jehoshaphat, *king of Judah,* 1 Ki 15:24, 22:50

Jehovah, *the personal name of God, probably means "the existing one,"* Ex 6:3, Psa 83:18, Isa 12:2

Jehu, *prophet,* 1 Ki 16:1; *king of Israel,* 1 Ki 19:16, 2 Ki 9:1, 10:1 ff

Jephthah, *judge,* Judg 11:4 ff

Jeroboam, *kings of Israel, (I)* 1 Ki 11:28 ff, 14:20; *(II)* 2 Ki 13:13, 14:23–29

Jeremiah, *prophet about 626–586 B.C.,* Jer 1:1 ff

Jericho, *city by Jordan,* Josh 2:1, 6:20

Jerusalem, *city made capital of Judah and Israel by David,* Josh 10:1 ff, 2 Sam 5:6, Lk 2:22, etc.

Jesse, *David's father,* Ruth 4:22, 1 Sam 16:5

Jesus, *shortened and Grecianized form of Joshua which means "savior,"* Mat 1:16,21,25, 2:1, Mk 1:9, Lk 1:31, Jno 1:29, etc.
See also for connection with Christ: Mat 1:1, Mk 1:1, Acts 2:38, etc.

Jethro, *Moses' father-in-law,* Ex 18:12

Jew, *shortened form of Judah; Israelites first called in* 2 Ki 16:6

jewels, *ornament, treasure*
lips of knowledge are *j*   Pro 20:15
when I make up my *j*   Mal 3:17

Jezebel, *wife of Ahab,* 1 Ki 16:31, 18:4, 21:1 ff, 2 Ki 9:30

Jezreel, *city and valley of northern Palestine,* Josh 17:16, 19:8, Hos 1:5

Joab, *David's general,* 2 Sam 8:16, 3:23, 18:14, 1 Ki 1:7, 2:5 ff

Joash, or Jehoash, *king of Judah,* 2 Ki 11:2, 12:1,20; *king of Israel, 2 Ki 13:9,25, 14:16*

Job, *hero of book of Job,* Job 1:1, Ezek 14:14

Jochebed, *Moses' mother,* Ex 6:20, Num 26:59

Joel, *prophet,* Joel 1:1 ff, Acts 2:16

John, *the Baptist,* Mat 3:1 ff, 4:12, 14:2, Mk 1:4 ff, Lk 1:60, 3:2 ff, 7:19 ff, Jno 1:6–8,15–36, *see also:* Isa 40:3, Mal 4:5; *the Apostle,* Mat 4:21, Mk 1:19, Lk 5:10, Jno 13:23, 19:27, Acts 3:1 ff, 1 Jno 1:1 ff, Rev 1:1 ff

John Mark, see Mark

join, *to unite*
let us *j* ourselves to   Jer 50:5
what God hath *j*   Mat 19:6, Mk 10:9
perfectly *j* in same   1 Cor 1:10
j to the Lord   6:17
the whole body fitly *j*   Eph 4:16

joint, *a fitting together*
thigh out of *j*   Gen 32:25
which every *j* supplieth   Eph 4:16
by *j* knit together   Col 2:19

Jonah, *prophet,* 2 Ki 14:25, Jonah 1:1, Mat 12:39

Jonathan, *son of Saul,* 1 Sam 13:2, 18:1, 31:2, 2 Sam 1:17

Joppa, *Jaffa, city west of Jerusalem on coast of Mediterranean,* 2 Chr 2:16, Acts 9:36, 10:5 ff

Jordan, *river flowing from Sea of Galilee to Dead Sea,* Josh 3, 2 Ki 5:10, Mat 3:5, etc.

Joseph, *son of Jacob,* Gen 30:34, 37:5 ff, 37:28; *Mary's husband,* Mat 1:19, Lk 1:27; *of Arimathaea,* Mat 27:57, Mk 15:42, Lk 23:50, Jno 19:38

Joshua, *son of Nun, and Moses' successor,* 1 Chr 7:27, Heb 4:8, Ex 17:9, 24:13, Num 13:16, 27:18, Josh 24:29

Josiah, *king of Judah,* 1 Ki 13:2, 2 Ki 22:1 ff, 23:29

Jotham, *son of Gideon,* Judg 9:5 ff; *king of Judah,* 2 Ki 15:32, 2 Chr 27:1 ff

journey, *walk, go about*

Lord make *j* prosperous Gen 24:21
took *j* into far country Lk 15:13
in *j* often 2 Cor 11:26

joy, *gladness*

j of Lord is strength Neh 8:10
j of hypocrite but for Job 20:5
sorrow is turned to *j* 41:22
restore *j* of salvation Psa 51:12
with *j* shall draw water Isa 12:3
meek shall increase *j* 29:19
ye shall go out with *j* 55:12
with *j* receiveth it Mat 13:20, 8:13
the *j* of thy Lord Mat 25:21
my *j* is fulfilled Jno 3:29

your *j* might be full 15:11, 16:24
kingdom of God is *j* Rom 14:17
fill you with all *j* 15:13
count it all *j* Jas 1:2
See also: Psa 112:1, Lk 1:14

joyful *(see joy)*

my soul shall be *j* in Psa 35:9
make a *j* noise 66:1, 95:1, 98:6
soul shall be *j* in God Isa 61:10
exceeding *j* in all 2 Cor 7:4

Jubal, *son of Lamech,* Gen 4:21

Judah, *son of Jacob,* Gen 29:35, 43:3, 49:8; *one of twelve tribes,* 1 Ki 12:21

Judas, *Iscariot, apostle who betrayed Jesus,* Mat 10:4, 26:14, Jno 13:26, 18:2, Mat 27:5, Acts 1:18; *for other Judases, see also:* Mat 10:3, 13:55, Mk 6:3, Jude 1:1 ff

judge (verb), *discern, decide*

Lord shall *j* people Deut 32:36, Psa 7:8, 50:4, Heb 10:30
he shall *j* world in righteousness Psa 96:13, 98:9, Acts 17:31
j not, that ye be not *j* Mat 7:1
j righteous judgment Jno 7:24
Let us not *j* another Rom 14:13
j every man according to Rev 20:13

judge (noun)

j of all the earth Gen 18:25
who made thee *j* Ex 2:14, Acts 7:27
God is *j* himself Psa 50:6
who made me *j* over Lk 12:14
j of quick and dead Acts 10:42
the Lord, righteous *j* 2 Tim 4:8
to God the *j* of all Heb 12:23
not doer of law, but *j* Jas 4:11

the *j* standeth at door   5:9

judgment, *justice*
  judge with just *j*   Deut 16:18
  ungodly not stand in *j*   Psa 1:5
  let *j* run down like   Amos 5:24
  in danger of *j*   Mat 5:21
  committed all *j* to Son   Jno 5:22
  judge righteous *j*   7:24
  now is *j* of this world   12:31
  reasoned of *j* to come   Acts 24:25
  stand in *j*   Rom 14:10, 2 Cor 5:10
  after this the *j*   Heb 9:27
  fearful looking for *j*   10:27
  j begin at house of   1 Pet 4:17

just, *upright, righteous*
  Noah was a *j* man   Gen 6:9
  that ruleth must be *j*   2 Sam 23:3
  a *j* man falleth   Pro 24:16
  way of *j* is uprightness   Isa 26:7
  j shall live by faith   Hab 2:4, Rom
              1:17, Gal 3:11, Heb 10:38
  sendeth rain on *j* and   Mat 5:45
  ninety and nine *j* persons   Lk 15:7
  not hearers of law *j*   Rom 2:13
  whatsoever things are *j*   Phil 4:8
  j recompense of reward   Heb 2:2

justice, *rightness*
  to do *j* is better   Pro 21:3
  establish throne in *j*   Isa 9:7

justification *(see justify)*
  Christ raised for our *j*   Rom 4:25
  free gift came on all to *j*   5:18

justify, *declare guiltless*
  in thy sight no man be *j* Psa 143:2
  wisdom is *j* of her children   Mat
              11:19, Lk 7:35
  by words thou shalt be *j* Mat 12:37
  willing to *j* himself   Lk 10:29

that believe are *j*   Acts 13:39
j freely by   Rom 3:24, Tit 3:7
a man *j* by faith   Rom 3:28
being *j* by faith   5:1
j in the Spirit   1 Tim 3:16

justly *(see justice)*
  Lord require of thee but to do *j*?
                                    Mic 6:8

K

Kadesh-Barnea, *city of southern Palestine,* Num 32:8, Deut 9:23, Josh 10:41, 14:7

keep, *keep, guard, perform*
  shall *k* the way of Lord Gen 18:19
  remember sabbath to *k*   Ex 20:8,
              31:13 ff, Deut 5:12,15
  Lord bless thee and *k*   Num 6:24
  k thy tongue from evil   Psa 34:13
  angels charge to *k*   91:11, Lk 4:10
  except Lord *k* city   Psa 127:1
  Lord shall *k* thy foot   Pro 3:26
  fear God *k* commandments   Ecc
                                    12:13
  in temple, let earth *k*   Hab 2:20
  shepherds *k* watch by   Lk 2:18
  Mary *k* in her heart   2:19,51
  blessed that hear word of God and
  k   11:28
  k my sayings shall never   Jno 8:51
  if ye love me *k* commandments
                                    14:15
  love me *k* my words   14:23
  k not my sayings   14:24

those thou gave me I *k* 17:12
let women *k* silent 1 Cor 14:34
k the unity of spirit Eph 4:3
peace of God *k* hearts Phil 4:7
k thyself pure 1 Tim 5:22
k that committed 6:20
k himself unspotted Jas 1:27
we know if we *k* commandments
1 Jno 2:3
love of God that we *k* 5:3
k yourselves in love Jude 21
are *k* by power of God 1 Pet 1:5
they which *k* the commandments
Rev 14:12

keeper *(see keep)*
am I my brother's *k*? Gen 4:9
Lord is thy *k* Psa 121:5
k of house tremble Ecc 12:3
chaste, *k* at home Tit 2:5

key, *key, opener*
k of the kingdom Mat 16:19
k of bottomless pit Rev 9:1, 20:21

kick, *kick, resist*
hard to *k* against Acts 9:5, 26:14

kill, *put to death*
thou shall not *k* Ex 20:13, Deut
5:17, Mat 5:21, Rom 13:9
k any man Lev 24:17, Num 35:30
for thy sake are we *k* Psa 44:22,
Rom 8:36
wrath *k* foolish man Job 5:2
time to *k*, time to heal Ecc 3:3
k prophets Mat 23:37, Lk 13:34
save life, or *k*? Mk 3:4
do not *k* 10:19, Lk 18:20, Jas 2:11
fear not them which *k* body Lk
12:4
rise Peter, *k* and eat Acts 10:13

k the Lord Jesus 1 Thes 2:15
letter *k*, spirit giveth 2 Cor 3:6
ye *k* and desire to have Jas 4:2
he that *k* with the sword Rev
13:10

kind, *useful, beneficial*
God is *k* to unthankful Lk 6:35
charity suffereth and is *k* 1 Cor
13:4
be *k* one to another Eph 4:32

kind, *species, type*
fruit after *k* Gen 1:11,12,21,25,
6:20
every beast after *k* 8:19
a *k* of firstfruits Jas 1:18

kindle, *to burn*
contentious man *k* strife Pro 26:21
a little fire *k* Jas 3:5

kindly, *tenderly*
k affectioned one to Rom 12:10

kindness, *love*
God of great *k* Neh 9:17
his merciful *k* is great Psa 117:2
he is of great *k* Joel 2:13
to brotherly *k* charity 2 Pet 1:7

kindred, *brother, relation*
get thee from *k* Gen 12:1, Acts 7:3
all *k* of earth blessed 3:25
all *k* of earth shall Rev 1:7

kine, *cows*
seven well-favored *k* Gen 41:2
hear this, ye *k* Amos 4:1

king, *ruler*
Melchizedek, *k* Gen 14:18, Heb
7:1
new *k* over Egypt Ex 1:8
trees went to anoint *k* Judg 9:8
no *k* over Israel 17:6, 18:1, 19:1,
21:25

make us a *k* to judge — 1 Sam 8:5
God save the *k* — 10:24
Lord is *k* forever — Psa 10:16, 29:10
Lord of hosts, he is *k* — 24:10
mine eyes seen *k* — Isa 6:5
creator is *k* — 43:15
God, everlasting *k* — Jer 10:10
k cometh — Zech 9:9, Mat 21:5
to make him *k* — Jno 6:15
behold thy *k* cometh — 12:15
Pilate said, art thou *K?* — 18:37
now to the *k* eternal — 1 Tim 1:17
k of kings, and Lord of — 6:15
fear God, honour *k* — 1 Pet 2:17
Lord of Lords, *k* — Rev 17:14, 19:16

kingdom, *rulership, nation*

ye shall be *k* of priests — Ex 19:6
thine is *k* — 1 Chr 29:11, Mat 6:13
k is the Lord's — Psa 22:28
thy *k* come — Mat 6:10
seek ye first *k* — 6:33
k divided is — 12:25
k is come unto you — 12:28
rich man to enter *k* — 19:24, Mk
— 10:23, Lk 18:24
inherit *k* prepared — Mat 25:34
my *k* is not of world — Jno 18:36
k of God is not meat — Rom 14:17
translated into *k* — Col 1:13
k cannot be moved — Heb 12:28
See also: Mk 1:14, Acts 8:12, 20:25,
28:31, Mk 10:24, 14:25, Lk 4:43,
17:20, 18:25, 21:31, 22:18, Rom 6:9

kingdom of heaven

k of *h* is at hand — Mat 3:2, 4:7, 10:7
theirs is the *k* of *h* — 5:3
give keys of *k* of *h* — 16:19

Kish, *father of Saul,* 1 Sam 9:1, 10:11,
14:51

kiss, *kiss, touch*

k of an enemy deceitful — Pro 27:6
thou gavest me no *k* — Lk 7:45
betray son of man with *k* — 22:48
salute with holy *k* — Rom 16:16
See also: 1 Cor 16:20, 2 Cor 13:12,
1 Thes 5:26, 1 Pet 5:14

knee

not bowed *k* to Baal — 1 Ki 19:18
every *k* shall bow — Isa 45:23, Rom
— 14:11, Phil 2:10

knew *(see know)*

profess, I never *k* — Mat 7:23
the world *k* him not — Jno 1:10
he *k* what was in man — 2:25
who *k* no sin — 2 Cor 5:21
by wisdom *k* not God — 1 Cor 1:21
because it *k* him not — 1 Jno 3:1

knit, *bind*

Jonathan *k* to David — 1 Sam 18:1
sheet *k* at four corners — Acts 10:11
hearts *k* together — Col 2:2,19

knock, *knock, beat*

k shall be opened — Mat 7:8, Lk
— 11:10
I stand at the door and *k* — Rev 3:20

know, *understand, recognize*

I *k* my redeemer liveth — Job 19:25
be still and *k* that — Psa 46:10
heart to *k* wisdom — Ecc 1:17, 7:25
living *k* they shall die — 9:5
all flesh shall *k* — Isa 49:26
I *k* works and thoughts — 66:18
I *k* way of man not — Jer 10:23
let not right hand *k* — Mat 6:3
ye err, not *k* scriptures — 22:29

ye *k* not hour	24:42
I *k* you not	25:12
ye *k* not scriptures	Mk 12:24
he shall *k* doctrine	Jno 7:17
sheep *k* his voice	10:4
I *k* my sheep	10:27
determined not to *k*	1 Cor 2:2
we *k* in part	13:9
I *k* in part	13:12
k the love of Christ	Eph 3:19
I *k* whom I believed	2 Tim 1:12
I *k* thy works	Rev 2:2,13, 3:8

knoweth *(see know)*

Lord *k* way of righteous	Psa 1:6
O God thou *k* my foolish	69:5
who *k* the spirit of man	Ecc 3:1
the ox *k* his owner	Isa 1:3
Lord *k* them trust in him	Nah 1:7
Father *k* what need	Mat 6:8
any man think he *k*	1 Cor 8:2
him that *k* to do good	Jas 4:12
the world *k* us not	1 Jno 3:21
k not God, for God is love	4:8

knowledge *(see know)*

tree of *k* of good and	Gen 2:9,17
night to night show *k*	Psa 19:2
such *k* too wonderful	139:6
fear of Lord beginning of *k*	Pro 1:7
fools hate *k*	1:22
wise men lay up *k*	10:14
a prudent man concealeth *k*	12:23
k increaseth sorrow	Ecc 1:18
people destroyed lack *k*	Hos 4:6
zeal, not according to *k*	Rom 10:2
k puffeth up	1 Cor 8:1
whether there be *k*, it shall vanish	13:8
filled with *k* of his	Col 1:19

come to *k* of	1 Tim 2:4, 2 Tim 3:7
wise, endured with *k*	Jas 3:13
to virtue *k*, to *k*	2 Pet 1:5
grow in *k* of Lord	3:18

known *(see know)*

you only have I *k*	Amos 3:2
that shall not be *k*	Mat 10:26, Lk 8:17, 12:2
tree *k* by fruits	Mat 12:33, Lk 6:44
k mind of God	Rom 11:34, 1 Cor 2:16
from a child *k* scriptures	2 Tim 3:15

Korah, *rebelled against Moses,* Num 16:1 ff, Jude 11

L

Laban, *Jacob's father-in-law,* Gen 24:29, 30:36, 31:2,12,55, 32:4

labour, *work, burden*

six days *l*	Ex 20:9, Deut 5:13
firstfruits of thy *l*	Ex 23:16
they *l* in vain	Psa 127:1
gathereth by *l* shall	Pro 13:11
in all *l* there is profit	14:23
l not to be rich	23:4
profit hath man of *l*	Ecc 1:3
sleep of *l* man sweet	5:12
rejoice in *l* this	5:19
l of foolish wearieth	10:15
I have *l* in vain	Isa 49:4
they shall not *l* in vain	65:23
come to me all that *l*	Mat 11:28
l not for meat which	Jno 6:27

your *l* is not in vain   1 Cor 15:58
I have not *l* in vain   Phil 2:16
and our *l* be in vain   1 Thes 3:5
l to enter into rest   Heb 4:11
I know why thy *l* and patience Rev
                                      2:2
See also: Gen 2:15, 3:19, Ecc 9:10,
Col 4:11, 2 Thes 3:10

labourer, *(see labour)*
harvest plenteous, but *l* few   Mat
                              9:37,38, Lk 10:2
l is worthy of his hire   10:7
l together with God   1 Cor 3:9
l worthy of reward   1 Tim 5:18

lack, *shortage, need*
if there shall *l* five   Gen 18:28
had no *l*   Ex 16:18, 2 Cor 8:15
destroyed for *l* of knowledge   Hos
                                       4:6
what *l* I yet?   Mat 19:20
one thing thou *l*   Mk 10:21, Lk
                                       18:22
supply *l* of service   Phil 2:30
that ye *l* nothing   1 Thes 4:12
l wisdom ask of God   Jas 1:5
l these things is blind   2 Pet 1:9
See also: Psa 34:9, 1 Jno 3:17, Rev
3:17

ladder, *ladder, stairs*
behold a *l* set up   Gen 28:12

lake, *pool, body of water*
Jesus stood by *l*   Lk 5:1 f, 8:23 f
both cast in *l* fire   Rev 19:20, 20:10
                                   ff, 21:8

lamb, *young sheep*
God will provide a *l*   Gen 22:8
they shall take a *l*   Ex 12:3,21
took poor man's *l*   2 Sam 12:4

as a *l* to slaughter   Isa 53:7, Jer
                                      11:19
behold *L* of God   Jno 1:29,36
Jesus saith, feed my *l*   21:15
l dumb before shearer   Acts 8:32
as *l* without blemish   1 Pet 1:19
midst of elders stood *L*   Rev 5:6

lame, *crippled*
legs of *l* are not equal   Pro 26:7
l walk   Mat 11:5, 15:31, Lk 7:22

Lamech, *descendant of Cain*, Gen 4:18;
father of Noah, Gen 5:25 ff

lamp, *torch, flame, light*
burning *l* that passed   Gen 15:17
thy word is *l* to feet   Psa 119:105
commandment is a *l*   Pro 6:23
candlestick and seven *l*   Zech 4:2
ten virgins look *l*   Mat 25:1 ff

land, *land, earth*
let the dry *l* appear   Gen 1:9
to *l* I show   12:1, Acts 7:3
thy seed will I give this *l*   Gen
   12:7, 15:18, 24:7, 48:4, Ex 32:13
l not able to bear them   Gen 13:6
unto thy seed *l*   17:8, 28:13, 35:12
from *l* of living   Jer 11:19
Barnabas having *l*   Acts 4:37

landmark, *border markers*
not remove *l*   Deut 19:14, Pro
                                22:28, 23:10

language, *dialect, tongue*
whole earth was one *l*   Gen 11:1
no *l* where voice is   Psa 19:3
See also: Mk 16:17, Acts 2:4, 1 Cor
14:2, Rev 5:9

languish, *become weak*
world *l* and fadeth   Isa 24:4

Laodicea, *city of Asia Minor, one of seven mentioned in Revelation*, Col 2:1, 4:13,15,16, Rev 3:14

large, *big, great*
l upper room   Mk 14:15, Lk 22:12
l letter I have written   Gal 6:11

lasciviousness, *excess*
out of heart proceed *l*   Mk 7:22
works of flesh, *l*   Gal 5:19

last, *last, latter*
Lord, first and *l*   Isa 41:4, 44:6, 48:12, Rev 1:11,17, 2:8, 22:13
l state worse   Mat 12:45, Lk 11:26
first shall be *l* and   Mat 19:30, 20:16, Mk 10:31, Lk 11:26
l error worse than first   Mat 27:64
raise it again at *l* Jno 6:39,40,44,54
l enemy is death   1 Cor 15:26
l day perilous times   2 Tim 3:1
spoken in *l* day by his Son Heb 1:2
come in *l* day scoffers   2 Pet 3:3
See also: Ecc 7:8, Mk 9:35, Rev 22:13

latter, *later than*
give first and *l* rain   Deut 11:14
stand at *l* day   Job 19:25
and *l* rain in season   Jer 5:24
in *l* times some depart   1 Tim 4:1

laugh, *laugh, scorn*
wherefore did Sarah *l?* Gen 18:13
in heavens shalt *l*   Psa 2:4
time to weep, time to *l*   Ecc 3:4
that weep, ye shall *l*   Lk 6:21
See also: Pro 17:22, Ecc 7:3,6

laughed *(see laugh)*
Abraham *l*   Gen 17:17, 18:12
l him to scorn Mat 9:24, Mk 5:40, Lk 8:53

laughter *(see laugh)*
l turned to mourning   Jas 4:9

launch, *go forth*
Simon *l* out into deep   Lk 5:4

law, *decree, commandment*
walk in my *l*   Ex 16:4
in his *l* doth he meditate   Psa 1:2
l of his God in his heart   37:31
out of Zion shall go *l* Isa 2:3, Mic 4:2
not to destroy *l*   Mat 5:17
great commandment in *l*   22:36
weightier matters of *l*   23:23
many as sinned without *l*   Rom 2:12
not hearers of *l* are   2:13
by deeds of *l*   3:20,28, Gal 2:16
ye are not under the *l*   Rom 6:14
dead to the *l*   7:4
another *l* warring   7:23
end of *l* for righteousness   10:4
love is fulfilling of *l*   13:10
brother goeth to *l* with   1 Cor 6:6
not just by works of *l*   Gal 2:16
no man justified by the *l*   3:11
l was our schoolmaster   3:24
put my *l* into the mind   Heb 8:10
put my *l* in their hearts   10:16
fulfil royal *l*   Jas 2:8
l of liberty   2:12

lawful *(see law)*
what is *l* and right   Ezek 18:5
do what is not *l*   Mat 12:2, Mk 2:24
is it *l* to heal on sabbath? Mat 12:10,12, Mk 3:4, 6:9, 14:3
not crown, except *l*   2 Tim 2:5

lay, *place, put*
   l up treasures   Mat 6:20, Lk 12:21
   to *l* hands on him   Mat 21:46, Lk
           20:19
   nowhere to *l* head   Mat 8:20, Lk
           9:58
   friends went to *l*   Mk 3:21
   l down life for   Jno 10:15,17
   l it down of myself   10:18
   l down life for friends   15:13
   l not this sin to   Acts 7:60
   I *l* in Sion a stumblingstone   Rom
           9:33
   l hands suddenly on   1 Tim 5:22
   l hold on eternal   6:12,19
   l hold on hope set   Heb 6:18
   l aside every weight   12:1
   l in Sion a chief   1 Pet 2:6
   l down lives for   1 Jno 3:16

laid *(see lay)*
   axe *l* to root   Mat 3:10, Lk 3:9
   firstborn *l* in manger   2:7
   never man was *l*   23:53, Jno 19:41
   l money at apostles'   Acts 4:37, 5:2
   l down their clothes   7:58
   l up for me a crown   2 Tim 4:8

laying *(see lay)*
   l on of apostles' hands   Acts 8:18
   with *l* on of hands   1 Tim 4:14
   not *l* again foundation   Heb 6:1
   l aside all malice   1 Pet 2:1

Lazarus, *hero of one of Jesus' stories,*
Lk 16:20; *man that Jesus raised,* Jno
11:2, 12:2,17

lead, *guide, cause to go*
   pillar of cloud *l* them   Ex 13:21
   l me in thy righteousness   Psa 5:8
   l beside still waters   23:2,3

   light and truth, let them *l*   43:3
   l to rock higher than I   61:2
   a little child shall *l*   Isa 11:6
   l us not into   Mat 6:13, Lk 11:4
   wide is way *l* to   Mat 7:13
   if blind *l* blind   15:14, Lk 6:39
   goodness of God *l* to repentance
           Rom 2:4
   we may *l* a quiet life   1 Tim 2:2
   See also: Psa 16:11, Pro 16:9, Jer
   3:4

leaf
   sew fig *l* made aprons   Gen 3:7
   in mouth was olive *l*   8:11
   his *l* shall not wither   Psa 1:3
   nothing but *l*   Mat 21:19, Mk 11:13
   l for healing nations   Rev 22:2

Leah, *first wife of Jacob,* Gen 29:16,
30:19, Ruth 4:11

learn, *gain knowledge*
   l war any more   Isa 2:4, Mic 4:3
   l of me, for I am meek   Mat 11:29
   l doth make thee mad   Acts 26:24
   written for our *l*   Rom 15:4
   ye have not so *l* Christ   Eph 4:20
   l in state to be content   Phil 4:11
   woman *l* in silence   1 Tim 2:11
   ever *l* and never able   2 Tim 3:7
   yet *l* he obedience   Heb 5:8
   See also: Pro 15:14, 16:16, 24:4,
   Hab 2:14

least, *smallest*
   l commandments   Mat 5:19
   l in kingdom   11:11, Lk 7:28
   l of these my brethren   Mat 25:40
   I am *l* of the apostles   1 Cor 15:9
   See also: Mat 13:31, Lk 16:10, Eph
   3:8

leave, *forsake, give*

l father and mother Gen 2:24, Mat 19:5, Mk 10:1, Eph 5:31

not *l* my soul in hell   Psa 16:10, Acts 2:27

and not to *l* other undone   Mat 23:23

not *l* you comfortless   Jno 14:18

my peace I *l* with you   14:27

I will never *l* thee   Heb 13:5

leaven, *yeast, fermenting agent*

kingdom is like *l*   Mat 13:33, Lk 13:21

beware of *l* Pharisees   Mat 16:6,11, Mk 8:15, Lk 12:1

little *l* leaveneth   1 Cor 5:6 ff, Gal 5:8 ff

leaving *(see leave)*

l principles of Christ   Heb 6:1

l an example   1 Pet 2:21

Lebanon, *white, snowy; country and mountains north of Palestine,* Deut 1:7, Josh 1:4, Judg 3:3, *etc.*

led *(see lead)*

Moses *l* flock to back of   Ex 3:1

l thee forty years   Deut 8:2, 29:5

l them with a cloud   Psa 78:14

l as sheep to slaughter   Acts 8:32

are *l* by Spirit of God   Rom 8:14

if ye be *l* by spirit   Gal 5:18

left *(see leave)*

l us a remnant   Isa 1:9, Rom 9:29

l nets   Mat 4:20,22

l not one stone   24:2, Mk 13:2, Lk 21:6

soul was not *l* in hell   Acts 2:31

leg

came and brake *l*   Jno 19:32

legion, *many, a troop*

name is *L*   Mk 5:9, Lk 8:30

lend, *give, make a loan*

not *l* on usury   Deut 23:19

if *l* them of whom   Lk 6:34,35

leopard

l shall lie with kid   Isa 11:6

can *l* change his spots?   Jer 13:23

leper, *one who has leprosy*

put out of camp every *l*   Num 5:2

Naaman was a *l*   2 Ki 5:1

there came a *l*   Mat 8:2, Mk 1:40

ten men that were *l*   Lk 17:12

leprous, *scabby, scaly*

hand was *l* as snow   Ex 4:6

Miriam became *l*   Num 12:10

less, *beneath, small*

l light to rule night   Gen 1:16

mother of James the *l*   Mk 15:40

more I love, *l* am I   2 Cor 12:15

let, *to prevent, hinder* (archaic)

but was *l* hitherto   Rom 1:13

now letteth, will *l*   2 Thes 2:7

let down, *to lower*

l d nets for   Lk 5:4

l him *d*, in basket   Acts 9:25, 2 Cor 11:33

four corners, *l d*   Acts 10:11

letter, *anything written*

by *l* transgress law   Rom 2:27

not in the oldness of the *l*   7:6

not of *l* but of Spirit   2 Cor 3:6

be not shaken by *l*   2 Thes 2:2

Levi, *son of Jacob,* Gen 29:34, Ex 1:2, Num 3:17; *another name for Matthew,* Mk 2:14, Lk 5:27

Levite, *a descendant of Levi,* Ex 4:14, 25:32, Num 1:47, etc.

liar, *deceiver*

all men are *l*	Psa 116:11
poor man better than *l*	Pro 19:22
and thou be found *l*	30:6
God true, every man a *l*	Rom 3:4
sinned, make him *l*	1 Jno 1:10
all *l* have part in	Rev 21:8

liberally, *freely, open-handedly*

God giveth all men *l*   Jas 1:5
See also: Pro 11:25, Lk 6:38, Acts 4:34, 2 Cor 9:7

libertines, *freed slaves*

called synagogue of *l*   Acts 6:9

liberty, *freedom*

set at *l* them bruised	Lk 4:18
from bondage into *l*	Rom 8:21
take heed lest *l* of	1 Cor 8:9
stand fast in the *l*	Gal 5:1
ye have been called to *l*	5:13
perfect law of *l*	Jas 1:25
be judged by the law of *l*	2:12
not using *l* for cloke	1 Pet 2:16
they promise them *l*	2 Pet 2:19

See also: Jno 8:22, Rom 7:6

lie, *deceit, falsehood*

such as turn aside to *l*	Psa 40:4
false witness will *l*	Pro 14:5
he that speaketh *l*	19:9
make people trust in *l*	Jer 28:15
changed truth unto *l*	Rom 1:25
I *l* not	9:1, 1 Tim 2:7
l not one to another	Col 3:9
shall believe a *l*	2 Thes 2:11
God cannot *l*	Tit 1:2, Heb 6:18
l in hypocrisy	1 Tim 4:2
l not against the truth	Jas 3:14

we *l* and do not truth	1 Jno 1:6
whatso maketh *l*	Rev 21:27, 22:15

lie, *recline, rest*

l down in green pastures   Psa 23:2

life

breathed the breath of *l*	Gen 2:7
flesh with *l*	9:4, Lev 17:14
will I require *l* of man	Gen 9:5
give *l* for *l*	Ex 21:23, Deut 19:21
blood is *l*, not eat *l*	Ex 12:23
no man sure of *l*	Job 24:22
out of heart are issues of *l*	Pro 4:23
whoso findeth me findeth *l*	8:35
followeth mercy, find *l*	21:21
wisdom giveth *l*	Ecc 7:12
no thought for *l*	Mat 6:25, Lk 12:22
lose his *l* shall find it	Mat 10:39, 16:25, Mk 8:35
into *l* with one	Mat 18:9, Mk 9:45
give *l* a ransom	Mat 20:28, Mk 10:45
l consisteth not in	Lk 12:15
l more than meat	12:23
I am the bread of *l*	Jno 6:35,48
words I speak to you, are *l*	6:63
resurrection and *l*	11:25, 14:6
men that have hazarded *l*	Acts 15:26
walk in newness of *l*	Rom 6:4
to be spiritually minded is *l*	8:6
no man *l* to self	14:7
if in this *l* only	1 Cor 15:19
spirit giveth *l*	2 Cor 3:6
your *l* is hid, with Christ	Col 3:3
receive crown of *l*	Jas 1:12
what is your *l*? a vapour	4:14

things pertaining to *l*   2 Pet 1:3
lay down *l* for brethren   1 Jno 3:16
I will give crown of *l*   Rev 2:10

lift, *raise*
   as Moses *l* up serpent   Jno 3:14
   I, if I be *l* up, will draw   12:32

light, *not heavy*
   l thing that should   Isa 49:6
   yoke easy, burden *l*   Mat 11:30
   l affliction worketh   2 Cor 4:17

light, *radiance*
   God said, Let there be *l*   Gen 1:3
   pillar gave *l* by night   Ex 14:20
   Lord is my *l* and salvation Psa 27:1
   and a *l* to my paths·   119:105
   seen great *l*   Isa 9:2, Mat 4:16
   l of world   5:14,15
   life was the *l* of men   Jno 1:4
   l is come into world   3:19
   one doeth evil hateth *l*   3:20
   I am *l* of world   8:12, 9:5
   l to the Gentiles   Acts 13:47
   Christ shall give *l*   Eph 5:14
   l shine in dark place   2 Pet 1:19
   walk in *l* as he   1 Jno 1:7
   he that saith he is in the *l*   2:9

lightning
   thunders *l* and cloud   Ex 19:16
   l cometh out   Mat 24:27, Lk 17:24
   his countenance was like *l*   Mat 28:3
   as *l* fall from heaven   Lk 10:18

lights *(see light)*
   let there be *l* in   Gen 1:14
   ye shine as *l* in world   Phil 2:15
   down from Father of *l*   Jas 1:17

like, *resembling, equal to*
   who is *l* unto thee?   Ex 15:11

that wavereth is *l* a wave   Jas 1:6
l precious faith   2 Pet 1:1
we shall be *l* him   1 Jno 3:2

like (verb), *to wish, desire*
   did not *l* to retain God   Rom 1:28

likeness *(see like)*
   make men after *l*   Gen 1:26, 5:1
   in *l* of his death   Rom 6:5
   See also: Psa 17:15, 1 Cor 15:49,
   2 Cor 4:4

lilies, *spring flowers*
   consider the *l*   Mat 6:28, Lk 12:27

line, *measuring cord*
   who stretched *l* of it   Job 38:5
   their *l* gone out   Psa 19:4
   l upon *l*   Isa 28:10

linen, *cloth woven of flax*
   wrapped it in a clean *l*   Mat 27:59,
   Jno 19:40

lintel, *top of door*
   strike *l* and two posts   Ex 12:22

lion
   calf and *l* lie down   Isa 11:6
   better than dead *l*   Ecc 9:4
   devil as *l* walk about   1 Pet 5:8

lip, *edge, mouth*
   poison under *l*   Psa 140:3, Rom 3:13
   l of righteous feed   Pro 10:21
   l abomination to Lord   12:22
   a man of unclean *l*   Isa 6:5
   honoureth with *l* Mat 15:8, Mk 7:6
   his *l* speak no guile   1 Pet 3:10

listen, *see:* Psa 13:3, Isa 55:3, Mat
   11:15, Rev 2:7

listeth, *wishes, wills*
   wind bloweth where it *l*   Jno 3:8
   whithersoever *l*   Jas 3:4

little, *small*

  l lower than angels Psa 8:5, Heb 2:7
  l sleep, *l* slumber Pro 6:10, 24:33
  better is *l* with fear of 15:16
  better is *l* with righteous 16:8
  here a *l*, there a *l* Isa 28:10
  O thou of *l* faith Mat 14:31
  to whom *l* is forgiven Lk 7:47
  been faithful in *l* 19:17
  l leaven 1 Cor 5:6, Gal 5:9
  exercise profiteth *l* 1 Tim 4:8
  a *l* lower than angels Heb 2:9
  tongue is a *l* member Jas 3:5
  a *l* fire kindleth 3:5

live, *to be alive*

  tree of life *l* for ever Gen 3:22
  no man see me and *l* Ex 33:20
  not *l* by bread alone Deut 8:3, Mat 4:4, Lk 4:4
  shall he *l* again? Job 14:14
  I know my Redeemer *l* 19:25
  seek me, ye shall *l* Amos 5:4,6
  just shall *l* by Hab 2:4, Rom 1:17
  this do and shall *l* Lk 10:28
  because I *l* ye Jno 14:19
  in him we *l* and move Acts 17:28
  in that the *l* he *l* to God Rom 6:10
  if ye *l* after flesh 8:13
  l peaceably with all men 12:18
  whether we *l* we *l* unto 14:8
  I *l*; yet not I Gal 2:20
  just *l* by faith Gal 3:11, Heb 10:38
  for me to *l* is Christ Phil 1:21

lively, *living*

  begot us to *l* hope 1 Pet 1:3
  as *l* stones, are built 2:5

living, *to be alive*

  she was mother of all *l* Gen 3:20
  Noah and every *l* thing 8:1
  found in land of *l* Job 28:13
  God of *l* Mat 22:32, Mk 12:27, Lk 20:38
  why seek ye *l* among dead 24:5
  I am the *l* bread Jno 6:51
  bodies a *l* sacrifice Rom 12:1
  by a new and *l* way Heb 10:20

locust, *grasshopper*

  tomorrow I will bring *l* Ex 10:4
  l have no king Pro 30:27
  hath *l* eaten where Joel 1:4
  meat was *l* and Mat 3:4, Mk 1:6

lodge, *dwell, spend night*

  where thou *l*, I will Ruth 1:16
  birds *l* in branches Mat 13:32, Mk 4:32, Lk 13:19
  See also: Mat 8:20, Jno 1:38

loins, *thighs, flanks*

  thicker than father's *l* 1 Ki 12:10, 2 Chr 10:10
  girdle of leather about his *l* 2 Ki 1:8, Mat 3:4, Mk 1:6
  gird up thy *l* 2 Ki 4:29, 9:1, Job 38:3, 40:7, Jer 1:17
  let your *l* be girded Lk 12:35
  your *l* girt about Eph 6:14

long, *abundance, length*

  that thy days may be *l* Ex 20:12
  that tarry *l* at wine Pro 23:30
  man go to his *l* home Ecc 12:5
  for pretence make *l* prayer Mat 23:14, Mk 12:40, Lk 20:47
  if a man have *l* hair 1 Cor 11:14
  mayest live *l* on earth Eph 6:3

long-suffering, *endurance, patience*

Lord God is *l*   Ex 34:6, Num
          14:18, Psa 86:15, 2 Pet 3:9
fruit of Spirit is *l*   Gal 5:22
l of God waited   1 Pet 3:20
l of Lord is   2 Pet 3:15

look, *appearance, to look*

l not behind thee   Gen 19:17
Moses afraid to *l* on God   Ex 3:6
Lord hateth a proud *l*   Pro 6:17
high *l* and proud heart   21:4
l not upon wine when it is red
                                  23:31
that *l* out at windows   Ecc 12:3
shall man *l* to his maker   Isa 17:7
l unto me and be saved   45:22
l back, not fit for kingdom Lk 9:62
l for that blessed hope   Tit 2:13
we *l* for the Saviour   Phil 3:20
l unto Jesus the author   Heb 12:2
we *l* for new heaven   2 Pet 3:13
See also: Gen 13:14, Ecc 11:7

loose, *unfasten*

ever silver cord be *l*   Ecc 12:6
be *l* in heaven   Mat 16:19, 18:18
who is worthy to *l* seals   Rev 5:2

Lord, *master*

earth is the *L*'s   Ex 9:29, Psa 24:1,
                              1 Cor 10:26
who is on the *L*'s side   Ex 32:26
L, let him do what seemeth good
      1 Sam 3:18, 2 Sam 10:12, 1 Chr
                    19:13, Jno 21:7
know ye that *L* he is God   Psa
                                  100:3
L our *L*, how excellent   8:1
prepare way of *L* Isa 40:3, Mat 3:4,
                          Mk 1:3, Lk 3:4

what doth *L* require?   Mic 6:8
that saith, *L, L*   Mat 7:21,22, Lk
                                  13:25
place where the *L* lay   Mat 28:6
L of Sabbath   Mk 2:28, Lk 6:5
why call me *L, L*, and do not 6:46
L to whom shall we go?   Jno 6:68
ye call me master and *L*   13:13
he is *L* of all   Acts 10:36
if the *L* will   1 Cor 4:19, Jas 4:15
one *L*, one faith   Eph 4:5
King of kings, *L* of *l*   1 Tim 6:15
L God omnipotent reigneth   Rev
                                  19:6

lordship, *rule, dominion*

they rule over Gentiles exercise *l*
                        Mk 10:42, Lk 22:25

lose

findeth life shall *l* it   Mat 10:39,
              16:25, Mk 8:35, Lk 9:24
l his own soul   Mat 16:26, Mk
              8:36, Lk 9:25, 12:25

loss

I counted *l* for Christ   Phil 3:7

lost

if salt *l* savour   Mat 5:13, Mk 9:50,
                              Lk 14:34
to the *l* sheep of Israel   Mat 10:6,
                                  15:24
Son is come to save what was *l*
                        18:11, Lk 19:10
he was *l* and is found   15:24
from them that are *l*   2 Cor 4:3

Lot, *nephew of Abraham,* Gen 11:27,
      12:4, 19:16, etc.

love, *affection, compassionate concern*

l covereth sins   Pro 10:12
continue ye in my *l*   Jno 15:9

greater *l* hath no man   15:13
God commended his *l*   Rom 5:8
separate from *l* of Christ?   8:35
l be without dissimulation   12:9
by *l* unfeigned   2 Cor 6:6
prove the sincerity of your *l*   8:8
faith which worketh by *l*   Gal 5:6
fruit of Spirit is *l*   5:22
to know the *l* of Christ   Eph 3:19
forbearing one another in *l*   4:2
but speaking the truth in *l*   4:15
edifying of itself in *l*   4:16
l of money is root   1 Tim 6:10
not fear, but *l*   2 Tim 1:7
brotherly *l* continue   Heb 13:1
behold what *l* Father   1 Jno 3:1
hereby percieve we *l* of   3:16
one another, *l* is of God   4:7
God is *l*   4:8
there is no fear in *l*   4:18
l of God that we keep   5:3

love (verb)
  l thy neighbour as thyself   Lev
      19:18,34, Mat 19:19, 22:39, Mk
      12:31, Rom 13:9, Gal 5:14, Jas
      2:8
  l Lord thy God with all thy heart
      Deut 6:5, 10:12, 11:1,13,22,
      19:9, 30:6
  time to *l*, time to hate   Ecc 3:8
  l thy neighbour   Mat 5:43
  l your enemies 5:44, Lk 6:27,32,35
  if ye *l* them which *l* you Mat 5:46
  l Lord thy God   22:37, Mk
      12:30,33, Lk 10:27
  if ye *l* me, keep my   Jno 14:15
  husbands *l* your wives as Christ *l*
      church Eph 5:25,28,33, Col 3:19

C.B.C.—7

whom not seen ye *l*   1 Pet 1:8
l one another with pure   1:22
l not the world   1 Jno 2:15
not *l* in word nor tongue   3:18
l him because he first   4:19
if a man say, I *l* God   4:20
loved (see love)
  God so *l* the world   Jno 3:16
  as Father *l* me, so I *l* you   15:9
  if God so *l* us   1 Jno 4:11
loveth (see love)
  little forgiven, *l* little   Lk 7:47
  l life shall lose   Jno 12:25
  whom Lord *l* he chasteneth   Heb
                                     12:6
  every one that *l* is   1 Jno 4:7
low, *humble, down*
  made him *l* than   Psa 8:5, Heb 2:7
  high and *l*, rich and poor Psa 49:2
  pride brings *l*   Pro 29:23
lowly (see low)
  giveth grace to *l*   Psa 3:34
  l, riding on ass   Zech 9:9
  for I am meek and *l*   Mat 11:29
  walk with *l* and meek   Eph 4:2
  See also: Isa 57:15, Mat 5:3, Lk
      14:11, Rom 12:16, Phil 2:3
lucre, *gain, profit*, 1 Sam 8:3, 1 Tim
      3:3,8, Tit 1:11, 1 Pet 5:2
Luke, *physician, companion of Paul,
  author of Luke-Acts*, Col 4:14, 2 Tim
      4:11, Phil 24
lukewarm, *tepid*
  because thou art *l*   Rev 3:16
lump, *bunch, mass*
  leaveneth whole *l*   1 Cor 5:6, Gal
                                      5:9
lust, *desire*

not fulfil *l* of flesh   Gal 5:16
crucified flesh with *l*   5:24
flee youthful *l*   2 Tim 2:22
when drawn of his *l*   Jas 1:14,15
ye *l* and have not   4:2
l of flesh, *l* of eye   1 Jno 2:16
Luz, *Bethel,* Gen 28:19
Lydia, *convert of Paul,* Acts 16:14 ff
lying, *false, deceitful*
   l lips put to silence   Psa 31:18
   proud look, *l* tongue   Pro 6:17
   l lips abomination to   · 12:22
   a righteous man hateth *l*   13:5
   swearing, *l* and killing   Hos 4:2
lying, *reclining*
   babe *l* in manger   Lk 2:12,16
Lystra, *town of Asia Minor where Paul was stoned,* Acts 14:8

M

Macedonia, *province of northern Greece,* Acts 16:9, 17:1, 2 Cor 8,9, Phil 4:15
mad, *foolish, insane*
   of laughter, it is *m*   Ecc 2:2
   hath a devil, and is *m*   Jno 10:20
   learning make thee *m*   Acts 26:24
   See also: Ecc 7:7, Hos 9:7, 1 Cor 14:23
made
   wisdom hast thou *m*   Psa 104:24
   the day Lord hath *m*   118:24
   I am wonderfully *m*   139:14
   God hath *m* man upright Ecc 7:29

all things were *m* by him   Jno 1:3
m him to be sin for   2 Cor 5:21
m of a woman, *m* under law   Gal 4:4
m in likeness of men   Phil 2:7
might be *m* manifest   1 Jno 2:19
magnify, *make great*
   what is man, thou shouldst *m*   Job 7:17
   O *m* the Lord with me   Psa 34:3
   my soul doth *m* the Lord   Lk 1:46
   speak, and *m* God   Acts 10:46
majesty, *greatness, honor*
   thine O Lord, is *m*   1 Chr 29:11
   voice of Lord full of *m*   Psa 29:4
   on right hand of *m*   Heb 1:3, 8:1
   eyewitnesses of his *m*   2 Pet 1:16
   to God be glory and *m*   Jude 25
maker, *creator*
   be more pure than *m?*   Job 4:17
   kneel before Lord our *m*   Psa 95:6
   striveth with his *m*   Isa 45:9
   Israel forgotten *m*   Hos 8:14
   builder and *m* is God   Heb 11:10
Malachi, *"my messenger," a prophet,* Mal 1:1
malice, *evil intention*
   not with leaven of *m*   1 Cor 5:8
   in *m* be ye children   14:20
   put away all *m*   Eph 4:31
   laying aside all *m*   1 Pet 2:1
mammon, *wealth, riches,* Mat 6:24, Lk 16:9 ff
Mamre, *dwelling place of Abraham,* Gen 13:18 ff
man, *human being*
   let us make *m*   Gen 1:26
   God formed *m* of dust   · 2:7

God is not a *m* — Num 23:19
said, thou art the *m* — 2 Sam 12:7
m is born to trouble — Job 5:7
m that is born of a woman — 14:1
God is greater than *m* — 33:12
not fear: what can *m* do — Psa 118:6
what is *m* that thou — 144:3
he is a *m* of sorrows — Isa 53:3
not in *m* to direct his — Jer 10:23
no *m* can serve two — Mat 6:24
Sabbath was made for *m* — Mk 2:27
behold the *m* — Jno 19:5
when I became a *m* — 1 Cor 13:11
put on the new *m* — Eph 4:24
found in fashion as a *m* — Phil 2:8
hidden *m* of the heart — 1 Pet 3:4

Manasseh, *son of Joseph,* Gen 41:51;
tribe of Israel, Num 1:34, 32:33, Josh
13:29; *king of Judah,* 2 Ki 21

manifest, *to show, make evident*
m counsels of heart — 1 Cor 4:5
works of flesh are *m* — Gal 5:19
God was *m* in flesh — 1 Tim 3:16
m to take away sins — 1 Jno 3:5
was *m* the love of God — 4:9

manifold, *many, abundant*
the *m* wisdom of God — Eph 3:10
through *m* temptations — 1 Pet 1:6
stewards of *m* grace of God — 4:10

manna, *food of Israelites in wilderness,*
Ex 16:4 ff, Deut 8:3, Num 11:6, Josh
5:12

manner, *custom, habit, kind*
is this *m* of man? — 2 Sam 7:19
all *m* of evil against — Mat 5:11
what *m* of man is this? — 8:27, Mk
4:41, Lk 8:25
as the *m* of some is — Heb 10:25

forgetteth what *m* of — Jas 1:24
what *m* of persons ought — 2 Pet 3:11
what *m* of love — 1 Jno 3:1

Mark (John), *evangelist and author of
Gospel bearing his name,* Acts
12:12,25, 13:5, 15:37, 2 Tim 4:11

mark, *sign, brand, goal*
Lord set a *m* on Cain — Gen 4:15
m the perfect man — Psa 37:37
m of the Lord Jesus — Gal 6:17
I press toward *m* — Phil 3:14

marrow, *bone center*
dividing joints and *m* — Heb 4:12

marry
neither *m* or are — Mat 22:30
let them *m* — 1 Cor 7:9
See also: Mat 19:6, Jno 2:1, Eph 5:31

Martha, *sister of Mary and Lazarus,*
Lk 10:38, Jno 11:5 ff

marvel, *be amazed, wonder*
Jesus *m* — Mat 8:10, Mk 6:6, Lk 7:9
m not if world hate — 1 Jno 3:13

marvellous, *wonderful*
m things without number — Job 5:9
into his *m* light — 1 Pet 2:9

Mary, *mother of Jesus,* Mat 1:18, Lk
1:26, Jno 2:1, Mat 27:56;
Magdalene, Lk 8:2, Mat 27:56, 28:1;
sister of Lazarus, Lk 10:42, Jno 11:5,
12:3

master, *lord, owner, teacher*
no man can serve two *m* — Mat 6:24
disciple not above *m* — 10:24
is your *m,* even Christ — 23:8,10
good *m,* what shall I — Mk 10:17, Lk
10:25, 18:18

ye call me *m*, and ye   Jno 13:13
as a wise *m* builder   1 Cor 3:10
m is in heaven   Eph 6:9, Col 4:1
be not many *m*   Jas 3:1

matter, *thing*
conclusion of whole *m*   Ecc 12:13
omitted weightier *m*   Mat 23:23
how great a *m* a little   Jas 3:5

Matthew, *apostle, also called Levi,* Mat
9:9, Mk 2:14, Lk 5:27

Matthias, *chosen to replace Judas,*
Acts 1:26

mean, *signify*
what *m* testimonies?   Deut 6:20
what *m* these stones?   Josh 4:6,21

means, *manner*
by all *m* save some   1 Cor 9:22
by any *m* attain   Phil 3:11

measure, *measure, length, quanitity*
just *m* shalt thou   Deut 25:15
to know *m* of my days   Psa 39:4
with what *m* ye mete   Mat 7:2
good *m* pressed down   Lk 6:38
every man *m* of faith·   Rom 12:3
m of gift of Christ   Eph 4:7
to the *m* of the stature   4:13
m themselves by   2 Cor 10:12

meat, *flesh, food*
m in due   Psa 145:15, Mat 24:45
life more than *m?*   6:25, Lk 12:23
worthy of his *m*   Mat 10:10
my *m* is to do will   Jno 4:34
labour not for *m* that   6:27
eat *m* with gladness   Acts 2:46
kingdom is not *m* and   Rom 14:17
m for the belly   1 Cor 6:13
strong *m* belongeth to   Heb 5:14

meddle, *to stir up*
m not with·him that   Pro 20:19
that *m* with strife   26:17

mediator, *middle man*
one *m*, Christ Jesus   1 Tim 2:5
m of a better covenant   Heb 8:6
the *m* of the new testament   9:15
Jesus *m* of new covenant   12:24

medicine, *healing, remedy*
doeth good like a *m*   Pro 17:22

meditate, *consider, ponder*
thou shalt *m* therein   Josh 1:8
in·his law doth he *m*   Psa 1:2
m on these things   1 Tim 4:15
See also: Psa 19:14, 104:34, 119:97

meek, *humble, mild*
m shall eat and   Psa 22:26
m shall inherit   37:11, Mat 5:5
Lord lifteth up the *m*   Psa 147:6
I am *m* and lowly   Mat 11:29
ornament of *m* and quiet 1 Pet 3:4

meekness *(see meek)*
by the *m* of Christ   2 Cor 10:1
fruit of Spirit is *m*   Gal 5:23
restore in the spirit of *m*   6:1
put on *m*, longsuffering   Col 3:12
follow after *m*   1 Tim 6:11
received with *m* the word   Jas 1:21
reason of hope with *m*   1 Pet 3:15

meet, *fitting, suitable* (archaic)
an help *m* for him   Gen 2:18
fruits *m* for repentance   Mat 3:8
works *m* for repentance Acts 26:20
make· *m* to be partakers   Col 1:12

meet, *to come together*
rich and poor *m* together   Pro 22:2
prepare to *m* thy God   Amos 4:12
in clouds to *m* Lord   1 Thes 4:17

Megiddo, *important fortress in plain of Jezreel,* Josh 17:11, Judg 1:27, 5:19, 2 Ki 23:29

Melchizedek, *king and priest,* Gen 14:18, Heb 5:6, 6:20, 7:1

Melita, *island near Italy where Paul was shipwrecked,* Acts 28:1

melody, *music*
  making *m* to the Lord   Eph 5:19

member, *part of a body*
  one of thy *m* should   Mat 5:29
  another law in *m*   Rom 7:23
  bodies are *m* of Christ   1 Cor 6:15
  the body is not one *m*   12:14
  we are *m* one of another Eph 4:25
  m of his body   5:30
  tongue is a little *m*   Jas 3:5
  lusts that war in your *m*   4:1

memory, *remembrance*
  m of the just is blessed   Pro 10:7

men *(see man)*
  in favour with Lord and *m* 1 Sam 2:26
  ye shall die like *m*   Psa 82:7
  shew yourselves *m*   Isa 46:8
  m should do to you, do ye even so Mat 7:12, Lk 6:31
  quit you like *m*   1 Cor 16:13
  not pleasing *m,* but God 1 Thes 2:4
  honour all *m*   1 Pet 2:17

mention, *speak of*
  m of you in my prayers Rom 1:9, Eph 1:16, 1 Thes 1:2

Mephibosheth, *son of Jonathan,* 2 Sam 4:4, 9:1, 16:1, 21:7

merchandise, *objects of trade*
  m of it better than   Pro 3:14

make *m* of you   2 Pet 2:3

merchant, *trader*
  like *m* seeking pearls   Mat 13:45

merciful, *compassionate*
  Lord God *m* and gracious Ex 34:6
  with *m,* shew thyself *m* 2 Sam 22:26, Psa 18:25
  the righteous is ever *m*   37:26
  God be *m* to us   67:1
  m man doeth good to   Pro 11:17
  I know thou art a *m* God Jonah 4:2
  God be *m* to me a sinner Lk 18:13
  I will be *m* to their   Heb 8:12

mercy, *compassion, pity*
  I will shew *m* on whom   Ex 33:19
  Lord is of great *m* Num 14:18, Psa 103:11, 145:8
  his *m* endureth forever   1 Chr 16:34,41, 2 Chr 5:13, 7:3,6, Ezra 3:11, Psa 106:1, 118:1, 136:1, Jer 33:11
  and *m* shall follow me   Psa 23:6
  all paths of Lord are *m*   25:10
  I trust in the *m* of God   52:8
  with the Lord there is *m*   130:7
  not *m* and truth forsake Pro 3:3
  after *m* findeth life   21:21
  m and not sacrifice   Hos 6:6, Mat 9:13
  do justly, and love *m*   Mic 6:8
  merciful shall obtain *m* Mat 5:7
  omitted judgment and *m*   23:23
  I will have *m* on whom   Rom 9:15,18
  the Father of *m*   2 Cor 1:3
  God, who is rich in *m*   Eph 2:4
  according to his *m* he   Tit 3:5

judgment without *m* that   Jas 2:13
and of tender *m*   5:11
his abundant *m*   1 Pet 1:3
merry, *happy, jovial*
let thine heart be *m*   Judg 19:6,
                              1 Ki 21:7
m heart maketh cheerful Pro 15:13
m heart doeth good like   17:22
to eat and be *m*   Ecc 8:15
ease, eat and be *m*   Lk 12:19
is any *m?*   Jas 5:13
Mesopotamia, *"between rivers," region
of Babylon,* Gen 11:31, Acts 2:9, 7:2
message, *word*
m we have heard   1 Jno 1:5, 3:11
Messiah, *anointed,* Isa 9:6, Dan 9:25,
Jno 1:41
Methuselah, *oldest man,* Gen 5:27
Micah, *prophet,* Jer 26:18, Mic 1:1 ff;
idol worshiper, Judg 17:1 ff
Micaiah, *prophet,* 1 Ki 22
Michael, *angel,* Dan 10:13, 12:1, Jude
9, Rev 12:7
Midian, *son and descendants of
Abraham,* Gen 25:4, Ex 2:15, Num
31:1
midst, *middle, among*
tree of life in the *m*   Gen 2:9
God is in the *m*   Psa 46:5
dwell in *m* of a people   Isa 6:5
child in *m*   Mat 18:2, Mk 9:36
there am I in the *m*   Mat 18:20
might, *strength*
do according to thy *m*   Deut 3:24
love thy God with all thy *m*   6:5
m of mine hand gotten wealth 8:17
do it with thy *m*   Ecc 9:10
strengthened with *m* Eph 3:16, Col
                                 1:11

glory and *m* be unto God Rev 7:12
mighty, *strong, powerful*
he was a *m* hunter   Gen 10:9
became a *m* nation   18:18
how are the *m* fallen   2 Sam 1:19
God is wise and *m*   Job 9:4
slow to anger better than *m*   Pro
                                16:32
their redeemer is *m*   23:11
the *m* One of   Isa 1:24, 30:29,
                       49:26, 60:16
m works   Mat 11:20, 13:54, 14:2,
                             Mk 6:2
m power of God   Lk 9:43
not many *m* called   1 Cor 1:26
weapons of warfare *m*   2 Cor 10:4
working of his *m* power   Eph 1:19
milk
I have fed you with *m*   1 Cor 3:2
such as have need of *m*   Heb 5:12
the sincere *m* of word   1 Pet 2:2
mind
serve with willing *m*   1 Chr 28:9
people had a *m* to work   Neh 4:6
fool uttereth his *m*   Pro 29:11
m is stayed on thee   Isa 26:3
love Lord with all thy *m*   Mat
             22:37, Mk 12:30, Lk 10:27
carnal *m* is enmity against   Rom
                                8:7
who known *m* of Lord?   11:34
we have *m* of Christ   1 Cor 2:16
be of one *m*   13:11, Phil 1:27, 2:2
spirit of sound *m*   2 Tim 1:7
put laws in their *m*   Heb 8:10
mindful, *to remember*
that thou art *m* of him?   Psa 8:4,
                              Heb 2:6

be *m* of words spoken   2 Pet 3:2
mine, *belonging to me*
  earth is *m*   Ex 19:5, Psa 50:12
  not *m* to give   Mat 20:23, Mk 10:40
  thine are *m*   Jno 17:10
minister, *servant*
  be your *m*   Mat 20:26, Mk 10:43
  he is the *m* of God   Rom 13:4
  is faithful *m*   Eph 6:21, Col 1:7
  a good *m* of Christ   1 Tim 4:6
minister (verb), *to serve*
  not to be *m* unto   Mat 20:28, Mk 10:45
  m grace to the hearers   Eph 4:29
  m to heirs of salvation   Heb 1:14
ministration, *service*
  widows neglected in *m*   Acts 6:1
ministry, *service*
  or *m* let us wait on   Rom 12:7
  m of reconciliation   2 Cor 5:18
  take heed to the *m*   Col 4:17
  full proof of thy *m*   2 Tim 4:5
  a more excellent *m*   Heb 8:6
miracle, *sign, acts of power*
  thine eyes have seen *m*   Deut 29:3
  a *m* in my name   Mk 9:39
  this beginning of *m*   Jno 2:11
  this is the second *m*   4:54
  approved of God by *m*   Acts 2:22
mirth, *joy*
  m of the land is gone   Isa 24:11
Miriam, *sister of Moses,* Ex 15:20, Num 12:1 ff, 20:1
miry, *boggy*
  brought me out of *m* clay   Psa 40:2
mischief, *perversity, evil*
  how long ye imagine *m*   Psa 62:3

as sport to fool to do *m*   Pro 10:23
wicked fall in *m*   24:16, 28:14
misery, *agony, suffering*
  the *m* of man is great   Ecc 8:6
  howl for your *m*   Jas 5:1
mixed, *mingled*
  not being *m* with faith   Heb 4:2
Moab, *son of Lot, and nation descended from him,* Gen 19:37, Deut 2:9, 34:5, Judg 3:12
mock, *scorn, deride*
  m poor, reproacheth Maker   Pro 17:5
  God is not *m*.   Gal 6:7
  See also: Pro 20:1, Jude 18
moment, *period of time*
  hid my face for *m*   Isa 54:8
  changed in a *m*   1 Cor 15:52
  affliction, but for *m*   2 Cor 4:17
money, *silver*
  putteth not out *m* to usury   Psa 15:5
  redeemed without *m*   Isa 52:3
  thy *m* perish with thee   Acts 8:20
  love of *m* the root   1 Tim 6:10
Mordecai, *cousin of Esther,* Esth 2:5 ff
morrow, *morning, tomorrow*
  m we die   Isa 22:13, 1 Cor 15:32
  take no thought for *m*   Mat 6:34
  what shall be on *m*   Jas 4:14
mortal, *subject to death*
  your *m* body   Rom 6:12, 8:11
  m must put on immortality   1 Cor 15:53
  Jesus manifest in *m*   2 Cor 2:11
Moses, *leader of Israel from Egypt,* Ex. 2 ff, 14:1, 19:25, Deut 34:5

mote, *chaff, splinter*
  m in brother's eye   Mat 7:3, Lk
                                       6:41

mother
  was *m* of all living   Gen 3:20
  a joyful *m* of children   Psa 113:9
  who is my *m* Mat 12:48, Mk 3:33
  Jerusalem, *m* of us all   Gal 4:26

mount, *mountain*
  the *m* of God   Ex 18:5, 1 Ki 19:8

mourn, *grieve*
  a time to *m*   Ecc 3:4
  to comfort all that *m*   Isa 61:2
  turn their *m* into joy   Jer 31:13
  blessed are they that *m*   Mat 5:4

mouth
  m of babes   Psa 8:2, Mat 21:16
  a fool's *m* is his   Psa 18:7
  m of righteous speaketh   37:30
  m of the just bringeth   Pro 10:31
  draw near with *m*   Isa 29:13, Mat
                                       15:8
  abundance of heart *m* speaketh
                        Mat 12:34, Lk 6:45
  give you *m* and wisdom   Lk 21:15
  with *m* confession is   Rom 10:10
  out of same *m* proceedeth Jas 3:10

move
  I shall not be *m*   Psa 10:6, 16:8,
                                30:6, 62:2
  in him we live and *m*   Acts 17:28
  none of these things *m*   20:24

multiply, *make abundant*
  fruitful and *m* Gen 1:22, 9:7, 35:11
  their sorrows shall be *m* Psa 16:4
  peace be *m*   Jude 2
  word of God grew and *m*   Acts
                                      12:24

multitude, *crowd, many*
  not follow a *m* to evil   Ex 23:2
  m of years should teach   Job 32:7
  m of mercy   Psa 5:7, 51:1, 69:13
  no king saved by *m* of   33:16
  hide a *m* of sins   Jas 5:20
  covereth *m* of sins   1 Pet 4:8

murmur, *complain*
  m not among yourselves   Jno 6:43
  all things without *m*   Phil 2:14

music
  his elder son heard *m*   Lk 15:25

mystery, *secret*
  to know *m* of kingdom   Mk 4:11
  revelation of *m*   Rom 16:25
  this is a great *m*   Eph 5:32
  great is *m* of godliness 1 Tim 3:16

N

Naaman, *Syrian officer cured of leprosy,* 2 Ki 5:1 ff, Lk 4:27

Nabal, *rich man of Maon who insulted
  David,* 1 Sam 25:3 ff

Naboth, *owner of vineyard Ahab
  wanted,* 1 Ki 21:1, 2 Ki 9:2

Nahor, *brother of Abraham,* Gen
  11:26; *grandfather of Abraham,* Gen
  11:22

nail, *pin, peg*
  Jael took a *n* of tent   Judg 4:21
  idol with *n*   Isa 41:7, Jer 10:4
  finger in print of *n*   Jno 20:25

nailing *(see nail)*
 n it to his cross   Col 2:14

naked, *unclothed*
 they were both *n*   Gen 2:25
 knew they were *n*   3:7, 10:11
 n came I out of womb   Job 1:21
 n shall he return   Ecc 5:15
 n and ye clothed me   Mat 25:36
 shall *n* separate us?   Rom 8:35
 all things are *n* to   Heb 4:13
 poor, and blind, and *n*   Rev 3:17

name, *name, fame*
 and called their *n* Adam   Gen 5:2
 a *n* lest we be scattered   11:4
 neither profane the *n* of thy God
     Lev 18:21, 19:12, 21:6, 22:2,32
 choose to place his *n* there   Deut
     14:23,24, 16:6,11, 26:2
 for his *n* sake   1 Sam 12:22, Psa
     23:3, 106:8, 1 Jno 2:12, 3 Jno 7
 n of Lord is tower   Pro 18:10
 good *n* to be chosen   22:1
 good *n* better than   Ecc 7:1
 his *n* called Wonderful   Isa 9:6
 three gathered in my *n*   Mat 18:20
 baptizing them in *n* of   28:19
 calleth his sheep by *n*   Jno 10:3
 baptized in *n* of   Acts 2:38
 none other *n* under heaven   4:12
 n of God blasphemed   Rom 2:24
 above every *n* named   Eph 1:21

names *(see name)*
 n written in heaven   Lk 10:20
 n are in book of life   Phil 4:3
 n not written   Rev 13:8, 17:8

Naomi, *mother-in-law of Ruth*, Ruth
 1:2

Naphtali, *son of Jacob, and tribe of Israel*, Gen 30:8, 35:25, 46:24, 49:21

narrow, *narrow, strait*
 strange woman is *n* pit   Pro 23:27
 n is way which leadeth to life Mat
                                  7:14

Nathan, *prophet who condemned David*, 2 Sam 5:14, 7:17, 12:1, 1 Ki 1:34

nation, *group of people*
 be a father of many *n*   Gen 17:4,5,
                    48:19, Rom 4:17,18
 all the *n* of earth be blessed   Gen
                    18:18, 22:18, 26:4
 be a holy *n*   Ex 19:6, 1 Pet 2:9
 bless is *n* whose God   Psa 33:12
 shall exalt *n*   Pro 14:34
 cease being *n*   Jer 31:36, 33:24
 n rise against *n*   Mat 24:7, Mk
                       13:8, Lk 21:10
 made one blood all *n*   Acts 17:26
 shall all *n* be blessed   Gal 3:8

natural *(see nature)*
 women change *n* use   Rom 1:26
 a man behold *n* face   Jas 1:23

nature, *character, essence*
 do by *n* things in law   Rom 2:14
 doth not *n* teach   1 Cor 11:14
 partakers of divine *n*   2 Pet 1:4

nay, *no*
 communication be yea, yea, *n*, *n*
     Mat 5:37, Jas 5:12, 2 Cor 1:17

Nazareth, *hometown of Jesus in Galilee*, Mat 2:23, 21:11, Mk 10:47, Lk
 1:26

Nazarite, *one with vow*, Num 6:1 ff

near, *nigh, at hand*
 call upon Lord while he is *n*   Isa
                                  55:6

our salvation *n* than   Rom 13:11

Nebo, *mount where Moses died,* Deut 33:49, 34:1

Nebuchadnezzar, *king of Babylon about 600 B.C.,* 2 Ki 24:11, 25:1, 2 Chr 36:6, Jer 39:1

necessity, *that which is necessary*
not grudgingly or of *n*   2 Cor 9:7
there must of *n* be death Heb 9:16

neck, *neck, throat*
thy rebellion and stiff *n* Deut 31:27
millstone about *n*   Mat 18:6, Mk 9:42, Lk 17:2

need, *lack, need*
ye have *n* of   Mat 6:8,32
n not a physician   9:12, Mk 2:17, Lk 5:31
as had *n*   Acts 2:45, 4:35
to give him that *n*   Eph 4:28
I have *n* of nothing   Rev 3:17
See also: 2 Cor 8:13 f, Phil 4:19

needle, *sewing instrument*
eye of *n* Mat 19:24, Mk 10:25, Lk 18:25

needs *(see need)*
ye must *n* be subject   Rom 13:5

needy *(see need)*
buy *n* for pair of shoes Amos 8:6
poor and *n*   Psa 35:10, 72:4,13

neglect, *disregard, be careless*
widows were *n* in daily   Acts 6:1
n not gift in thee   1 Tim 4:14
how escape, if *n*   Heb 2:3
See also: Pro 21:13, Heb 2:1, Jas 4:17

Nehemiah, *governor of Judah about 444 B.C.,* Ezra 2:2, Neh 7:7

neighbour, *friend, companion*

not bear false witness against *n* Ex 20:16 f, Deut 5:20
love thy *n* as thyself   Lev 19:18
whoso slandereth his *n*   Psa 101:5
hypocrite destroy his *n*   Pro 11:9
better is a *n* that is near   27:10
love thy *n* Mat 5:43, 19:19, 22:39, Mk 12:31, Lk 10:27, Rom 13:9, Gal 5:14, Jas 2:8
love *n* as himself   Mk 12:31
who is my *n?*   Lk 10:29
See also: Eph 4:25, Phil 2:4, 1 Thes 4:12

nest, *nest, roosting place*
birds have *n*   Mat 8:20, Lk 9:58

net, *snare, fishing net*
cast *n* into   Mat 4:18, Mk 1:16
kingdom is like *n*   Mat 13:47
forsook *n* follow him   Mk 1:18
I will let down the *n*   Lk 5:5
cast *n* on right side   Jno 21:6

never
it was *n* so seen in Israel Mat 9:33
answered him to *n* a word   27:14

new
arose a *n* king over   Ex 1:8
Lord make *n* thing   Num 16:30
no *n* thing under sun   Ecc 1:9
n things I declare   Isa 42:9, 48:6
n heavens *n* earth   65:17, 66:22
I will put *n* spirit   Ezek 11:19
n cloth to an old   Mat 9:16, Mk 2:21, Lk 5:36
n wine into Mat 9:17, Mk 2:22, Lk 5:38
my blood of *n* testament   Mat 26:28, Mk 14:24, Lk 22:20, 1 Cor 11:25

Joseph laid body in *n* tomb, Mat 27:60

what *n* doctrine   Mk 1:27

n commandment I give   Jno 13:34

these men full of *n* wine   Acts 2:13

he is a *n* creature   2 Cor 5:17

a *n* creature   Gal 6:15

put on *n* man   Eph 4:24, Col 3:10

by *n* and living way   Heb 10:20

as *n* born babes, desire   1 Pet 2:2

n heavens, *n* earth   2 Pet 3:13

write no *n* commandment   1 Jno 2:7

not as though I wrote *n*   2 Jno 5

n name written   Rev 2:17

I saw *n* heaven and *n* earth   21:1

I make all things *n*   21:5

newness *(see new)*

shall walk in *n* of life   Rom 6:4

should serve in *n* of spirit   7:6

Nicodemus, *Pharisee friendly to Jesus*, Jno 3:1, 7:50, 19:39

nigh, *near*

salvation *n* them that fear   Psa 85:9

day of Lord is *n* at hand   Joel 2:1

kingdom of God is *n*   Lk 21:31

made *n* by blood   Eph 2:13

night, *night, darkness*

the darkness he called *n*   Gen 1:5

rain 40 days, 40 *n*   7:4,12

fire by *n*   Num 9:16

fire by *n* to show way   Deut 1:33

n unto *n* uttereth   Psa 19:2

not be afraid by *n*   91:5

this *n* thou shalt deny   Mat 26:34

watch over flock by *n*   Lk 2:8

Nicodemus came by *n*   Jno 3:2, 19:39

n cometh, no man can work   9:4

n is spent   Rom 13:12

n he was betrayed   1 Cor 11:23

as thief in the *n*   1 Thes 5:2, 2 Pet 3:10

we are not of the *n*   1 Thes 5:5

be no *n* there   Rev 21:25, 22:5

Nimrod, *mighty hunter*, Gen 10:8, 1 Chr 1:10

nine

where are the *n*?   Lk 17:17

ninety-nine

leave the *n* and seek?   Mat 18:12, Lk 15:4

Nineveh, *capital of Assyria*, Gen 10:11, Jonah 1:2, Nah 1:1

ninth

darkness unto *n* hour   Mat 27:45, Mk 15:33

Noah, or Noe, survivor of flood, Gen 5:29, 6:8 ff, Mat 24:37, 1 Pet 3:20

noble, *honorable*

These more *n*   Acts 17:11

not many *n* are called   1 Cor 1:26

noise, *sound*

make a joyful *n*   Psa 66:1, 81:1, 95:1,2, 98:4,6, 100:1

pass away with *n*   2 Pet 3:10

noon, *midday*

at *n*, I will pray   Psa 55:17

darkness be as *n*   Isa 58:10

about *n*, a light   Acts 22:6

north

he stretched out the *n*   Job 26:7

cold cometh out of the *n*   37:9

shall come from *n*   Lk 13:29

nostrils, *nose*

breathed into man's *n*   Gen 2:7

notable, *very manifest*
   n day of Lord   Acts 2:20
note, *take notice of*
   n that man   2 Thes 3:14
nothing, *no thing*
   hanged the earth upon *n*   Job 26:7
   n that not be revealed   Mat 10:26,
                  Mk 4:22, Lk 12:2
   n shall be impossible   Mat 17:20,
                         Lk 1:37
   I should lose *n*   Jno 6:39
   without me ye can do *n*   15:5
   I know *n* by myself   1 Cor 4:4
   and have not charity, I am *n* 13:2
   do *n* against truth   2 Cor 13:8
   shall profit you *n*   Gal 5:2
   be careful for *n*, but   Phil 4:6
   and entire, wanting *n*   Jas 1:4
   ask in faith, *n* wavering   1:6
nourish, *sustain*
   but *n* his flesh   Eph 5:29
   n up in words of faith   1 Tim 4:6
novice, *newly planted*
   not *n* less lifted   1 Tim 3:6
numbered, *counted*
   thy seed be *n*   Gen 13:16, 16:10
   hairs of head are *n*   Mat 10:30, Lk
                      12:7
nurture, *instruction*
   bring them up in *n*   Eph 6:4

O

oak, *oak, terebinth*
   Jacob hid gods under *o*   Gen 35:4
   Absalom hanged in an *o*   2 Sam
                        18:10
   See also: Amos 2:9, Isa 1:30
oath, *promise, swearing*
   o which I sware to Abraham   Gen
      26:3, Deut 7:8, Psa 105:9, Jer
                      11:5
   perform to Lord *o*   Mat 5:33
   swear not by any other *o*   Jas 5:12
   See also: Isa 19:21, 62:8, Zech 8:17,
   Heb 7:21
Obadiah, *minister of Ahab,* 1 Ki 18:3;
   prophet, Ob 1:1
obedience *(see obey)*
   by *o* of one many be   Rom 5:19
   or of *o* unto righteousness   6:16
   learned *o* by things   Heb 5:8
   See also: Num 15:39, 1 Sam 15:22,
   Mat 7:21
obedient *(see obey)*
   so is wise reprover on *o* ear   Pro
                      25:12
   he became *o* to death   Phil 2:8
   wives, be *o* to husbands   Tit 2:5
obey, *hearken, do as commanded*
   if ye will *o* my   Ex 19:5
   to *o* is better than   1 Sam 15:22
   amend your ways, *o*   Jer 26:13
   winds and sea *o* him?   Mat 8:27,
                  Mk 1;41, Lk 8:25
   unclean spirits *o* him   Mk 1:27
   o God rather than men   Acts 5:29

and do not *o* the truth   Rom 2:8
whom to *o*, his servants ye *o*   6:16
o from heart doctrine   6:17
you should not *o*?   Gal 3:1, 5:7
children *o* parents   Eph 6:1
salvation to all that *o*   Heb 5:9
that *o* not gospel?   1 Pet 4:17
See also: Jno 7:17, 1 Pet 1:21, Rev
22:14

observe, *keep, watch*
o sabbath   Ex 31:16
o that which I command   34:11,
                    Deut 12:28, 24:8
teaching them to *o*   Mat 28:20
o from my youth   Mk 10:20

obstinate, *stubborn*
I knew that thou art *o*   Isa 48:4

obtain, *acquire, possess*
through mercy *o* mercy Rom 11:31
so, run, that ye *o*   1 Cor 9:24
o more excellent name   Heb 1:4
elders *o* good report   11:2,39
ye kill and cannot *o*   Jas 4:2

occasion, *opportunity*
use not liberty for *o*   Gal 5:13
none *o* of stumbling   1 Jno 2:10
See also: Esth 4:14, Rom 14:13,
1 Tim 5:14

occupation, *work, profession,* Gen
46:33, Jno 1:8, Acts 18:3

odour, *smell, perfume*
o of a sweet smell   Phil 4:18

offence, *stumbling block, sin*
conscience void of *o*   Acts 24:16
delivered for our *o*   Rom 4:25
for through *o* for one   5:18
mark them which cause *o*   16:17
sincere and without *o*   Phil 1:10

offend, *cause to stumble*
a brother *o* is harder   Pro 18:19
if thy right eye *o*   Mat 5:29
not be *o*   11:6, Lk 7:23
whoso *o* one of these   Mat 18:6,
                    Mk 9:42, Lk 17:2
whereby brother is *o*   Rom 14:21
meat make brother *o*   1 Cor 8:13
yet *o* in one point   Jas 2:10

offer, *give, sacrifice*
Cain brought *o* unto Lord Gen 4:3
sanctify the *o*   Ex 29:27
Nadab and Abihu, *o* strange fire
            Lev 10:1, 16:1, Num 3:4, 26:61
o sacrifices of Deut 63:19, Psa 4:5
cheek, *o* also other   Lk 6:29
things *o* to idols 1 Cor 8:1 ff, 10:19
give self as *o* for us   Eph 5:2
I am ready to be *o*   2 Tim 4:6
o spiritual sacrifices   1 Pet 2:5
no more *o* for sin   Heb 10:18
See also: Deut 16:17, Psa 51:17,
Pro 21:3, Hos 6:6, Mat 12:33, 2 Cor
8:12

office, *function, work*
members have not same *o*   Rom
                              12:4
if a man desire *o*   1 Tim 3:1
let them use *o* of deacon   3:10,13

oft, *often*
how *o* my brother sin?   Mat 18:21
as *o* as ye drink   1 Cor 11:25
in deaths *o*   2 Cor 11:23

oil, *oil, ointment*
anoint my head with *o*   Psa 23:5
the foolish took no *o*   Mat 25:3
with *o* didst not   Lk 7:46
hurt not wine and *o*   Rev 6:6

ointment *(see oil)*

good name better than *o* Ecc 7:1
dead flies cause *o* to stink 10:1
box of precious *o* Mat 26:7, Mk
  14:3, Lk 7:37
the Lord with *o* Jno 11:2, 12:3

old, *aged*

Abraham died in *o* age Gen 25:8
new cloth to *o* Mat 9:16,17
the *o* is better Lk 5:39
man be born when *o*? Jno 3:4
o things passed away 2 Cor 5:17
refuse *o* wives fables 1 Tim 4:7
purged from his *o* sins 2 Pet 1:9
not serve in *o* of letter Rom 7:6

olive

in mouth was *o* leaf Gen 8:11
I am like green *o* tree Psa 52:8
fatness of *o* Rom 11:17
fig tree bear *o* berries? Jas 3:12

omega, *last letter of the Greek alphabet,*
Rev 1:8

omer, *Hebrew measure, one-tenth of
ephah,* Ex 16:16,36

omit, *let go, neglect*

o matters of the law Mat 23:23
See also: Josh 11:15, Mat 23:3,
25:45, Jas 4:17

omnipotent, *all-powerful*

Lord God *o* reigneth Rev 19:6
See also: Psa 62:11, Col 1:11

Omri, *king of Israel, father of Ahab,*
1 Ki 16:16

once, *one time, once for all*

he died unto sin *o* Rom 6:10
appointed *o* to die Heb 9:27
suffered *o* for sins 1 Pet 3:18
faith *o* delivered Jude 3

one

shall be *o* flesh Gen 2:24, Mat
  19:5, Mk 10:8, 1 Cor 6:16
Lord our God is *o* Lord Deut 6:4,
  Mk 12:29
o jot or tittle not pass Mat 5:18
hate *o* and 6:24, Lk 16:13
none good but *o* Mat 19:17, Mk
  10:18, Lk 18:19
o thing lack Mk 10:21, Lk 18:22
there is *o* God Mk 12:32, 1 Tim
  2:5, Jas 2:19
o thing I know Jno 9:25
I and Father are *o* 10:30
none righteous, no not *o* Rom 3:10
o faith, *o* Lord, *o* baptism Eph 4:5

Onesimus, *slave of Philemon,* Col 4:9,
Philem 10

only, *one, alone*

God *o* wise, be glory Rom 13:27,
  1 Tim 1:17, Jude 25
not to me *o* but to all 2 Tim 4:8

open, *uncovered*

throat is *o* sepulchre Psa 5:9, Rom
  3:13
ears *o* to their cry Psa 34:15
o rebuke than secret love Pro 27:5
heaven *o* Ezek 1:1, Mat 3:16, Mk
  1:10, Lk 3:21, Acts 7:56
it shall be *o* Mat 7:7, Lk 11:9,10
great door is *o* unto me 1 Cor
  16:9, 2 Cor 2:12
put him to *o* shame Heb 6:6
ears are *o* to prayers 1 Pet 3:12
o and no man shutteth Rev 3:7
I have set *o* door 3:8

openly, *in public*

Father reward *o* Mat 6:4,6,18

have beaten us *o*   Acts 16:37
operation, *working,* 1 Cor 12:6, Col 2:12
Ophir, *prob. province of south Arabia,* 1 Ki 9:28, 1 Chr 29:4
opinion, *thinking,* 1 Ki 18:21
opportunity, *a fit season*
   o to betray   Mat 26:16, Lk 22:6
   as we have *o*, do good   Gal 6:10
   See also: Esth 4:14, Jer 8:20, Lk 19:13, Jno 4:35, 2 Cor 6:2, Rev 22:17
oppose, *set against*
   when they *o* themselves Acts 18:6
   those that *o* themselves 2 Tim 2:25
   See also: Acts 26:1, Eph 6:12
oppositions *(see oppose),* 1 Tim 6:20
oppress, *afflict, bruise*
   the Egyptians *o* them   Ex 3:9
   not *o* one another   Lev 25:14
   neither *o* strange   22:21, 23:9
   Lord looked on our *o*   Deut 26:7
   he was *o* and afflicted   Isa 53:7
   do not rich men *o* you? Jas 2:6
   See also: Pro 14:31, Jno 15:20
oppressor *(see oppress)*
   envy not *o* choose none   Pro 3:31
oracles, *words, revelation*
   committed *o* of God   Rom 3:2
   first principles of *o* of   Heb 5:12
   speak of the *o* of God   1 Pet 4:11
ordain, *appoint, select*
   out of mouths of babes *o*   Psa 8:2
   moon and stars which thou *o*   8:3
   Jesus *o* twelve   Mk 3:14
   o to eternal life   Acts 13:48
   powers *o* of God   Rom 13:1
   God hath before *o*   Eph 2:10
   I am *o* preacher to God   1 Tim 2:7

shouldest *o* elders   Tit 1:5
order
   after *o* of Melchizedek   Psa 110:4,
          Heb 5:6,10, 6:20, 7:11,17,21
   See also: Psa 37:23, 119:133
ordinance, *commandment*
   passover an *o* for ever Ex 12:14,24,
          13:10
   shalt teach them *o*   18:20
   power resists *o* of God   Rom 13:2
   submit to every *o* of   1 Pet 2:13
   blotting out handwriting of *o*   Col
          2:14
ornament
   an *o* of grace   Pro 1:9
   o of meek, quiet spirit   1 Pet 3:4
   See also: Pro 11:22, 20:15, Isa 49:18, Jer 2:32
Osee, *Greek spelling of Hosea,* Rom 9:25
other, *another*
   none *o* but God   Gen 28:17
   is salvation in any *o*   Acts 4:12
Othniel, *first judge of Israel,* Josh 15:11, Judg 1:13, 3:9,11
ought, *obliged, indebted*
   o have done   Mat 23:23, Lk 11:42
   to pray for as we *o*   Rom 8:26
   how thou *o* to behave 1 Tim 3:15
   speak things *o* not   5:13
   these *o* not to be   Jas 3:10
   ye *o* to say, If the Lord   4:15
ought, *anything at all, aught*
   brother hath *o* against   Mat 5:23
outer, *outside*
   o darkness   Mat 8:12, 22:13, 25:30
outrun, *run before*
   other disciple *o* Peter   Jno 20:4

outside, *externally*
  o of cup   Mat 23:25, Lk 11:39
  See also: Mk 7:15, 2 Cor 7:5

outstretched, *stretched out*
  us out with an *o* arm   Deut 26:8

outward, *outside*
  appear beautiful *o*   Mat 23:27
  Jew which is one *o*   Rom 2:28
  our *o* man perish   2 Cor 4:16
  not that *o* adorning   1 Pet 3:3

oven, *oven, furnace*
  cast into *o*   Mat 6:30, Lk 12:28

overcome, *conquer, prevail*
  I have *o* the world   Jno 16:33
  be not *o* of evil, but *o* evil   Rom 12:21
  of whom man is *o*   2 Pet 2:19
  are of God, have *o*   1 Jno 4:4
  born of God *o* world, victory *o* world 5:4,5
  o will I give tree of   Rev 2:7
  Lamb shall *o* them   17:14

overseers, *those who watch over*
  Holy Ghost made you *o*   Acts 20:28

overshadow, *cover over*
  bright cloud *o* them   Mat 17:5, Mk 9:7, Lk 9:34

oversight, *put in charge*
  taking *o* not by   1 Pet 5:2

overtake, *draw near*
  plowman *o* the reaper   Amos 9:13
  should *o* you as thief   1 Thes 5:4
  if man be *o* in a fault   Gal 6:1

overthrow, *break down*
  God *o* these cities   Gen 19:25,29
  when God *o* Sodom and   Isa 13:19, Jer 50:40, Amos 4:11

Jesus *o* tables of   Mat 21:12, Mk 11:15, Jno 2:15
ye cannot *o*   Acts 5:39
o the faith of some   2 Tim 2:18
See also: Pro 24:16, Mat 21:44

owe, *be obliged*
  o no man anything   Rom 13:8

own, *that which belongs to one*
  came to his *o*   Jno 1:11
  ye are not your *o*   1 Cor 6:19
  let no man seek his *o*   10:24
  charity seeketh not her *o*   13:5
  See also: 1 Cor 3:21 ff, 6:19

owner, *proprieter*
  the ox knoweth his *o*   Isa 1:3

ox, *bullock, cow*
  not covet neighbor's *o*   Ex 20:17
  not muzzle *o* treadeth out corn   Deut 25:4, 1 Cor 9:9, 1 Tim 5:18
  hewed yoke of *o*   1 Sam 11:7
  a stalled *o*, and   Pro 15:17
  o knoweth his owner   Isa 1:3
  o or ass fall into pit   Lk 14:5

P

pacify, *cause to rest*
  a wise man *p* wrath   Pro 16:14
  a gift in secret *p* anger   21:14
  See also: Isa 9:6, Mat 5:9, Rom 14:19

pain, *pain, writhing*
  loosed the *p* of death   Acts 2:24
  creation travaileth in *p*   Rom 8:22

neither be any more *p*   Rev 21:4
painted, *painted, colored*
Jezebel *p* her face   2 Ki 9:30
palace, *castle, temple*
shall enter king's *p*   Psa 45:15
strong man keepeth *p*   Lk 11:21
palm, *hand, palm tree*
flourish like *p* tree   Psa 92:12
smote Jesus with *p* of hands   Mat 26:67, Mk 14:65
branches of *p* and went   Jno 12:12
Pamphylia, *province of Asia Minor,* Acts 13:13,14,24
pant, *long for*
a hart *p* for water brooks   Psa 42:1
p after the dust   Amos 2:7
parable, *story, similitude*
why speak in *p*   Mat 13:10
See also: Pro 26:7, 13:34, Mk 4:11, Lk 8:10
paradise, *garden-like dwelling place for the departed souls of the righteous*
today be with me in *p*   Lk 23:43
was caught up into *p*   2 Cor 12:4
tree of life in *p* of God   Rev 2:7
pardon, *forgive, pass over*
p our iniquity Ex 34:9, Num 14:19
a God ready to *p*   Neh 9:7
for thy name's sake *p*   Psa 25:11
he will abundantly *p*   Isa 55:7
See also: Mic 7:18, Mat 6:14, Lk 17:3
parents, *begetters, progenitors*
children rise against *p*   Mat 10:21
who did sin, this man or *p* Jno 9:2
disobedient to *p* Rom 1:30, 2 Tim 3:2
children obey *p* Eph 6:1, Col 3:20

See also: Ex 20:12, Pro 20:20, 2 Cor 12:14, 2 Tim 3:2
part, *piece, portion*
we have no *p* in David 2 Sam 20:1
they *p* my garments   Psa 22:18
Mary hath chosen good *p* Lk 10:42
thou hast no *p* with me   Jno 13:8
we know in *p* and   1 Cor 13:9
partaker, *one who shares in*
p of spiritual things   Rom 15:27
p of heavenly calling   Heb 3:1
p of Christ's sufferings 1 Pet 4:13
p of divine nature   2 Pet 1:4
See also: Phil 1:7, Col 1:12
partial, *showing favoritism, biased*
doing nothing by *p*   1 Tim 5:21
are ye not *p* in yourselves Jas 2:4
See also: Gen 25:28, Lev 19:15
partition, *fence, hedge*
middle wall of *p*   Eph 2:14
pass, *to go on*
see the blood I will *p*   Ex 12:13
heaven and earth shall *p* Mat 9:18
let this cup *p*   26:39, Mk 14:36
fashion of world *p* away   1 Cor 7:31, 1 Jno 2:17
old things *p* away   2 Cor 5:17
love of Christ which *p*   Eph 3:19
peace of God which *p* understanding   Phil 4:7
heavens shall *p* away   2 Pet 3:10
past *(see pass)*
ask of days *p*   Deut 4:23
the harvest is *p*   Jer 8:20
ways *p* finding out   Rom 11:33
time *p* ye walked   Eph 2:2
God spake in time *p*   Heb 1:1
See also: Ecc 7:10, Isa 43:18, 46:9

pastor, *shepherd, feeder*

woe to *p* that destroy   Jer 23:1
gave some *p* and teachers Eph 4:11
See also: Jno 10:13, 1 Pet 5:2,3

pasture, *feeding place*

me lie down in green *p*   Psa 23:2
sheep of *p*   74:1, 79:13, 100:3
flock of *p* are men   Ezek 34:31
in and out and find *p*   Jno 10:9

path, *customary road.*

shew me the *p* of life   Psa 16:11
word is a light to my *p*   119:105
p of just is shining   Pro 4:18
we will walk in his *p*   Isa 2:3, Mic
                    4:2
make his *p* straight   Mat 3:3, Mk
                 1:3, Lk 3:4
See also: Mat 7:14, 1 Cor 12:31

patience, *forbearance, endurance*

p in spirit is better than   Ecc 7:8
tribulation worketh *p*   Rom 5:3
faith, charity, *p*   Tit 2:2
through *p* inherit promises   Heb
                  6:12
ye have need of *p*   10:36
let us run with *p*   12:1
trying of faith worketh *p*   Jas 1:3
be *p* unto coming of Lord   5:7
ye have heard of *p* of   Job 5:11
add to temperance *p*   2 Pet 1:6
See also: Rev 1:9, 2:2

patiently *(see patience)*

when buffeted, take it *p* 1 Pet 2:20
See also: Rom 2:7, 12:12, 1 Thes
5:14

pattern, *model, standard*

make them after *p*   Ex 25:40
show thyself a *p* of good words Tit
                  2:7

See also: Mat 5:16, Jno 13:15, Heb
8:5

Paul, *the apostle to the Gentiles, origi-
nally known as Saul,* Acts 7:58, 9:1
ff, 13:1 ff *to end of the book of Acts.
See also his thirteen letters, Romans
through Philemon*

pay, *give, reward*

ye *p* tithe of mint   Mat 23:23
for this cause *p* tribute   Rom 13:6
See also: Rom 6:23, 2 Cor 9:6, 1
Tim 5:18

peace, *rest, ease*

my covenant of *p*   Num 25:12
lay me down in *p*   Psa 4:8
seek *p* and   4:14, 1 Pet 3:11
end of upright man is *p* Psa 37:37
time of war, time of *p*   Ecc 3:8
prince of *p*   Isa 9:6
thy *p* as a river   48:18
no *p* to the wicked   48:22, 57:21
way of *p* they   59:8, Rom 3:17
saying *p*, *p* when   Jer 6:14, 8:11
my *p* I give   Jno 14:27
we have *p* with God   Rom 5:1
spiritually minded is *p*   8:6
gospel of *p*   10:15, Eph 6:15
kingdom of God is *p*   Rom 14:17
things which make for *p*   14:19
God called us to *p*   1 Cor 7:15
fruit of spirit is joy, *p*   Gal 5:22
he is our *p*   Eph 2:14
unity of spirit in bond of *p*   4:3
p of God which passeth   Phil 4:7
let the *p* of God rule   Col 3:15
righteousness is sown in *p* Jas 3:18
See also: Isa 2:4, Mat 5:9, 1 Thes
5:13

peaceable (see peace)
  lead quiet and *p* life   1 Tim 2:2
  wisdom from above is *p*   Jas 3:17

pearl
  cast *p* before swine   Mat 7:6
  one *p* of great price   13:46
  not with *p*, or costly   1 Tim 2:9

Pekah, *king of Israel,* 2 Ki 15:25, 2 Chr 28:6, Isa 7:1

Pekahiah, *king of Israel,* 2 Ki 15:22

Pentecost, *feast 50 days after Passover,* Lev 23:9, Deut 16:9, Acts 2:1

people
  I will take you for a *p*   Ex 6:7,
       Deut 4:20, 2 Sam 7:24, Jer
                           13:11
  thy *p* shall be my *p*   Ruth 1:16
  sin is reproach to *p*   Pro 14:34
  a rebellious *p*   Isa 30:9, 65:2
  p prepared for the Lord   Lk 1:17
  purify a peculiar *p*   Tit 2:14
  they shall be to me a *p*   Heb 8:10

perceive, *understand, discern*
  shall see, and *p* not Mat 13:14, Mk
              4:12, Acts 28:26
  p we love of God   1 Jno 3:16
  See also: Job 33:14, Ecc 2:14, Isa 64:4

perdition, *destruction*
  none lost but son of *p*   Jno 17:12

perfect, *complete, whole*
  be thou *p*   Gen 17:1
  the law of Lord is *p*   Psa 19:7
  mark the *p* man   37:37
  in *p* peace whose mind is Isa 26:3
  be *p* as your Father   Mat 5:48
  if thou wilt be *p*   19:21
  that *p* will of God   Rom 12:2

  till we come unto *p* man   Eph 4:13
  charity bond of *p*   Col 3:14
  man of God may be *p*   2 Tim 3:17
  make *p* through sufferings   Heb
                             2:10
  being made *p*   5:9
  let patience have *p* work   Jas 1:4
  every good and *p* gift   1:17
  the *p* law of liberty   1:25
  by faith works made *p*   2:22
  the same is *p* man   3:2
  p love casteth out fear   1 Jno 4:18

perfection (see perfect)
  let us go on to *p*   Heb 6:1

perform, *to do, finish*
  zeal of Lord will *p*   Isa 9:7
  how to *p* which is good   Rom 7:18
  See also: 2 Cor 8:11, Phil 1:6

Perga, *city of Asia Minor,* Acts 13:13, 14:25

Pergamos, *one of seven churches of Asia,* Rev 1:11, 2:12

peril, *danger*
  shall *p* separate us   Rom 8:35
  in *p* of waters   2 Cor 11:26
  See also: Acts 15:26, 1 Cor 15:30, 2 Tim 3:1

perish, *to be lost, die*
  a Syrian ready to *p*   Deut 26:5
  who *p* being innocent   Job 4:7
  shall *p* with sword   Mat 26:52
  carest not that we *p*   Mk 4:38
  believeth in him not *p*   Jno 3:15 f
  not willing that any *p*   2 Pet 3:9

Perizzites, *one of pre-Israelite tribes of Palestine,* Gen 13:7, Judg 1:4, 2 Chr 8:7

persecute, *pursue, oppress*

blessed when men *p* you Mat 5:11
pray for them that *p* you 5:44·
p me, they will *p* you Jno 15:20
why *p* thou me? Acts 9:4
bless them which *p* you Rom 12:14
being *p*, we suffer it 1 Cor 4:12
p but not forsaken 2 Cor 4:9
See also: Psa 44:22, Lk 11:47, 2 Cor 12:10

persecution *(see persecute)*
shall *p* separate us Rom 8:35
live godly suffer *p* 2 Tim 3:12

Persia, *eastern empire established by Cyrus,* 2 Chr 36:20, Esth 1:3,. Isa 21:2, Dan 5:28

person, *man, individual*
God respect any *p* 2 Sam 14:14
regardest not *p* of men Mat 22:16, Mk 12:14
express image of his *p* Heb 1:3
what manner of *p* ought 2 Pet 3:11

persuade, *convince, entice*
almost thou *p* me Acts 26:28
I am *p* that neither Rom 8:38
we *p* men 2 Cor 5:11
am *p* that he is able 2 Tim 1:12

pertain, *concern*
that *p* to this life 1 Cor 6:3
things that *p* to life 2 Pet 1:3

perverse, *turned about*
a *p* generation Deut 32:5
p tongue falleth into Pro 17:20
p generation Mat 17:17, Lk 9:41
midst of *p* generation Phil 2:15
See also: 2 Sam 19:6, Pro 28:6, Ecc 1:15

pervert, *to turn aside, distort*
gift doth *p* words Deut 16:19

have *p* words of God Jer 23:36
would *p* the gospel Gal 1:7

Peter, *apostle, also called Simon and Cephas,* Mat 4:18, 16:16, 17:1 ff, 26:69,75, Mk 1:16, Lk 5:3 ff, Jno 1:35, Acts 1:15, 2:14 ff, 10:1 ff, 15:7, Gal 2:14, *See also:* 1 & 2 Pet

Pharaoh, *title of Egyptian kings,* Gen 12:15, 40:1 ff, Ex 1:8 ff, 1 Ki 3:1, 2 Ki 23:29 ff

Pharisees, *sect of Jews who believed in resurrection,* Mat 5:20, 23:1 ff, Mk 2:18, 8:15, Lk 11:37, 12:1, Jno 7:32 ff, Acts 2:8

Phebe, *servant of church of Cenchrea,* Rom 16:1

Phenice, *Phoenicia,* Acts 11:19, 15:3, 27:12

Philadelphia, *one of seven churches of Asia,* Rev 1:11, 3:7

Philemon, *friend of Paul to whom Onesimus was sent back,* Philem 1

Philip, *an apostle,* Mat 10:3, Jno 1:43, 14:8; *deacon of Jerusalem church,* Acts 6:5, 8:5, 27, 21:8; *brother of Herod,* Mat 14:3, Mk 6:17, Lk 3:1,19

Philippi, *city of Macedonia,* Acts 16:2, *see also Paul's epistle to Philippians*

Philistia, *southwest portion of Palestine,* Gen 21:34, Ex 13:17, Josh 13:2, 2 Ki 8:2

Philistines, *invaders of Palestine,* Gen 10:14, 28:14, Josh 13:2,3, Judg 14:15, 1 Sam 4:1, 2 Chr 21:16

philosophy, *lit., love of wisdom*
spoil you through *p* Col 2:8

Phrygia, *province of central Asia Minor,* Acts 16:6, 18:23

physician, *healer*
whole need not *p*	Mat 9:12, Mk 2:17, Lk 5:31
p heal thyself	4:23
Luke the beloved *p*	Col 4:14

pierce, *to stab through*
p my hands and my feet	Psa 22:16
whom thy have *p*	Zech 12:10, Jno 19:37
p themselves with	1 Tim 6:10
p to dividing asunder	Heb 4:12

Pilate, *governor of Judea who allowed crucifixion of Jesus,* Mat 27:2,13 ff, Mk 15:1 ff, Lk 23:1 ff, Jno 18:29 ff, 19:1 ff

pillar, *column, support*
a *p* of salt	Gen 19:26
leddest by cloudy *p*	Neh 9:12
p and ground of truth	1 Tim 3:15
I will make a *p* in temple	Rev 3:12

pillow, *mattress, cushion*
Jacob put stones for *p*	Gen 28:11
Jesus was asleep on *p*	Mk 4:38

pipe, *flute*
we have *p* unto you	Mat 11:17, Lk 7:32

Pisgah, *mount where Moses died,* Num 23:14, Deut 3:27, 34:1

Pisidia, *province of Asia Minor,* Acts 13:14, 14:24

pit, *grave, ditch*
go down into the *p*	Num 16:30,33, Psa 28:1, 143:7, Pro 1:12
fall into his own *p*	28:10
p on sabbath	Mat 12:11, Lk 14:5

C.B.C.–8

pitcher, *pitcher, vessel*
p broken at fountain	Ecc 12:6

pity, *compassion*
hath *p* on poor	Pro 19:17
See also: Psa 69:20, Mat 5:7, Jas 5:11, 1 Pet 3:8	

place
eyes of Lord in every *p*	Pro 15:3
give *p* to wrath	Rom 12:19
neither give *p* to devil	Eph 4:17

plague, *a smiting, pestilence*
p of his own heart	1 Ki 12:13
God shall add *p* written	Rev 22:18

plain, *clear; level place*
p to him who understand	Pro 8:9
way of righteous made *p*	15:19
rough places made a *p*	Isa 40:4
be Christ, tell us *p*	Jno 10:24

plant, *herb*
God made every *p*	Gen 2:4
grow up as tender *p*	Isa 53:2
every *p* my Father hath	Mat 15:13

plant (verb), *to sow*
have been *p* together	Rom 6:5
I *p*, Apollos watered	1 Cor 3:6

play, *play instrument, act as children*
rose up to *p*	Ex 32:6, 1 Cor 10:7
I will *p* before Lord	2 Sam 6:21
p skilfully with	Psa 33:3
boys and girls *p* in	Zech 8:5

plead, *beg, implore*
p with your mother	Hos 2:2
I will *p* with them for	Joel 3:2

pleasant, *desirable*
p to the eyes	Gen 3:6
p for brethren to dwell	Psa 133:1
knowledge is *p* to soul	Pro 2:10
bread eaten in secret is *p*	9:17

p words are as honeycomb   16:24
that hath *p* voice   Ezek 33:32

please, *to satisfy*

p Lord to bruise him   Isa 53:10
in flesh cannot *p* God   Rom 8:8
even Christ *p* not self   15:3
p God by foolishness   1 Cor 1:21
without faith impossible to *p* Heb
                                  11:6

pleasure *(see please)*

p in uprightness   1 Chr 29:17
p in wickedness   Psa 5:4
taketh *p* in his people   149:4
I have no *p* in them   Ecc 12:1
p of Lord shall prosper   Isa 53:10
I have no *p* in you   Mat 1:10
choked with *p* of life   Lk 8:14
to will and do his *p*   Phil 2:13

plenty, *abundance*

p of corn and wine   Gen 27:28
gladness from *p* field   Jer 48:33
the harvest truly is *p*   Mat 9:37
ground brought forth *p*   Lk 12:16
See also: Lev 26:5, Pro 3:9,10, Joel
2:26

plow

p with my heifer   Judg 14:18
they that *p* iniquity reap   Job 4:8
a sluggard will not *p*   Pro 20:4
p of wicked is sin   21:4
swords into *p* shares   Isa 2:4, Mic
                                   4:3
p shares into swords   Joel 3:10
ye have *p* wickedness   Hos 10:13
hand to *p* and look back   Lk 9:62

pluck, *snatch away*

a time to *p* up   Ecc 3:2
firebrand *p* out of fire   Amos 4:11,
                                   Zech 3:3

if eye offend thee, *p* it out   Mat
                           5:29, 18:9, Mk 9:37
p them out of my hand   Jno 10:28

point, *thing, matter*

in all *p* tempted as we   Heb 4:15
yet offend in one *p*   Jas 2:10

poison, *venom*

p is under their lips   Psa 140:3
tongue full of deadly *p*   Jas 3:8

pollute, *contaminate*

p yourselves with idols Ezek 20:31,
                           23:30, 36:18
hath *p* this holy place   Acts 21:28
See also: Tit 1:15, 2 Pet 2:20, Rev
22:11

ponder, *weigh, consider*

p the path of thy feet   Pro 4:26
Mary *p* in her heart   Lk 2:19

poor, *destitute*

p shall never cease   Deut 15:11
deliver the *p* and needy   Psa 82:4
mercy on *p*, happy is   Pro 14:21
whoso mocketh *p*, reproacheth 17:5
lest I be *p* and steal   30:9
p and contrite spirit   Isa 66:2
sold *p* for a pair of   Amos 2:6
blessed are *p* in spirit   Mat 5:3
have *p* always with you 26:11, Mk
                           14:7, Jno 1:18
our sakes he became *p*   2 Cor 8:9
hath God chosen the *p*   Jas 2:5

portion, *part, piece*

Lord's *p* is his people   Deut 32:9
p of goods that falleth   Lk 15:12

possess, *take charge of*

p iniquities of youth   Job 13:26
patience *p* your souls   Lk 21:19

possession, *inheritance, acquired*
for an everlasting *p* Gen 17:8, 48:4
had great *p* Mat 19:22, Mk 10:22
sold their *p* Acts 2:45
See also: Pro 28:10, Lk 12:15, 1 Cor 3:21

possible, *able, capable*
with God all things are *p* Mat 19:26, Mk 10:27
if *p*, let this cup pass Mat 26:39, Mk 14:35
all things are *p* to him 9:23
all things are *p* 14:36, Lk 18:27
if *p*, live peaceably Rom 12:18
See also: Mat 17:20, 19:26, Phil 4:13

pot, *kettle, vessel*
take a *p* of manna Ex 16:33
there is death in *p* 2 Ki 4:40
washing of cups and *p* Mk 7:4

Potiphar, *Joseph's master,* Gen 39

pour, *to empty, spill*
now my soul is *p* out Job 30:16
I *p* out my soul Psa 42:4
p out your heart before 62:8
I will *p* out my Spirit Pro 1:23, Isa 44:3, Joel 2:28, Acts 2:17
will not *p* out blessing Mat 3:10

poverty, *lack, destitution*
p to him that refuseth Pro 13:18
neither *p* nor riches 30:8
through his *p* be rich 2 Cor 8:9
I know thy works and *p* Rev 2:9
See also: Deut 15:11, 1 Sam 2:7, Psa 37:16, Lk 6:20, Jas 2:5

powder, *dust*
ground to *p*^ Mat 21:44, Lk 20:18

power, *strength, ability, authority*
my strength and *p* 2 Sam 22:33
thine is *p* 1 Chr 29:11, Mat 6:13
redeem my soul from *p* Psa 49:15
p belongeth unto God 62:11
made earth by his *p* Jer 10:12, 51:16
delivered from *p* of evil Hab 2:9
son of man hath *p* to forgive Mat 9:6, Mk 2:10, Lk 5:24
all *p* is given Mat 28:18
kingdom of God came with *p* Mk 9:1
this *p* will I give thee Lk 4:6
p to cast into hell 12:5
endued with *p* from high 24:49
p to become sons of God Jno 1:12
receive *p* after Holy Ghost Acts 1:8
eternal *p* and Godhead Rom 1:20
p of his resurrection Phil 3:10
delivered us from *p* of Col 1:13
p, love, and sound mind 2 Tim 1:7
but denying the *p* 3:5
by word of his *p* Heb 1:3
word of God quick and *p* 4:12
worthy to receive *p* Rev 4:11, 5:12
See also: Isa 40:29, Rom 8:37, Heb 7:16

praise, *commendation, thanksgiving*
p is comely Psa 33:1, 147:1
let heaven and earth *p* him 69:34
let them *p* thy great name 99:3
enter his courts with *p* 100:4
who can shew forth his *p* 106:2
p ye the name of Lord Joel 2:26
earth was full of his *p* Hab 3:3
loved *p* of men Jno 12:43

whose *p* is in gospel   2 Cor 8:18
if there be any *p*   Phil 4:8
church I will sing *p*   Heb 2:12

pray, *praise, petition, implore*
  p for them which   Mat 5:44
  love to *p* standing in   6:5
  apart to *p*   14:23, Mk 6:46, Lk
                        6:12, 9:28
  p enter not into temptation   Mat
      26:41, Mk 14:38, Lk 22:40
  Lord, teach us to *p*   11:1
  I *p* for them, not for   Jno 17:9
  I will *p* with Spirit   1 Cor 14:15
  p without ceasing   1 Thes 5:17

prayer, *praise, petition*
  p of upright his delight   Pro 15:8
  house of *p* Isa 56:7, Mat 21:13, Mk
             11:17, Lk 19:46
  by *p* and fasting   Mat 17:21, Mk
                        9:29
  whatsoever ye ask in *p*   Mat 21:22
  thy *p* is heard   Acts 10:31
  by *p* let your requests   Phil 4:6
  p of faith shall save   Jas 5:15
  fervent *p* of righteous man   5:16
  the *p* of saints   Rev 5:8, 8:3

preach, *to tell, announce good news*
  appointed prophets to *p*   Neh 6:7
  anointed me to *p* good   Isa 61:1
  Jesus began to *p*   Mat 4:17
  John did *p* the baptism   Mk 1:4
  ceased not to *p*   Acts 5:42
  p a man should not   Rom 2:21
  how shall they *p* except   10:15
  p Christ crucified   1 Cor 1:23
  if I *p* not the Gospel   9:16
  when I have *p* to others   9:27
  so we *p* and so ye believed   15:11

p the word, be instant   2 Tim 4:2
See also: Acts 4:20, Col 4:3

preacher *(see preach)*
  how hear without a *p*?   Rom 10:14
  ordained a *p*   1 Tim 2:7, 2 Tim
                        1:11
  Noah, a *p* of   2 Pet 2:5

precious, *valuable, rare*
  word of Lord was *p*   1 Sam 3:1
  redemption of soul is *p*   Psa 49:8
  p in sight of Lord is   116:15
  wisdom more *p* than rubies   Pro
                        3:15
  lips of knowledge are *p*   20:15
  good name better than *p*   Ecc 7:1
  man more *p* than gold   Isa 13:12
  p blood of Christ   1 Pet 1:19
  obtained like *p* faith   2 Pet 1:1
  great and *p* promises   1:4

preeminence, *to be first*
  that he might have *p*   Col 1:18
  Diotrephes, loveth *p*   3 Jno 9
  See also: Mk 9:35, Rev 22:13

prefer, *to set forward, exalt*
  in honour *p* another   Rom 12:10

preparation *(see prepare)*
  feet shod with *p* of   Eph 6:15

prepare, *make ready*
  p your hearts   1 Sam 7:3
  p a table for me   Psa 23:5
  p the way of the Lord   Isa 40:3,
      Mal 3:1, Mat 3:3, Mk 1:3, Lk
                        1:76
  p to meet thy God   Amos 4:12
  my messenger shall *p*   Mal 3:1
  a people *p* for Lord   Lk 1:17
  I go to *p* a place for   Jno 14:2
  things God hath *p*   1 Cor 2:9

presbytery, *assembly of elders*
  laying on hands of *p*   1 Tim 4:14

presence
  hid from *p* of the Lord   Gen 3:8
  my *p* shall go with thee   Ex 33:14
  cast me not from thy *p*   Psa 51:11
  shall I flee from thy *p?*   139:7
  from *p* of the Lord   Acts 3:19
  his bodily *p* is weak   2 Cor 10:10

present, *near to*
  God is a very *p* help   Psa 46:1
  evil is *p* with me   Rom 7:21
  to be *p* with the Lord   2 Cor 5:8
  deliver us from *p* world   Gal 1:4
  godly in this *p* world   Tit 2:12

present (verb), *to give*
  p your bodies a living   Rom 12:1
  to *p* you holy   Col 1:22

preserve, *to save, keep*
  might *p* us alive   Deut 6:24
  Let integrity *p* me   Psa 25:21
  Lord shall *p* thy   121:8
  I will *p* thee   Isa 49:8
  lose his life, shall *p*   Lk 17:33

press, *crowd, push*
  good measure *p* down   Lk 6:38
  I *p* toward the mark   Phil 3:14

presumptuous, *proud, presuming*
  keep servant from *p* sins Psa 19:13
  p are they, self-willed   2 Pet 2:10
  See also: Pro 27:1, Ob 1:4, Job 20:6

pretence, *false claim, pretext*
  for a *p* make Mat 23:14, Mk 12:40
  whether in *p* or in truth   Phil 1:18
  See also: Isa 32:6, Lk 12:1, Tit 1:16

prevail, *to be strong, overcome*
  by strength no man *p*   1 Sam 2:9
  gates of hell not *p*   Mat 16:18

prevent, *to go before* (archaic)
  snares of death *p*   2 Sam 22:6, Psa 18:5
  not *p* them asleep   1 Thes 4:15

prey, *victim of aggressor*
  shall *p* be taken from   Isa 49:24
  flock no more be *p*   Ezek 34:22

price, *reward, value*
  her *p* far above rubies   Pro 31:10
  and milk without *p*   Isa 55:1
  one pearl of great *p*   Mat 13:46
  bought with a *p*   1 Cor 6:20
  meek spirit of great *p*   1 Pet 3:4

pricks, *goads, thorns*
  hard to kick against *p*   Acts 9:5, 26:14

pride, *arrogance, presumption*
  p do I hate   Pro 8:13
  by *p* cometh contention   13:10
  p goeth before destruction   16:18
  p of thine heart hath   Jer 49:16
  out of heart, *p*, foolishness Mk 7:22
  lifted up with *p*   1 Tim 3:6
  p of life is not of   1 Jno 2:16
  See also: 2 Chr 26:16, Pro 3:7, 30:13, Isa 65:5, Dan 4:30, Lk 18:11, Rom 2:19

priest, *a mediator between God and man*
  raise up a faithful *p*   1 Sam 2:35
  p for ever after Psa 110:4, Heb 5:6
  as people, so *p*   Isa 24:2
  came down a *p*   Lk 10:31
  made us *p* to God   Rev 1:6, 5:10

priesthood *(see priest)*
  hath an unchangeable *p*   Heb 7:24
  an holy *p*   1 Pet 2:5

ye are a royal *p*   2:9

prince, *ruler*
who made thee a *p*   Ex 2:14
p is fallen in Israel   2 Sam 3:38
the *p* of peace   Isa 9:6
casteth out devils through *p*   Mat
        9:34, 12:24, Mk 3:22
p of world Jno 12:31, 14:30, 16:11
killed the *p* of life   Acts 3:15
nor wisdom of *p* of   1 Cor 2:6

principality, *rulership*
neither *p* nor powers   Rom 8:38
far above all *p*   Eph 1:21
we wrestle against *p*   6:12

print, *mark*
except I see *p* of nails   Jno 20:25

prison, *dungeon, jail*
butler and baker in *p*   Gen 40:3
in *p* and ye came   Mat 25:36

prisoner, *captive*
p of hope   Zech 9:12
release *p*   Mat 27:15
p of Jesus   Eph 3:1, 4:1, Philem 9

private, *one's own*
of *p* interpretation   2 Pet 1:20

privily, *privately*
p slandereth neighbour   Psa 101:5
p bring in heresies   2 Pet 2:1

prize, *crown, reward*
one receiveth *p*   1 Cor 9:24
I press for the *p*   Phil 3:14
See also: Psa 58:11, 2 Tim 4:8

proceed, *go out, forward*
thing *p* from the Lord   Gen 24:50
p out of mouth of God   Deut 8:3,
                                Mat 4:4
which *p* out of mouth defile   15:18,
                                Mk 7:21

same mouth *p* blessing   Jas 3:10

proclaim, *to declare*
p liberty to captives   Isa 61:1
shall be *p* on housetops   Lk 12:3

prodigal, *wasteful, See:* Pro 21:20, 29:3,
        Lk 15:13 ff

profane, *to make common, irreverent*
neither *p* name of God   Lev 18:21,
        19:12, 20:3, 21:6, 22:2
avoid *p* babblings   1 Tim 6:20,
                                2 Tim 2:16
lest be any *p* person   Heb 12:16

profess, *say, assert, affirm*
p I never knew you   Mat 7:23
p selves to be wise   Rom 1:22
p a good profession   1 Tim 6:12
they *p* they know God   Tit 1:16
hold fast our *p*   Heb 4:14

profit (noun), *value, gain*
in all labour is *p*   Pro 14:23
what *p* hath   Ecc 1:3, 3:9, 5:11
no *p* under the sun   2:11
by wisdom there is *p*   7:11
what *p* of circumcision?   Rom 3:1

profit (verb)
cannot *p*, nor deliver   1 Sam 12:21
treasures of wickedness *p*   Pro 10:2
riches *p* not in the day   11:4
what is a man *p* if   Mat 16:26, Mk
                                8:36
Christ shall *p* you   Gal 5:2
exercise *p* little   1 Tim 4:8
what doth it *p*?   Jas 2:14

profitable *(see profit)*
can a man be *p* to God?   Job 22:2
wisdom is *p* to direct   Ecc 10:10
godliness is *p* to all   1 Tim 4:8
scripture is *p* for   2 Tim 3:16

prolong, *to lengthen*

  p your days   Deut 4:26, 30:18

  fear of Lord *p* days   Pro 10:27

promise, *word, agreement*

  doth his *p* fail?   Psa 77:8

  p is to you and your   Acts 2:39

  p is made of none effect Rom 4:14

  make *p* of none effect   Gal 3:17

  having *p* of the life that now is

                  1 Tim 4:8

  through faith inherit *p*   Heb 6:12

  great and precious *p*   2 Pet 1:4

  where is the *p* of coming?   3:4

  Lord not slack concerning *p*   3:9

promise (verb)

  p before the world began   Tit 1:2

  faithful that *p*   Heb 10:23, 11:11

promote, *cause to prosper*

  wisdom shall *p* thee   Pro 4:8

proof, *evidence, token*

  shewed himself alive by *p* Acts 1:3

  ye seek *p* of Christ   2 Cor 13:3

  make full *p*   2 Tim 4:5

  See also: Jno 4:48, 2 Cor 8:24, 1 Jno
4:1

prophecy, *message*

  p shall fail   1 Cor 13:8

  more sure word of *p*   2 Pet 1:19

  p came not by will of man   1:21

  any take from this *p*   Rev 22:19

prophesy, *to speak forth*

  prophets *p* falsely   Jer 5:31

  prophets *p* lies   14:14, 23:25

  sons shall *p* Joel 2:28, Acts 2:17

  whether prophecy let us *p*   Rom
12:6

  we *p* in part   1 Cor 13:9

prophet, *one who speaks forth*

  Aaron shall be thy *p*   Ex 7:1

  Lord's people were *p* Num 11:29

  Lord will raise up a *p* Deut 18:15,

               Acts 3:22, 7:37

  do my *p* no harm 1 Chr 16:2, Psa
105:15

  I was no *p*, nor *p*'s son Amos 7:14

  the *p* is a fool   Hos 9:7

  no *p* is accepted in   Lk 4:24

  he gave some *p*   Eph 4:11

propitiation, *that which appeases*

  set forth to be a *p*   Rom 3:25

  p for our sins   1 Jno 2:2, 4:10

  See also: 1 Cor 15:3, Eph 2:16, Col
1:19

proportion, *equality*

  according to *p* of faith Rom 12:6

prosper, *get gain, increase*

  he doeth shall *p*   Psa 1:3

  covereth sins not *p*   Pro 28:13

  pleasure of Lord *p*   Isa 53:10

prosperity *(see prosper)*

  when I saw *p* of wicked Psa 73:3

  p of fools shall destroy Pro 1:32

  in day of *p* be joyful   Ecc 7:14

proud *(see pride)*

  every one that is *p*   Job 40:11

  respecteth not the *p*   Psa 40:4

  him that hath a *p* heart   101:5

  contempt of the *p*   123:4

  the *p* he knoweth afar off 138:6

  the Lord hateth a *p* look Pro 6:17

  high look and *p* heart is   21:4

  better than *p* in spirit   Ecc 7:8

  we call the *p* happy   Mal 3:15

  God resisteth *p* Jas 4:6, 1 Pet 5:5

prove, *test*

examine me, O Lord, *p* me   Psa 26:2

I go to *p* them   Lk 14:19
p what is good will of   Rom 12:2
p all things   1 Thes 5:21

proverb, *saying*

become *p,* and byword   Deut 28:37
set in order many *p*   Ecc 12:9
no more speak *p*   Jno 16:25

provide, *supply*

God will *p* a lamb   Gen 22:8
p things honest   Rom 12:17
p not for own house   1 Tim 5:8

provision, *allowance*

make not *p* for flesh   Rom 13:14

provoke, *anger, stir up*

how long people *p* me? Num 14:11
p to jealousy   Rom 10:19, 11:11
charity not easily *p*   1 Cor 13:5
p not children to wrath   Eph 6:4
p to love and good   Heb 10:24

prudent, *wise, intelligent*

p man covereth shame   Pro 12:16
p man concealeth knowledge 12:23
wisdom of *p* is to understand 14:8
a *p* wife is from the Lord   19:14
p man foreseeth evil   22:3, 27:12
woe to them *p* in own   Isa 5:21
hid from wise and *p* Mat 11:25, Lk 10:21
the understanding of *p*   1 Cor 1:19

psalms, *songs of praise*

make a joyful noise with *p* Psa 95:2
David saith in *p*   Lk 20:42
speaking to yourselves in *p*   Eph 5:19
one another in *p*   Col 3:16

let him sing *p*   Jas 5:13

publican, *tax collector*

do not even *p* the same? Mat 5:46
a friend of *p*   11:19, Lk 7:34
p go into kingdom of God   Mat 21:31
one a Pharisee, other *p*   Lk 18:10

publish, *tell, declare abroad*

p it not in Askelon   2 Sam 1:20
that *p* peace   Isa 52:7, Nah 1:15
word of Lord was *p*   Acts 13:49

pull, *draw, tug*

p mote out   Mat 7:4, Lk 6:42
I will *p* down my barns   12:18
p him out on Sabbath   14:5
p them out of the fire   Jude 23

pulpit, *high place*

stood upon a *p* of wood   Neh 8:4

punish, *smite, avenge*

to *p* just is not good   Pro 17:26
to *p* inhabitants of earth. Isa 26:21
p with everlasting   2 Thes 1:9
of judgment to be *p*   2 Pet 2:9

punishment *(see punish)*

my *p* is greater than   Gen 4:13
man of wrath suffer *p*   Pro 19:19
bear *p* of iniquity   Ezek 14:10
into everlasting *p*   Mat 25:46
of how much sorer *p*   Heb 10:29

purchase, *buy*

Abraham *p* of sons of   Gen 25:10
this man *p* a field   Acts 1:18
p with his own blood   20:28
redemption of *p* possession   Eph 1:14

pure, *clean, sincere*

words of Lord are *p*   Psa 12:6
commandment of Lord is *p*   19:8

words of *p* pleasant   Pro 15:26
who say, I am *p* from sin?   20:9
every word of God is *p*   30:5
blessed are *p* in heart   Mat 5:8
all things are *p*   Rom 14:20
whatsoever things are *p*   Phil 4:8
p conscience   1 Tim 3:9, 2 Tim 1:3
keep thyself *p*   1 Tim 5:22
to *p* all things are *p*   Tit 1:15
p religion   Jas 1:27
wisdom from above first *p*   3:17
love with *p* heart   1 Pet 1:22
even as he is *p*   1 Jno 3:3

purge, *to purify, refine*
p me with hyssop   Psa 51:7
he will *p*   Mat 3:12, Lk 3:17
beareth fruit, he *p*   1 Cor 5:7
p your conscience   Heb 9:14
hath forgotten he was *p*   2 Pet 1:9

purify *(see pure)*
p to himself, peculiar   Tit 2:14
p your hearts, ye double   Jas 4:8

purpose, *intention, goal*
a time to every *p*   Ecc 3:1,17, 8:6
with *p* of heart   Acts 11:23
called according to *p*   Rom 8:28
as he *p* in his heart   2 Cor 9:7
eternal *p* in Christ   Eph 3:11
according to his *p* and grace 2 Tim
1:9
for this *p* the Son   1 Jno 3:8

pursue, *to follow, seek for*
seek peace and *p* it   Psa 34:14
that *p* evil, *p* death   Pro 11:19
evil *p* sinners   13:21
wicked flee when no man *p*   28:1

put, *place*
I will *p* enmity between   Gen 3:15

p all things under feet Psa 8:6, Eph
1:22, Heb 2:8
p my spirit upon him Isa 42:1, Mat
12:18
let no man *p* asunder   19:6, Mk
10:9
p all enemies under   1 Cor 15:25
p off old man   Eph 4:22, Col 3:9
p him to an open shame   Heb 6:6
will *p* you in remembrance   Jude 5

Q

quails, *See:* Ex 16:13, Num 11:3 ff, Psa
105:40

quake, *tremble*
whole mount *q* greatly   Ex 19:18
host trembled, earth *q* 1 Sam 14:15
earth shall *q* before   Joel 2:10
the mountains *q* at him   Nah 1:5
earth did *q* and rocks   Mat 27:51

quarrel, *complaint*
he seeketh *q* against me   2 Ki 5:7
if any have *q*   Col 3:13
See also: Lev 26:25, Mk 6:19, 1 Cor
11:16, 2 Cor 12:20

queen
q of Sheba   1 Ki 10:1, 2 Chr 9:1
removed Maacah from being *q*
1 Ki 15:13, 2 Chr 15:16
Vashti the *q* made feast   Est 1:9
incense to *q* of heaven Jer 44:17,25
q of south shall rise Mat 12:42, Lk
11:31
Candace *q* of Ethiopia   Acts 8:27

quench, *extinguish, destroy*

   q not light of Israel   2 Sam 21:17
   they are *q* as fire   Psa 118:12
   waters cannot *q* love   S of S 8:7
   flax not be *q*   Isa 42:3, Mat 12:20
   where fire is not *q*   Mk 9:44 ff
   able to *q* fiery darts   Eph 6:16
   q not Spirit   1 Thes 5:19

question, *to ask, inquiry, matter*

   lawyer asked him a *q*   Mat 22:35
   I will ask you one *q*   Mk 11:29
   q of words and names   Acts 18:15
   no *q* of conscience   1 Cor 10:25
   but doting about *q*   1 Tim 6:4
   foolish and unlearned *q* 2 Tim 2:23

quick, *living* (archaic)

   judge of *q* and dead   Acts 10:42
   shall judge *q* and dead   2 Tim 4:1,
                 1 Pet 4:5
   the word of God is *q*   Heb 4:12

quicken, *to give or preserve life*

   q me according to thy word   Psa
                 119:25,149
   as father *q* them even   Jno 5:21
   it is the Spirit that *q*   6:63
   even God who *q* the dead   Rom
                  4:17
   shall also *q* your mortal   8:11
   See also: Ezek 37:5 ff, Jno 11:25,
   2 Cor 3:6, Eph 2:5, Col 2:13, 1 Tim
   6:13

quickly, *speedily, hastily*

   agree with adversary *q*   Mat 5:25
   that thou doest, do *q*   Jno 13:27
   come *q* and remove candlestick
                  Rev 2:5
   behold, I come *q*   3:11, 22:7,12
   surely I come *q*   22:20

quiet, *calm, silent*

   words of wise heard in *q*   Ecc 9:17
   be *q* fear not   Isa 7:4
   study to be *q*   1 Thes 4:11
   sorrow on sea, cannot be *q*   Jer
                  49:32
   lead a *q* and peaceable   1 Tim 2:2
   a meek and *q* spirit   1 Pet 3:4
   See also: Psa 4:8, Ecc 9:11, Lk
   10:41, Heb 4:9

quietness, *peace, security, calmness*

   better a dry morsel and *q* Pro 17:1
   better is handful with *q*   Ecc 4:6
   in *q* and confidence   Isa 30:15
   exhort that with *q*   2 Thes 3:12

quit, *to act or conduct self*

   q yourselves like men   1 Sam 4:9
   1 Cor 16:13; *in sense of innocent or*
   free, see: Ex 21:28, Josh 34:29, Job
   34:29

R

rabbi, *master,* Mat 23:7, Jno 1:38, 3:2

raca, *fool,* Mat 5:22

race, *course, contest*

   a strong man to run a *r*   Psa 19:5
   r is not to the swift   Ecc 9:11
   they which run a *r*   1 Cor 9:24
   run with patience *r*   Heb 12:1

Rachel, *wife of Jacob,* Gen 29:10, 31:1

rage, *show violent anger*

   why do heathen *r*   Psa 2:1, Acts
                  4:25
   fool *r*, and is confident   Pro 14:16

raging *(see rage)*

thou rulest the *r* of sea	Psa 89:9
strong drink is *r*	Pro 20:1
rebuked *r* of the water	Lk 8:24

rags, *tatters*

our righteousness as *r*	Isa 64:6

Rahab, *prostitute of Jericho,* Josh 2:1,
6:17, Heb 11:31, Jas 2:25

raiment, *clothing*

r waxed not old	Deut 8:4
r of camel's hair	Mat 3:4
body more than *r*	6:25, Lk 12:23
clothed in soft *r*	Mat 11:8, Lk 7:25
r white as light	Mat 17:2, Mk 9:3, Lk 9:29
parted his *r*	23:34, Jno 19:24
having food and *r* let	1 Tim 6:8
a poor man in vile *r*	Jas 2:2

rain

had not caused it to *r*	Gen 2:5
r from heaven was	8:2
I will *r* bread from	Ex 16:4
r in due season	Lev 26:4, Deut 11:14, 28:12
doctrine drop as *r*	32:2
who giveth *r* upon	Job 5:10
and *r* down manna	Psa 78:24,27
like clouds without *r*	Pro 25:14
clouds return after *r*	Ecc 12:2
as *r* cometh down	Isa 55:10
and *r* righteousness	Hos 10:12
sendeth *r* on just and	Mat 5:45
r descended, and floods	7:25
earth drinketh in the *r*	Heb 6:7

raise, *to lift up*

r up a prophet	Deut 18:15, Acts 3:22
dead are *r* up	Mat 11:5, Lk 7:22

three days I will *r* it	Jno 2:19
r him up at the last day	6:40
was *r* again for	Rom 4:25
as Christ was *r* from dead	6:4
r us by his power	1 Cor 6:14
trust God who *r* dead	2 Cor 1:9
he shall *r* us by Jesus	4:14
hath *r* us up together	Eph 2:6
the Lord shall *r* him up	Jas 5:15

Ramoth-Gilead, *city of Gilead, east of
the Jordan,* 1 Ki 4:13, 22:4

ransom, *price of freedom*

for the *r* of his life	Ex 21:30
r of a man's life are	Pro 13:8
his life a *r* for	Mat 20:28, Mk 10:45
gave himself a *r* for	1 Tim 2:6

rash, *hasty*

be not *r* with thy mouth	Ecc 5:2

rather, *rather, more*

go *r* to the lost sheep	Mat 10:6
yea *r*, that is risen	Rom 8:34

reach, *touch, stretch*

tower may *r* to heaven	Gen 11:4
r forth to those things	Phil 3:13

read

have ye not *r*	Mat 12:3, Mk 2:25, Lk 6:3
epistle, known and *r*	2 Cor 3:2
blessed is he that *r*	Rev 1:3

ready, *prepared*

a Syrian *r* to perish	Deut 26:5
all things *r*	Mat 22:4, Lk 14:17
be also *r*	Mat 24:44, Lk 12:40
spirit is *r*, flesh	Mk 14:38
I am *r* to preach the	Rom 1:15
I am *r* to be offered	2 Tim 4:6
r to every good work	Tit 3:1

be *r* to give an answer   1 Pet 3:15

reap, *gather harvest*
sow in tears, *r* in joy   Psa 126:5
regardeth clouds not *r*   Ecc 11:4
shall *r* the whirlwind   Hos 8:7
sow righteousness, *r*   10:12
sow not, neither *r*   Mat 6:26, Lk
                 12:24
r where I sowed   Mat 25:26, Lk
                 19:22
soweth sparingly, shall *r*   2 Cor 9:6

reason, *explanation*
a *r* of the hope   1 Pet 3:15

reason, *weigh, discuss*
let us *r* together   Isa 1:18
why *r* ye among   Mat 16:8
as he *r* of righteousness   Acts 24:25

rebel, *turn against*
r not against the Lord   Num 14:9
r against words of God   Psa 107:11

rebellious *(see rebel)*
let not the *r* exalt   Psa 66:7
a *r* generation   78:8
people hath a *r* heart   Jer 5:23

rebuke, *correct*
r a wise man, and he will   Pro 9:8
a scorner heareth not *r*   13:1
open *r* is better than   27:5
better hear *r* of wise   Ecc 7:5
Peter began to *r*   Mat 16:22, Mk
                 8:32
r not an elder   1 Tim 5:1
r with longsuffering   2 Tim 4:2
r sharply   Tit 1:13, 2:15

receive, *accept*
if thou wilt *r* my words   Pro 2:1
able to *r* it   Mat 19:12
believe ye *r*   Mk 11:24

as many as *r* him   Jno 1:12
can *r* nothing except   3:27
ask, and ye shall *r*   16:24
blessed to give than *r*   Acts 20:35
shall *r* his own reward   1 Cor 3:8
every one *r* things done   2 Cor 5:10
ye ask and *r* not   Jas 4:3
whatsoever we ask, we *r*   1 Jno
                 3:22

reckon, *take account of*
Reward is not *r* of grace   Rom 4:4
I *r* the sufferings of   8:18

recompense, *repay*
say not, I will *r* evil   Pro 20:22
r them according   Jer 25:14, Hos
                 12:2
r to do man evil for   Rom 12:17
great *r* of reward   Heb 10:35

reconcile, *reunite, appease*
be *r* to thy brother   Mat 5:24
God was in Christ, *r*   2 Cor 5:19
be ye *r* to God   5:20
might *r* both to God   Eph 2:16
to *r* all things to   Col 1:20
See also: 2 Cor 5:18, Heb 2:17

record, *testify, write*
call heaven to *r*   Deut 30:19
I bear them *r* they have   Rom 10:2
three that bear *r*   1 Jno 5:7

red, *red, fiery*
eyes be *r* with wine   Gen 49:12
the wine is *r*   Psa 75:8
not on wine when *r*   Pro 23:31
sins be *r* like crimson   Isa 1:18

redeem, *free*
I will *r* you   Ex 6:6
God went to *r*   2 Sam 7:23
r us from the curse   Gal 3:13

r us from all iniquity — Tit 2:14
not *r* with corruptible — 1 Pet 1:18
thou hast *r* us to God — Rev 5:9

redeemer *(see redeem)*
I know my *r* liveth — Job 19:25
I am thy *r* — Isa 49:26, 60:16
thou art our Father, our *r* — 63:16

redemption *(see redeem)*
r of soul is precious — Psa 49:8
them that looked for *r* — Lk 2:38
r though blood — Eph 1:7, Col 1:14

refrain, *withhold*
I have not *r* my lips — Psa 40:9
I *r* my feet from — 119:101
r his lips is wise — Pro 10:19
r his tongue from — 1 Pet 3:10

refresh, *rest*
Lord rested, and was *r* — Ex 31:17
times of *r* shall come — Acts 3:19

refuge, *place of safety*
eternal God is thy *r* — Deut 33:27
my high tower and *r* — 2 Sam 22:3
the Lord is his *r* — Psa 14:6
my *r* in day of trouble — 59:16

refuse, *reject*
stone which builders *r* — Psa 118:22
he that *r* instruction — Pro 15:32
nothing to be *r* — 1 Tim 4:4
r not him that speaketh — Heb 12:25

regard, *observe, consider*
r not iniquity — Job 36:21
fear not God, nor *r* man — Lk 18:4
he that *r* day, *r* it — Rom 14:6

rehearse, *retell*
they *r* all that God — Act 14:27

Rehoboam, *king of Judah,* 1 Ki 11:43, 2 Chr 9:31

reign, *rule*

Lord shall *r* for ever — Ex 15:18
trees said, *r* thou — Judg 9:8
king shall *r* over — 1 Sam 12:12
Lord of hosts shall *r* — Isa 24:23
shall *r* in life by — Rom 5:17
let not sin *r* in your — 6:12
we shall also *r* with — 2 Tim 2:12
he shall *r* for ever and — Rev 11:15
Lord God omnipotent *r* — 19:6
they shall *r* for ever and — 22:5

reins, *kidneys*
God trieth the hearts and *r* — Psa 7:9
girdle of his *r* — Isa 11:5

reject, *loathe, disapprove*
ye have *r* God — 1 Sam 10:19
he is *r* of men — Isa 53:3
stone which builders *r* — Mat 21:42, Mk 12:10, Lk 20:17
be *r* of elders — Mk 8:31, Lk 9:22
be *r* of this generation — 17:25

rejoice, *to be joyful*
shall *r* in all ye — Deut 12:7
heart *r* that seek — 1 Chr 16:10, Psa 105:3
r as a strong man — 19:5
statutes are right, *r* heart — 19:8
let the heavens *r* — 96:11
let the earth *r* — 97:1
I *r* at thy word — 119:162
r not when thine enemy — Pro 24:17
many shall *r* at his — Lk 1:14
went on his way *r* — Acts 8:39
r in hope — Rom 12:12
r with them that do *r* — 12:15
r not in iniquity — 1 Cor 13:6
r in the Lord — Phil 3:1, 4:4
r evermore — 1 Thes 5:16
r of hope firm unto end — Heb 3:6

ye *r* with joy unspeakable 1 Pet 1:8

relieve, *rescue*

brother be poor, *r* him   Lev 25:35
r the oppressed   Isa 1:17

religion, *to live by rule*

profited in Jew's *r*   Gal 1:14
pure *r* and undefiled·   Jas 1:27

remain, *to be left*

while earth *r*   Gen 8:22
body not *r* on tree   Deut 21:23
I only, *r* a prophet   1 Ki 18:22
who *r* unto coming   1 Thes 4:15
r no more sacrifice   Heb 10:26
strengthen things which *r*   Rev 3:2

remember, *be reminded*

r sabbath day   ╱   Ex 20:8
r all the commandments   Num 15:39
r now thy Creator   Ecc 12:1
r Lot's wife   Lk 17:32
Lord, *r* me when   23:42
r them that have rule   Heb 13:7

remembrance, *recollection*

in death there is no *r*   Psa 6:5
righteous be everlasting *r*   112:6
no *r* of the wise   Ecc 2:16
this do in *r*   Lk 22:19, 1 Cor 11:24
all things to your *r*   Jno 14:26
alms. are had in *r*   Acts 10:31
put them in *r*   2 Tim 2:14
pure minds by way of *r*   2 Pet 3:1

remission, *to send away*

shed for *r* of sins   Mat 26:28
repentance for *r*   Mk 1:4, Lk 3:3
baptized for *r*   Acts 2:38
shall receive *r*   10:43
without blood no *r*   Heb 9:22

remnant, *what is left over*

prayer for the *r* 2 Ki 19:4, Isa 37:4
r shall be very small   16:14

remove, *take away*

not *r* landmark   Deut 19:14
though the earth be *r*   Psa 46:2
righteous never be *r*   Pro 10:30
hills shall be *r*   Isa 54:10
r hence, it shall *r*   Mat 17:20
I could *r* mountains   1 Cor 13:2
I marvel ye are so soon *r*   Gal 1:6

rend, *tear*

a time to *r*   Ecc 3:7
lest they turn and *r* you   Mat 7:6
not *r* it, but cast   Jno 19:24

render, *to give*

r to every man Pro 24:12, Rom 2:6
r unto Caesar   Mat 22:21, Mk 12:17, Lk 20:25
not *r* evil for evil   1 Thes 5:15, 1 Pet 3:9

renew, *make new*

r a right spirit within   Psa 51:10
wait on Lord shall *r*   Isa 40:31
inward man is *r*   2 Cor 4:16
r in spirit of your   Eph 4:23
new man, *r* in knowledge Col 3:10
if fall away, to *r* them   Heb 6:6

renown, *fame*

men of *r*   Gen 6:4, Num 16:2

rent, *a tear (see rend)*

r is made worse Mat 9:16, Mk 2:21
veil of temple was *r* Mat 9:16, Mk 15:38, Lk 23:45

repay, *give back*

Vengeance is mine, I will *r*   Rom 12:19

repent, *to turn back*

it *r* the Lord   Gen 6:6
Lord *r* of   Ex 32:14, 2 Sam 24:16,
                     1 Chr 21:15, Jer 26:19
if turn, I will *r*   18:8, 26:13
that men should *r*   Mk 6:12
except ye *r*   Lk 13:3
if brother *r*, forgive   17:3
r and be baptized   Acts 2:38
r ye therefore and   3:19
r of this thy wickedness   8:22
commandeth all men to *r*   17:30
they should *r*, and turn   26:20
r, or else I will   Rev 2:16

repentance *(see repent)*
fruits meet for *r*   Mat 3:8, Lk 3:8,
                            Acts 26:20
to call sinners to *r*   Mat 9:13, Mk
                         2:17, Lk 5:32
leadeth thee to *r*   Rom 2:4
godly sorrow worketh *r* 2 Cor 7:10
the foundation of *r*   Heb 6:1
renew them again to *r*   6:6
all should come to *r*   2 Pet 3:9

repetitions, *saying again and again*
use not vain *r* as   Mat 6:7

report, *word, testimony*
evil *r* of the land   Num 13:32
who hath believed our *r*   Isa 53:1
things are of good *r*   Phil 4:8
bishop must have good *r* 1 Tim 3:7
r for good works   5:10

reproach, *disgrace*
oppresseth, *r* his   Pro 14:31, 17:5
sin is *r* to people   14:34
fear not *r* of men   Isa 51:7
r you for my sake   Lk 6:22
we labour and suffer *r* 1 Tim 4:10
r of Christ greater   Heb 11:26

if ye be *r* of Christ's   1 Pet 4:14

reprobate, *disapproved*
gave them to a *r* mind   Rom 1:28

reproof, *rebuke*
regardeth *r* is prudent   Pro 15:5
profitable for *r*   2 Tim 3:16

reprove *(see reproof)*
r not a scorner, lest   Pro 9:8
lest he *r* thee, and thou   30:6
r, rebuke, exhort   2 Tim 4:2

reputation, *honor*
r for wisdom   Ecc 10:1
made himself of no *r*   Phil 2:7

request, *ask, seek*
every prayer making *r*   Phil 1:4
let your *r* be made known to   4:6

require, *ask, demand*
blood will I *r*   Gen 9:5
what doth Lord *r* Deut 10:12, Mic
                               6:8
two things have I *r*   Pro 30:7
blood will I *r*   Ezek 3:18, 33:6
thy soul shall be *r*   Lk 12:20

requite, *give, repay*
so God hath *r* me   Judg 1:7
Lord will *r* good for   2 Sam 16:12

resemble, *to be like, liken*
whereunto shall I *r*   Lk 13:18

reserve, *keep back*
r day of destruction   Job 21:30
inheritance *r* in heaven   1 Pet 1:4
mist of darkness *r*   2 Pet 2:17
to whom is *r* blackness   Jude 13

resist, *to oppose*
ye *r* not evil   Mat 5:39
whosoever *r* the power   Rom 13:2
God *r* proud   Jas 4:6, 1 Pet 5:5
r the devil, and he   Jas 4:7

whom *r* stedfast in   1 Pet 5:9

resort, *to go*
    Jesus ofttimes *r* thither   Jno 18:2

respect, *accept, regard*
    the Lord had *r* to Abel   Gen 4:4
    God had *r* unto them   Ex 2:25
    no *r* of persons with God   2 Chr
      19:7, Rom 2:11, Eph 6:9, Col
      3:25
    blessed is man that *r* not   Psa 40:4
    not good to *r* person   Pro 24:23,
      28:21
    without *r* of persons   1 Pet 1:17

rest, *stillness, remainder*
    he *r* on seventh day   Gen 12:2
    the Sabbath of *r*   Ex 25:4
    I will give thee *r*   33:14
    return to thy *r*   Psa 116:7
    find *r* for souls   Jer 6:16
    I will give you *r*   Mat 11:28
    they *r* not, day and night   Rev 4:8
    may *r* from labours   14:13

restore, *to give back*
    he *r* my soul   Psa 23:3
    r the joy of salvation   51:12
    I *r* him fourfold   Lk 19:8
    r such an one in meekness   Gal 6:1

restrain, *hold back*
    rain from heaven was *r*   Gen 8:2
    scarce *r* that the   Acts 14:18

resurrection, *cause to stand*
    Sadducees say there is no *r*   Mat
      22:23, Mk 12:18, Acts 23:8,
      1 Cor 15:12
    I am *r* and life   Jno 11:25
    preached Jesus and *r*   Acts 17:18
    in likeness of his *r*   Rom 6:5
    know power of his *r*   Phil 3:10

obtain a better *r*   Heb 11:35
this is the first *r*   Rev 20:5

retain, *to keep*
    gracious woman *r* honour   Pro
      11:16
    no man hath power to *r*   Ecc 8:8
    whose soever sins ye *r* they   Jno
      20:23
    did not like to *r* God   Rom 1:28

return, *turn back*
    to dust shalt thou *r*   Gen 3:19
    naked shall I *r*   Job 1:21
    and *r* to the dust   Psa 104:29
    as dog *r* to his vomit   Pro 26:11
    naked shall he *r*   Ecc 5:15
    dust *r* to earth, and spirit   12:7
    not *r* to me void   Isa 55:11
    r to give glory to   Lk 17:18
    now *r* to the shepherd   1 Pet 2:25

Reuben, *son of Jacob,* Gen 29:32,
    35:23, Ex 1:2, Num 1:20

reveal, *make known*
    a talebearer *r* secrets   Pro 11:13
    God that *r* secrets   Dan 2:28
    he *r* his secret   Amos 3:7
    that shall not be *r*   Mat 10:26
    and blood hath not *r*   16:17
    when Son of man is *r*   Lk 17:30
    wrath of God is *r* from   Rom 1:18
    when Lord shall be *r*   2 Thes 1:7
    that man of sin be *r*   2:3
    glory that shall be *r*   1 Pet 5:1

revelation *(see reveal)*
    r of the mystery   Rom 16:25
    r of Jesus Christ   Rev 1:1

revellings, *carousing*
    works of flesh are *r*   Gal 5:21
    we walked in lusts, *r*   1 Pet 4:3

revenge, *to exact justice*
　r all disobedience　2 Cor 10:6
　See also: Num 35:19, Rom 13:4

revenue, *income*
　my *r* is better than　Pro 8:19
　is better than great *r*　16:8

reverence, *fear, awe, veneration*
　they will *r* my son　Mat 21:37, Mk
　　12:6, Lk 20:13
　serve God with *r*　Heb 12:28

revile, *to speak injuriously*
　when men shall *r* you　Mat 5:11
　they that passed by *r* him　27:39
　they *r* him　Mk 15:32
　being *r* we bless　1 Cor 4:12
　when he was *r, r* not　1 Pet 2:23
　See also: Isa 51:7, 1 Cor 6:10

revive, *cause to live again*
　wilt thou not *r* us again　Psa 85:6
　to *r* spirit of humble　Isa 57:15
　Christ died, rose and *r*　Rom 14:9

revolt, *to turn aside, against*
　oppression and *r*　Isa 59:13

reward, *recompense, wages*
　I will *r* them that hate　Deut 32:41
　the Lord *r* thee　1 Sam 24:19
　hireling looketh for *r*　Job 7:2
　the *r* of the wicked　Psa 91:8
　not *r* us according to　103:10
　your *r* in heaven　Mat 5:12
　what *r* have ye　5:46
　they have their *r*　6:2,5,16
　he shall *r* every man　16:27
　your *r* shall be great　Lk 6:35
　r is not reckoned of　Rom 4:4
　shall receive his own *r*　1 Cor 3:8
　worthy of his *r*　1 Tim 5:18
　recompence of *r*　Heb 2:2, 10:35,
　　11:26

rich, *rich, wealthy*
　Lord maketh poor and *r* 1 Sam 2:7
　hand of diligent maketh *r* Pro 10:4
　the *r* hath many friends　14:20
　the *r* answereth roughly　18:23
　loveth wine not *r*　21:17
　labour not to be *r*　23:4
　r man is wise in　28:11
　curse not the *r* in thy　Ecc 10:20
　let not the *r* man glory　Jer 9:23
　not *r* toward God　Lk 12:21
　for he was very *r*　18:23
　yet making many *r*　2 Cor 6:10
　r, yet for your sakes he　8:9
　God who is *r* in mercy　Eph 2:4
　be *r* in good works　1 Tim 6:18
　chosen poor, *r* in faith　Jas 2:5
　thou sayest, I am *r*　Rev 3:17

riches, *wealth*
　he heapeth up *r*　Psa 39:6
　trusted in abundance of *r*　52:7
　if *r* increase, set not　62:10
　the ungodly increase in *r*　73:12
　r profit not in day of　Pro 11:4
　ransom of life are *r*　13:8
　neither poverty, nor *r*　30:8
　I give thee hidden *r*　Isa 45:3
　deceitfulness of *r*　Mat 13:22, Mk
　　4:19, Lk 8:14
　they that have *r*　Mk 10:23
　unsearchable *r* of Christ　Eph 3:8
　nor trust in uncertain *r* 1 Tim 6:17
　reproach of Christ greater *r*　Heb
　　11:26

right, *just, proper*
　shall not Judge do *r*　Gen 18:25
　Lord led men in *r*　24:48
　do that is *r* Deut 6:18, 12:25, 21:9

God of truth, just and *r* 32:4
I will teach you good and *r* 1 Sam
12:23
forcible are *r* words Job 6:25
not lay on man more than *r* 34:23
statutes of Lord are *r* Psa 19:8
renew a *r* spirit within me 51:10
led thee in *r* paths Pro 4:11
thoughts of righteous are *r* 12:5
way that seemeth *r* 14:12, 16:25
r in his own eyes 21:2
getteth riches, not by *r* Jer 17:11
till he comes whose *r* Ezek 21:27
in his *r* mind Mk 5:15
obey parents, this is *r* Eph 6:1
forsaken the *r* way 2 Pet 2:15

righteous, *upright, just*
destroy *r* with wicked Gen 18:23
let me die death of *r* Num 23:10
the congregation of the *r* Psa 1:5
Lord knoweth way of the *r* 1:6
the *r* God trieth the hearts 7:9
r cry and Lord heareth 34:17
r speaketh wisdom 37:30
there is a reward for *r* 58:11
the Lord loveth the *r* 146:8
r never be removed Pro 10:30
r hath hope in his death 14:32
he heareth prayer of *r* 15:29
when *r* are in authority 29:2
be not *r* overmuch Ecc 7:16
not come to call *r* Mat 9:13, Mk
2:17, Lk 5:32
outwardly appear *r* Mat 23:28
trusted they were *r* Lk 18:9
certainly this was a *r* man 23:47
there is none *r*, not one Rom 3:10
eyes of Lord are over *r* 1 Pet 3:12

if *r* scarcely be saved 4:18
righteously *(see righteous)*
he that walketh *r* shall Isa 33:15
we shall live soberly, *r* Tit 2:12
righteousness *(see righteous)*
he shall judge world in *r* Psa 9:8
leadeth me in paths of *r* 23:3
r tendeth to life Pro 11:19
r exalteth a nation 14:34
better is a little with *r* 16:8
work of *r* shall be peace 32:17
let *r* run down as stream Amos
9:24
to fulfil all *r* Mat 3:15
hunger and thirst after *r* 5:6
except your *r* exceed *r* of 5:20
he that worketh *r* Acts 10:35
as he reasoned of *r* 24:25
as instruments of *r* Rom 6:13
the *r* of faith 9:30
kingdom of God is *r*, peace 14:17
the breastplate of *r* Eph 6:14
a crown of *r* 2 Tim 4:8
wrath of man worketh not *r* Jas
1:20
fruit of *r* is sown 3:18
should live unto *r* 1 Pet 2:24
wherein dwelleth *r* 2 Pet 3:13
rightly *(see right)*
said, thou hast *r* judged Lk 7:43
r dividing word of 2 Tim 2:15
riot, *revelry, squander*
walk not in *r* Rom 13:13
that you run not to *r* 1 Pet 4:4
rise, *go up*
sceptre shall *r* out of Num 24:17
r at voice of bird Ecc 12:4
r early and protesting Jer 11:7

.maketh sun to *r* on   Mat 5:45
third day shall *r* again   20:19, Mk
9:31, 10:34, Lk 18:33, 24:7
the Lord is *r* indeed   24:34
Christ died, is *r* again   Rom 8:34
if the dead *r* not   1 Cor 15:15
if ye be *r* with Christ   Col 3:1
dead in Christ *r* first   1 Thes 4:16

river
stretch hand on *r*   Ex 7:19, 8:5
a tree planted by the *r*   Psa 1:3
a *r*, the streams   46:4
all *r* run into sea   Ecc 1:7
I will make *r* in desert   Isa 43:19

roar, *roar, shriek*
let the sea *r*   1 Chr 16:32, Psa
96:11, 98:7
Lord shall *r* out   Joel 3:16, Amos
1:2
the sea of waves *r*   Lk 21:25
the devil as a *r* lion   1 Pet 5:8

rob, *to snatch away*
r not the poor   Pro 22:22
will a man *r* God   Mal 3:8

robe, *cloak, garment*
on Jesus a scarlet *r*   Mat 27:28
bring forth the best *r*   Lk 15:22

rock, *stone, cliff*
speak to the *r*   Num 20:8
water out of the *r*   Deut 8:15
he is the *R*   32:4
r that is higher than I   Psa 61:2
r of salvation   89:26, 95:1
founded upon *r* Mat 7:25, Lk 6:48
upon this *r* I will build my church
Mat 16:18
lay in Sion a *r* Rom 9:33, 1 Pet 2:8
drank of spiritual *r*   1 Cor 10:4

rod, *stick*
thy *r* and staff comfort   Psa 23:4
he that spareth the *r*   Pro 13:24

Rome, *capital of Italy and Roman Empire,* Acts 2:10, Rom 1:7, 2 Tim 1:17

roof, *covering*
not worthy thou come under my *r*
Mat 8:8
they uncovered the *r*   Mk 2:4

room
man's gift maketh *r* for   Pro 18:16
large upper *r* Mk 14:15, Lk 22:12
no *r* for them in inn   2:7

root
seen foolish taking *r*   Job 5:3
r thee out of the land of the living
Psa 52:5
branch grow out of his *r*   Isa 11:1
r of Jesse   11:10, Rom 15:12
r out of a dry ground   Isa 53:2
axe is laid to *r*   Mat 3:10, Lk 3:9
had no *r*   Mat 13:6, Mk 4:6, Lk
8:13
shall be *r* up   Mat 15:13
r and grounded in love   Eph 3:17
r and build up in him   Col 2:7
love of money is *r* of   1 Tim 6:10
any *r* of bitterness   Heb 12:15

rose, *narcissus*
I am the *r* of Sharon   S of S 2:1
desert blossom as *r*   Isa 35:1

rose *(see rise)*
not persuaded, though one *r*   Lk
16:31
Christ both died and *r*   Rom 14:9
buried, and *r* again   1 Cor 15:4

rough, *rugged*
  r places be made plain   Isa 40:4
  r ways be made smooth   Lk 3:5

royal, *belonging to a king*
  if ye fulfil the *r* law   Jas 2:8
  ye are a *r* priesthood   1 Pet 2:9

rubies, *red gem*
  price of wisdom is above *r*   Job
          28:18, Pro 8:11

rudiments, *elements, first step*
  the *r* of the world   Col 2:8,20

ruin, *overthrow*
  flattering mouth worketh *r*   Pro
                   26:28
  r of house was great   Lk 6:49

rule, *restrain, govern*
  thy husband shall *r*   Gen 3:16
  he that *r* over men must be just
                  2 Sam 23:3
  servant to have *r* over   Pro 19:10
  no *r* over his own spirit   25:28
  walk by the same *r*   Phil 3:16
  that have *r* over   Heb 13:7,17
  peace of God *r* in   Col 3:15
  how to *r* his house   1 Tim 3:5

ruler, *leader*
  not curse *r* of   Ex 22:28
  have any of *r* believed   Jno 7:48
  r are not a terror to   Eph 6:12

rumour, *report, tidings*
  wars and *r* of wars   Mat 24:6

run, *go, flow, run*
  as a strong man to *r*   Psa 19:5
  my cup *r* over   23:5
  their feet *r* to evil   Pro 1:16
  I should *r*, or had *r*   Gal 2:2
  let us *r* with patience   Heb 12:1

rush, *hasten*
  nations *r* like *r* of   Isa 17:13
  sound as *r* mighty wind   Acts 2:2

rust, *eat away, decay*
  when moth and *r* doth Mat 6:19,20
  the *r* of them shall be   Jas 5:3

Ruth, *ancestress of David,* Ruth 1–4,
Mat 1:5

S

sabbath, *day of rest*
  Remember the *s* day   Ex 20:8
  ye shall keep the *s*   31:14,16
  call *s* a delight   Isa 58:13
  when will the *s* be gone Amos 8:5
  s was made for man   Mk 2:27
  Son is Lord of *s*   2:28, Lk 6:5

sacrifice, *slaughter, offering*
  s to the Lord   Ex 5:17, 8:8
  obey better than *s*   1 Sam 15:22
  offer *s* of righteousness   Psa 4:5
  s thou didst not   40:6, 51:16
  s of God, a broken spirit   51:17
  more acceptable than *s*   Pro 21:3
  to what purpose your *s*   Isa 1:11
  nor are your *s* sweet   Jer 6:20
  I desired mercy rather than *s* Hos
            6:6, Mat 9:13, 12:7
  they *s*, but the Lord   Hos 8:13
  to love is more than *s*   Mk 12:33
  present bodies a living *s* Rom 12:1
  s to God for a sweet   Eph 5:2
  s of your faith   Phil 2:17
  s acceptable, to God   4:18

put away sin by the *s*   Heb 9:26

no more *s* for sin   10:26

offer the *s* of praise   13:15

to offer spiritual *s*   1 Pet 2:5

things *s* to idols   Rev 2:14,20

See also: Mk 8:34, Lk 21:3, Jno 15:13, 1 Cor 13:3, 2 Cor 12:15

sad, *to be dark, gloomy, unhappy*

be not of *s* countenance   Mat 6:16

he was *s* at that saying   Mk 10:22

See also: 1 Thes 4:13, Rev 7:17

Sadducees, *conservative aristocratic Jewish sect,* Mat 16:6, 22:23, Acts 4:1, 23:8

safe

trusteth in Lord be *s*   Pro 29:25

safety

horse is vain thing for *s*   Pro 33:17

multitude of counsellors is *s* 11:14, 24:6

shall say, peace and *s*   1 Thes 5:3

See also: Psa 23:5, 1 Pet 3:13

saints, *set apart, holy*

Lord forsaketh not *s*   Psa 37:28

he preserveth his *s*   97:10

called to be *s*   Rom 1:7, 1 Cor 1:2

the necessity of *s*   Rom 12:13

s shall judge world   1 Cor 6:2

· perfecting of *s*   Eph 4:12

once delivered to *s*   Jude 3

prayers of *s*   Rev 5:8, 8:3

sake, *on account of*

cursed ground for thy *s*   Gen 3:17

not curse ground for man's *s*   8:21

for his name's *s*   Psa 23:3

for thy *s* are we killed 44:22, Rom 8:36

loseth life for my *s*   Mat 10:39, 16:25, Mk 8:35, Lk 9:24

for elect's *s*   Mat 24:22, Mk 13:20, 2 Tim 2:10

body's *s*, the church   Col 1:24

esteem for work's *s*   1 Thes 5:13

for truth's *s*   2 Jno 2

salt

a pillar of *s*   Gen 19:26

s of the earth   Mat 5:13

speech seasoned with *s*   Col 4:6

s water and fresh   Jas 3:12

salute, *bless, embrace*

if *s* your brethren only   Mat 5:47

s one another with kiss   Rom 16:16

s every saint in Christ   Phil 4:21

See also: Mat 23:5, Mk 12:38, Lk 1:29, 1 Cor 16:21

salvation, *safety, ease*

I have waited for *s*   Gen 49:18

s belongeth to the Lord   Psa 3:8

Lord is my *s*   27:62, Isa 12:2

restore the joy of *s* Psa 51:12, 70:4

shew forth his *s*   96:2

ends of earth hath seen *s*   98:3

s is far from wicked   119:155

earth shall see the *s*   Isa 52:10

helmet of *s* on his head   59:17

all flesh shall see *s*   Lk 3:6

s is of the Jews   Jno 4:22

power of God unto *s*   Rom 1:16

now is day of *s*   2 Cor 6:2

work out your *s* with   Phil 2:12

make wise to *s*   2 Tim 3:15

grace that bringeth *s*   Tit 2:11

if neglect so great *s*   Heb 2:3

author of eternal *s*   5:9

end of faith, *s* of   1 Pet 1:9

longsuffering is *s*   2 Pet 3:15

See also: Mat 16:25, Lk 13:24, Rom 6:23, Eph 2:8, 2 Pet 3:9

Samaria, *capital of Israel,* 1 Ki 16:24, 20:1, 2 Ki 6:24; *district between Judaea and Galilee,* Lk 17:11

same, *this, itself*
thou art the *s*   Psa 102:27, Heb 1:12
s yesterday, today   13:8

Samson, *judge (leader) from tribe of Dan,* Judg 13:24 ff

Samuel, *judge and prophet,* 1 Sam 1:19,26, 3:1 ff, 10:1 ff, 25:1 ff, 13:13 ff, 16:1 ff

Sanballat, *governor of Samaria,* Neh 2:10, 6:2, 13:28

sanctify, *separate, make holy*
s them through truth   Jno 17:17
being *s* by Holy Ghost   Rom 15:16
might *s* and cleanse the church
      Eph 5:26
it is *s* by word of God   1 Tim 4:5
s for master's use   2 Tim 2:21
s Lord God in heart   1 Pet 3:15
See also: Lev 19:2, 20:7, 1 Cor 1:30, 2 Thes 2:13, 1 Pet 1:2

sand
multiply as *s*   Gen 22:17, 32:12
more in number than *s* Psa 139:18
built his house on *s*   Mat 7:26

Sarah, *wife of Abraham,* Gen 12:14, 20:2, 23:1 ff

sat
not *s* with vain persons   Psa 26:4
people who *s* in darkness Mat 4:16
s on right hand of God   Mk 16:19

Satan, *an adversary*
S provoke David   1 Chr 21:1
S went from presence of   Job 1:12
if *S* cast out *S*   Mat 12:26, Mk 3:23, Lk 11:18

get behind me, *S*   Mat 16:23, Mk 8:33, Lk 4:8
tempted of *S*   Mk 1:13
S as lightning fall   Lk 10:18
God shall bruise *S*   Rom 16:20
turned aside after *S*   1 Tim 5:15
seat where *S* dwelleth   Rev 2:13
See also: 1 Pet 5:8, Rev 20:7

satisfy, *to fill, content*
my soul shall be *s*   Psa 63:5
a good man shall be *s*   Pro 14:14
open eyes, and be *s*   20:13
three things never *s*   30:15
eye is not *s* with seeing   Ecc 1:8
shall eat, and not be *s*   Isa 9:20, Mic 6:14
Lord shall *s* thy soul   Isa 58:11
See also: Pro 25:25, Ecc 4:6, Isa 55:1, Phil 4:11

Saul, *king of Israel,* 1 Sam 9–10, 16:14, 18:1 ff; *see also Paul*

save, *give life or safety*
he shall *s* the humble   Job 22:29
God who *s* the upright   Psa 7:10
s (those) of contrite spirit   34:18
s children of needy   72:4
Lord's hand is not shortened that it cannot *s*   Isa 59:1
summer ended, we not *s*   Jer 8:20
s people from sins   Mat 1:21
whosoever will *s* his life 16:25, Mk 8:35, Lk 9:24
to seek and to *s*   Mat 18:11, Lk 19:10
who can be *s*   Mat 19:25, Mk 10:26, Lk 18:26
he *s* others   Mat 27:42, Mk 15:31
is it lawful to *s*   3:4, Lk 6:9

s yourselves from this   Acts 2:40
whereby we must be *s*   4:12
what must I do to be *s*   16:30
we are *s* by hope   Rom 8:24
foolishness of preaching to *s* 1 Cor
                      1:21
Christ came to *s* sinners   1 Tim
                      1:15
thou shalt *s* thyself   4:16
able to *s* your souls   Jas 1:21
can faith *s* him   2:14
prayer of faith shall *s* sick   5:15
shall *s* a soul from death   5:20
righteous scarcely *s*   1 Pet 4:18

saviour, *preserver*
forgot God their *s*   Psa 106:21
he shall send them a *s*   Isa 19:20
born in city of David a *s*   Lk 2:11
Christ, the *S* of the world Jno 4:42
Christ is *s* of body   Eph 5:23
God is *S* of all   1 Tim 4:10
adorn doctrine our *S*   Tit 2:10

savour, *smell, aroma*
Lord smelled sweet *s*   Gen 8:21
salt lost its *s*   Mat 5:13, Lk 14:34
sacrifice for sweet-smelling *s*   Eph
                      5:2
See also: Mat 16:23, Mk 8:33

saw *(see see)*
sea *s* it, and fled   Psa 114:3
under fig tree I *s*   Jno 1:48
Abraham *s* my day   8:56

say, *speak, reply*
think not to *s*   Mat 3:9, Lk 3:8
whom *s* ye that I am   Mat 16:15,
           Mk 8:29, Lk 9:20
they *s*, and do not   Mat 23:3
ought to *s*, if Lord will   Jas 4:15

saying, *that which is said, proverb, teaching*
my dark *s* on harp   Psa 49:4
utter dark *s* of old   78:2
cannot receive *s*   Mat 19:11
let *s* sink into   Lk 9:44
hard *s*   Jno 6:60
keepeth not my *s*   14:24
this is a faithful *s*   1 Tim 1:15
these *s* are faithful   Rev 22:6

scarcely, *hardly*
s for a righteous   Rom 5:7
See also: Gen 27:30, Deut 8:9, Acts
14:18

scatter, *spread*
did Lord *s* them   Gen 11:9
I will *s* you among   Lev 26:33
workers of iniquity be *s* Psa 92:9
pastors that *s* sheep   Jer 23:1
sheep shall be *s*   Zech 13:7, Mat
           26:31, Mk 14:27
s as sheep having no   Mat 9:36
he that gathereth not, *s*   12:30, Lk
                    11:23
wolf *s* the sheep   Jno 10:12

sceptre, *staff, royal symbol*
s shall not depart from   Gen 49:10
s of thy kingdom Psa 45:6, Heb 1:8

scholar, *one who is taught*
the teacher as the *s*   1 Chr 25:8

science, *knowledge*
avoiding oppositions of *s* falsely so
called   1 Tim 6:20

scorner, *derider, ridiculer*
reprove not a *s* lest   Pro 9:8
s loveth not one that   15:12
smite a *s*   19:25
s is abomination to men   24:9

See also: Psa 1:1, 44:13, 79:4, Pro 19:28, Isa 28:14

scourge, *whip, flog*

shall *s* him   Mat 20:19, Mk 10:34, Lk 18:33
a *s* of small cards   Jno 2:15
Lord *s* every son he   Heb 12:6

scribe, *copyist, teacher of the Law*

a wise man and a *s*   1 Chr 27:32
where is the *s*   Isa 33:18
exceed righteousness of *s* Mat 5:20
woe unto *s*, Pharisees   23:13 ff
beware of *s*   Mk 12:38, Lk 20:46
where is the *s*   1 Cor 1:20

scrip, *bag, purse*

not *s* for your journey   Mat 10:10, Mk 6:8, Lk 9:3, 10:4
take his purse and *s*   22:36

scripture, *that which is written*

not knowing the *s*   Mat 22:29
have ye not read this *s*   Mk 12:10
search the *s*   Jno 5:39
what saith *s*   Rom 4:3
comfort of *s*   15:4
all *s* is by inspiration   2 Tim 3:16
do ye think the *s* saith   Jas 4:5
it is contained in *s*   1 Pet 2:6
no *s* is of private   2 Pet 1:20
See also: Deut 8:3, Isa 34:16, Heb 4:12, Jas 1:21, Rev 22:19

search, *seek, investigate*

the Lord *s* all hearts   1 Chr 28:9
number of his years be *s* Job 36:26
s me, know my heart   Psa 139:23
heart to *s* wisdom   Ecc 1:13, 7:25
I the Lord *s* the heart   Jer 17:10
s the scriptures   Jno 5:39
Spirit *s* all things   1 Cor 2:10

seared, *branded, burned*

s with hot iron   1 Tim 4:2

season, *appointed time*

light be for signs, and *s* Gen 1:14
give rain in his *s*   Deut 28:12
word spoken in due *s*   Pro 15:23
to every thing is a *s*   Ecc 3:1
changeth times and *s*   Dan 2:21
not to know time or *s*   Acts 1:7
a convenient *s*   24:25
be instant in *s* and   2 Tim 4:2
pleasures of sin for *s*   Heb 11:25
See also: Mk 9:50, Lk 14:34, Col 4:6

seat, *chair, throne*

s of the scornful   Psa 1:1
s of them that sold doves .   Mat 21:12, Mk 11:15
chief *s* in synagogues   Mat 23:6, Mk 12:39
mighty from their *s*   Lk 1:52

secret, *hidden, concealed*

s things belong to God Deut 29:29
hast heard *s* of God   Job 15:8
cleanse me from *s*   Psa 19:12
s of Lord is with .   25:14
his *s* is with righteous   Pro 3:32
a gift in *s* pacifieth anger   21:14
better than *s* love   27:5
every *s* thing   Ecc 12:14
knoweth *s* of heart   44:21
Father who seeth in *s*   Mat 6:4
putteth candle in *s*   Lk 11:33
s of his heart   1 Cor 14:25
See also: Jno 3:20, Eph 5:11

secretly *(see secret)*

a disciple, but *s*   Jno 19:38

sect, *party*

s of the Sadducees	Acts 5:19
s of the Pharisees	15:5
s of the Nazarenes	24:5
straitest *s* of religion	26:5
s everywhere spoken against	28:22
See also: 1 Cor 1:10, 1:13	

secure, *safe*

that provoke God are *s*	Job 12:6
seeing he dwelleth *s*	Pro 3:29

see, *look, observe*

Lord came down to *s*	Gen 11:5
when I *s* the blood	Ex 12:13
no man *s* me, and live	33:20
in my flesh *s* God	Job 19:26
taste and *s* the Lord	Psa 34:8
lest they *s* with	Isa 6:10
shall *s* eye to eye	52:8
pure in heart *s* God	Mat 5:8
we would *s* a sign	12:38
ye shall *s*.	13:14, Mk 4:12, Acts
	28:26
having eyes, *s* not	Mk 8:18
blind, now I *s*	Jno 9:25
s through a glass	1 Cor 13:12
we shall *s* him as he is	1 Jno 3:2
every eye shall *s* him	Rev 1:7

seed, *seed; often: descendants*

enmity between thy *s*	Gen 3:15
s of dust of earth	13:16
bear precious *s*	Psa 126:6
s of righteous	Pro 11:21
s to the sower	Isa 55:10
him that soweth *s*	Amos 9:13
s by the way side	Mat 13:19
s is the word of God	Lk 8:11
not of corruptible *s*	1 Pet 1:23

seek, *search, inquire*

s him with all	Deut 4:29
prepared heart to *s* God	2 Chr
	19:3, 30:19
we *s* your God as	Ezra 4:2
s welfare of Israel	Neh 2:10
s peace and	Psa 34:14, 1 Pet 3:11
early will I *s* thee	Psa 63:1
s him with the whole heart	119:2
s me early shall find	Pro 8:17
s Lord while may be found	Isa
	55:6
shall *s* me and find	Jer 29:13
they shall *s* peace	Ezek 7:25
s ye me, and ye shall	Amos 5:4
s word of Lord	8:12
these the Gentiles *s*	Mat 6:32
s ye first	6:33, Lk 12:31
s, and ye shall	Mat 7:7, Lk 11:9
all men *s* thee	Mk 1:37
things the nations *s*	Lk 12:30
many will *s* to enter in	13:24
s diligently till	15:8
s to save his life	17:33
to *s* and to save	19:10
ye shall *s* me, and	Jno 7:34
let no man *s*	1 Cor 10:24
charity *s* not her own	13:5
s things are above	Col 3:1
shall men *s* death	Rev 9:6

seem, *appear*

way that *s* right	Pro 14:12
if any *s* to be wise	1 Cor 3:18
any man *s* religious	Jas 1:26

seen

I have *s* God face to	Gen 32:30
die, because *s* God	Judg 13:22
mine eyes have *s* Lord	Isa 6:15

neither eyes *s*   64:4, 1 Cor 2:9
no man hath *s* God   Jno 1:18
hath *s* me, hath *s* Father   14:9
because thou hast *s*   20:29
of things not *s*   Heb 11:1
God whom hath not *s*   1 Jno 4:20

sell
  s me thy birthright   Gen 25:31
  buy truth, and *s* not   Pro 23:23
  let him *s* his garment   Lk 22:36
  we will buy and *s*   Jas 4:13

send
  s me to preserve life   Gen 45:5
  s out light and truth   Psa 43:3
  whom shall I *s*   Isa 6:8
  s labourers   Mat 9:38, Lk 10:2

Sennacherib, *king of Assyria,* 2 Ki
18:13, 19:9 ff, Isa 36:37

sent *(see send)*
  God *s* me before you   Gen 45:7
  I AM hath *s* me unto you   Ex 3:14
  s to lost sheep of ·   Mat 15:24
  do will of him that *s*   Jno 4:34
  works of him that *s* me   9:4
  preach except be *s*   Rom 10:15
  s his only begotten Son   1 Jno 4:9

sentence, *judgment*
  Pilate gave *s*   Lk 23:24
  we had the *s* of death   2 Cor 1:9

separate, *divide*
  s friends   Pro 16:28, 17:9
  s us from love of   Rom 8:35
  be ye *s*   2 Cor 6:17

serpent, *snake*
  s was more subtil   Gen 3:1
  Moses made *s* of brass   Num 21:9
  like poison of a *s*   Psa 58:4
  at last biteth like *s*   Pro 23:32

give him a *s*   Mat 7:10, Lk 11:11
they shall take up a *s*   Mk 15:18
as Moses lifted up *s*   Jno 3:14

Sergius Paulus, *a convert of Paul,* Acts
13:7

servant, *minister, slave, server*
  borrower is *s* to lender   Pro 22:7
  chief, let him be *s*   Mat 20:27, Mk
                                9:35
  good and faithful *s*   Mat 25:21
  at season he sent *s*   Lk 20:10
  s abideth not in house   Jno 8:35
  there shall my *s* be   12:26
  I made myself *s* of all   1 Cor 9:19
  as *s* of Christ   Eph 6:6
  he took form of *s*   Phil 2:7
  not as *s,* but above   Philem 16

serve, *to wait on, aid*
  elder shall *s* younger   Gen 25:23,
                               Rom 9:12
  not bow down nor *s*   Ex 20:5
  fear Lord, and *s* him   Deut 6:13,
    10:12, 11:13, 13:4, Josh 22:5,
      24:14, 1 Sam 7:3, 12:14
  choose whom ye will *s*   Josh 24:15
  no man can *s* two masters   Mat
                     6:24, Lk 16:13
  if any man *s* me, let   Jno 12:26
  should *s* in newness   Rom 7:6
  by love *s* one another   Gal 5:13
  s God acceptably   Heb 12:28
  See also: Lk 9:24, Acts 20:35, Rom
    12:1, 15:1, Jas 2:15

service *(see serve)*
  your reasonable *s*   Rom 12:1
  doing *s* as to Lord   Eph 6:7

set, *place*
  I *s* my bow in cloud   Gen 9:13

I *s* before thee life   Deut 30:15
I *s* before you way of   Jer 21:8
a city *s* on a hill   Mat 5:14
on hope *s* before us   Heb 6:18

settle, *establish*
thou *s* the furrows   Psa 65:10
s it in your heart   Lk 21:14
faith, grounded and *s*   Col 1:23

sew
s fig leaves together   Gen 3:7
time to rend, time to *s*   Ecc 3:7
s new cloth on old   Mk 2:21

shade
the Lord is thy *s*   Psa 121:5

shadow, *shade, shelter*
he fleeth as a *s*   Job 14:2
hide me under *s* of wings   Psa 17:8
days are like a *s* 102:11, 144:4, Ecc
                8:13
as *s* of a great rock   Isa 32:2
under *s* we shall live   Lam 4:20
a *s* of things to come   Col 2:17
law having *s* of good   Heb 10:1
no *s* of turning   Jas 1:17

Shadrach, *one of three cast in fiery furnace,* Dan 1:3

shake, *agitate*
though the mountains *s*   Psa 46:3
to *s* the earth   Isa 2:19
s heavens   13:13, Hag 2:6,21
I will *s* all nations   2:7
s dust off your feet   Mat 10:14, Mk
                6:11, Lk 9:5
good measure *s* together   6:38
be not soon *s* in mind   2 Thes 2:2
I *s* not earth only   Heb 12:26

Shalmaneser, *king of Assyria,* 2 Ki 17:3, 18:9

shame, *embarrass, dishonor*
how long turn glory to *s*   Psa 4:2
worthy to suffer *s*   Acts 5:41
whose glory is in their *s*   Phil 3:19
put him to an open *s*   Heb 6:6
endured cross, despising *s*   12:2
See also: Lk 9:26, Rom 1:16

Shaphan, *in charge of temple repair under King Josiah (c. 621 B.C.),* 2 Ki 22:3, 2 Chr 34:8

Sharon, *coastal plain of Palestine,* S of S 2:1, 1 Chr 5:16, 27:29, Isa 33:9, 35:2, 65:10

sharp, *pointed, cutting*
arrows *s* in the heart   Psa 45:5
tongue like a *s* razor   52:2
their tongue a *s* sword   57:4
false witness is *s* arrow   Pro 25:18
right is *s* than   Mic 7:4
contention was *s*   Acts 15:39
word of God *s* than sword   Heb
                4:12

Sheba, *possibly the south coast of Arabia,* Gen 25:3, Job 6:19, Psa 72:10, Jer 6:20, Ezek 27:22, 38:13

Shechem, *a Canaanite man,* Gen 34:2 ff; *center of Northern Kingdom, later called Sychar,* Gen 35:4, Josh 24:1, Judg 9:1, 1 Ki 12:1, Psa 60:6

shed, *pour out*
s for many for remission Mat 26:28
love of God is *s* in   Rom 5:5
without *s* of blood no remission
                Heb 9:22

sheep
Abel was keeper of *s*   Gen 4:2

as *s* which have no shepherd Num
27:17, 1 Ki 22:17, 2 Chr 18:16,
Mat 9:36, Mk 6:34
like *s* have gone astray Isa 53:6
like *s* for slaughter Jer 12:3
false prophets in *s* clothing Mat
7:15
as *s* having no shepherd 9:36
go to lost *s* of Israel 10:6
feed my *s* Jno 21:16

Shem, *son of Noah,* Gen 9:26, 10:21,
11:10, 1 Chr 1:17

shepherd, *keeper of sheep*
s is abomination to Gen 46:34
the Lord is my *s* Psa 23:1
feed his flock like *s* Isa 40:11
s caused to go astray Jer 50:6
woe to *s* of Israel Ezek 34:2,8
smite the *s* Zech 13:7
s abiding in fields Lk 2:8
by the door is the *s* Jno 10:2
I am the good *s* 10:11
chief *S* shall appear 1 Pet 5:4

Sheshbazzar, *governor of Judah,* Ezra
1:8, 5:14

shew, *show* (archaic)
thou will *s* me path of life Psa
16:11
for *s* make long prayers Lk 20:47
do *s* Lord's death 1 Cor 11:26
to make a fair *s* in flesh Gal 6:12

shield, *armor*
Lord, *s* of thy help Deut 33:29
Lord is our *s* Psa 33:20, 59:11,
84:9
a sun and *s* 84:11
truth shall be thy *s* 91:4
s to them that trust Pro 30:5

taking the *s* of faith· Eph 6:16

Shiloh, *site of tabernacle in time of
Judges,* Josh 18:1, Judg 21:19, 1 Sam
1:3, 2:1 f, 3:21, Psa 78:60, Jer 7:12,
26:6

shine, *be bright*
Lord make his face *s* Num 6:25
upon them hath the *s* Isa 9:2
let your light so *s* Mat 5:16
righteous *s* as sun 13:43
face did *s* as sun 17:2
light *s* in a dark 2 Pet 1:19

Shishak, *king of Egypt,* 1 Ki 14:25,
2 Chr 12:2 ff

shoe
put off thy *s* Ex 3:5
sold poor for pair of *s* Amos 2:6
s not worthy to bear Mat 3:11

short
triumph of wicked is *s* Job 20:5
come *s* of glory of God Rom 3:23
the time is *s* 1 Cor 7:29
See also: Isa 28:20, 59:1, Mat 24:22,
Mk 18:20

shout, *loud cry*
all the people shall *s* Josh 6:5
God is gone up with a *s* Psa 47:5
Lord descend with *s* 1 Thes 4:16

Shushan, *capital of Medo-Persia,* Neh
1:1, Esth 2:8, 3:15

shut, *close in*
Lord *s* him in Gen 7:16
he *s* up tender mercies Psa 77:9
s kingdom of heaven Mat 23:13

sick, *weak, diseased, ill*
Hope deferred maketh *s* Pro 13:12
s, and ye visited me Mat 25:36
but they that are *s* Mk 2:17

prayer of faith save *s*   Jas 5:15

sickness *(see sick)*
   thou wilt make his bed in *s*   Psa 41:3
   himself bare our *s*   Mat 8:17

side
   who is on Lord's *s*   Ex 32:26
   Lord is on my *s*   Psa 118:6
   troubled on every *s*   2 Cor 4:8

sift, *shake, sift out*
   s nations with sieve   Isa 30:28
   Satan desired to *s* you   Lk 22:31

sight, *appearance, view*
   turn and see this great *s*   Ex 3:3
   better is *s* of eyes   Ecc 6:9
   recovering of *s* to blind   Lk 4:18
   walk by faith, not *s*   2 Cor 5:7

sign, *wonder, token*
   let them be for *s*   Gen 1:14
   ask thee a *s* of Lord   Isa 7:11
   we would see a *s* Mat 12:38, 16:1, Mk 8:11, Lk 11:16
   what shall be the *s*   Mat 24:3
   approved of God by *s*   Acts 2:22
   See also: Gen 9:13, Lk 11:29

Sihon, *king of Amorites,* Num 21:21, Deut 1:4, 2:26, Psa 135:11, 136:19

Silas, *companion of Paul,* Acts 15:22, 16:22, 17:4

silence, *quietness*
   let all earth keep *s*   Hab 2:20
   put to *s* foolish men   1 Pet 2:15
   See also: Psa 94:17, Zech 2:13, 1 Tim 2:12

silly, *foolish*
   slayeth the *s* one   Job 5:2
   Ephraim is like *s* dove   Hos 7:11

Siloam, *pool in Jerusalem,* Jno 9:7

Simeon, *son of Jacob,* Gen 29:33, 34:1 ff, 42:24, 46:10, Ex 6:15; *old man in temple at Jesus' presentation,* Lk 2:25

similitude, *likeness, similarity*
   after the *s* of God   Jas 3:9

Simon, *at least eight men bear the name in the N.T.:* (1) *brother of Jesus,* Mat 13:55, Mk 6:3; (2) *Zelotes, apostle,* Mat 10:4, Mk 3:18, Lk 6:15; (3) *Pharisee,* Lk 7:36; (4) *leper,* Mat 26:6, Mk 14:3; (5) *of Cyrene,* Mat 27:32, Mk 15:21, Lk 23:26; (6) *tanner,* Acts 9:43, 10:6; (7) *sorcerer,* Acts 8:9,18; (8) *see Peter*

simple, *harmless, often: sincere*
   making wise the *s*   Psa 19:7
   Lord preserveth the *s*   116:6
   giveth understanding to *s*   119:130
   s concernng evil   Rom 16:19

sin (noun), *guilt, error, missing the mark*
   s lieth at the door   Gen 4:7
   put to death for his own *s*   Deut 24:16, 2 Ki 14:6, 2 Chr 25:4
   my *s* is ever before me   Psa 51:3
   fools mock at *s*   Pro 14:9
   s is reproach   14:34
   your *s* be as scarlet   Isa 1:18
   he bare the *s* of many   53:12
   all manner of *s* shall   Mat 12:31
   forgive us our *s*   Lk 11:4
   taketh away the *s* of   Jno 1:29
   without *s*, cast first stone   8:7
   lay not this *s* to   Acts 7:60
   whose *s* are covered   Rom 4:7

shall we continue in *s*   6:1
not of faith is *s*   14:23
made him to be *s* for   2 Cor 5:21
concluded all under *s*   Gal 3:22
he appeared to put away *s*   Heb
                                              9:26
s that so easily beset   12:1
his own self bare our *s*   1 Pet 2:24
cleanseth us from all *s*   1 Jno 1:7
if we say we have no *s*   1:8
See also: Isa 59:2, Eph 4:22

sin (verb) *(see sin, noun)*
I have *s* Ex 9:27, Num 22:34, Josh
    7:20, 1 Sam 15:24, 26:21, 2 Sam
    12:13, Job 7:20, Psa 41:4, Mat
    27:4, Lk 15:18
soul that *s*, shall die   Ezek 18:4
s no more   Jno 5:14
shall we *s* because   Rom 6:15
be angry, and *s* not   Eph 4:26
if we *s* wilfully after   Heb 10:26
cannot *s*, because born of 1 Jno 3:9
Sinai, *mountain where O.T. law was
given,* Deut 33:2, Judg 5:5, Psa 68:8,
Gal 4:24

sincere, *pure, genuine*
fear Lord and serve in *s*   Jas 24:14
may be *s* and   Phil 1:10
desire *s* milk of word   1 Pet 2:2
See also: Josh 24:14, 1 Cor 5:8,
2 Cor 2:17, Eph 6:6, 1 Pet 2:22

sing
s to the Lord   Ex 15:21, 1 Chr
             16:23, Psa 30:4, 95:1, 98:1,
                  149:1, Isa 12:5
time of *s* of birds   S of S 2:12
s in your hearts Eph 5:19, Col 3:16

single, *simple, sincere, without du-
plicity*
if eye be *s*   Mat 6:22, Lk 11:34
See also: Acts 2:46, Eph 6:5, Col
3:22

sinner *(see sin)*
standeth not in way of *s*   Psa 1:1
s shall be converted   51:13
if *s* entice thee   Pro 1:10
one *s* destroyeth much   Ecc 9:18
not to call righteous, but *s*   Mat
                                        9:13, Mk 2:17
friend of *s*   Mat 11:19, Lk 7:34
woman who was a *s*   7:37
joy in heaven over one *s*   15:7
God be merciful to me a *s*   18:13
while we were yet *s*   Rom 5:8
converteth *s*, save soul   Jas 5:20
See also: Job 4:8, Ezek 8:12, 1 Jno
3:4

Sisera, *general of Canaanite army,*
Judg 4:2,21, 5:24, 1 Sam 12:9, Psa
83:9

sister
same in my brother and *s*   Mat
                            12:50, Mk 3:35

sit
s we here till we die   2 Ki 7:3
s thou at my right   Psa 110:1
s every man under his   Mic 4:4
s on my right   Mat 20:23, Mk
                                         10:37
s here in good place   Jas 2:3

skin
s of his face shone   Ex 34:29
s of my teeth   Job 19:20
can Ethiopian change *s*   Jer 13:23
wandered in sheep *s*   Heb 11:37

skip, *spring, dart*

he cometh, *s* upon hills   S of S 2:8

slack, *slow, tardy, feeble*

Lord is not *s* concerning   2 Pet 3:9

slain *(see slay)*

I have *s* a man   Gen 4:23

by wicked hands have *s*   Acts 2:23

having *s* the enmity   Eph 2:16

slaughter *(see slay)*

as sheep for *s* Psa 44:22, Rom 8:36

as lamb to *s*   Isa 53:7, Jer 11:19

valley of *s*   7:32, 19:6

slay, *kill*

though he *s* me, yet   Job 13:15

sleep

God caused a deep *s* to   Gen 2:21

lay me down in peace and *s*   Psa 4:8

lest I *s* the *s* of death   13:3

keepeth Israel shall never *s*   121:4

they *s* not, except   Pro 4:16

yet a little *s*   6:10, 24:33

Love not *s*   20:13

s of labouring man sweet   Ecc 5:12

my *s* was sweet   Jer 31:26

many that *s* in the dust   Dan 12:2

time to awake out of *s*   Rom 13:11

we shall not all *s*   1 Cor 15:14

them which *s* in Jesus   1 Thes 4:14

slip, *move, let go*

lest we should let them *s*   Heb 2:1

slothful, *idle, lazy*

way of *s* man is   Pro 15:19

s is brother to waster   18:9

wicked and *s* servant   Mat 25:26

not *s* in business   Rom 12:11

be not *s*   Heb 6:11

See also: Pro 20:4

slow, *sluggish, delay*

a God *s* to anger   Neh 9:17

s to wrath, is of great   Pro 14:29

s to anger appeaseth strife   15:18

s to speak, *s* to wrath   Jas 1:19

See also: Pro 16:32, Nah 1:3

slumber, *sleep*

keepeth thee will not *s*   Psa 121:3

none shall *s* nor sleep   Isa 5:27

small, *little*

still *s* voice   1 Ki 19:12

a *s* one shall become   Isa 60:22

See also: Pro 15:16, 16:8, Mic 5:2, Mat 18:3, Jas 3:3 ff

smell

see, nor eat, nor *s*   Deut 4:28

but they *s* not   Psa 115:6

where were the *s*   1 Cor 12:17

an odour of sweet *s*   Phil 4:18

smite, *strike, beat*

sun shall not *s* thee   Psa 121:6

s thee on right cheek   Mat 5:39

smitten *(see smite)*

my heart is *s*   Psa 102:4

s of God   Isa 53:4

smoke

as *s* of a furnace   Gen 19:28

as *s* is driven away   Psa 68:2

days consumed like *s*   102:3

as *s* to the eyes   Pro 10:26

house was filled with *s*   Isa 6:4

s flax shall he not quench   42:3

heavens vanish like *s*   51:6

smooth, *even, plain*

words were *s* than butter   Psa 55:21

speak unto us *s* things   Isa 30:10

rough ways be made *s*   Lk 3:5

smote *(see smite)*

Moses *s* the rock   Num 20:11
publican *s* his breast   Lk 18:13

Smyrna, *city of Asia,* Rev 2:8

snare, *trap, net*

s of death prevented   2 Sam 22:6
s of his soul   Pro 18:7
fall into *s* of devil   1 Tim 3:7
rich fall into a *s*   6:9
out of *s* of devil   2 Tim 2:26

snow

I shall be whiter than *s*   Psa 51:7
giveth *s* like wool   147:16
as *s* in summer   Pro 26:1
sins shall be white as *s*   Isa 1:18
raiment white as *s*   Mat 28:31, Mk
    9:3

sober, *serious, sensible*

words of truth and *s*   Acts 26:25
think *s,* as God   Rom 12:3
watch and be *s*   1 Thes 5:6,8
bishop be *s*   1 Tim 3:2, Tit 1:8
be *s,* and watch   1 Pet 4:7
be *s,* be vigilant   5:8
See also: Tit 2:4,6,12, 1 Pet 1:13

Sodom, *city of the plain, destroyed by
God,* Gen 13:13, 18:20, 19:4 ff

soft

will he speak *s* words   Job 41:3
maketh my heart *s*   23:16
s answer turneth wrath   Pro 15:1
a *s* tongue breaketh bone   25:15
I shall go *s*   Isa 38:15
clothed in *s* raiment   Mat 11:8
See also: Psa 55:21, Acts 27:13

sojourn, *dwell temporarily*

s in the land   Gen 47:4
went to Egypt to *s*   Isa 52:4

by faith he *s* in   Heb 11:9
time of *s* here   1 Pet 1:17

sold *(see sell)*

s his birthright   Gen 25:33
no devoted things be *s*   Lev 27:28
ye have *s* yourselves for   Isa 52:3
s righteous for silver   Amos 2:6
are not two sparrows *s*   Mat 10:29
went and *s* all   13:46
s under sin   Rom 7:14

soldier

the *s* demanded, what   Lk 3:14
a devout *s*   Acts 10:7
hardness as good *s*   2 Tim 2:3
chosen him to be a *s*   Tit 2:4

sole, *bottom of the foot*

dove found no rest for *s*   Gen 8:9
from *s* of foot to crown   2 Sam
    14:25, Isa 1:6

solitary, *lonely*

departed to a *s* place   Mk 1:35

Solomon, *son of David by Bath-sheba,*
2 Sam 12:24, 1 Ki 1:2,24,
1 Chr 28:9,29, etc.

son

wise *s* maketh glad Pro 10:1, 15:20
unto us a *s* is given   Isa 9:6
the *S* of God   Dan 3:25, Lk 3:38,
    Jno 1:34, Acts 9:20
no man knoweth the *S*   Mat 11:27
this is my beloved *S*   17:5
Christ, whose *s* is he?   22:42
my *s* was dead   Lk 15:24
only begotten *S*   Jno 1:18, 3:18
if *S* make you free   8:36
God sending his own *S*   Rom 8:3
spared not his own *S*   8:32
God hath spoken by his *S* Heb 1:2

though he were a *S*, yet   5:8
he that hath *S* hath   1 Jno 5:12

song

sing a new *s*   Psa 33:3, Isa 42:10
singeth *s* to heavy heart   Pro 25:20
s of *s* which is   S of S 1:1
as a very lovely *s*   Ezek 33:32
in psalms and spiritual *s*   Eph 5:19,
    Col 3:16

soon, *quickly, shortly*

not *s* angry   Tit 1:7

sore, *very, mightily* (archaic)

they were *s* displeased   Mat 21:15
wept *s*   Acts 20:37

sorrow, *sadness, grief*

s is turned into   Job 41:22
he addeth no *s*   Pro 10:22
who hath *s*   23:29
bread of *s*   127:2
knowledge increaseth *s*   Ecc 1:18
s is better than laughter   7:3
remove *s* from thy heart   11:10
s and sighing shall   Isa 35:10, 51:11
a man of *s*   53:3
s, yet always rejoicing   2 Cor 6:10,
    7:10
no death, neither *s*   Rev 21:4

sorrowful *(see sorrow)*

a woman of a *s* spirit   1 Sam 1:15
went away *s*   Mat 19:22, Lk 18:28
he began to be *s*   Mat 26:37
my soul is *s*   25:38, Mk 14:34
as *s*, yet always   2 Cor 6:10

sort, *kind*

two of every *s*   Gen 6:19
after a godly *s*   2 Cor 7:11, 3 Jno 6

sought *(see seek)*

I *s* the Lord, and   Psa 34:4, 77:2

pastors have not *s* the   Jer 10:21
he *s* to see Jesus   Lk 19:3
they *s* it not by faith   Rom 9:32

soul, *life*

man became a living *s*   Gen 2:7
love Lord with all thy *s*   Deut 6:5
serve him with all your *s*   11:13
with all your *s*   13:3, Josh 22:5
set your *s* to seek   1 Chr 22:19
not leave my *s* in hell   Psa 16:10
law perfect converting *s*   19:7
He restoreth my *s*   23:3
Lord redeemeth *s* of   34:22
panteth my *s* after thee   42:1 f
bless the Lord, O my *s*   103:1,
    104:1
He satisfieth longing *s*   107:9
he shall preserve thy *s*   121:7
winneth *s* is wise   Pro 11:30
s without knowledge is   19:2
all *s* are mine   Ezek 18:4
destroy *s* and body   Mat 10:28
in exchange for *s*   16:26, Mk 8:36
s, thou hast goods   Lk 12:19
let every *s* be subject   Rom 13:1
an anchor of the *s*   Heb 6:19
shall save a *s* from death   Jas 5:20
salvation of your *s*   1 Pet 1:9
fleshly lusts war against *s*   2:11
bishop of your *s*   2:25
commit keeping of *s* to him   4:19
See also: 2 Cor 4:16

sound, *noise*

s of a shaken leaf   Lev 26:36
s of grinding is low   Ecc 12:4
there came *s* from heaven   Acts 2:2
s went into all earth   Rom 10:18
trumpet give uncertain *s*   1 Cor
    14:8

trumpet shall *s*, dead shall   15:52
See also: Psa 66:1, Ezek 1:24, 1 Cor 13:1

sound (adj.), *perfect, complete*
  s heart is life of flesh   Pro 14:30
  s doctrine   1 Tim 1:10, 2 Tim 4:3,
                         Tit 1:9, 2:1
  spirit of a *s* mind   2 Tim 1:7
  form of *s* words   1:13

sow, *plant*
  s wickedness reap same   Job 4:8
  s not among thorns   Jer 4:3
  s in righteousness, reap   Hos 10:12
  they *s* not   Mat 6:26
  he that *s* sparingly   2 Cor 9:6
  whatsoever man *s*, that   Gal 6:7

spake *(see speak)*
  he *s*, and it was done   Psa 33:9
  never man *s* like this   Jno 7:46
  I *s* as a child   1 Cor 13:11
  God who *s* in time past   Heb 1:1
  men of God *s* as moved   2 Pet 1:21

spare, *keep back, save*
  he that *s* the rod   Pro 13:24
  bread enough and to *s*   Lk 15:17
  he that *s* not his Son   Rom 8:32

spark, *flame, firebrands*
  as *s* fly upward   Job 5:7

sparrow, *small bird*
  more value than *s*   Mat 10:31, Lk 12:7

speak *(see also say)*
  as a man *s* to his friend   Ex 33:11
  s, Lord, thy servant   1 Sam 3:9
  s not in the ears of a fool   Pro 23:9
  a time to *s*   Ecc 3:7
  to *s* a word in season   Isa 50:4
  s the truth   Zech 8:16, Eph 4:25

heard for much *s*   Mat 6:7
idle word that men *s*   12:36
when men *s* well of you   Lk 6:26
all *s* same things   1 Cor 1:10
evil *s* be put away   Eph 4:31
s not as pleasing   1 Thes 2:4
slow to *s*   Jas 1:19
s great swelling words   Jude 16
See also: Col 4:6, Jas 3:6

spear, *lance, javelin*
  beat *s* into pruninghooks   Isa 2:4,
                        Mic 4:3
  s pierced his side   Jno 19:34

speech, *language, words*
  whole earth was one *s*   Gen 11:1
  I am slow of *s*   Ex 4:10
  day unto day uttereth *s*   Psa 19:2
  thy *s* betrayeth thee   Mat 25:73
  not excellency of *s*   1 Cor 2:1
  let your *s* be with grace   Col 4:6
  sound *s* that cannot   Tit 2:8
  See also: Psa 19:14, Pro 18:21, Mat 12:34, 2 Tim 1:13

speed, *haste*
  neither bid him God *s*   2 Jno 10

spend, *use*
  s our years as tale   Psa 90:9
  why *s* money for   Isa 55:2
  gladly *s* and be spent   2 Cor 12:15

spent *(see spend)*
  my life is *s* with grief   Psa 31:10
  I have *s* my strength   Isa 49:4
  s their time to tell   Acts 17:21
  night is far *s*   Rom 13:12

spirit, *breath, inner man*
  My *s* shall not always strive   Gen 6:3
  a man in whom is *s*   Num 27:18

into thy hand I commit my *s*   Psa
31:5, Lk 23:46

in whose *s* no guile   Psa 32:2

a right *s* within me   51:10

shall I go from thy *s*   139:7

he that is hasty of *s*   Pro 14:29

haughty *s* goeth before   16:32

s of man is candle of   20:27

who knoweth *s* of man   Ecc 3:21

s shall return to God   12:7

S of Lord is   Isa 61:1, Lk 4:18

s is willing   Mat 26:41, Mk 14:38

S descending   1:10, Jno 1:32

God is a *S*   4:24

S that quickeneth   6:63

Sadducees say neither *s*   Acts 23:8

walk after the *S*   Rom 8:1

have not *s* of Christ   8:9

S maketh intercession   8:26

joined to Lord is one *s*   1 Cor 6:17

letter killeth, but *S*   2 Cor 3:6

where *S* of Lord is, there   3:17

walk in the *S*   Gal 5:16 f

if ye be led of *s*   5:18

if we live in *s*   5:25

soweth to *S* shall of   6:8

we have access by one *S*   Eph 2:18

one body, and one *S*   4:4

be filled with the *S*   5:18

take sword of the *S*   6:17

quench not the *S*   1 Thes 5:19

justified in the *S*   1 Tim 3:16

body without *s* is dead   Jas 2:26

a meek and quiet *s*   1 Pet 3:4

live according to God in *s*   4:6

try the *s* whether   1 Jno 4:1

S and bride say, come   Rev 22:17

spiritual, *nonphysical*

comparing *s* things with   1 Cor 2:13

ye which are *s*, restore   Gal 6:1

and hymns, and *s* songs   Eph 5:19,
Col 3:16

spoil, *seize, destroy*

he shall divide *s*   Gen 49:27

findeth great *s*   Psa 119:162

foxes that *s* vines   S of S 2:15

lest any man *s* you   Col 2:8

having *s* principalities   2:15

spoken *(see speak)*

glorious things are *s*   Psa 87:3

a word fitly *s*   Pro 25:11

way of truth be evil *s*   2 Pet 2:2

spot, *blemish, mark*

can leopard change *s*   Jer 13:23

church, not having *s*   Eph 5:27

commandment without *s*   1 Tim
6:14

himself without *s*   Heb 9:14

as a lamb without *s*   1 Pet 1:19

may be found without *s*   2 Pet 3:14

sprang *(see spring)*

fruit that *s* up   Mk 4:8, Lk 8:8

spread, *scatter*

God *s* out the heavens   Job 9:8

s out my hands to   Isa 65:2

your faith is *s* abroad   1 Thes 1:8

spring, *rise up*

truth shall *s* out   Psa 85:11

a well of water *s* up   Jno 4:14

sprinkle

hearts *s* from an evil   Heb 10:22

spy, *search out*

Moses sent to *s* land   Josh 2:1

to *s* out our liberty   Gal 2:4

See also: Num 13:2, 2 Sam 10:3

staff, *rod, support*

thy rod and *s* comfort me Psa 23:4

Lord hath broken *s* of wicked   Isa 14:5

leaning on top of *s*   Heb 11:21

stagger, *go astray, doubt*

s like a drunken   Job 12:25, Psa 107:27

he *s* not at promise   Rom 4:20

stand, *stand still, steady*

s still and see   Ex 14:13, 2 Chr 20:17

s at latter day on   Job 19:25

ungodly not *s* in judgment   Psa 1:5

s in awe and sin not   4:4

counsel of Lord *s* for ever   33:11

word of God shall *s*   Isa 40:8

s in ways, ask for old   Jer 6:16

house divided shall not *s*   Mat 12:25, Mk 3:25, Lk 11:17

why *s* ye all day idle   Mat 20:6

why *s* gazing into heaven   Acts 1:11

grace wherein we *s*   Rom 5:2

s fast in the faith   1 Cor 16:13

s fast in the liberty   Gal 5:1

having done all, to *s*   Eph 6:13

s fast in one spirit   Phil 1:27

s fast in Lord   4:1, 1 Thes 3:8

foundation of God *s*   2 Tim 2:19

grace wherein we *s*   1 Pet 5:12

I *s* at the door and   Rev 3:20

who shall be able to *s*   6:17

star

he made *s* also   Gen 1:16

a *S* out of Jacob   Num 24:17

morning *s* sang together   Job 38:7

have seen his *s* in east   Mat 2:2

wandering *s*   Jude 13

See also: Psa 147:4, 148:3, Rev 8:10

state, *condition*

man at best *s* is vanity   Psa 39:5

last *s* worse than   Mat 12:45, Lk 11:26

stature, *measure, size*

not add to *s*   Mat 6:27, Lk 12:25

Jesus increased in *s*   2:52

s of fulness of Christ   Eph 4:13

statute, *law, ordinance*

s of the Lord are right   Psa 19:8

walk in the *s* of life   Ezek 33:15

See also: Mat 5:17, Rom 7:6, 1 Jno 5:3

stay, *support, held*

whose mind is *s* on thee   Isa 26:3

steal

lest I be poor, and *s*   Pro 30:9

break through and *s*   Mat 6:19

him that stole, *s* no   Eph 4:28

stedfast, *faithful, firm*

words by angels was *s*   Heb 2:2

hold confidence *s* to end   3:14

hope as anchor, sure and *s*   6:19

whom resist *s* in   1 Pet 5:9

See also: Mat 10:22, 24:13, Jno 8:31, 1 Cor 16:13, Gal 6:9

step, *pace, pathway*

s between me and death   1 Sam 20:3

s of good man   Psa 37:23

Lord directeth his *s*   Pro 16:9

not in man to direct *s*   Jer 10:23

walk in *s* of that faith   Rom 4:12

that ye should follow his *s*   1 Pet 2:21

See also: Mic 6:8, Rom 6:4

steward, *trusted manager*
  faithful and wise *s*   Lk 12:42
  s of mysteries of God   1 Cor 4:1 f
  s of grace of God   1 Pet 4:10
  See also: Lk 12:48, 1 Tim 6:20

stick, *piece of wood*
  gathered *s* on sabbath   Num 15:32

stick (verb), *to cling*
  friend that *s* closer   Pro 18:24

stiff, *hard, rigid*
  a *s*necked people   Ex 32:9, 34:9,
               Deut 9:13, 10:16
  ye *s*necked, ye resist   Acts 7:51

still, *calm, quiet*
  beside the *s* waters   Psa 23:2
  be *s*, and know that I am God
                         46:10
  said to sea, peace, be *s*   Mk 4:39

sting
  s like an adder   Pro 23:32
  death, where is thy *s* 1 Cor 15:55

stir, *agitate*
  wrathful man *s* up strife Pro 15:18,
                         29:22
  s up gift of God   2 Tim 1:6

Stoics, *Greek philosophers who believed
in passive life in hands of fate,* Acts
17:18

stolen *(see steal)*
  s waters are sweet   Pro 9:17

stone, *rock*
  the water wear the *s*   Job 14:19
  heart is firm as *s*   41:24
  dash thy foot against *s* Psa 91:12,
              Mat 4:6, Lk 4:11
  s which builders refused   Psa
    118:22, Mat 21:42, Mk 12:10
  he that rolleth a *s*   Pro 26:27

s is heavy, fool's wrath   27:3
tried *s*, a precious corner *s*   Isa
          28:16, 1 Pet 2:6
take *s* heart out   Ezek 11:19
will he give him a *s*   Mat 7:9, Lk
                  11:11
fall on this *s* shall   21:44
one *s* upon another Mat 24:2, Mk
       13:2, Lk 19:44, 21:6
found the *s* rolled away Mk 16:4,
                 Lk 24:2
s that it be made bread   4:3
s would cry out   19:40
Cephas, by interpretation, a *s* Jno
                1:42
lively *s*, are built up   1 Pet 2:5
  See also: Isa 51:1

stood *(see stand)*
  Abraham *s* before Lord Gen 18:22
  commanded, and it *s* fast Psa 33:9

stoop, *bend low*
  Jesus *s* down, and wrote   Jno 8:6

stop, *close, end, restrain*
  windows of heaven were *s* Gen 8:2
  they *s* their ears   Acts 7:57
  whose mouths must be *s* Tit 1:11

store, *save up, treasure*
  let every one lay by him in *s* 1 Cor
                 16:2
  laying in *s* a good   1 Tim 6:19
  See also: Lk 12:24

straight, *upright, not crooked*
  make thy way *s*   Psa 5:8
  s in desert a highway   Isa 40:3
  crooked shall be made *s*   40:4,
        42:16, 45:2, Lk 3:5
  make his paths *s* Mat 3:3, Mk 1:3,
         Lk 3:4, Jno 1:23

street is called *S*   Acts 9:11

make *s* paths for   Heb 12:13

strain, *separate*

s at a gnat   Mat 23:24

strait, *narrow, difficult*

enter in at *s* gate   Mat 7:13, Lk 13:24

in a *s* betwixt two   Phil 1:23

strange, *alien, different*

put away *s* gods that   Gen 35:2

stranger in *s* land   Ex 2:22

offered *s* fire   Lev 10:1, Num 3:4, 26:61

way of man *s*   Pro 21:8

setter forth of *s* gods   Acts 17:18

carried with *s* doctrines   Heb 13:9

stranger *(see strange)*

s in the earth   Psa 119:19

I was a *s*, and ye took   Mat 25:35

to entertain *s*   Heb 13:2

See also: Eph 2:12–19

stream, *river, brook*

s in the desert   Isa 35:6

righteousness mighty *s*   Amos 5:24

street

wisdom uttereth voice in *s*   Pro 1:20

prayers in *s*   Mat 6:5

s called Straight   Acts 9:11

s of city was gold   Rev 21:21

strength, *power*

the Lord is my *s*   Ex 15:2, 2 Sam 22:33, Psa 18:2, 28:7, 118:14, Isa 12:2

out of mouth of babes hast thou ordained *s*   Psa 8:2

Lord is *s* of my life   27:1

God is refuge and *s*   46:1, 81:1

way of Lord is *s* to   Pro 10:29

wisdom is better than *s*   Ecc 9:16

s is to sit still   Isa 30:7

love God with all *s*   Mk 12:30

when we were without *s*   Rom 5:6

See also: Psa 55:22, 121:1, Mat 7:25

strengthen *(see strength)*

s ye the weak hands   Isa 35:3

through Christ which *s*   Phil 4:13

stretch, *spread out*

he hath *s* out the heavens   Jer 10:12, 51:15

s forth thine hand   Mat 12:13

strive, *struggle, contend*

Spirit shall not always *s*   Gen 6:3

s not without cause   Pro 3:30

not *s* nor cry   Mat 12:19

s to enter strait gate   Lk 13:24

servant of Lord not *s*   2 Tim 2:24

See also: Pro 6:19, 20:3, Lk 21:10, Eph 6:12

strong, *mighty*

as a *s* man run a race   Psa 19:5

the Lord *s* and mighty   24:8

love is *s* as death   S of S 8:6

s in faith   Rom 4:20

s ought to bear infirmities   15:1

need milk, not *s* meat   Heb 5:12

study, *meditate, be diligent*

much *s* is a weariness   Ecc 12:12

ye *s* to be quiet   1 Thes 4:11

s to shew self approved   2 Tim 2:15

See also: Psa 1:2, Pro 4:7, 12:1

stumble, *fall*

at what they *s*   Pro 4:19

if walk in day, *s* not   Jno 11:9

whereby thy brother *s*   Rom 14:21

that *s* at the word   1 Pet 2:8
See also: Isa 59:10, 1 Pet 2:8, 1 Jno 2:10

stumbling block, *obstacle*
not put *s b* before   Lev 19:14
take *s b* out of way   Isa 57:14
I lay in Sion a *s b*   Rom 9:33
no man put *s b*   14:13
unto Jews a *s b*   1 Cor 1:23
liberty become *s b*   8:9

subdue, *humble, conquer*
he will *s* iniquities   Mic 7:19
all things *s* unto him   1 Cor 15:28
able to *s* all things   Phil 3:21

subject, *ruled by*
it is not *s* to law   Rom 8:7
be *s* to higher powers   13:1
as church is *s* to Christ   Eph 5:24
all things in *s* under   Heb 2:8
be *s* one to another   5:5
being made *s* to him   1 Pet 3:22
See also: 1 Cor 9:27

submit, *to yield to*
wives *s* yourselves to husbands   Eph 5:22, Col 3:18
s yourselves to God   Jas 4:7
s to every ordinance   1 Pet 2:13
See also: Mat 6:10, 26:39, Eph 5:21

substance, *possession, foundation*
wasted his *s*   Lk 15:13
in heaven a better *s*   Heb 10:34
faith is *s* of things hoped   11:1

subtil, *subtle, crafty* (archaic)
serpent was more *s* than   Gen 3:1
s of heart   Pro 7:10

sudden, *unexpected, quickly*
not afraid of *s* fear   Pro 3:25
s destruction cometh   1 Thes 5:3

See also: Pro 29:1, Mal 3:1, Mk 13:36, 1 Tim 5:22

suffer, *permit* (archaic); *endure*
s thy foot to be moved   Psa 121:3
Jesus said, *s* it to be   Mat 3:15
must *s* many things   16:21, Mk 10:14, Lk 18:16
behoved Christ to *s*   24:45, Acts 3:18
if we *s* with him   Rom 8:17
not *s* to be tempted   1 Cor 10:13
charity *s* long   13:4
to *s* for his sake   Phil 1:29
if we *s*, we shall reign   2 Tim 2:12
to *s* affliction   Heb 11:25
Christ *s* for us, leaving   1 Pet 2:21
See also: 2 Cor 4:17, 1 Pet 4:1,19, Rev 2:10

sufficient, *enough*
s to day is evil   Mat 6:34

sumptuously, *richly*
fared *s* every day   Lk 16:19

sun
s stand thou still   Josh 10:12
Lord is a *s* and shield   Psa 84:11
s shall not smite thee   121:6
no new thing under the *s*   Ecc 1:9
pleasant for eyes to behold *s*   11:7
s to rise on evil and   Mat 5:45
righteous shine as the *s*   13:43
one glory of *s*   1 Cor 15:41
s go down on your wrath   Eph 4:26
city had no need of *s*   Rev 21:23
See also: Gen 1:16

sup, *take evening meal*
took cup when he had *s*   1 Cor 11:25
I will *s* with him   Rev 3:20

supplication, *entreaty, pleading*
with all prayer and *s*	Eph 6:18
in every thing by *s*	Phil 4:6
s be made for all men	1 Tim 2:1

support, *uphold*
ye ought to *s* weak	Acts 20:35,
	1 Thes 5:14

sure, *firm, secure, know*
s your sin will find	Num 32:23
no man is *s* of life	Job 24:22
his commandments are *s*	Psa 111:7
foundation standeth *s*	2 Tim 2:19
calling and election *s*	2 Pet 1:10
more *s* word of prophecy	1:19

swallow, *drink down*
s up death in victory	Isa 25:8
strain gnat, and *s* camel	Mat 23:24
death *s* in victory	1 Cor 15:54
mortality be *s* up	2 Cor 5:4

swear, *take oath*
not *s* by my name	Lev 19:12
s not at all	Mat 5:34

sweat, *perspiration*
in *s* of face eat bread	Gen 3:19
s was as blood	Lk 22:44

sweet
though wickedness be *s*	Job 20:12
how *s* are thy words	Psa 119:103
stolen waters are *s*	Pro 9:17
pleasant words are *s*	16:24
bread of deceit is *s* to	20:17
to hungry bitter thing is *s*	27:7
sleep of labouring man *s*	Ecc 5:12
s water and bitter	Jas 3:11

swelling, *puffed up*
s words of vanity	2 Pet 2:18

swift, *quick*
my days *s* than	Job 7:6

s in running to mischief	Pro 6:18
race is not to *s*	Ecc 9:11
feet *s* to shed blood	Rom 3:15
s to hear, slow to	Jas 1:19
s destruction	2 Pet 2:1

sword, *weapon*
Cherubims, and flaming *s*	Gen 3:24
tongue is a sharp *s*	Psa 57:4
beat *s* into plowshares	Isa 2:4
not lift *s* against nation	Mic 4:3
not peace, but *s*	Mat 10:34
he that hath no *s*	Lk 22:36
s of the Spirit	Eph 6:17
sharper than two-edged *s*	Heb 4:12
out of his mouth went a sharp *s*	
	Rev 1:16, 19:15
killeth with *s*, must	13:10

synagogue, *gathering place*
taught in *s*	Mat 13:54, Mk 6:2
put out of the *s*	Jno 12:42
put you out of *s*	16:2

T

tabernacle, *tent*
set a *t* for the sun	Psa 19:4
salvation is in *t* of	118:15
let us make three *t*	Mat 17:4
this *t* be dissolved	2 Cor 5:1
in this *t* do groan	5:4
t of God is with men	Rev 21:3

table, *board, slab*
thou preparest a *t*	Psa 23:5
write on *t* of heart	Pro 3:3, 7:3
crumbs from master's *t*	Mat 15:27,
	Mk 7:28

fleshy *t* of the heart   2 Cor 3:3

take, *receive, capture, use*
 I will *t* you for a people   Ex 6:7
 t name of Lord in vain   20:7, Deut 5:11
 t not Holy Spirit from   Psa 51:11
 soul, *t* thine ease   Lk 12:19
 any man *t* away from   Rev 22:19

tale, *story (measure, in Ex 5:8)*
 we spend our years as a *t* Psa 90:9
 that carry *t* to shed blood   Ezek 22:9
 seemed as idle *t*   Lk 24:11

talent, *cake, weight*
 a *t* of silver   2 Ki 5:22
 owed ten thousand *t*   Mat 18:24
 I went and hid thy *t*   25:25

talk, *say, speak*
 t of them when sittest   Deut 6:7
 entangle him in his *t*   Mat 22:15
 See also: Eph 5:4, Tit 1:10, Jas 5:12

tame, *subdue*
 nor could any man *t* him   Mk 5:4
 tongue can no man *t*   Jas 3:8

tarry, *wait, linger*
 t long at wine   Pro 23:30
 while the bridegroom *t*   Mat 25:5
 why *t* thou? Arise   Acts 22:16
 t one for another   1 Cor 11:33

taste
 t of manna like wafers   Ex 16:31
 t and see Lord is good   Psa 34:8
 thy words to my *t*   119:103
 which shall not *t* death Mat 16:28, Mk 9:1, Lk 9:27
 shall never *t* death   Jno 8:52
 touch not, *t* not   Col 2:21
 have *t* of heavenly gift   Heb 6:4

t Lord is gracious   1 Pet 2:3

taught *(see teach)*
 their fear is *t* by   Isa 29:13
 he *t* as one having authority   Mat 7:29, Mk 1:22
 they shall be *t* of God   Jno 6:45

teach, *instruct, cause to understand*
 may *t* their children   Deut 4:10
 t me thy paths   Psa 25:4
 t trangressors thy ways   51:13
 t no more every man neighbour Jer 31:34, Heb 8:11
 priests *t* for hire   Mic 3:11
 t all nations   Mat 28:19
 t us to pray   Lk 11:1
 ceased not to *t* and   Acts 5:42
 t thou not thyself?   Rom 2:21
 t and admonishing one   Col 3:16
 suffer not woman to *t*   1 Tim 2:12
 apt to *t*   3:2, 2 Tim 2:24
 things command and *t*   1 Tim 4:11
 able to *t* others   2 Tim 2:2
 have need that one *t*   Heb 5:12

teacher, *instructor*
 t as the scholar   1 Chr 25:8
 a *t* come from God   Jno 3:2
 desiring to be *t* of   1 Tim 1:7
 shall be false *t*   2 Pet 2:1

tears, *weeping*
 sow *t*, reap joy   Psa 126:5
 will wipe away *t*   Isa 25:8
 to wash his feet with *t*   Lk 7:38
 to warn with *t*   Acts 20:31
 God wipe away *t*   Rev 7:17, 21:4

teeth
 t shall be white   Gen 49:12
 escaped with skin of *t*   Job 19:20
 as vinegar to *t*   Pro 10:26

children's *t* set on edge   Jer 31:29,
       Ezek 18:2

tell, *to say, relate*
  t it not in Gath   2 Sam 1:20
  who can *t* if God will   Jonah 3:9
  will *t* us all things   Jno 4:25

temperance, *self-restraint*
  fruit of Spirit is *t*   Gal 5:22 f
  add to knowledge *t*   2 Pet 1:6
  See also: Pro 23:29

tempest, *hurricane, storm*
  darkness and *t*   Heb 12:18
  clouds carried with *t*   2 Pet 2:17
  See also: Ecc 1:6, Hos 8:7, Mat 8:27

temple, *house of God (or gods)*
  train filled the *t*   Isa 6:1
  Lord is in his Holy *t*   Psa 11:4
  found him in the *t*   Lk 2:46
  destroy this *t*   Jno 2:19
  t made with   Acts 7:48, 17:24
  ye are the *t* of God   1 Cor 3:16,
       2 Cor 6:16
  body is *t* of Holy   1 Cor 6:19
  groweth into a holy *t*   Eph 2:21

temporal, *temporary, of this world*
  things seen are *t*   2 Cor 4:18

tempt, *to entice, try, prove*
  God did *t* Abraham   Gen 22:1
  shall not *t* the Lord   Deut 6:16,
       Mat 4:7, Lk 4:12
  suffer you to be *t*   1 Cor 10:13
  lest thou also be *t*   Gal 6:1
  in all points *t* like   Heb 4:15
  God cannot be *t*, neither Jas 1:13 f
  See also: Pro 1:10, Mat 4:1, Rev 3:10

temptation *(see tempt)*
  as in day of *t*   Psa 95:8, Heb 3:8

not into *t*   Mat 6:13, Lk 11:4
lest ye enter into *t* Mat 26:41, Mk
       14:38, Lk 22:46
hath no *t* taken   1 Cor 10:13
rich fall into *t*   1 Tim 6:9
count it joy when fall into *t*   Jas
       1:2,3
blessed that endure *t*   1:12

tender, *soft, timid*
  great are thy *t* mercies   Psa
       119:156
  grow up as a *t* plant   Isa 53:2
  be kind, *t* hearted   Eph 4:32
  Lord of *t* mercy   Jas 5:11

tents
  how goodly are thy *t*   Num 24:5
  to your *t*, O Israel   1 Ki 12:16

terrible, *fearful, reverenced*
  mighty God and *t*   Deut 7:21,
       10:17, Neh 1:5, 4:14, 9:32
  the Lord most high is *t*   Psa 47:2
  thy great and *t* name   99:3
  day of the Lord is *t*   Joel 2:11

terrify *(see terror)*
  in nothing *t* by   Phil 1:28

terror, *fear, reverence*
  the *t* of God   Gen 35:5
  sword without, *t* within Deut 32:25
  t shall not be near   Isa 54:14
  t of shadow of death   Job 24:17
  rulers are not a *t* to   Rom 13:3
  knowing *t* of Lord   2 Cor 5:11
  See also: Psa 55:5, 73:19, 91:5

testament, *dispensation*
  my blood of new *t* Mat 25:28, Mk
       14:24
  cup of new *t*   Lk 22:20, 1 Cor
       11:25

surety of a better *t*　　　　Heb 7:22
where a *t* is, there　　　　　　9:16
See also: Jer 31:31, Heb 8:6,13,
Rom 15:4

testify, *answer, bear witness*
our sins *t* against us　　　Isa 59:12
pride of Israel doth *t* Hos 5:5, 7:10
Scriptures *t* of me　　　　Jno 5:39
t the gospel of　　　　Acts 20:24

testimony, *witness*
thy *t* are sure　　　　　　Psa 93:5
we know his *t* is　　　　　Jno 21:24
See also: Jer 20:9, Mk 15:39, 2 Cor
4:13

thank, *express gratitude*
I *t* thee, O Father　Mat 11:25, Lk
　　　　　　　10:21, Jno 11:41
God be *t* ye were　　　Rom 6:17

thanks, *bless, praise, be grateful*
good thing to give *t*　　　Psa 92:1
he took cup, and gave *t* Mat 26:27,
　　　　　　　　　　Lk 22:17
t to God who giveth　1 Cor 15:57
t be to God for　　　2 Cor 9:15
he giveth God *t*　　　Rom 14:6
giving *t* for all　　　Eph 5:20
See also: Lk 17:17,18

thanksgiving, *expression of gratitude*
his presence with *t*　　　Psa 95:2
enter into gates with *t*　　100:4
with *t* let your requests　Phil 4:6
be received with *t*　　1 Tim 4:3

thief, *robber*
partner with *t*, hateth　Pro 29:24
t cometh in, and robbers　Hos 7:1
as the *t* is ashamed　　　Jer 2:26
enter windows like *t*　　Joel 2:9
what hour *t*　Mat 24:43, Lk 12:39

are ye come as against a *t*　Mat
　　　　26;55, Mk 14:48, Lk 22:52
same is a *t* and robber　Jno 10:1
day of Lord cometh as a *t*　1 Thes
　　　　　　　5:2, 2 Pet 3:10
See also: Pro 28:24, Mal 3:8, Eph
4:28

thigh, *upper leg*
hollow of Jacob's *t*　　　Gen 32:25

thine, *yours* (archaic)
t, O Lord, is the　　　1 Chr 29:11
we are *t*　　　　　　　Isa 63:19
not my will, but *t*　　　Lk 22:42
all mine are *t*, and *t*　　Jno 17:10

thing, *matter, word, object*
better is end of *t* than　　Ecc 7:8
shall the *t* framed　　　Isa 29:16
not the *t* of God　　　Mat 16:23
t which are Caesar's　　　22:21
weak *t* of world　　1 Cor 1:27 f
let us mind same *t*　　　Phil 3:16

think, *ponder, meditate*
as he *t* in his heart　　　Pro 23:7
t not to say within　　　Mat 3:9
t not I am come to destroy　5:17
what *t* ye of Christ　　　22:42
not to *t* more highly　　Rom 12:3
that *t* he standeth　　1 Cor 10:12
t himself some thing　　　Gal 6:3
above all we ask or *t*　　Eph 3:20
t on these things　　　Phil 4:8

thirst
t for God　　Psa 42:2, 63:1, 143:6
shall not hunger nor *t*　Isa 49:10
t after righteousness　　Mat 5:6
shall never *t*　　Jno 4:14, 6:35
if any man *t*, let him　　　7:37
if enemy *t*, give him　Rom 12:20

thirsty *(see thirst)*

as cold waters to *t*	Pro 25:25
t land become springs	Isa 35:7
I was *t*, ye gave me	Mat 25:25

thistle, *bramble*

thorns and *t* shall it	Gen 3:18
t in Lebanon	2 Ki 14:9, 2 Chr 25:18
men gather figs of *t*	Mat 7:16

thorn, *brier*

slothful as hedge of *t*	Pro 15:19
t in way of froward	22:5
as the lily among *t*	S of S 2:2
grapes of *t*	Mat 7:16, Lk 6:44
fell among *t*	Mat 13:7, Mk 4:7
platted a crown of *t*	Mat 27:29, Mk 15:17, Jno 19:2
a *t* in the flesh	2 Cor 12:7

thought *(see think)*

t of heart only evil	Gen 6:5
ye *t* evil against me	50:20
Lord understandeth *t*	1 Chr 28:9
Lord knoweth *t* of man	Psa 94:11
know my *t*	139:23
t of righteous are right	Pro 12:5
unrighteous forsake *t*	Isa 55:7
my *t* are not your *t*	55:8
out of heart evil *t*	Mat 15:19, Mk 7:21
t a thing incredible	Acts 26:8
Lord knoweth *t* of wise	1 Cor 3:20
I *t* as a child	13:11
t it not robbery	Phil 2:6
discerner of the *t*	Heb 4:12
become judges of evil *t*	Jas 2:4

throat, *gullet*

their *t* is an open sepulchre	Psa 5:9, Rom 3:13

knife to thy *t*	Pro 23:5

throne, *seat*

Lord's *t* is in heaven	Psa 11:4
God sitteth on *t* of	47:8
heaven is my *t*	Isa 55:1, Acts 7:49
heaven, it is God's *t*	Mat 5:34
boldly to *t* of grace	Heb 4:16
grant to sit on my *t*	Rev 3:21
great white *t*	20:11

thrust, *cast away, drive out*

shall surely *t* you out	Ex 11:1
t hand into his side	Jno 20:25

tidings, *report, news*

not be afraid of evil *t*	Psa 112:7
I bring you good *t* of	Lk 2:10
glad *t* of kingdom	8:1
glad *t* of good things	Rom 10:15
See also: Pro 25:25, Isa 61:1, Tit 1:11	

time

t not hidden from Almighty	Job 24:1
t when mayest be found	Psa 32:6
deliver in *t* of trouble	41:1
an acceptable *t*	69:13, Isa 49:8
a *t* to every purpose	Ecc 3:1
t and chance happen to all	9:11
thy *t* was *t* of love	Ezek 16:8
it is *t* to seek Lord	Hos 16:3
my *t* is not yet come	Jno 7:6
it is high *t* to awake	Rom 13:11
the *t* is short	1 Cor 7:29
redeeming the *t*	Eph 5:16, Col 4:5
t of my departure is	2 Tim 4:6
help in *t* in need	Heb 4:16
appeareth a little *t*	Jas 4:14
pass *t* of sojourning	1 Pet 1:17
be *t* no longer	Rev 10:6

See also: 2 Pet 3:8

title, *sign*
to give flattering *t*   Job 32:22
Pilate wrote a *t*   Jno 19:19
See also: Isa 9:6, Jer 10:16, Mat 1:23, Lk 1:32

tittle, *a small stroke made in writing*
t shall not pass Mat 5:18, Lk 16:17

together, *as one*
or three gathered *t*   Mat 18:20
all things work *t* for   Rom 8:28

token, *sign, proof*
t of perdition   Phil 1:28
t of righteous judgment 2 Thes 1:5

tongue, *tongue, language*
keep *t* from   Psa 34:13, 1 Pet 3:10
t of the just as   Pro 10:20
t of wise is   12:18, 31:26
lying *t* is but for   12:19
death and life in *t*   18:21
whoso keepeth his *t*   21:23
given me *t* of learned   50:4
and bridleth not his *t*   Jas 1:26
the *t* is a little member   3:5
the *t* is a fire   3:6
the *t* can no man tame   3:8
nor let us love in *t*   1 Jno 3:18

torment, *test, affliction*
art thou come to *t* us   Mat 8:29
being in *t*   Lk 16:23
fear hath *t*   1 Jno 4:18
the smoke of their *t*   Rev 14:11

toss, *shake, throw about*
t with tempest   Isa 54:11
children *t* to and fro   Eph 4:14
like a wave *t*   Jas 1:6

touch
t not mine anointed   1 Chr 16:22, Psa 105:15

lo, this hath *t* thy lips   Isa 6:7
t no unclean   52:11, 2 Cor 6:17
the Lord *t* my mouth   Jer 1:9
t his garment   Mat 9:21, Mk 5:28
t me not   Jno 20:17
t not, taste not   Col 2:21

tower, *watchtower, castle*
let us build city and *t*   Gen 11:4
Lord is a strong *t*   Pro 18:10
built a *t*   Isa 5:2, Mat 21:33, Mk 12:1
intending to build *t*   Lk 14:28

tradition, *that which is handed down*
t of the elders   Mat 15:2, Mk 7:5
zealous of *t* of fathers   Gal 1:14
spoil you after *t* of men   Col 2:8
See also: Jer 18:15, Mat 15:6, Mk 7:8

train, *instruct*
t child in way he   Pro 22:6
See also: Deut 6:7, Eph 6:4

train (noun), *flowing robe*
his *t* filled the temple   Isa 6:1

traitor, *betrayer*
Judas was a *t*   Lk 6:16
men shall be *t*   2 Tim 3:1 ff
See also: Pro 25:19, Lk 11:23, Mk 13:12

trample, *tread on*
t them under foot   Mat 7:6

transfigured, *transformed, changed*
he was *t*   Mat 17:2, Mk 9:2

transformed, *changed, renewed*
t by renewing of mind   Rom 12:2
Satan is *t* into   2 Cor 11:14
See also: Eph 4:23, Phil 3:20, 1 Jno 3:14

TRANSGRESS

transgress, *rebel, go against*
- *t* commandments of Lord — Num 14:41, 2 Chr 24:20
- come to Bethel and *t* — Amos 4:4
- sin, *t* the law — 1 Jno 3:4
- *See also:* Gen 6:5, *and below*

transgression *(see transgress)*
- whose *t* is forgiven — Psa 32:1
- fools because of *t* — 107:17
- he was wounded for our *t* — Isa 53:5
- where no law is, no *t* — Rom 4:15

transgressor *(see transgress)*
- then will I teach *t* — Psa 51:13
- way of *t* is hard — Pro 13:15
- numbered with *t* — Mk 15:28, Lk 22:37
- thou art become a *t* — Jas 2:11

translated, *cause to pass over*
- *t* us into kingdom — Col 1:13
- Enoch was *t* — Heb 11:5

travail, *labor, toil, pain*
- he *t* with iniquity — Psa 7:14
- whole creation *t* — Rom 8:22
- destruction as *t* — 1 Thes 5:3

travel, *to go*
- kingdom of heaven is as a man *t* — Mat 25:14
- *See also:* Pro 27:8, Mk 13:34

treacherously, *deceptively*
- dealeth *t* — Isa 21:2, 24:16
- why happy that deal *t* — Jer 12:1
- they have dealt *t* against — Hos 5:7
- deal not *t* — Mal 2:10
- *See also:* Ex 20:16, 2 Cor 11:26

tread, *trample*
- not muzzle ox when he *t* corn — Deut 25:4, 1 Cor 9:9, 1 Tim 5:18

- as they that *t* grapes — Jer 25:30
- loveth to *t* out corn — Hos 10:11
- he *t* winepress of wrath — Rev 19:15

treasure, *thing of value*
- dig more than for hid *t* — Job 3:21
- *t* of snow, *t* of hail — 38:22
- *t* of wickedness — Pro 10:2
- great *t* and trouble — 15:16
- fear of Lord is his *t* — Isa 33:6
- *t* upon earth — Mat 6:19
- where your *t* is — 6:21, Lk 12:34
- out of good *t* of — Mat 12:35, Lk 6:45
- *t* hid in a field — Mat 13:44
- bringeth out of his *t* — 13:52
- *t* in heaven — 19:21, Mk 10:21, Lk 18:22
- *t* in earthen vessels — 2 Cor 4:7
- hid *t* of wisdom — Col 2:3
- greater riches than *t* in — Heb 11:26
- ye have heaped *t* together — Jas 5:3
- *See also:* Pro 27:24

treasury, *storehouse*
- not lawful to put in *t* — Mat 27:6
- casting money into *t* — Mk 12:41, Lk 21:1

tree
- given you every *t* — Gen 1:29
- *t* of life — 3:22, Pro 3:18, 11:30, 13:12, 15:4
- *t* planted by rivers — Psa 1:3, Jer 17:8
- good *t* bringeth — Mat 7:17, Lk 6:43
- hangeth on *t* — Gal 3:13
- eat of *t* of life — Rev 2:7

tremble, *shake, shudder*
- the pillars of earth *t* — Job 9:6
- pillars of heaven *t* — 26:11

keepers of house shall *t*　Ecc 12:3
your salvation with *t*　Phil 2:12
devils believe and *t*　Jas 2:19

trespass, *be guilty*
if forgive men their *t*　Mat 6:14
if ye forgive not *t*　18:35
if brother *t* against　Lk 17:3
dead in *t* and sins　Eph 3:1
having forgiven all *t*　Col 2:13
See also: Isa 59:2, 2 Cor 5:19

trial, *proving, testing*
a great *t* of affliction　2 Cor 8:2
the *t* of your faith　1 Pet 1:7
fiery *t* which is　4:12
See also: Jno 16:33, Jas 1:12

tribulation, *distress, affliction*
when *t* ariseth　Mat 13:21
in world shall have *t*　Jno 16:33
through much *t* enter　Acts 14:22
t worketh patience　Rom 5:3
shall *t* separate us　8:35
patient in *t*　12:12
exceeding joyful in *t*　2 Cor 7:4
See also: Mat 24:7, 1 Cor 15:57

tribute, *tax, custom*
to give *t* unto Caesar　Mat 22:17,
　Mk 12:14, Lk 20:22
render *t* to whom due　Rom 13:7

triumph, *victory*
he hath *t* gloriously.　Ex 15:1
how long shall wicked *t*　Psa 94:3
causeth us to *t* in Christ　2 Cor
　2:14
See also: 1 Cor 15:55, 1 Jno 5:4

trodden *(see tread)*
I have *t* winepress　Isa 63:3
salt be *t* under foot　Mat 5:13
fell by way side, and was *t*　Lk 8:5

hath *t* under foot Son　Heb 10:29

trouble, *distress, evil*
when they in *t*　2 Chr 15:4, Neh 9:27
he that *t* Israel　1 Ki 18:17
neither doth *t* spring　Job 5:6
man of few days, and *t*　14:1
refuge in times of *t*　Psa 9:9
very present help in *t*　46:1
salvation in time of *t*　Isa 33:2
wicked like *t* sea　57:20
Jesus was *t* Jno 11:33, 12:27, 13:21
let not your heart be *t*　14:1,27
comfort them in *t*　2 Cor 1:4
t on every side　4:8, 7:5
lest bitterness *t*　Heb 12:15

true, *genuine, sure*
tell me nothing but *t*　1 Ki 22:16
judgments of Lord *t*　Psa 19:9
t from the beginning　119:160
the Lord is the *t* God　Jer 10:10
thou art *t*　Mat 22:16, Mk 12:14
the *t* riches　Lk 16:11
that was the *t* light　Jno 1:9
the *t* bread　6:32
the *t* vine　15:1
as God is *t*　2 Cor 1:18
whatsoever things are *t*　Phil 4:8
draw near with a *t* heart Heb 10:22

truly *(see true)*
t this was Son of God　Mat 27:54

trump *(see trumpet)*
last *t*, dead be　1 Cor 15:52
shall descend with *t*　1 Thes 4:16

trumpet, *horn, cornet*
lift up voice like *t*　Isa 58:1
not sound a *t* before　Mat 6:2
t give an uncertain sound　1 Cor 14:8

voice as of a *t*   Rev 1:10, 4:1

trust, *have confidence, lean upon*
in him will I *t*   2 Sam 22:3, Psa
                  18:2, 91:2
yet will I *t* in him   Job 13:15
t in him at all times   Psa 62:8
better to *t* in Lord   118:8
Lord knoweth them that *t* Nah 1:7
them that *t* in riches   Mk 10:24
certain *t* in themselves   Lk 18:9
not *t* in ourselves   2 Cor 1:9
we *t* in living God   1 Tim 4:10

truth
a God of *t*   Deut 32:4
t of Lord endureth   Psa 117:2
thy law is *t*   119:142
buy the *t*   Pro 23:23
t is fallen in street   Isa 59:14
full of grace and *t*   Jno 1:14
t shall make you free   8:32
I am the way, the *t,* and   14:6
what is *t*?   18:38
who hold *t* in   Rom 1:18
judgment of God is *t*   2:2
rejoiceth in *t*   1 Cor 13:4
do nothing against *t*   2 Cor 13:8
speaking the *t* in love   Eph 4:15
pillar and ground of *t*   1 Tim 3:15
rightly dividing the word of *t*
                  2 Tim 2:15
come to knowledge of *t*   3:7
lie not against the *t*   Jas 3:14
if any err from the *t*   5:19
the Spirit is *t*   1 Jno 5:6

try, *test, prove*
t me, and know   Psa 139:23
fire shall *t* every   1 Cor 3:13
t the spirits   1 Jno 4:1

turn, *repent, turn about*
t unto the Lord   Psa 22:27
soft answer *t* wrath   Pro 15:1
t ye from evil way   Jer 25:5
repent and *t*   Ezek 2:12
t the other also   Mat 5:39
repent and *t* to God   Acts 26:20
no shadow of *t*   Jas 1:17

twain, *two*
with *t* he covered face   Isa 6:2
go mile, go with him *t*   Mat 5:41
no more *t*   19:6, Mk 10:8
veil rent in *t* Mat 27:51, Mk 15:38
to make of *t* one new   Eph 2:15

twice, *two times*
before the cock crow *t*   Mk 14:30
I fast *t* in the week   Lk 18:12
t dead, plucked up   Jude 12

twinkling, *sudden motion*
in the *t* of an eye   1 Cor 15:52

two
went in *t* by *t*   Gen 7:9
can *t* walk together   Amos 3:3
if *t* agree   Mat 18:19
t shall be one flesh   1 Cor 6:16
any *t*-edged sword   Heb 4:12

U

unawares, *without knowledge*
destruction come on him *u*   Psa
                  35:8
that day come on you *u* Lk 21:34
entertained angels *u*   Heb 13:2

unbelief, *lack of faith (see believe)*
help thou mine *u*	Mk 9:24
shall their *u* make faith?	Rom 3:3
an evil heart of *u*	Heb 3:12
not enter because of *u*	3:19, 4:6

See also: Jno 20:27, 1 Tim 1:13, Tit 1:15

unbelievers *(see unbelief)*
him his portion with *u*	Lk 12:36
goeth to law before *u*	1 Cor 6:6
unequally yoked with *u*	2 Cor 6:14

unblameable, *blameless*
present you holy, *u*	Col 1:22
stablish hearts *u*	1 Thes 3:13

uncertain, *hesitating, undependable*
so run, not as *u*	1 Cor 9:26
trumpet give an *u*	14:8
nor trust in *u* riches	1 Tim 6:17

uncircumcised *(see circumcise)*
stiffnecked, *u* in heart	Acts 7:51
thou wentest in to men *u*	11:3

uncircumcision *(see circumcise)*
thy circumcision made *u*	Rom 2:25
circumcision nothing, nor *u*	1 Cor 7:18

unclean, *impure*
between *u* and clean	Lev 10:10, 11:47
man of *u* lips, and dwell	Isa 6:5
discern clean and *u*	Ezek 44:23
power against *u* spirits	Mat 10:1, Mk 6:7
to him it is *u*	Rom 14:14
touch not *u* thing	2 Cor 6:17

uncleanness *(see unclean)*
full of bones, and *u*	Mat 23:7
gave them up to *u*	Rom 1:24
u and covetousness	1 Thes 4:7

unction, *anointing*
we have an *u*	1 Jno 2:20

undefiled, *not polluted, clean*
pure religion and *u*	Jas 1:27
an inheritance *u*	1 Pet 1:4

under, *beneath*
all *u* sin	Rom 3:9, Gal 3:22
not *u* law, but *u* grace	Rom 6:15
brought *u* power of	1 Cor 6:12
I keep *u* my body and bring	9:27
our fathers were *u* cloud	10:1
things *u* the earth	Phil 2:10

understand, *comprehend, consider*
evil men *u* not judgment	Pro 28:5
lest they *u*	Isa 6:10, Jno 12:40
neither do they *u*	Mat 13:13
not yet *u*	15:17, 16:9, Mk 8:17,21
I *u* all mysteries	1 Cor 13:2
through faith we *u*	Heb 11:3

See also: Pro 4:7, 1 Cor 14:20

understandest *(see understand)*
Philip said, *u* thou	Acts 8:30

understanding *(see understand)*
apply thine heart to *u*	Pro 2:2
lean not on thine own *u*	3:5
happy is man that getteth *u*	3:13
slow wrath is great *u*	14:29
love him with all *u*	Mk 12:33
without *u*, unmerciful	Rom 1:31
sing with *u*	1 Cor 14:15
having *u* darkened	Eph 4:18
which passeth *u*	Phil 4:7

understood *(see understand)*
I *u* as a child	1 Cor 13:11
things hard to be *u*	2 Pet 3:16

undone, *lost, turned aside, not done*
woe is me, for I am *u*	Isa 6:5
not to leave the other *u*	Mat 23:23

unequal, *unfair*
  not your ways *u*? Ezek 18:25,29
  be not *u* yoked with 2 Cor 6:14

unfeigned, *not pretended*
  pure heart and faith *u* 2 Cor 6:6
  u love of brethren 1 Pet 1:22

unfruitful *(see fruit)*
  u riches, choke word Mat 13:22,
    Mk 4:19
  understanding is *u* 1 Cor 14:14
  fellowship with *u* works Eph 5:11
  be barren nor *u* in 2 Pet 1:8

ungodliness, *wickedness, irreverence*
  wrath of God against *u* Rom 1:18
  denying *u* and worldly Tit 2:12

ungodly *(see ungodliness)*
  in the counsel of the *u* Psa 1:1
  u man diggeth up evil Pro 16:27
  Christ died for the *u* Rom 5:6
  where shall the *u* and sinner? 1 Pet
    4:18

unholy, *profane, common*
  the law is for *u* 1 Tim 1:9
  shall be unthankful, *u* 2 Tim 3:2
  covenant an *u* thing Heb 10:29

unity, *oneness*
  to dwell together in *u* Psa 133:1
  endeavouring to keep the *u* Eph
    4:3
  come in the *u* of the faith 4:13
  See also: Deut 6:4, 1 Cor 1:13, Eph
  2:15

unjust, *preverse, evil*
  deliver me from the *u* Psa 43:1
  u man is an abomination Pro 29:27
  u knoweth no shame Zeph 3:5
  rain on the just and *u* Mat 5:45
  go to law before the *u* 1 Cor 6:1

Christ suffered for *u* 1 Pet 3:18
reserve *u* to day 2 Pet 2:9

unknown *(see known)*
  to the *u* God Acts 17:23
  speaketh in *u* tongue 1 Cor 14:2 ff

unlearned, *uneducated*
  u questions avoid 2 Tim 2:23
  which *u* wrest 2 Pet 3:16

unloose, *untie*
  not worthy to *u* Mk 1:7, Lk 3:16,
    Jno 1:27

unmerciful, *without mercy*
  implacable, *u* Rom 1:31
  See also: Amos 2:6, Mat 23:23,
  25:42

unmoveable, *stable*
  be ye stedfast, *u* 1 Cor 15:58

unprofitable, *worthless*
  cast out the *u* servant Mat 25:30
  we are *u* servants Lk 17:10
  altogether become *u* Rom 3:12
  for that is *u* for you Heb 13:17

unpunished *(see punish)*
  wicked shall not be *u* Pro 11:21
  proud shall not be *u* 16:5

unquenchable, *that cannot be put out*
  burn up the chaff with *u* fire Mat
    3:12, Lk 3:17

unreasonable, *irrational*
  delivered from *u* men 2 Thes 3:2

unrighteous *(see righteous)*
  hand to be an *u* witness Ex 23:1
  u man forsake his way Isa 55:7
  hold truth in *u* Rom 1:18
  members as instruments of *u* 6:13
  is there *u* with God? 9:14
  u shall not inherit 1 Cor 6:9
  what fellowship with *u* 2 Cor 6:14

cleanse us from all *u*   1 Jno 1:9
all *u* is sin   5:17

unruly, *unrestrained*
   tongue is an *u* evil   Job 3:8
   warn them that are *u*   1 Thes 5:14

unsearchable, *beyond comprehension*
   Lord, his greatness *u*   Psa 145:3
   how *u* are his judgments   Rom 11:33
   the *u* riches of Christ   Eph 3:8

unseemly, *shameless, rude*
   working that which is *u*   Rom 1:27
   doth not behave *u*   1 Cor 13:5

unskilful, *inexperienced*
   is *u* in the word   Heb 9:13

unspeakable, *beyond description*
   to God for his *u*   2 Cor 9:15
   rejoice with joy *u*   1 Pet 1:8

unspotted, *not contaminated*
   keep himself *u* from   Jas 1:27

unstable, *not settled*
   double minded man is *u*   Jas 1:8
   unlearned and *u* wrest   2 Pet 2:14

unthankful, *ungrateful*
   blasphemers, *u*, unholy   2 Tim 3:2

untoward, *crooked, perverse*
   save from this *u*   Acts 2:40

unwashen, *unwashed*
   eat with *u* hands   Mat 15:20, Mk 7:2

unwise, *without common sense*
   to the wise and *u*   Rom 1:14
   not *u* but understanding   Eph 5:17

unworthily *(see worthy)*
   and drinketh *u*   1 Cor 11:27,29

upbraideth, *reproaches*
   all men liberally and *u*   Jas 1:5

upharsin, *divided (prob. a coin)*
   mene, tekel, *u*   Dan 5:25

uphold, *support*
   u me with thy free   Psa 51:12
   u me according to word   119:116
   honour shall *u* the humble   Pro 29:23
   my servant whom I *u*   Isa 42:1
   u all things by word   Heb 1:3

upper, *above*
   love the *u*most rooms   Mat 23:6, Mk 12:29, Lk 11:43
   large *u* room   Mk 14:15, Lk 22:12
   up into an *u* room   Acts 1:13

upright, *having integrity and truth*
   and behold the *u*   Psa 37:37
   u shall dwell in   140:13
   Lord is strength to *u*   Pro 10:29
   the prayer of *u* is   15:8

uproar, *tumult*
   all the city in *u*   Acts 17:5
   all Jerusalem was in *u*   21:31

upside down
   wipeth a dish turning it *u d*   2 Ki 21:13
   turned world *u d*   Acts 17:6

upward
   as the sparks fly *u*   Job 5:7
   spirit that goeth *u*   Ecc 3:21

Ur, *city of Mesopotamia, first home of Abraham,* Gen 11:28, 15:7, Neh 9:7

Uriah, *husband of Bath-sheba,* 2 Sam 11:3 ff, 12:9, Mat 1:6

Urim, *divine oracle "Urim and Thummim,"* Ex 28:30, Lev 8:8, Num 27:21, Deut 33:8, Ezra 2:63

use
   tongue of the wise *u*   Pro 15:2

that despitefully *u*   Mat 5:44, Lk
6:28
when you pray, *u* not   Mat 6:7
u not liberty   Gal 5:13, 1 Pet 2:16
meet for master's *u*   2 Tim 2:21
every one that *u* milk   Heb 5:13

usurp, *seize power*
woman to *u* authority   1 Tim 2:12

utter, *say, speak*
day unto day *u* speech   Psa 19:2
who can *u* mighty acts   106:2
false witnesses *u* lies   Pro 14:5
a fool *u* all his mind   29:11
which cannot be *u*   Rom 8:26

Uzziah, *leper king of Judah*, 2 Chr
26:21, 2 Ki 14:21

V

vagabond, *wanderer*
fugitive and *v*   Gen 4:12,14
certain *v* Jews took   Acts 19:13

vain, *hollow, empty*
not take name of Lord in *v*   Ex
20:7, Deut 5:11
I hate *v* thoughts   Psa 119:113
take name of God in *v*   Pro 30:9
favour is deceitful, beauty *v*   31:30
use not *v* repetitions   Mat 6:7
v in imagination   Rom 1:21
is our preaching *v* 1 Cor 15:14,17
desirous of *v* glory   Gal 5:26
nothing done through *v*   Phil 2:3
spoil through *v* deceit   Col 2:8
man's religion is *v*   Jas 1:26

valley, *cleft, deep place*
walk through *v* of death   Psa 23:4
lily of the *v*   S of S 2:1
every *v* be exalted   Isa 40:4
in *v* full of bones   Ezek 37:1
multitudes in *v* of decision   Joel
3:14
every *v* shall be filled   Lk 3:5

value, *weight, worth*
wisdom cannot be *v*   Job 28:16,19
ye are of more *v*   Mat 10:31, Lk
12:7

vanish, *go away, disappear*
heavens shall *v* away   Isa 51:6
knowledge, shall *v*   1 Cor 13:8
life a vapour that *v*   Jas 4:14

vanity *(see vain)*
wealth gotten by *v*   Pro 13:11
soweth iniquity reap *v*   22:8
v of vanities, all is *v*   Ecc 1:2,14,
3:19, 11:8, 12:8
speak words of *v*   2 Pet 2:18

vapour, *mist, smoke*
what is your life? a *v*   Jas 4:14

variableness, *change*
with whom is no *v*   Jas 1:17

Vashti, *queen of Persia*, Esth 1:9,
12,19, 2:17

vaunt, *exalt*
charity *v* not itself   1 Cor 13:4

veil, *covering*
make a *v* of blue   Ex 26:31
Moses put a *v* on face   34:33,35
v of temple was rent   Mat 27:51,
Mk 15:38, Lk 23:45

vengeance, *revenge*
to me belongeth *v* Deut 32:35, Psa
94:1, Heb 10:30

not spare in day of *v*   Pro 6:34
v is mine, saith Lord   Rom 12:19
fire, taking *v*   2 Thes 1:8

venom, *poison*
wine is *v* of asps   Deut 32:33

very, *truly*
this is *v* Christ Jno 7:26, Acts 9:22
v God of peace   1 Thes 5:23

vessel, *utensil*
I am like a broken *v*   Psa 31:12
wise took oil in *v*   Mat 25:4
he is a chosen *v*   Acts 9:15
make one *v* to honour   Rom 9:21,22
treasure in earthen *v*   2 Cor 4:7

vesture, *clothing*
they cast lots upon my *v*   Psa 22:18, Mat 27:35, Jno 19:24
how long will ye *v* soul   Job 19:2
v of spirit   Ecc 1:14, 2:11,17
Lot *v* with   2 Pet 2:7,8

victory, *conquest*
v that day was turned   2 Sam 19:2
thine is the *v*   1 Chr 29:11
swallow up death in *v*   Isa 25:8, 1 Cor 15:54
grave, where thy *v?*   15:55
God, who giveth us the *v*   15:57
this is the *v* even   1 Jno 5:4
See also: Rom 8:37, 2 Cor 2:14

vigilant, *watchful*
a bishop must be *v*   1 Tim 3:2
be *v* because adversary   1 Pet 5:8
See also: Amos 6:1, Mat 24:42

vile, *despised, filthy*
God gave them up to *v*   Rom 1:26
shall change *v* body   Phil 3:21
poor man in *v* raiment   Jas 2:2

vine, *grapevine*
binding his foal to *v*   Gen 49:11
trees said to *v*, reign   Judg 9:12
man under his *v*   1 Ki 4:25
v have tender grapes   S of S 2:15
Israel is an empty *v*   Hos 10:1
every man under his *v*   Mic 4:4
not drink of fruit of *v*   Mat 26:29, Mk 14:25, Lk 22:18
I am the true *v*   Jno 15:1,5
can *v* bear figs?   Jas 3:12

vinegar, *sour wine*
gave *v*   Psa 69:21
as *v* to the teeth   Pro 10:26
sponge filled with *v* Mat 27:48, Mk 15:36, Lk 23:36, Jno 19:29,30

vineyard, *grape or olive arbor*
Noah planted a *v*   Gen 9:20
hire labourers in his *v*   Mat 20:1
certain householder planted *v* 21:33, Mk 12:1, Lk 20:9

violence, *force, strife*
earth filled with *v*   Gen 6:11,12
I have seen *v* and strife   Psa 55:9
they drink wine of *v*   Pro 4:17
he had done no *v*   Isa 53:9
do *v* to no man   Lk 3:14

violent *(see violence)*
delivered me from *v* man   2 Sam 22:49, Psa 18:48
preserve me from *v*   140:1,4
v take it by force   Mat 11:12

viper, *serpent*
generation of *v*   Mat 3:7, 12:34, 23:33, Lk 3:7
v fasten, on Paul's hand   Acts 28:3

virgin, *chaste maiden*
v shall conceive Isa 7:14, Mat 1:23

v of Israel is fallen   Amos 5:2
is like to ten *v*   Mat 25:1
angel was sent to a *v*   Lk 1:27

virtue, *strength*
   v had gone out of him Mk 5:30, Lk
                6:19, 8:46
   if there be any *v*   Phil 4:8
   called to glory and *v*   2 Pet 1:3
   add to faith *v*   1:5

virtuous *(see virtue)*
   thou art a *v* woman   Ruth 3:11
   v woman is a crown   Pro 12:4
   who can find a *v* woman?   31:10
   daughter have done *v*   31:29

visible, *able to be seen*
   all things created, *v*   Col 1:16

vision, *sight, dream*
   God spake in *v*   Gen 46:2
   there was no open *v*   1 Sam 3:1
   where no *v*, people perish   Pro
                   29:18
   burden of valley of *v*   Isa 22:1,5
   I saw *v*, a vessel descend Acts 11:5
   See also: Acts 9:3, 16:10

visit, *inspect, look after, afflict*
   v iniquity of fathers   Ex 20:5, 34:7,
             Num 14:18, Deut 5:9
   thou *v* him   Psa 8:4, Heb 2:6
   sick and ye *v* me   Mat 25:36
   God hath *v* his people   Lk 7:16
   v fatherless and widows   Jas 1:27

vocation, *calling*
   walk worthy of the *v*   Eph 4:1
   See also: 1 Cor 7:20, 2 Pet 1:10

voice, *sound*
   v of brother's blood   Gen 4:10
   v is Jacob's but hands   27:22
   a still small *v*   1 Ki 19:12

a fool's *v* is known   Ecc 5:3
he shall rise at *v* of bird   12:4
v of turtle is heard in   S of S 2:12
v crieth in wilderness Isa 40:3, Mat
      3:3, Mk 1:3, Lk 3:4, Jno 1:23
v from heaven   Mat 3:17, Mk 1:11,
                    Lk 3:22
v out of cloud, this is my Son   Mat
      17:5, Mk 9:7, Lk 9:35,36
sheep hear his *v*.   Jno 10:3,16,27
then came a *v* saying   12:28
so many *v* in world   1 Cor 14:10
with *v* of archangel   1 Thes 4:16

void, *empty*
   earth without form and *v*   Gen 1:2,
                   Jer 4:23
   v of wisdom despiseth   Pro 11:12
   my word shall not return *v*   Isa
                   55:11
   do we make *v* law?   Rom 3:31

vow, *promise*
   when thou *v* a *v*   Deut 23:21
   Jephthah *v* a *v*   Judg 11:30
   when thou *v* a *v*   Ecc 5:4
   better thou shouldest not *v*   5:5
   head, for he had a *v*   Acts 18:18

vulture, *scavenger bird*
   there *v* be gathered   Isa 34:15

W

wages, *hire, reward*
   what shall thy *w* be?   Gen 29:15
   changed my *w* ten times   31:7,41
   be content with your *w*   Lk 3:14

the *w* of sin is death   Rom 6:23

w of unrighteousness   2 Pet 2:15

See also: Hag 1:6, 1 Tim 5:18

wagging

passed by reviled him, *w* heads
               Mat 27:39, Mk 15:29

wail, *mourn, cry out*

w shall be in streets   Amos 5:16

w and gnashing   Mat 13:42,50

wait

w on Lord shall inherit   Psa 37:7

w for salvation of   Lam 3:26

w for promise of Father   Acts 1:4

w for adoption   Rom 8:25

w for coming of Lord   1 Cor 1:7

w for hope   Gal 5:5

patient *w* for Christ   2 Thes 3:5

longsuffering of God *w*   1 Pet 3:20

wake, *awaken*

he *w* mine ear   Isa 50:4

whether *w* or sleep   1 Thes 5:10

See also: 1 Cor 15:34, Eph 5:14,
1 Thes 5:6

walk, *step, go about*

w before me   Gen 17:1

take heed *w* in ways   Josh 22:5

though I *w* through valley Psa 23:4

will *w* in mine integrity   26:11

can two *w* except   Amos 3:3

Rise, and *w*   Mat 9:5, Mk 2:9, Lk
        5:23, Jno 5:8,11,12, Acts 3:6

the lame *w*   Mat 11:5

not *w* in darkness but   Jno 8:12

w in newness of life   Rom 6:4

we *w* by faith   2 Cor 5:7

w in the Spirit   Gal 5:16,25

w worthy of vocation   Eph 4:1

w in love   5:2

see ye *w* circumspectly   5:15

mark them which *w*   Phil 3:17

w worthy of Col 1:10, 1 Thes 2:12

so *w* in him   Col 2:6

which *w* disorderly   2 Thes 3:11

to *w* as he walked   1 Jno 2:6

walked *(see walk)*

Enoch *w* with God   Gen 5:22,24

Peter *w* on the water   Mat 14:29

disciples *w* no more   Jno 6:66

ought to walk as he *w*   1 Jno 2:6

walketh *(see walk)*

spirit is gone out, *w* through dry
places   Mat 12:43, Lk 11:24

brother *w* disorderly   2 Thes 3:6

devil *w* about seeking   1 Pet 5:8

hate brother *w* in   1 Jno 2:11

walking *(see walk)*

voice of Lord *w* in garden Gen 3:8

Jesus went *w* on sea   Mat 14:25

I see men as trees *w*   Mk 8:24

wall, *enclosure, rampart*

she dwelt upon *w*   Josh 2:15

w of city shall fall   6:5,20

so built we *w*   Neh 4:6

as high *w* in conceit   Pro 18:11

Saul down by the *w* in basket Acts
             9:25, 2 Cor 11:33

Christ broken down *w*   Eph 2:14

w of Jericho fell   Heb 11:30

See also: Pro 25:28, Isa 62:6

wander, *go to and fro*

shall *w* in wilderness   Num 14:33,
             32:13, Psa 107:40

w from house to house 1 Tim 5:13

w stars   Jude 1:13

See also: Psa 119:176, Lam 4:14

want, *lack*

die for *w* of wisdom   Pro 10:21
he began to be in *w*   Lk 15:14

want, *need*

shepherd, I shall not *w*   Psa 23:1
he began to be in *w*   Lk 15:14
See also: Deut 8:9, Psa 34:10, Pro 10:15

wanting *(see want)*

set in order things *w*   Tit 1:5
and entire, *w* nothing   Jas 1:4

wanton, *lewd*

not chambering and *w*   Rom 13:13
wax *w* against Christ   1 Tim 5:11
allure through much *w*   2 Pet 2:18

war, *conflict*

people repent when see *w*   Ex 13:17
nor learn *w*   Isa 2:4, Mic 4:3
hear of *w* and rumours of *w*   Mat 24:6, Mk 13:7, Lk 21:9
king going to *w*?   14:31
from whence come *w*?   Jas 4:1

war (verb), *to fight*

do not *w* after flesh   2 Cor 10:3
w entangleth himself   2 Tim 2:4
lusts *w* against soul   1 Pet 2:11

warfare, *conflict*

her *w* is accomplished   Isa 40:2
weapons of *w* not carnal   2 Cor 10:4
might war a good *w*   1 Tim 1:18

warmed, *to heat*

Peter *w* himself   Mk 14:54, Jno 18:18,25
depart in peace, be *w*   Jas 2:16

warn, *to advise*

Joseph being *w* of God   Mat 2:12

who hath *w* you?   3:7, Lk 3:7
w that are unruly   1 Thes 5:14

was, *has been*

walked with God *w* not   Gen 5:24
is and which *w*   Rev 1:4,8, 4:8

wash, *bathe, cleanse*

w in Jordan seven times   2 Ki 5:10
w me from mine iniquity   Psa 51:2
when fastest, *w* face   Mat 6:17
began to *w* his feet   Lk 7:38
to *w* disciples' feet   Jno 13:5
w away thy sins   Acts 22:16
See also: Psa 51:7, 1 Cor 6:11

washed *(see wash)*

Pilate *w* his hands   Mat 27:24
having our bodies *w*   Heb 10:22

waste, *ruin, consume*

man dieth, *w* away   Job 14:10
Lord maketh earth *w*   Isa 24:1
w and destruction are   59:7
to what purpose is this *w*?   Mat 26:8, Mk 14:4
w his substance   Lk 15:13
See also: Pro 12:27, Mat 7:6

watch, *observe, guard*

Lord *w* between me   Gen 31:49
thousand years as a *w*   Psa 90:4
w in watchtower   Isa 21:5
all that *w* for iniquity   29:20
w therefore   Mat 24:42, 25:13, Mk 13:35, Lk 21:36, Acts 20:3
w and pray   Mat 26:41, Mk 13:22, 14:38, Col 4:2
shepherds keeping *w*   Lk 2:8
w ye, stand fast   1 Cor 16:13
let us *w*   1 Thes 5:6, 1 Pet 4:7

watched *(see watch)*

w whether he would heal   Mk 3:2,
                          Lk 6:7, 14:1
w gates day and might   Acts 9:24

watching *(see watch)*

when come, find w   Lk 12:37
in labours, in w, in   2 Cor 6:5
w with perseverance   Eph 6:18

watchman, *guard, lookout*

made thee a w   Ezek 3:17, 33:7
set him up for w   33:2,6
I have set w on walls   Isa 62:6
set w over you, saying   Jer 6:17

water

unstable as w not excel   Gen 49:4
shall come w out of rock   Ex 17:6
land drinketh w of   Deut 11:11
bread and w of affliction   1 Ki
                      22:27, 2 Chr 18:26
drink iniquity like w   Job 15:16
leadeth me beside still w Psa 23:2
hart panteth after w   42:1
will pour w on thirsty   Isa 44:3
knees weak as w   Ezek 7:17, 21:7
baptize you with w   Mat 3:11, Mk
                    1:8, Lk 3:16, Jno 1:26
give cup of w   Mat 10:42, Mk 9:41
thou gavest me no w   Lk 7:44
may dip his finger in w   16:24
except man be born of w   Jno 3:5
living w   4:10
here is w   Acts 8:36
can any forbid w   10:47
washed with pure w   Heb 10:22
yield salt w and fresh   Jas 3:12
wells without w   2 Pet 2:17
came by w and blood   1 Jno 5:6
Spirit, w, blood   5:8

clouds without w   Jude 12

watered

mist w face of ground   Gen 2:6
Jordan that it was well w   13:10
I planted, Apollos w   1 Cor 3:6

waters

moved upon face of w   Gen 1:2
a flood of w on earth   6:17
not cut off any more by w   9:11
by east wind the w   Ex 14:21
w of Jordan were cut off   Josh 4:7
smote rock that w gushed   Psa
          78:20, 105:41, 114:8, Isa 48:21
stolen w are sweet   Pro 9:17
as cold w to thirsty soul   25:25
cast thy bread upon w   Ecc 11:1
tree planted by the w   Jer 17:8

wavereth, *to be uncertain*

he that w is like wave   Jas 1:6

wavering *(see wavereth)*

hold faith without w   Heb 10:23
ask in faith, nothing w   Jas 1:6

waves

as w of sea   Isa 48:18

wax, *to become, to grow*

w old as garment   Psa 102:26, Isa
                    50:9, 51:6, Heb 1:11

waxed *(see wax)*

famine w sore in Egypt   Gen 41:56
people's heart w gross   Mat 13:15,
                          Acts 28:27

way, *road, path, direction*

to walk in his w   Deut 8:6, 26:17,
                   28:9, 30:16, 1 Ki 2:3
w of all earth   2:2
nor standeth in the w   Psa 1:1
knoweth w of righteous   1:6
teach me thy w   27:11, 86:11

teach transgressors thy _w_ 51:13
refrain frim evil _w_ 119:101
hate every false _w_ 119:104
Lord is right in all his _w_ 145:17
_w_ of wicked darkness Pro 4:19
_w_ of life 6:23
train up child in the _w_ 22:6
_w_ fool right in own eyes 12:15
sayest my _w_ is hid? Isa 40:27
will make _w_ in wilderness 43:19
let wicked forsake his _w_ 55:7
_w_ of peace they know not 59:8,
Rom 3:17
_w_ of man is not in himself Jer
10:23
agree while in the _w_ Mat 5:25
broad is _w_ to destruction 7:13
prepare thy _w_ before thee 11:10,
Mk 1:2, Lk 7:27
teach _w_ of God in truth Mat 22:16,
Mk 12:14, Lk 20:21
_w_ ye know Jno 14:4
expounded unto him the _w_ of God
Acts 18:26
misery are in their _w_ Rom 3:16
his _w_ past finding 11:33
a more excellent _w_ 1 Cor 12:31
unstable in all his _w_ Jas 1:8
See also: Acts 19:9,23, 24:14

wayfaring, _traveling_
_w_ men not err therein Isa 35:8

way side, _pathway_
seeds fell by _w_ s Mat 13:4,19, Mk
4:4,15, Lk 8:5,12

weak, _feeble, without strength_
let the _w_ say Jonah 3:10
flesh _w_ Mat 26:41, Mk 14:38
him that is _w_ Rom 14:1

bear infirmities of _w_ 15:1
we also are _w_ Col 13:4
support the _w_ 1 Thes 5:14
weakness _(see weak)_
_w_ of God is stronger 1 Cor 1:25
sown in _w_ raised in power 15:43
out of _w_ made strong Heb 11:34
wealth, _riches, substance_
trust in _w_, boast in riches Psa 49:6
_w_ gotten by vanity Pro 13:11
_w_ maketh many friends 19:4
See also: Pro 22:1, 23:4, Mat 19:24,
1 Tim 6:7
weapons
wisdom better than _w_ Ecc 9:18
_w_ of warfare not carnal 2 Cor 10:4
See also: Rev 12:11, 13:10
wear, _to wear away_
waters _w_ the stones Job 14:19
wear _to be clothed_
woman shall not _w_ Deut 22:5
not be _w_ of gold 1 Pet 3:3
wearied, _exhausted, tired_
labour of foolish _w_ Ecc 10:15
lest ye be _w_ and faint Heb 12:3
weariness _(see weary)_
study is a _w_ of flesh Ecc 12:12
_w_ and painfulness 2 Cor 11:27
weary, _tired_
my soul is _w_ of Job 10:1
shadow of rock in _w_ land Isa 32:2
God fainteth not, nor _w_ 40:28
let us not be _w_ in Gal 6:9, 2 Thes
3:13
weather
fair _w_ come out of Job 37:22
fair _w_, for sky is red Mat 16:2
See also: Gen 8:22, Psa 148:8, S of
S 2:11

weaver, *one who plaits*
 days swift as *w* shuttle   Job 7:6
wedding, *marriage*
 had not on *w* garment   Mat 22:11
 See also: Jno 2:2, *and marry*
week, *seven days*
 first day of *w* Mat 28:1, Mk 16:2,9,
           Lk 24:1, Jno 20:1,19
 first day of *w* Paul   Acts 20:7
 on first day of *w* let   1 Cor 16:2
weep, *mourn, cry*
 a time to *w* a time to   Ecc 3:4
 there shall be *w*   Mat 8:12, 22:13,
           24:51, 25:30, Lk 13:38
 blessed are ye that *w*   6:21
 w not   7:13, 8:52, Rev 5:5
 woman stood at feet *w*   Lk 7:38
 w with them that *w*   Rom 12:15
 See also: Isa 25:8
weigh, *balance, test*
 let me be *w* in even   Job 31:6
 thou art *w* in balance   Dan 5:27
weight, *balance stone, burden*
 a just *w* and   Pro 16:11
 eternal *w* of glory   2 Cor 4:17
 lay aside every *w*   Heb 12:1
weightier *(see weight)*
 omitted *w* matters   Mat 23:23
well, *cistern, water source*
 righteous man is *w* of   Pro 10:11
 Jacob's *w* was there   Jno 4:6
 are *w* without water   2 Pet 2:17
well, *good, acceptable*
 that it may go *w* with   Deut 4:40,
       5:16, 6:3,18, 12:25,28, 19:13,
           22:7, Ruth 3:1, Eph 6:3
 w done, good and faithful   Mat
           25:21,23, Lk 19:1

went *(see go)*
 Jesus *w* about teaching   Mat 4:23,
              9:35, Mk 6:6
 w away sorrowful   Mat 19:22, Mk
                   10:22
 I go, sir, but *w* not   Mat 21:30
 many disciples *w* back   Jno 6:66
 Jesus *w* doing good   Acts 10:38
 they *w* out from us   1 Jno 2:19
west, *sun setting*
 far as east from *w*   Psa 103:12
 he-goat came from *w*   Dan 8:5
 come from east and *w*   Mat 8:11,
                   Lk 13:29
 as lightning shineth to *w* Mat 24:27
whale, *great sea monster*
 God created great *w*   Gen 1:21
 three days in *w*   Mat 12:40
whatsoever
 w I command   Deut 12:32
 w ye would men should   Mat 7:12
 w ye shall ask   Jno 15:16, 16:23
wheat, *small grain*
 have sown *w*, but   Jer 12:13
 gather *w* into my barn   Mat 13:30
 Satan may sift you as *w*   Lk 22:31
wheel, *turning, rolling*
 w broken at cistern   Ecc 12:6
 w in midst of *w*   Ezek 1:16, 10:10
when
 w will ye be wise?   Psa 94:8
 who can tell *w* it shall be? Ecc 8:7
where
 Lord said, *w* art thou?   Gen 3:9
 w is he?   Jno 7:11, 9:12
 w I am   7:34, 12:26, 14:3, 17:24

wherefore
w art thou come?   Mat 26:50

whereto
prosper w I sent it   Isa 55:11

wherewithal
w shall we be clothed?   Mat 6:31

whirlwind, *hurricane*
take up Elijah by a w   2 Ki 2:1,11
reaped the w   Hos 8:7
destruction cometh as w   Pro 1:27

whisperer, *gossiper, slanderer*
w separateth friends   Pro 16:28
debate, deceit, w   Rom 1:29
See also: 2 Cor 12:20

white, *bright, shining*
w than snow   Psa 51:7
sins shall be w as snow   Isa 1:18
make hair w or black   Mat 5:36
his raiment was w   17:2, Mk 9:3,
Lk 9:29
raiment w as snow   Mat 28:3, Acts
1:10
fields are w to harvest   Jno 4:35
great w throne   Rev 20:11

whole, *entire*
w duty of man   Ecc 12:13
they that be w need not   Mat 9:12,
Mk 2:17, Lk 5:31
faith hath made thee w   Mk 5:34
Christ maketh thee w   Acts 9:34
if w body were eye   1 Cor 12:17
w armour of God   Eph 6:11
See also: Eph 4:13, Jas 1:4

whoremonger, *adulterer*
no w hath any inheritance   Eph 5:5
without are w, murderers   Rev
22:15

whosoever
w will, let him take   Rev 22:17

wicked, *evil*
I will not justify the w   Ex 23:7
wherefore do the w live?   Job 21:7
w shall be turned to hell   Psa 9:17
w will not seek God   10:4
deliver my soul from w   17:13
seen the w in great power   37:35
salvation is far from w   119:155
all w will he destroy   145:20
w not inhabit earth   Pro 10:30
w shall not be unpunished   11:21
Lord is far from the w   15:29
w flee when no man pursueth   28:1
let w forsake his way   Isa 55:7
w are like the troubled sea   57:20
w generation seeketh sign   Mat
16:4
by w hands hath slain   Acts 2:23
fiery darts of the w   Eph 6:16

wickedness, *iniquity, evil*
God saw w was great   Gen 6:5
they that sow w reap   Job 4:8
though w be sweet   20:12
they eat bread of w   Pro 4:17
treasures of w profit nothing   10:2
turn not from his w   Ezek 3:19
turneth from his w   33:12
out of heart proceed w   Mk 7:22
repent of this thy w   Acts 8:22
being filled with w   Rom 1:29
whole world lieth in w   1 Jno 5:19
See also: Isa 48:22, Mat 6:34, 15:19

wide, *broad*
w is gate that leadeth   Mat 7:13

wife, *woman*
whoso findeth a w   Pro 18:22

prudent *w* is from the Lord 19:14
remember Lot's *w* Lk 17:32
husband is head of *w* Eph 5:23
See also: Gen 2:18, Rev 21:2

wilderness, *desert, wilds*
  through terrible *w* Deut 1:19
  voice of him that crieth in the *w*
        Isa 40:3, Mat 3:3, Mk 1:3,
        Lk 3:4, Jno 1:23
  w to be tempted Mat 4:1

wiles, *deceit, craftiness*
  against *w* of devil Eph 6:11

will, *wish*
  thy *w* be done Mat 6:10, Lk 11:2
  w of my Father Mat 7:21, 12:50
  thy *w* be done 26:42
  good *w* toward men Lk 2:14
  do *w* of him that sent me Jno 4:34
  to *w* is present with me Rom 7:18
  not him that *w*, nor 9:16
  both to *w* and to do Phil 2:13

willing, *acting cheerfully, intending*
  whosoever is *w* heart Ex 35:5
  serve God with *w* mind 1 Chr 28:9
  the Spirit is *w* Mat 26:41
  if thou be *w*, remove Lk 22:42
  be first a *w* mind 2 Cor 8:12
  not *w* that any perish 2 Pet 3:9
  See also: Judg 5:2, 1 Chr 28:9

willingly *(see willing)*
  w, not of necessity Philem 14,
        1 Pet 5:2

win, *gain*
  he that *w* souls Pro 11:30
  that I may *w* Christ Phil 3:8

wind
  he shall inherit *w* Pro 11:29
  prophesy unto the *w* Ezek 37:9

they have sown *w* Hos 8:7
w bloweth where it listeth Jno 3:8
every *w* of doctrine Eph 4:14
wave driven with *w* Jas 1:6

windows, *opening*
  w of heaven were opened Gen 7:11
  look out *w* be darkened Ecc 12:3
  See also: Isa 60:8, Mal 3:10

wine, *fermented grape juice*
  w maketh glad heart Psa 104:15
  w is a mocker Pro 20:1
  look not on *w* when red 23:31
  till *w* inflame them Isa 5:11
  have erred through *w* 28:7
  he transgresseth by *w* Hab 2:5
  these men full of new *w* Acts 2:13
  new *w* in old bottles Lk 5:37
  be not drunk with *w* Eph 5:18
  not given to *w* 1 Tim 3:3, Tit 1:7,
        2:3
  w for stomach's sake 1 Tim 5:23
  walked in excess of *w* 1 Pet 4:3
  See also: Pro 31:6

wings
  bare you on eagles' *w* Ex 19:4
  shadow of thy *w* Psa 17:8, 36:7,
        57:1, 61:4, 91:4
  fly on *w* of the wind 18:10, 104:3
  that I had *w* like a dove! 55:6
  if I take *w* of morning 139:9
  with healing in his *w* Mal 4:2
  as hen gathereth chickens under *w*
        Mat 23:37, Lk 13:34

wink, *blink*
  wicked *w* with his eyes Pro 6:13
  ignorance God *w* at Acts 17:30

winter, *season of year*
  summer and *w* Gen 8:22, Psa 74:17

lo, the *w* is past S of S 2:11

wipe, *smear, wipe away*
w Jerusalem as dish 2 Ki 21:13
Lord will *w* away tears Isa 25:8,
  Rev 7:17, 21:4

wisdom, *understanding, skill*
fear of Lord beginning of *w* Psa
  111:10
apply our hearts to *w* 90:12
get *w* get understanding Pro 4:5
w is the principal thing 4:7
w is better than rubies 8:11
better get *w* than gold 16:16
he that getteth *w* loveth 19:8
in much *w* is grief Ecc 1:18
w of wise shall perish Isa 29:14
w is justified of Mat 11:19
Jesus increased in *w* Lk 2:52
not with *w* of words 1 Cor 1:17
Christ the *w* of God 1:24
w of world is foolishness 3:19
not with fleshly *w* 2 Cor 1:12
the manifold *w* of God Eph 3:10
walk in *w* toward them Col 4:5
if any lack *w* Jas 1:5
w from above is pure 3:17

wise *(see wisdom)*
a tree to make one *w* Gen 3:6
great men not always *w* Job 32:9
be not *w* in own eyes Pro 3:7
the *w* shall inherit glory 3:35
he that winneth souls is *w* 11:30
he that walketh with *w* 13:20
w in their own eyes Isa 5:21
be ye *w* as serpents Mat 10:16
professing to be *w* Rom 1:22
be not *w* in own conceits 12:16
where is the *w?* 1 Cor 1:20

not as fools, but *w* Eph 5:15
w unto salvation 2 Tim 3:15

wiser *(see wisdom)*
Solomon was *w* than 1 Ki 4:31
foolishness of God is *w* 1 Cor 1:25

withdraw, *to draw away*
w from disorderly 2 Thes 3:6
See also: Pro 25:17, 1 Tim 6:5

wither, *to dry up*
his leaf shall not *w* Psa 1:3
the grass *w* Isa 40:7, 1 Pet 1:24
having no root, *w* Mat 13:6, Mk
  4:6
the fig tree *w* away Mat 21:19, Mk
  11:21
cast forth as a branch, and *w* Jno
  15:6

withhold, *to hold back*
w not good from Pro 3:27
w not correction from 23:13

within, *inside*
thy law is *w* my heart Psa 40:8
from *w* proceed evil Mk 7:21

without, *outside*
w the true God 2 Chr 15:3
them that are *w* Col 4:5, 1 Thes
  4:12, 1 Tim 3:7
w are dogs Rev 22:15

withstand, *endure*
able to *w* in evil day Eph 6:13

witness, *to testify*
covenant be a *w* Gen 31:44
not bear false *w* Ex 20:16
a faithful *w* Pro 14:5
a *w* to the people Isa 55:4
the same came for a *w* Jno 1:7
ye shall be *w* Acts 1:8
this *w* is true Tit 1:13

compassed with cloud of w   Heb
                              12:1
Jesus Christ faithful w   Rev 1:5

wits, *mind*
stagger at w end   Psa 107:27

wolf, *wolf or jackal*
w shall dwell with   Isa 11:6
w and lamb shall feed   65:25
inwardly they are w.   Mat 7:15
as sheep in midst of w   10:16
hireling seeth w   Jno 10:12
w shall enter among   Acts 20:29

woman, *female, wife*
made he a w   Gen 2:22
enmity between thee and w   3:15
born of w   Job 14:1
foolish w is clamorous   Pro 9:13
virtuous w   12:4, 31:10
brawling w in wide house   21:9,19
w that feareth the Lord   31:30
w is the glory of man   1 Cor 11:7
suffer not w to teach   1 Tim 2:12

womb, *"belly" in Hebrew and Greek*
formed thee from w   Isa 44:2, 49:5

women *(see woman)*
blessed above w   Judg 5:24
among them born of w   Mat 11:11,
                              Lk 7:28
blessed art thou among w   1:28

wonder, *sign, miracle*
a sign and w   Deut 13:1, 28:46
I will show w in heaven   Joel 2:30,
                              Acts 2:19

wonderful, *full of wonder*
talk of his w works 1 Chr 16:9, Psa
       26:7, 105:2, 119:27, 145:5
his name shall be called W   Isa 9:6

wont, *accustomed*
governor was w to   Mat 27:15
prayer was w to   Acts 16:13

wood, *tree, fuel*
no w is, fire goeth out   Pro 26:20
See also: Pro 26:21, 1 Cor 3:12

wool, *sheep's wool*
he giveth snow like w   Psa 147:16
your sins be as w   Isa 1:18

word, *saying, thing*
not add to w I command Deut 4:2
every w of God   8:3, Mat 4:4
every w is nigh   Deut 30:14, Rom
                              10:8
let w of my mouth   Psa 19:14
w spoken in due season Pro 15:23
w of man's mouth   18:4
a w fitly spoken   25:11
multitude of w   Ecc 5:3
trust not lying w   Jer 7:4
nor shall the w perish   18:18
By thy w   Mat 12:37
my w shall not pass away   24:35
in the beginning was W   Jno 1:1
the W was made flesh   1:14
thou has w of eternal life   6:68
w of reconciliation   2 Cor 5:19
law fulfilled in one w   Gal 5:14
whatsoever do in w or   Col 3:17
comfort one another with these w
                              1 Thes 4:18
preach the w   2 Tim 4:2
w spoken by angels was   Heb 2:2
w of God is quick and   4:12
receive the engrafted w   Jas 1:21
be ye doers of w   1:22
sincere milk of the w   1 Pet 2:2
not love in w but   1 Jno 3:18

work, *effort, accomplishment*

God rested from his *w*	Gen 2:3
six days do all *w*	Ex 20:9, 23:12, Deut 5:13
render according to his *w*	Pro 24:12
a time for every *w*	Ecc 3:17
every *w* into judgment	12:14
we are *w* of thy hand	Isa 64:8
mighty in *w*	Jer 32:19
this is *w* of God, that	Jno 6:29
w of darkness	Rom 13:12, Eph 5:11
w together with him	2 Cor 6:1
by *w* of law no flesh justified	Gal 2:16
every man prove his own *w*	6:4
good word and *w*	2 Thes 2:17
patience have perfect *w*	Jas 1:4
faith, if it hath not *w*	2:17
by *w* faith made perfect	2:22
I know thy *w*	Rev 2:19
their *w* do follow them	14:13

See also: Lk 2:49, Rom 3:28

work (verb)

six days thou shalt *w*	Ex 34:21
people had a mind to *w*	Neh 4:6
flattering mouth *w* ruin	Pro 26:28
w hitherto, and I *w*	Jno 5:17
night, when no man *w*	9:4
all things *w* together	Rom 8:28
w a far more exceeding weight	2 Cor 4:17
faith which *w* by love	Gal 5:6
w out your salvation	Phil 2:12

workman, *worker*

the *w* is worthy of	Mat 10:10
w not be ashamed	2 Tim 2:15

world, *land, habitable earth*

w and they that	Psa 24:1, 98:7
the *w* is mine	50:12
w in their heart	Ecc 3:11
light of the *w*	Mat 5:14
care of this *w*	13:22
gain whole *w*	16:26, Mk 8:36, Lk 9:25
God so loved the *w*	Jno 3:16
I am light of *w*	8:12, 9:5
I came not to judge *w*	12:47
turned *w* upside down	Acts 17:6
be not conformed to *w*	Rom 12:2
friendship of the *w*	Jas 4:4
love not the *w*	1 Jno 2:15
w lieth in wickedness	5:19

wormwood, *plant, bitterness*

star is called *w*	Rev 8:11

worse, *more displeasing*

last state *w*	Mat 12:45, 27:64, Lk 11:26
not better, but *w*	1 Cor 11:17
latter end is *w*	2 Pet 2:20

worship, *bow down, adore*

w the Lord in beauty of holiness	1 Chr 16:29, Psa 29:2, 96:9
neither *w* strange god	81:9
in vain they do *w* me	Mat 15:9
w in spirit	Jno 4:23

See also: Eph 3:14, 5:19

worthy, *fitting, suitable*

workman is *w* of his	Mat 10:10
fruits *w* of repentance	Lk 3:8
labourer is *w*	10:7, 1 Tim 5:18
no more *w* to be called	Lk 15:19
walk *w*	Eph 4:1, Col 1:10, 1 Thes 2:12
w of acceptation	1 Tim 1:15, 4:9

w to receive   Rev 4:11, 5:12

would, *willing, desire*
  whatsoever ye w Mat 7:12, Lk 6:31
  good that I w I do not   Rom 7:19
  cannot do things ye w   Gal 5:17

wound, *hurt*
  give w for w   Ex 21:25
  w spirit who can bear?   Pro 18:14
  w for our transgressions Isa 53:5

wrath, *anger, transgression*
  w killeth foolish man   Job 5:2
  soft answer turneth w   Pro 15:1
  from w to come   Mat 3:7, Lk 3:7
  give place to w   Rom 12:19
  children of w   Eph 2:3
  not sun go down on w   4:26
  provoke not children to w   6:4
  put off w   Col 3:8
  slow to speak, slow to w Jas 1:19

wrest, *twist*
  that are unstable w   2 Pet 3:16

wrestle, *struggle*
  there w a man with him Gen 32:24
  we w not against flesh   Eph 6:12

wretched, *miserable*
  w man that I am   Rom 7:24
  knowest not thou art w   Rev 3:17

wrinkle
  not having spot or w   Eph 5:27

write, *inscribe, engrave, record*
  w them on posts   Deut 6:9, 11:20
  w on table of heart   Pro 3:3, 7:3
  I will w law in their hearts   Jer
                      31:33, Heb 8:10

written *(see write)*
  w with finger of God   Ex 31:18
  it is w   Mat 4:4
  w for our admonition 1 Cor 10:11

it is w be ye holy   1 Pet 1:16

wrong, *to do violence, injustice*
  w his own soul   Pro 8:36
  do no w, do no violence Jer 22:3
  he that doeth w   Col 3:25

wrote *(see write)*
  man's hand w on the wall Dan 5:5

wroth *(see wrath)*
  why art thou w?   Gen 4:6
  Naaman was w   2 Ki 5:11
  I was w with my people   Isa 47:6

wrought, *to do, make*
  hand of Lord hath w   Job 12:9
  things Christ hath not w   Rom
                           15:18
  faith w with works   Jas 2:22

Y

yea, *yes* (archaic)
  conversation be y   Mat 5:37, Jas
                            5:12
  be y, y and nay   2 Cor 1:17

year
  atonement once a y   Lev 16:34
  continue there a y   Jas 4:13
  See also: Ex 12:1, Lev 23:5

years
  for seasons, days, y   Gen 1:14
  Abraham died full of y   25:8
  thousand y in thy sight Psa 90:4
  our y as a tale   90:9
  y are threescore and ten   90:10
  nor y draw nigh   Ecc 12:1
  bound Satan thousand y Rev 20:2

yesterday, *day past*
  thousand years but as *y*   Psa 90:4
  same *y* and for ever   Heb 13:8

yield, *give*
  to whom ye *y* yourselves   Rom
                    6:16
  no fountain *y* salt water and   Jas
                    3:12

yoke, *beam for attaching oxen to plow*
  take my *y* upon you   Mat 11:29
  be not entangled with *y*   Gal 5:1

yoked, *paired, attached*
  be not unequally *y*   2 Cor 6:14

youth, *young*
  remember thy Creator in *y*   Ecc
                    12:1
  kept from my *y*   Mat 19:20, Mk
               10:20, Lk 18:21

youthful *(see youth)*
  flee also *y* lusts   2 Tim 2:22

Z

Zaccheus, *a tax collector,* Lk 19:2
Zachariah, *king of Israel,* 2 Ki 14:29
Zacharias, *father of John the Baptist,*
  Lk 1:6
Zadok, *priest,* 2 Sam 8:17
zeal, *eagerness*
  z of Lord   2 Ki 19:31, Isa 37:32
  z of thy house   Psa 69:9, Jno 2:17
  they have *z* of God   Rom 10:2
zealous *(see zeal)*
  all *z* of law   Acts 21:20
  z towards God   22:3, Gal 1:14

  z of spiritual gifts   1 Cor 14:12
  people, *z* of good works   Tit 2:14

Zebedee, *father of James and John,*
  Mat 4:21, 10:2, 26:37, Mk 1:19,
  3:17, 10:35, Lk 5:10, Jno 21:2

Zebulun, *tribe of Israel,* Gen 30:20,
  49:13, Num 1:30, Josh 19:10

Zechariah, *king,* 2 Chr 24:20; *prophet,*
  Zech 1:1 ff

Zedekiah, *prophet,* 1 Ki 22:11; *king,*
  2 Ki 24:17; *and others*

Zephaniah, *priest,* Jer 29:25; *prophet,*
  Zeph 1:1 ff

Zerubbabel, *prince of Judah,* Ezra 2:2
  ff, Hag 1:1, Zech 4:6

Zidon, *Sidon, city of Phoenicia,* Gen
  49:13, Josh 11:8, 1 Ki 11:1, Lk 4:26

Ziklag, *city given David by Philistines,*
  1 Sam 27:6

Zimri, *king of Israel,* 1 Ki 16:9

Zion, or Sion, *another name for*
  Jerusalem, 2 Sam 5:7, 1 Ki 8:1, Rom
  11:26, Heb 12:22, Rev 14:1